Literature of the Somali Diaspora

BLACK LITERARY AND CULTURAL EXPRESSIONS

Bloomsbury's **Black Literary and Cultural Expressions** series provides a much-needed space for exploring dimensions of Black creativity as its local expressions in literature, music, film, art, etc., interface with the global circulation of culture. From contemporary and historical perspectives, and through a multidisciplinary lens, works in this series critically analyse the provenance, genres, aesthetics, intersections and modes of circulation of works of Black cultural expression and production.

Series Editors
Toyin Falola and Abimbola A. Adelakun, University of Texas at Austin, USA

Advisory Board
Nadia Anwar, University of Management and Technology, Lahore, Pakistan
Adriaan van Klinken, University of Leeds, UK
Alain Lawo-Sukam, Texas A&M University, USA
Nathaniel S. Murrell, University of North Carolina, Wilmington, USA
Mukoma wa Ngugi, Cornell University, USA
Bode Omojola, Mount Holyoke and the Five College Consortium, USA
Nduka Otiono, Carleton University, Canada
Bola Sotunsa, Babcock University, Nigeria
Nathan Suhr-Sytsma, Emory University, USA

Volumes in the Series:
Wole Soyinka: Literature, Activism, and African Transformation by Bola Dauda and Toyin Falola
Social Ethics and Governance in Contemporary African Writing: Literature, Philosophy, and the Nigerian World by Nimi Wariboko
The Birth of Breaking: Hip Hop History from the Floor Up by Serouj 'Midus' Aprahamian
Literature of the Somali Diaspora: Space, Language and Resistance in Somali Anglophone and Italian Novels by Marco Medugno
The Epic Poetry of Mazisi Kunene by Dike Okoro (forthcoming)
The Decolonizing Work of Jessica Huntley: The Political Roots of a Radical Black Activist by Claudia Tomlinson (forthcoming)

Literature of the Somali Diaspora

Space, Language and Resistance in Somali Novels in English and Italian

Marco Medugno

BLOOMSBURY ACADEMIC
NEW YORK • LONDON • OXFORD • NEW DELHI • SYDNEY

BLOOMSBURY ACADEMIC
Bloomsbury Publishing Inc, 1359 Broadway, New York, NY 10018, USA
Bloomsbury Publishing Plc, 50 Bedford Square, London, WC1B 3DP, UK
Bloomsbury Publishing Ireland, 29 Earlsfort Terrace, Dublin 2, D02 AY28, Ireland

BLOOMSBURY, BLOOMSBURY ACADEMIC and the Diana logo
are trademarks of Bloomsbury Publishing Plc

First published in the United States of America 2024
This paperback edition published in 2026

Copyright © Marco Medugno, 2024

For legal purposes the Note on Permissions on p. viii constitute
an extension of this copyright page.

Cover design by Eleanor Rose
Cover image: Modern day buildings coming up in the ancient neighbourhood of Xamar
Weyne, Mogadishu, Somalia © Fardosa Hussein / fardosahussein.visura.co

All rights reserved. No part of this publication may be: i) reproduced or transmitted in any form, electronic or mechanical, including photocopying, recording or by means of any information storage or retrieval system without prior permission in writing from the publishers; or ii) used or reproduced in any way for the training, development or operation of artificial intelligence (AI) technologies, including generative AI technologies. The rights holders expressly reserve this publication from the text and data mining exception as per Article 4(3) of the Digital Single Market Directive (EU) 2019/790.

Bloomsbury Publishing Inc does not have any control over, or responsibility for, any third-party websites referred to or in this book. All internet addresses given in this book were correct at the time of going to press. The author and publisher regret any inconvenience caused if addresses have changed or sites have ceased to exist, but can accept no responsibility for any such changes.

Whilst every effort has been made to locate copyright holders
the publishers would be grateful to hear from any person(s) not here acknowledged.

Library of Congress Cataloging-in-Publication Data
Names: Medugno, Marco, author.
Title: Literature of the Somali diaspora : space, language and resistance in Somali novels in English and Italian / Marco Medugno.
Other titles: Black literary and cultural expressions.
Description: New York : Bloomsbury Academic, 2024. | Series: Black literary and cultural expressions | Includes bibliographical references and index.
Identifiers: LCCN 2023058290 (print) | LCCN 2023058291 (ebook) | ISBN 9798765107485 (hardback) | ISBN 9798765107492 (paperback) | ISBN 9798765107508 (ebook) | ISBN 9798765107515 (pdf)
Subjects: LCSH: Somali fiction (English)–History and criticism. | Somali fiction (Italian)–History and criticism. | Somali fiction–Foreign countries–History and criticism. | Somali diaspora.
Classification: LCC PJ2533.5 .M43 2024 (print) | LCC PJ2533.5 (ebook) | DDC 820.996773–dc23
LC record available at https://lccn.loc.gov/2023058290
LC ebook record available at https://lccn.loc.gov/2023058291

ISBN:	HB:	979-8-7651-0748-5
	PB:	979-8-7651-0749-2
	ePDF:	979-8-7651-0751-5
	eBook:	979-8-7651-0750-8

Series: Black Literary and Cultural Expressions

Typeset by Integra Software Services Pvt. Ltd.

For product safety related questions contact productsafety@bloomsbury.com.

To find out more about our authors and books visit www.bloomsbury.com
and sign up for our newsletters.

Contents

List of Figures	vi
Acknowledgements	vii
Note on Permissions	viii
Note on Text	ix
Introduction: Writing the Diaspora	1
1 Key Places in the Somali Diasporic Imaginary	27
2 Literary Cartographies of Mogadishu	69
3 Multilingualism in Farah's *Links* and *Crossbones*	105
4 The Spoken Word Meets the Script: Somali, Italian and the Role of Orature	141
5 Resistance and *impegno:* Postcolonial Somali Novels in Italian and *Letteratura della Resistenza*	163
Conclusion: Re-inventing *Somalias*	203
Appendix	210
Bibliography	211
Index	231

Figures

2.1 Italian Somaliland: Mogadishu, demonstrative plan of the new constructions carried out and started on 1 October 1912. *Società Geografica Italiana*   85

2.2 Map of Mogadiscio, 1938. From the *Guida dell'Africa Orientale Italiana*   87

Acknowledgements

The idea behind this book goes way back and has been patiently nurtured by numerous people, to whom I am greatly indebted. My interest in postcolonial theories and writings, which underpins this book but also set the course for my academic journey, is owed to Annalisa Oboe, Carli Coetzee and Enio Sartori, who were great sources of inspiration when I was a student at the University of Padova. I extend my deepest gratitude to my former PhD supervisors, Neelam Srivastava and James Procter, for their patience, honest and kind feedback, guidance and stimulating discussions that pushed me to continually challenge ideas, even the most steadfast ones. A special thanks is reserved for Neelam, whose advice, support and encouragement have been invaluable. Heartfelt thanks to Francesca Orsini and Robbie McLaughlan for their feedback on my dissertation and their assistance with the book proposal, essential for developing this book – and for its very existence, in both material and electronic forms. My gratitude also goes to the School of English Literature, Language and Linguistics at Newcastle University for the support they provided to me as an early career researcher. And to my fellow PhD candidates too, now colleagues, with whom I shared my first teaching experience at the university. I feel particularly lucky to work in SELLL with brilliant people who helped make Newcastle my second home. Many thanks to those tireless colleagues who have been – or still are – part of the Newcastle Postcolonial Research Group. I am also indebted to the University of Glasgow and, in particular, to Maria-Daniella Dick and Richard Stacey for their support during the time I virtually spent there. Thank you for enduring long videocalls that, as we have all come to realize, can really be disheartening. A special word of gratitude goes to Erica Bellia, Gianmarco Mancosu, Jennifer Burns and, of course, Shirin Ramzanali Fazel for the fruitful talk we had about postcolonial writings, the Somali diaspora and Italian studies at the University of Cambridge. Thank you once again for inviting me. Also, thanks to those colleagues and friends I met around the world who, in one way or another, decided to stay in touch despite lengthy periods of isolation and nothing less than a global pandemic: Anita Virga, Lucio De Capitani, Alice Girotto, Simone Calabrò, Antony Jiang and Teresa Colliva.

A special thanks goes to Barbara Franchi – and her wonderful family, Marco, Elio and Paolo – for her support, wit and all the chats about literature, living abroad and the struggle of working in too-often precarious academic positions. To all my friends in Padova and those scattered across the globe whom I haven't seen much or met in a while but feel close to: thank you for being present, even virtually, when circumstances would not allow otherwise. Thanks to my parents and my sister Enrica: you have always shown me understanding and supported all my choices with love and kindness. Last but not least, I want to express my massive and heartfelt thanks to Steffen for standing by me through distance and extended periods of intense work that, too often, invaded weekends, summers and holidays. *Tausend Dank*!

Note on Permissions

Previous versions of Chapter 3 were published in Medugno, Marco. 2020. 'Dante in Mogadishu: *The Divine Comedy* in Nuruddin Farah's *Links*'. *Tydskrif vir Letterkunde* 57(1): 45–55. DOI: dx.doi.org/10.17159/2309-9070/tvl.v.57i1.8060. And in Medugno, Marco. 2018. 'The Distinctive Use of the Italian Language in Nuruddin Farah's Late Production'. *From the European South* 3: 71–84. Earlier drafts of selected material from Chapter 2 appeared in Medugno, Marco. 2018. 'A Contested Spatiality: The Representation of Mogadishu in Somali Anglophone and Italian Literature.' *Italian Studies in Southern Africa* 31(1): 110–34.

The articles are all published under a Creative Commons Attribution License. I am grateful to the editors of *Tydskrif vir Letterkunde*, *From the European South* and *Italian Studies in Southern Africa*, for their permission to reproduce this material.

Figure 2.1 is published under a Creative Commons Attribution License and made available by Società Geografica Italiana. Full reference below:

G. Gandolfi and M. Checchi, 'Somalia italiana: Mogadiscio, pianta dimostrativa delle nuove costruzioni eseguite ed iniziate al 1 ottobre 1912'. 1912, *Archivio Somalia*, ArcAdiA Archivio Aperto di Ateneo. Rome, http://hdl.handle.net/2307/3391.

Figure 2.2 is the reproduction of a map in *Guida dell'Africa Orientale Italiana*. 1938. Milan: Consociazione Turistica Italiana, p. 571.

Note on Text

Concerning orthography, I have tried to follow the Somali writing conventions to transcribe names, both proper and common, toponymy, sentences and titles of books, poems and songs. This led to the use of *x* as the aspirated *h* (as in Ubax instead of Ubah), *c* for the consonant 'ayn (as in Caydiid instead of 'Aidid), *q* for *k* (as in *qat* instead of *khat*) and double vocals to long vowel sound (as in Siyaad instead of Siad). The same occurs in the case of geographic names, such as Weebi Shabeelle (Shebelle River) and Xamar Weyne (Hamar Weyne). In the case of authors' names, I left the more conventional transliteration whether the latter was the only one provided or preferred by the authors themselves. This strategy led to different outcomes, as in the case of Ali Mumin Ahad, which falls in the first case, and Axmed Cali Abokor, which fits in the second. Likewise, since Nuruddin Farah never appears as Nuuradiin Faarax in published works, here it is written accordingly. In both cases, in the bibliography, I refer to published Somali authors using their grandfather's name as their last name. Finally, I left in quotation marks any nicknames, as the latter are often regarded as the formal name. Since other sources use different conventions, the reader should be aware of some inconsistencies in terms of orthography between this book and other texts. Any errors or inconsistencies that remain are, of course, my own.

When quoted passages in Italian are provided with an English translation, it means that the translation is my own. In all the other cases, translated texts and passages are referenced accordingly.

Introduction: Writing the Diaspora

In the literary history of Somalia, the novel is a relatively recent form, whose development has been anything but untroubled since the formalization of orthography in 1972 and the subsequent dissemination of written literature. After an initial period marked by a strong reliance on themes and forms belonging to the well-recognized and established oral tradition, novels have initiated a more autonomous expansion by loosening the ties with orature and venturing into the representation of 1970s cosmopolitan city life. This literary urban setting, introduced, for example, through the prose works of Axmed Cartan Xaange and Shire Jaamac Axmed, was a significant innovation in Somali literary tradition, typically – yet not exclusively – centred on folktales, fables and pastoral life (Andrzejewski 2011a, 73–4). Quite quickly, novels started circulating in periodicals and newspapers, such as *Xiddigta Oktoobar* (October Star), *Waaga Cusub* (The New Era) and *Kacaan* (Revolution). Nuruddin Farah, now an acclaimed writer whose novels have been translated and celebrated worldwide, took his first step in the literary world by publishing a novel in Somali, serialized in *Xiddigta Oktoobar* in 1973 (Farah 1988, 1593–6).[1]

The swift growth of prose production, however, faced severe setbacks throughout Maxamed Siyaad Barre's dictatorship (1969–91). After seizing power through a coup, Barre established an increasingly oppressive authoritarian rule that brought about political and religious persecution, political opponents' imprisonment and censorship. As a result, those authors and intellectuals who did not bow to Barre's rules, or did not turn their works into tools of socialist propaganda to survive the regime's suppression, fled the country. Nuruddin Farah, for example, following the publication of *A Naked Needle* (1976), became *persona non grata* with the regime after being warned, once in Rome, that Somali authorities planned to arrest him over the novel's content (Ali Farah 2018b). Farah did not return to Somalia, as did many other Somalis who decided to remain abroad or leave under threats and increasing intimidation from the regime. Emigration numbers and expulsions of Somali nationals rose steeply following the implementation of the National Security Law No. 54 (1970), which granted the National Security Service (NSS) the authority to indefinitely detain individuals if they expressed critical views about the government, all without facing proper trials.

The civil war that erupted with the fall of Siyaad Barre's regime in the early 1990s deteriorated the already compromised moral authority of Barre's rule, which began to weaken after ruinous military operations and the brutal repression of clan-affiliated political movements. The long dictatorship and the following civil war 'wipe[d] out most of the intellectual and material progress of the preceding thirty years' (Ahad 2004, 18). The escalating violence caused a rupture in the lives of the Somali people and produced displacements, expulsions and copious casualties among both civilians and military personnel.

Besides deeply affecting the Somali people, the civil war reshaped the trajectory of national development and the project of a unified nation-state, thus making Somalia decline into 'a collection of warring clans reminiscent of pre-industrial times' (Ahad 2004, 18). The power vacuum that followed the end of Barre's regime led to a resurgence of clan-based territorial control, as various groups vied for supremacy over the collapsed centralized state (Ingiriis 2016, 2018). When foreign powers, including the United States and the United Nations, interjected in Somalia's domestic affairs, the already unstable environment further deteriorated until 2004. It was in this year that a Transitional Federal Government (TFG) was established, leading to a relative decrease in the intensity of the fighting (Guglielmo 2013, 148–52; Gerrard 2016, 49–51).

Nevertheless, the newly formed Islamic Courts Union (ICU) took control of the southern regions after fighting the the TFG and the peacekeeping force operated by the African Union for control of the country. Kenyan troops entered southern Somalia to fight the newly-formed group of al-Shabaab, a military wing of the Islamic Courts, and succeeded in establishing a buffer zone inside Somalia. A new federal government was established in 2012, becoming the country's first permanent central government since the start of the civil war (Gerrard 2016, 51). Due to this prolonged instability and frail political institutions, Somalia has often been considered a 'failed state', a derogatory term that connotes the country as the epitome of dysfunctionality and economic decline (Myers 2011, 139; Scego 2023, 17).

Against this backdrop, literature endured and flourished abroad. Somali authors began to write from the diaspora in the language of their host countries (German, Finnish, Dutch and French), in the former colonial tongue (English and Italian) and in Somali, often weaving together the themes of war, memory, homelessness, nationhood, displacement and the idea of return. The Somali literary landscape, therefore, has now become physically unbound and centripetally pulled to Somalia, reflecting the political situation of the nation, which no longer denotes a unified or stable entity in political or geographical terms. Abdourahman Waberi, the Djiboutian author and scholar, reflects on this fragmentation by saying that Somalia is, in fact, 'a cultural area [...] of Somaliphone groups and [...] others as well' (1998, 780).[2]

Despite Somalia's *de facto* partition into federal regions, diaspora authors have symbolically referenced it as a single nation-state, using the term 'Somalia' as a synonym for 'Somali Republic'. The ongoing political and geographical break-up has not led these authors to perpetuate the narrative of Somalia as the quintessential example of a failed state or, more recently, the land of piracy and terrorism. Neither has this fragmentation disaffected the idea of nation, as they often consider it a unifying concept that binds them together. Rather than fixating on political resolutions, such as federal systems, centralized states with autonomous regions, clan-based territories or various forms of Islamic states, diasporic authors investigate what the solution may be for restoring the lost unity and reinvigorating the sense of nationhood at the societal level. They aim to counteract divisive clan narratives and foster transnational connections within the diaspora that transcend sectarian affiliations.

This intention seems to be pursued through the novel form, which has become a successful tool for reflecting on historical events, private and collective traumas, and for negotiating non-normative ideas of Somaliness or *Soomaalinimo* (Kabir 2010, 145; Fotheringham 2020, 56–7). As a dialogic, polyphonic and heteroglossic genre, the novel is a suitable form for syncretism, but also for enhancing the hybridity between languages, cultures and identities so ingrained in the diasporic condition. In this regard, I argue that through the novel form, Somali authors contemplate a urban and cosmopolitan ethos that can unite citizens, thus bridging divisions rooted in clan ideology and social fragmentation 'to recalibrate the vision of Somalia along the more positive lines of the moral nationhood inscribed by the concept of *Soomaalinimo*' (Fotheringham 2020, 59). This attempt is particularly evident in the novels of the 2000s selected here, which primarily focus on the fictionalization of the civil war and were written during the delicate period between the TFG (2004–12) and the current Federal Government of Somalia.[3] Even though some novels do not address the civil war directly, such as Farah's *Crossbones* (set in 2006) and Scego's *Adua* (set in the 1930s and 1970s), that period of violence and destruction creeps into the narrative as an unresolved and haunting event in Somalia's recent history. These novels, then, are fruitful resources to initiate a dialogue about a complex moment in the hope of reconstructing the idea of a nation and rebuilding a traumatized society. Anglophone and Italophone Somali diasporic authors try to explore and suggest ideas of nationhood that, even though fragmented and partial, represent an attempt at unity.[4] By promoting a narrative of Somalia as a political and cultural entity (not without problems), they challenge monolithically articulated concepts of Somaliness and attempt to envision potential sociopolitical alternatives for the future.

With a sense of both nostalgia and criticism towards the post-independence period, when Somalia was constituted from the unification of the former British protectorate and the Italian trusteeship administration in 1960, diasporic novels serve as conduits for encouraging a self-reflecting and self-questioning discussion about the country's tumultuous past, the post-war present and possible futures (Di Maio 2011, XXII; Mari 2018, 33). The novel form provides the Somali people with a means to recreate a country from abroad, as Nuruddin Farah suggested about his commitment to 'keep [Somalia] alive by writing about it' (Jaggi 2012). Due to the trajectory of the post-independence state, the novel form 'gained new traction from abroad by achieving *outside*' Somalia and the African continent and provided a space to investigate and make sense of the civil unrest (Hodapp 2020, 6). Vivian Gerrard remarks upon this point, noticing that literature can be a space for individual reflection and, at the same time, enable 'cultural survival' for the Somali people (2016, 11).

This necessarily simplified historical-literary summary establishes the context of this book, which aims to explore how Somalia is not only 'kept alive' from the diaspora but also how Somali authors try to find ways of addressing the civil war and the subsequent disruption of Somalia as a nation-state and as a society. Paying particular attention to novels written in two languages, English and Italian, this book breaks away from the confines of monolingual and nation-centric approaches, which are often prevalent in scholarly works within this field. *Literature of the Diaspora*, on the contrary, wishes to offer a comparative, transnational and multilingual examination of the network between texts, authors and contexts that inform Somali diasporic literature, with specific attention to the post-2000 novels that address the civil war and its aftermath. When taken together, these novels form a literary space where Somali authors share analogous aesthetic strategies and ethical concerns about Somaliness during a political moment that represents an attempt to restore national institutions in Somalia after the 1991 collapse of Siyaad Barre's regime and the resulting civil war.[5]

Avtar Brah's idea of 'diaspora space' becomes a functional conceptual category here, as it explains how diasporic experiences are internally related and accrued to the multiplicity of localities that they inhabit (Brah 1996, 209). Through their novels, Somali diasporic authors showcase the paradox of every diaspora – the simultaneous preservation of ties with their homeland and its reterritorialization in their host country through metaphorical symbolization (Ghorashi 2003, 189; Smith 2004, 256; McLeod 2018, XV). Being sites of confluence and convergence – of people, languages and cultures – diaspora spaces prompt an understanding of diasporas as both spatial and temporal events that should not be considered monolithically but according to their own history and internal differentiations (Brah 1996, 183). This idea however, should not be related to a physical, well-defined and enclosed territory, nor should it inevitably suggest the presence of identifiable borders and boundaries. I would like to think of diaspora spaces as flexible and fluid, with oceanic attributes, thus emphasizing constant movements, flows and currents between people, languages and cultures across different shores. Accordingly, this book examines the distant shores of the Somali diaspora and explores how they are connected through aesthetic forms and ethical concerns. It examines exchanges and mutual influences within the diaspora space without necessarily looking only at bifocal investigative models centred on the creative tension between 'home' and 'abroad'. Post-civil war novels, connected through their 'commitment to recording the memory and experiences of the Somali people, as well as celebrating their Somali literary heritage', have become a valuable tool to allow these exchanges and mutual influences to circulate (Fotheringham 2020, 57). In this sense, novels can be considered 'contested cultural and political terrains where individual and collective memories collide, reassemble and reconfigure' (Brah 1996, 193). Therefore, they will be the preferred form to investigate cultural and linguistic connections across the diaspora and link Somali authors living in the United States (such as Garane Garane and Afdhere Jama) to those living in Europe and writing in Italian (Igiaba Scego and Cristina Ali Farah) or German (Fadumo Korn) and those living in Africa (such as Nuruddin Farah).

In the case of Ali Farah and Scego, translations of their novels from Italian to English (specifically *Little Mother* and *Adua*, respectively) further encourage us to think about a potential dialogue between authors and their works, especially those coming from a relatively smaller circuit than those written in English. However, in certain instances, the term 'novel' is employed with flexibility. Garane's *Il latte è buono*, referred to as a novella here, and Ali Farah's *Little Mother* may retain elements that can be linked to the authors' real-life experiences, thus blurring the distinction between fiction and autobiography. I believe they also show a remarkable degree of invention and creativity that would be reductive to consider as autobiographies *tout court*. Another exception concerns Somali poems, analysed here via their English translations; they will be juxtaposed with prose works to offer a broader perspective on the civil war and engage in a dialogue with the texts under consideration, hopefully suggesting a cross-genre discussion that has yet to be explored.

In the vast and dynamic space of the diaspora, multiple languages and cultures coexist, as well as different experiences of migration, including those who personally lived through displacement and those who are post-migratory subjects. As scholar Khachig Tölölyan suggests, 'diaspora […] now shares meanings with a larger semantic domain that includes words like immigrant, expatriate, refugee, guest-worker, exile, community, overseas community, ethnic community' (1991, 4–5). Regardless of the distinctions between individual experiences and geographies, abodes (Italy, the United States and the UK), citizenships, cultural references and writing languages (English and Italian), the Somali writers considered here elected Somalia as their main subject of scrutiny. In other words, the idea of Somalia never really disappeared in the diaspora but 'rather remained present as a constitutive feature of the "imagined communities" that emerged amongst groups of migrants' (Singh 2021, 62).

This focus on Somalia across languages and nations makes the Somali diaspora a 'translocal circuit of contact' between authors and texts, which 'forms rhizomatic relays of new and renewed engagement for disparate participants' (McLeod 2018, XIV). This book draws upon this circuit of contact, which offers the opportunity to reflect on an idea of literature that is 'at once hybrid, national, transnational and global' (Comberiati and Luffin 2018, 15). In the diasporic and multilingual production, Somalia itself takes centrestage as an 'imaginary homeland', remembered, reimagined and contested in an interlocutory exchange between authors (Rushdie 1991). Importantly, it is worth underlining that this notion of homeland is not only a mythical place of longing but a physical place that, in Brah's terms, represents a 'lived experience of a locality', mediated by everyday social relations and subjectively experienced (1996, 192). Nuruddin Farah succinctly elaborates on this creative tension between the ideas of physical and conceptual homes, affirming that:

> I have not set foot in Mogadiscio for eighteen years and I have kept writing about this country. My connection with Somalia has always been through other places, other memories; even when I lived in Somalia, I often asked myself questions that made me use Somalia as a metaphor.
>
> (1993b, 62)

In the pursuit of investigating Somalia as a metaphor and as a homeland imagined from other places through private and collective memories, this book leverages a range of critical methodologies, including postcolonial theories, transnationalism, diaspora studies and literary geography. Opting for a single theory as the exclusive methodological approach, I believe, would restrict the goal of broadening and enriching the existing body of knowledge on Somali diasporic literature, a still-growing corpus of written and oral texts produced by different authors and from various places (Burns 2001). Therefore, I will refer to specific theories as suggested by the texts in question and engage with multiple approaches according to their relevance in my discussion. For example, the analysis of Nuruddin Farah, Garane Garane and Cristina Ali Farah's novels draws upon spatial literary studies but is also intertwined with notions of home, Blackness and multiple belongings, concepts that will benefit from the insights provided by postcolonial and diaspora studies. By emphasizing the complex network of interliterary references that may otherwise be overlooked if Somali authors and texts were grouped solely by nationality or language, the following analysis also combines diaspora and transnational studies. As the scholar Thomas Faist explains, 'While diaspora studies have mainly spoken to issues of cultural distinctiveness and its relevance for religious communities, nationhood and social practices such as entrepreneurship, transnational studies have come to focus on issues of mobility and networks' (2010, 17). Nonetheless, this book attempts to bridge the gap between these two concepts, which, I believe, despite having some conceptual and methodological differences, also exhibit intersections, similarities and reciprocal influences in how they approach shared themes, such as mobility, displacement, border crossing, and the tension between home and abroad (Tölölyan 1991, 5; Faist 2010, 20). Crucially, both diasporic and transnational perspectives acknowledge that social and cultural processes span multiple localities and national borders. Therefore, this book focuses not only on the relationship between home and abroad but also investigates the links between texts and contexts, meaning languages, literary traditions, intertextual references and aesthetic manifestations. It aims to elucidate how these elements play a role in constructing new narratives about Somalia from abroad in the post-civil war era.

Among the authors considered here (Ubax Cristina Ali Farah, Shirin Ramzanali Fazel, Igiaba Scego, Garane Garane, Afdhere Jama and Abdirazak Y. Osman), Nuruddin Farah (1945–) assumes a prominent position, owing to his esteemed status as an internationally acclaimed and award-winning author. Over his long literary career, he has produced plays, non-fiction, short stories and a substantial body of novels. Furthermore, Farah's work has been (and still is) a crucial reference point for the younger generation of Somali authors who started writing in the 1990s and 2000s, and he holds a revered position as a fatherly figure whose work has been a source of inspiration and influence, particularly for authors writing in Italian (Di Maio 2011; Dodgson-Katiyo 2020; Lazzari 2021).[6]

While Somali authors' literary production indicates 'biographical or imaginative association[s] to diaspora' through strong literary and cultural affinities, the following analysis will show that Somali literature slips away from too-narrow categorizations (Lazzari 2021, 66). Even though it is indeed global, produced outside Somalia and written in European languages, it 'is […] centred on national, ethnic, or religious questions' (Hodapp 2020, 5). In this regard, Farah seems to ratify these words, stating that 'stories are never told simply about the characters alone, but about a whole nation, which is the more important story' (1989, 186). A comparative and multilingual approach, then, is suitable to investigate how the local is transnationally mediated in the novels of Somali diasporic authors and how the global, conversely, is often disputed – as in the case of Western representations about Somalia – and addressed.

Concerning transnationalism, scholars Adele Parker and Stephenie Young argue that:

> Instead of emphasizing traditional national boundaries, [it] places importance on the 'trans': it marks movements across or beyond prescribed cultural and national spaces without privileging those spaces. It grows out of local sites of production but acknowledges that the local must have a conversation with the global.
>
> (2013, 1)

This book, accordingly, aims to shed light on transnational points of contact and tension across and beyond national spaces, shared aesthetics and ethics (in other words, discursive relations) within the multilingual and transnational diaspora space, without losing sight of local affiliations. As noticed, transnationalism is not necessarily 'a counter to nationalism' (Parker and Young 2013, 3), and transnational practices 'frequently bolster the formation and reconstitution of the nation-state' (Khan 2005, 2). This is the case of Somali diasporic novels, whose shared imagination is intrinsically connected to a nation-building project. Therefore, probing this dialogue between authors, texts and contexts will hopefully suggest new ways to look at Somali diasporic literature that, although multifaceted and challenging to encompass, presents similarities and intersections.

Some scholars have already moved towards this direction. Gabriele Lazzari, for example, has observed that Somali authors 'shared [the] attempt to narrativize the diasporic experience through an engagement with practices of border production' and try, at the same time, to articulate 'a minimally coherent identity through cultural and linguistic attachments (due to the absence of a stable political entity)' by framing 'identit[ies] in a transnational perspective' (2021, 63). Christopher Fotheringham, too, has recently studied points of contact between the novels of Nuruddin Farah and Nadifa Mohamed and Italophone writers of the Somali diaspora (2020, 56). Pauline Dodgson-Katiyo, similarly, has investigated the 'constructive linkages between Farah's work and that of [...] younger Somali writers', such as Cristina Ali Farah, Nadifa Mohamed, Diriye Osman and Abdourahman A. Waberi (2020, 67).

This book builds on and expands these views beyond border epistemologies (Lazzari 2021, 68) and the fictionalization of Somaliness through 'the strikingly harsh landscape of Somalia' (Fotheringham 2020, 63) to explore other cognate points of contact that hold equal importance in Somali diasporic novels. *Literature of the Somali Diaspora* thus puts in dialogue three main themes that have emerged as collective, recurrent and interrelated in the diasporic novels about the civil war: spatiality (with specific attention to the urbanscape), multilingualism (not necessarily bound by colonial binary oppositions) and resistance (by engaging with the literary canon and recovering the idea pf *impegno*). These three aspects allow us (and Somali authors) to develop and discuss configurations of the nation and the self across the diaspora and against the backdrop of the civil war. Specifically, through the literary representation of colonial architecture and its importance in the making of Somali identity, the creative use of multiple languages (English, Somali and Italian) and their engagement with the representation of nationhood in post-civil war periods (after Mussolini's and Barre's regimes in Italy and Somalia, respectively), *Literature of the Somali Diaspora* examines parallels and meeting points between Somali diasporic authors and texts, how they approach and resist their local realities, and how they interact with their cultural roots and each other.

Nowadays, Somalis are reshaping and rebuilding their national identity in a complex skein that rekindles and dismantles old social relations and political formations. Somali authors struggle with defining Somalia, as it is now a contested space that fights to survive in both geopolitical (Somalia as the Somali Democratic Republic, a sovereign country with defined borders and a centralized government, with Mogadishu as its capital city) and symbolical terms (the idea of Somalia as a collective and heterogeneous socio-cultural community whose inhabitants identify themselves as Somalis). While reassessing nationhood and the idea of homeland, Somali authors also navigate the challenges of resettlement in the former metropole, addressing identity-related issues such as ethnicity, race and gender. Their effort is both arduous and laudable. On the one hand, it engages with a country (or homeland) without stable borders, composed of people dispersed globally. On the other hand, it deals with a state that lacks centralized infrastructure and institutions, has limited readership and little public debate about the events that occurred during the civil war. As scholar Alexander Weheliye explains:

> Diaspora enables the desedimentation of the nation from the 'interior' by taking into account the groups that fail to comply with the reigning definition of the people as a cohesive political subject due to sharing one culture, one race, one language, one religion, and so on, and from the 'exterior' by drawing attention to the movements that cannot be contained by the nation's administrative and ideological borders.
>
> (2009, 162)

In literary terms, these practices of narrating an imaginary homeland from both internal and external perspectives have resulted in specific approaches and particular modes of representing Somalia, which *Literature of the Somali Diaspora* aims to analyse. This struggle to define Somalia and to position themselves in relation to the nation-state has become a distinctive feature of Somali diasporic authors, especially those who narrate the civil war and its aftermath, thus creating a specific poetics. In order to explore them, *Literature of the Somali Diaspora* suggests looking at Somali novels as 'signifier[s], not simply of transnationality and movement, but of political struggles to define the local, as a distinctive community, in historical contexts of displacement' instead of focusing predominantly on migration, displacement and resettlement in the host countries (Clifford 1994, 308).

As a way of retrieving and discussing nationhood, literature emerges as a means that allows for a transnational network of ideas and provides multifaceted representations of Somalia from both external and internal viewpoints. By enriching their narratives with several interpretations, combined with multiple languages and time settings, Somali novels look back at history by collecting multiple and often contrasting memories to both rebuild a sense of national unity and refashion the idea of Somalia on a global scale, in contrast to the one shaped during colonialism and the one that informs the Western narrative.[7] In this regard, Edward Said underlines that 'national identity always involves narratives of the nation's past, its founding fathers and documents, seminal events [...] Nevertheless, these narratives are never undisputed or merely a matter of the neutral recital of facts' (2000, 177). The idea that national identity comprises multiple narratives and languages informs most of the Somali novels of the diaspora, often characterized by contingent perspectives to overcome sectarian angles in favour of *tolerance*, as Farah observes, and 'the recognition of a necessary heterogeneity and diversity' (1993b, 63; Hall 1994, 401). Thus, one of the aims of this book is to investigate how these narratives and representations circulate through specific aesthetic strategies and how texts and context interact with one another.[8]

For example, the protagonist of Nuruddin Farah's novel *Links* (2005), Jeebleh, is pleased that Shirin Ramzanali Fazel, a real-life Somali Persian and Italian author, has authored a book about the civil war from a Somali perspective and by not following clan ideology and affiliation:

Reading the slim volume had been salutary, because unlike many books by authors with clan-sharpened axes to grind, this was not a grievance-driven pamphlet. It was charming, in that you felt that the author was the first to write a book about the civil war from a Somali perspective.

(Farah 2005, 226)[9]

As this passage shows, the emphasis is placed on the *Somali* perspective against, for example, clan-based narratives. Still, this fictional and metaliterary meeting sparks a discussion about nationhood and the diaspora, thus showing how Shirin Ramzanali Fazel's autobiography, *Lontano da Mogadiscio* (*Far from Mogadishu*, 1994), written and published in Italian, can dialogue with a novel of the 2000s written in English and contribute to the political discussion about Somalia within the diaspora. Similarly, another of Farah's novels, *From a Crooked Rib* (1970), is the intertextual reference to Cristina Ali Farah's *Le stazioni della luna* (Phases of the Moon, 2021), which rewrites the story of the same protagonist, Ebla, set in the Mogadishu of the 1930s and 1950s. Nuruddin Farah, recently interviewed for a special issue of *Tydskrif vir Letterkunde* for his fifty-year-long literary career, declared that he reads Cristina Ali Farah's and Igiaba Scego's works in Italian (Moolla 2020, 24). As mentioned, Nuruddin Farah represents a well-established literary antecedent, so it is not surprising that his quotation also appears as the epigraph of Igiaba Scego's *La mia casa è dove sono* (Home Is Where I Am, 2010) and Ali Farah's *Little Mother*.

Ali Farah acknowledges Farah's literary authority and role in influencing her imagination about Somalia by saying that, from the diaspora, 'literature is a dialogue with other texts and novels' (2015, 3; Einashe 2021). Interestingly, Ali Farah also elaborates on her role as a writer by making a helpful comparison:

> I protagonisti della diaspora si sentono come 'una collana incisa, in cui tutte le perle sono rimbalzate in più direzioni'. Con il mio romanzo e la mia scrittura, narro la storia di queste perle, quella delle tessere di un mosaico: il mio tentativo è fare in modo che le perle ritornino ad essere parte della stessa collana.
>
> (2007)

> The protagonists of the diaspora feel like 'a necklace that has been cut, whose beads have bounced away in several directions'. With my novel and my writing, I tell the story of these pearls, the story of the ties of a mosaic: I am trying to put the beads together again into a necklace.

It is evident here that Ali Farah is attempting to foster a dialogue between diasporic voices and experiences to reach a form of (comm)unity in the displacement. Ali Farah offers a creative elaboration of the etymology of the term 'diaspora', coming from the Greek verb *diaspeírein*, from *dia-* + *speírein*, meaning 'to scatter, spread, disperse, sow' (Baumann 2010, 20). She also echoes Farah's words in the preface of his non-fictional reportage about Somali refugees, *Yesterday, Tomorrow: Voices from the Somali Diaspora* (2000), in which he aims 'to impose a certain order on Somalia's anarchy' by collecting the 'voices of the refugees, the exiles and the internally displaced' to offer 'a nation of narratives held to ransom' (2000, VIII).

Therefore, there are clear connections between Somali Italian authors and Nuruddin Farah, but the transnational network of authors and texts unravels beyond Farah, Scego and Ali Farah's reciprocal references and develops in less evident and incredibly productive ways through shared themes and tropes that compose a specific Somali diasporic imaginary. Among these, urbanscapes, multilingualism and the concept of resistance and *impegno* will be the basis for the analysis conducted here.

The Nation, the City and Ourselves

Ato Quayson and Yoon Sun Lee claim that 'the diasporic imaginary rests on space' and that the question of identity in the novels of the diaspora is 'necessarily entangled with [it]' (2013, 148). Somali diasporic novels are no exception, and it is unsurprising that due to dispersion and resettlement, they are concerned with the (symbolical) restoration and re-imagination of different spaces.

One of the key aspects of the diasporic imagination concerning space is the representation of the lost homeland, which, in the case of Somali diasporic authors, is unambiguously defined in time and space, more than being related to a mythical or ancestral land. Somalia is then both a physical and imagined space in which a plurality of stories and languages converges, giving birth to a multilingual literature that is related to 'a notion of national identity and culture rooted in transnationalism and dishomogeneity' (Lombardi-Diop and Romeo 2014, 428).

This reflection on the meaning of Somalia as a nation from abroad, which involves the narrativization and elaboration of a sense of place and the mediation between diverse ways of belonging, is often filtered through the representation of Mogadishu. The capital city seems to have a centripetal pull on the writers of the diaspora and appears as an important site in which diasporic and transnational connections play out. Author Abdourahman Waberi, accordingly, has noticed that 'Mogadiscio [...] functions as an "actant" in its own right, with its own life, genealogy, personality, feelings, worries, etcetera' (1998, 776). Hence, the geographic mooring of this book is due to the noticeable significance that diasporic novels give to Mogadishu and its spatiality as to save it from the physical destruction of the civil war and counteract the detrimental narrative of the Western media about the city. As Iman Mohamed emphasizes in her useful essay about the colonial legacies in Mogadishu during independence and the civil war:

> The capital city has an understandably central place in the Somali national imaginary; claiming and moulding space in the city has always been a form of asserting and representing the state's broader power within and outside of Mogadishu.
>
> (2023, 3)

This central place is examined here, drawing upon Mohamed's investigation but expanding it beyond archival sources and personal accounts to read novels and maps. For example, looking more closely at Farah's literary production, Mogadishu emerges as the primary setting of almost all his English novels, from the first one, *From a Crooked Rib* (1970), to the latest trilogy, titled 'Past Imperfect', comprising *Links* (2004), *Knots* (2007) and *Crossbones* (2011). Appropriately, Ali J. Ahmed labels Farah as 'primarily an urban writer' (1996a, 35), a definition that Farah seems to have chosen for himself.[10] The capital city is not only a contextual setting but is addressed as a character itself – at times personified, as we will see – receiving close attention to its materiality. Farah affirms that he tries 'to view the city as the principal character, and the people living in it or visiting it become secondary characters' (Appiah 2004).

Indeed, Mogadishu also appears in other texts of the diaspora, such as *Nomad Diaries* (2009) by Yasmeen Maxamuud (born in Ceerigaabo, northern Somalia, and residing in San Diego) and *Liido Beach* (2018) by Afdhere Jama (born and raised in Somalia, now living in San Francisco), in the articles of *Guban*'s author Abdi Latif Ega (2012) and Mohamed Osman Omar's memoir, *The Road to Zero: Somalia's Self-destruction* (1993). Mogadishu also features in postcolonial Somali novels in Italian, such as Garane Garane's *Il latte è buono* (2005), Ubax Cristina Ali Farah's (born in Verona, 1973) *Little Mother* (2011) and Igiaba Scego's (born in Rome) *La mia casa è dove sono* (2010),

Adua (2015) and her latest, the Strega Prize-shortlisted novel, *Cassandra a Mogadiscio* (Cassandra in Mogadishu, 2023); in the short stories by Kaha Mohamed Aden, such as *Fra-intendimenti* (Misunderstandings, 2010); in the works by Shirin Ramzanali Fazel, such as *Far from Mogadishu* ([1994] 2017) and *Clouds Over the Equator* (2017) and in Mohamed Aden Sheikh's *Arrivederci a Mogadiscio* (Farewell, Mogadishu, 1994). Even though each writer has a distinctive cultural background, education, generation and location (not all writers were born in Mogadishu), the fictionalization of the capital city seems to be one of the nodes that tie Somali diasporic production and combine social and architectural aspects in ways that are reciprocally and inextricably formative (Crowley 2015, 26). Accordingly, among the Somali diasporic texts published in the post-civil war period, I selected those that are connected to reflections on nationhood and, at the same time, feature Mogadishu as a significant, if not essential, part of the plot and the ongoing debate about national identity.

To explore these reciprocally and inextricably productive ways, we should bring the critical concept of spatiality to the fore. In what follows, spatiality denotes the sociopolitical and fictional dimension of space, and it can be read as 'the product of interrelations' and interactions between individuals and groups regarding one another and their environment (Massey 2005, 9). Spatiality is employed here in the context of Somali diasporic novels to unveil not only the physical features of the city but also the connections between colonial and neocolonial powers, as well as global and local influences. Representing and reimagining Mogadishu, besides keeping it alive by writing about it, allow Somali authors to 'resist the dehumanising structures of oppression imposed by global capitalist modernity that is determined by forms of neocolonialism and post-Empire' (Leetsch 2021, 5). As I will show in the case of Farah's novels *Links* and *Crossbones*, their emphasis on urban spatiality is a crucial aesthetic feature to unsettle the dominant narrative about the city as ground zero. At the same time, the novels reclaim the importance of the very same spatiality at the local level. The representation of Mogadishu's urbanscape in several novels allows us to explore how:

> [...] the lived spaces of the cit[y], with the very particular geographies, traditions of spatial usage, cultural identities, histories of migration, and colonial legacies, affect diasporic identity construction.
>
> (Ilott, Mendes and Newns 2018, xxix)

In other words, the dramatization of Mogadishu becomes a fundamental means to retrieve both the material and symbolic legacies of Italian colonialism and to demystify the detrimental neocolonial narrative imposed upon the city (and the whole country), regarded by the American media as 'the world-capital of things gone to hell' (Myers 2011, 138). By analysing Mogadishu as the 'inner landscape for the imagination', to paraphrase Italo Calvino, we can consider how Somali authors register the configurations of the city over time and enable a sense of community that simultaneously emerges as local and global, transnational and multilingual (2004, 167).

The result is a description of Mogadishu that can be broadly labelled as 'multilingual local', at the same time deeply grounded in the local social organization of space and understanding of territoriality and related to global institutional forces that sidestep the national scale (Orsini 2015). The novels will reveal that the description of Mogadishu as a cosmopolitan city parallels the recurrent presence of polyglot and city-dweller characters and underpins the 'struggle over different articulations of the structure of social relations [...] appropriate for the present-into-the-future of the Somali people and nation' (Garuba 2017a, 19). As I will show, the idea of nationhood that diasporic authors elaborate on stems from a cosmopolitan and urban ethos that eschews any grounding in same-blood and clan-based belonging, patriarchal family structures and non-secularized ideologies.

The presence of Rome parallels the frequent occurrence of Mogadishu in Somali diasporic fiction, one of the centres of the Somali diaspora and, most importantly, a recurring setting of diasporic novels. Given its status as the former capital city of the short-lived Italian Empire, Rome has become 'the symbol of the past and present controversial relationship between Somalis and Italians' (Lori 2016, 77). However, the presence of the two cities in the diasporic imaginary suggests the importance of looking thoroughly not only at Mogadishu and Rome and their literary representations but also at specific, recurring spatial nodes around which the plots of the novels unravel, and diasporic subjectivities are assessed. The airports in Mogadishu and Rome, Stazione Termini (Rome) and the market in Mogadishu will be analysed here with a perspective that considers how these public sites, famously identified as *non-lieux* (non-places), are reshaped and reworked according to their locales (Augé 1995).[11] *Non-lieux* have been often used to define Western or (post)modern urbanscapes, such as motorways, hotel rooms, airports and shopping malls, but have been rarely employed in the African context. Alternatively, this study provides a focal point for understanding how Somali writers resist Western-centric definitions and propose alternative visions of spatiality and spatial relations, thus showing how some so-called non-places play, in fact, a primary role in shaping diasporic identities and retrieving the nation's past. The focus on the spatiality of these diasporic nodes also allows us to examine the impact of the Italian colonial era, a period of almost a century in which urban plans, cartography, architecture and spatial forms of ghettoization moulded and shaped Mogadishu and Somalis.

By retrieving the vestigial colonial presence in toponymy, sociocultural references and physical objects, Somali authors describe a multi-layered urbanscape in which native social practices juxtapose Italian customs. For example, the Italian refurbishment of Mogadishu in Garane's novella *Il latte è buono* reveals how colonial discourse was still at work in the late 1960s. The production of space emerges in *Il latte è buono* as a social and political action led by colonial dynamics. Through his protagonist, Gashan, the author shows how the dominant interference of colonial discourse disrupted the *genius loci* (the spirit of the place) and provided it with new meanings and identity articulations. As Rashid Ali and Andrew Cross have noticed, 'the café culture, cuisine (pasta became a staple Somali diet) and the unhurried Mediterranean tradition of the evening strolling to shop, see and be seen' were adopted in Somali everyday life, suggesting that the influence of the built form was not confined to the architectural level but linked to cultural and social practices (2016, 13). By physically alienating the colonized subjects through the imposition of new names in a foreign language and by tangibly modifying local habits, 'colonialism [brought] with it a sense of dislocation between the environment and the imported language now used to describe it, a gap between the "experienced" place and the descriptions the language provides' (Ashcroft, Griffith and Tiffin 2000, 161). This gap, particularly evident in Mogadishu, represents a key feature of the diasporic imaginary and allows us to unravel the connections between colonialism and Somali national and personal identities and to explore the consequences of the processes of independence and decolonization that awkwardly occurred under the aegis of Italian rule (1950–60).

The effort to reimagine the lost nation is also evident in postcolonial Somali novels in Italian. However, this imaginative and creative attempt coexists with issues related to displacement and the unwelcoming society of the former metropole. Rome has become another centre of the diaspora and, appropriately, is the other focus of this book's geocritical analysis. As the city where Somali people gathered from the 1980s to the late 1990s, Rome is twinned with Mogadishu in Garane's, Ali Farah's and Scego's texts but, interestingly, also in Nuruddin Farah's and Fadumo Korn's. The two capital cities epitomize the long-lasting influences and relationships that have characterized Italy and Somalia's history, from colonialism to the civil war and throughout independence.

The Languages of Diasporic Subjectivities

The close relationship between spatiality and memory implies an association between materiality and narrative. The process of remembering is enabled and empowered by the act of writing, which is necessary to preserve Somalia's existence. The Mogadishu imagined and written in the novels of the diaspora can be considered an example of what Henri Lefebvre calls *architexture*, a space in which monuments and buildings are viewed in their surroundings and contexts as part of a network that includes their materiality and their social and symbolic relevance (1991, 118, 131). As the urbanscape can be read as a text in which physical elements (streets, buildings, houses, monuments and stations) have symbolic meanings, language plays a pivotal role in creating and reimaging not only space but also the interrelations between the people (or characters) who inhabit both literary and physical spaces. Again, the concept of spatiality is productive in incorporating several interweaved notions: social relations, power dynamics, memory, architecture and the writing process, all articulated through the polyphonic and multilingual feature of the novel form.

This mode of storytelling, in which multiple languages and viewpoints are employed for representing and interpreting events, does not necessarily conclude with a final denouement or a neat resolution. This aligns with what Ali Jimale Ahmed highlights as a prominent feature within Somali literary production:

Somali literature considers opposing views [...] a healthy sign indicative of the superstructure's ability to compromise on certain issues which do not jeopardize the essence of the social system's existence. The social system permits the expression of the different views of its different components.

(1996, 44)

By enriching their texts with multiple viewpoints and languages to accommodate several characters with distinct experiences and varying connections to diasporic realities, Somali novels succeed in refashioning an idea of Somalia as more composite and multi-layered than the one propagated by the Western narrative. As Colin Davis suggests, there are compelling links between the diaspora, the loss of home and (the lack) of language because the diasporic writer, split between two or more languages and cultures, navigates a new literary space where experiences of dispersion and unsettlement coexist with the yearning for an understanding of the individual and national self (2018, 122). Thus, multilingualism arises as the second meeting point of contemporary Somali novels and the second main subject of analysis. I aim to show, against any assumption of linguistic hegemony, the 'interwoven aesthetics and politics of [Somali] postcolonial novels' in English and Italian 'and how they have been in dialogue with each other' and with local forms of expression, not necessarily associated to the colonial presence (Laachir, Marzagora and Orsini 2018, 4). In other words, this book investigates how Somali novels are both globally influenced and locally concerned, without supporting the idea of the latter as a synonym for 'provincial' or hierarchically inferior to the former.[12]

On the contrary, the analysis will illustrate how, for example, Somali novels in Italian engage with and relate to their local background with 'strategies that are specifically tailored to seeking recognition in the Italian literary field', such as 'the explicit engagement with writers that any Italian reader would unmistakably perceive as part of the national canon' (Lazzari 2021, 72). However, they also foster a dialogue with the Somali language and literary forms, as in the case of Garane's novel *Il latte è buono*, which reinvents the oral form of the *gabay*, or in Scego's and Ali Farah's novels, which use Somali words, glossed and unglossed, in the Italian syntax in a creative coexistence between languages. This engagement with multiple languages and Italian is also present in Farah's novels, such as *Links* and *Crossbones*. Although mainly set in Somalia, they show a strong bond to Italy and the Italian culture and unsettle the colonial binary hierarchy by illustrating how it breaks down when a specific setting (Somalia) allows two colonial languages to compete (English and Italian) and Somali to be the medium of the factions during the civil war.

It should be emphasized that part of Somalia's actual social and political fragmentation is the result of colonialism and political interference that extended beyond Italian occupation. Even though it officially ended with the Trust Territory of Somaliland (in Italian: *Amministrazione fiduciaria italiana della Somalia* or AFIS), the relationship with Italy after Somali independence did not cease. In fact, the Italian government played a significant role during and after Barre's dictatorship, even with some illicit traffic connected to hazardous waste dumping. Maxamed Siyaad Barre was a former member of the Italian colonial police during the 1930s and a cadet of the Carabinieri Training School in Florence in the 1950s (Del Boca 1993; Chiapparoni 2009). Italy supported his dictatorial rule after 1969 and offered no asylum to those escaping the dictatorship or the war (Del Boca 1993). This reluctance to grant Somali people the status of political refugees, both during Barre's regime (1969–91) and the civil war (1991–), contributed to expanding the geographic borders of the diaspora, as Somali people, instead of choosing the hostile and unwelcoming metropole, mainly settled in African countries (Kenya and Ethiopia), Europe (the UK, Sweden, Norway, Germany and the Netherlands) or Canada and the United States.

However, although Italy showed little interest in welcoming its former colonized subjects, it should be noted that the presence of Italy emerges as a shared theme in the writings of Somali diasporic authors. The legacy left by the Italian occupation strongly resonates in both Anglophone and Italophone novels, despite their limited (Nuruddin Farah) or non-existent (Nadifa Mohamed, Afdhere Jama, Abdi Latif Ega or Yasmeen Maxamuud) experience in or of Italy (Di Maio 2017). Recent works have looked more closely at these authors and their relationship with Italianness, emphasizing their specificity within the Italian literary scene (Curti 2007; Proglio 2011; Brioni 2015; Lori 2016; Di Maio 2017). Vivian Gerrard's recent monograph, *Possible Spaces of Somali Belonging* (2016), detaches itself from language-based approaches and steps further in the direction of a comparative approach, as it examines how Somali communities resettled in two nations, Italy and Australia, via a visual and literary analysis.[13]

Literature of the Somali Diaspora further develops and enlarges the comparative trend but also shifts the focus from the experience and representation of resettlement and belonging to investigate multiple affiliations across the diaspora. This book, accordingly, examines Somali novels' strategies towards English, Italian and Somali without assuming the latter's 'dependence and subordination from the putative metropolitan centres' (Laachir, Marzagora and Orsini 2018, 293). Uncovering the *long durée* of Italian colonialism to investigate it through the eyes of Somali authors also means deprovincializing Italian studies and showing how diasporic texts play a significant role in retrieving the forgotten memories of Italian colonialism. In this sense, they can be considered 'part of a multilingual diasporic postcolonial tradition with an urgent ethic of remembrance' intended to address 'Italian colonial discourses and the history and stories of the victims of Italian imperialism' (Fotheringham 2019a, 111). Italy, therefore, can be considered a 'mobile cultural symbol' or 'a signifier [...] detached from its original national parameters of territory' (Bond 2022, 97). Building on Emma Bond's idea of 'looking sideways', a method to examine literary representations 'to show how they can put pressure on what (and where)' a culture resides, the present analysis wishes to explore how Italy is reproduced from outside the national canon. By including texts neither written in Italian nor by Italian authors, this book also implicitly proposes expanding the borders of national literature and welcoming voices from elsewhere who may 'offer sideways insight into Italian history and culture' (Bond 2022, 95).

In Farah's 'Past Imperfect' trilogy, for example, Italy surfaces through the generation of characters who grew up during the AFIS era and were exposed to Italian culture during the democratic period (1960–9). As Zoe Norridge notes, 'Italian rule has left multiple legacies: from *spaghetti* lunches to Farah's preferred spelling of the capital as Mogadiscio' (2012). These multiple legacies surface at the linguistic and physical levels, as the analysis of Farah's *Links* and *Crossbones* will show. The case of Garane Garane, who wrote his semi-autobiographical novella in Italian, is emblematic in showing the deep-rooted relationship between Italy and post-independence Somalia in terms of education, language and culture.

Garane's *Il latte è buono* will be examined with specific attention towards the use of the Italian language to describe a pre-colonial context (the Ajuran's sultanate in the eighteenth century) and in relation to the oral feature of his novella. In this regard, orature has been applied uncritically in Italian postcolonial studies, with little investigation of the specificity of Somali orature. While described as a characteristically African trait, orature has been disconnected from its literary and cultural context and inscribed in an ahistorical framework (Negro 2013, 57). In other words, the latter generalization has allowed Italian scholars to employ it as an all-purpose critical tool to denote the 'Africanness' of a text against Western norms.[14]

Ultimately, multilingualism also emerges in relation to another form of intertextuality, which does not involve the Somali language and orature but the use of Italian literary tradition. Indeed, this study will explore the composite network of intra-textual and intertextual references to Dante's *The Divine Comedy* in Farah's *Links*. Dante's work represents another transnational point of contact between the diaspora novels, as it is explicitly evoked in Scego's *La mia casa è dove sono* and *Adua* and in Garane's *Il latte è buono*. The presence of Dante's *Comedy* as the primary source text for Farah and Italian authors, beyond showing the literary connections between texts, indicates the transnational scope of the Somali diaspora. Farah's intense use of the *Comedy* raises several questions concerning intertextuality in the diasporic context, particularly when viewed comparatively with other Italophone texts and authors who consider Dante the epitome of Italian literary tradition. The analysis will suggest that, on the one hand, Farah employs Dante's well-known poem to represent the civil-war context of Somalia through the protagonist's point of view, thus deterritorializing the local context of Somalia. On the other hand, by placing Somalia and Mogadishu in relation to Hell, he subverts and re-contextualizes *Inferno*, generates new meanings and distances his novel from Dante's literary antecedent.

To better understand the multilingual context of Somalia, it is essential to show how diasporic novels interact with the linguistic backgrounds of where they are produced, the author's country of birth and their knowledge of the language employed for literary purposes. Most importantly, the understudied interrelation between Somali and Italian culture and literary tradition should also be addressed. For example, by examining orature and intertextuality, *Literature of the Somali Diaspora* shows how the novels relate to multilocal literary contexts and engage with the transnational feature of the Somali diaspora. In other words, it proposes an approach that takes multilingualism and multilocalism into account and 'holds both *local* and *cosmopolitan* perspectives in view' (Orsini 2015, 345). Somali diasporic novels, in particular, are 'at once carriers of national and familial traditions and emblems of cultural and personal identity' but also 'identity-grounding homes under conditions of displacement and means of intervention into identity-fixing cultural agendas' (Bammer 1994, XVI). This definition combines the concepts of diaspora, identity and nationhood as intertwined with language. It also leads us to the last aspect explored in this study: the fictionalization of historical events – dictatorship and the civil war – through aesthetic practices and ethical concerns that engage with canonical authors of the Italian literary tradition.

Resistenza and *Impegno* in Somali Novels in Italian

By moving the analysis beyond the intertextuality between a 'global' text, such as Dante's *Comedy*, and Somali writings and beyond the creative reuse of 'local' oral forms related to Somali orature, this study examines the interplay between postcolonial Somali writings in Italian and Italian literary traditions. In doing so, this book proposes reading Ali Farah's *Little Mother* and Scego's *Adua* and *Letteratura della Resistenza* (Resistance Literature or Literature of the Resistance) together. Paraphrasing Salman Rushdie's words used to describe the case of Indian authors in English, Somali writers 'have access to a second tradition' (1991, 124), which is made up of displacement, cross-cultural connections and multilingualism but, at the same time, is related to the history, culture and society of the host country. This second tradition allows us to consider them not just as either Somali or Italian but both, simultaneously, thus inscribing them 'within Italian frames of reference' (Gerrard 2016, 153).

By reading Somali novels in Italian in relation to the Italian literary tradition and their affinities with the aesthetic practices and ethical commitment of the *Resistenza*, we can overcome any strictly 'one-nation, one-state, one-language ideologies' that consider the Italian literary tradition as a homogeneous and monolingual corpus of literary works in which, thus far, only Italian-born (and white) authors are included (Beswick 2010, 134). The comparison between Igiaba Scego's *Adua* and Cristina Ali Farah's *Little Mother* with texts of the Italian literary canon, namely Italo Calvino's *Il sentiero dei nidi di ragno* (*The Path of the Spiders' Nests*, 1947) and Luigi Meneghello's *I piccoli maestri* (*The Outlaws*, 1964), aims to retrieve under-explored interrelations and exchanges between the post-war poetics of the *Resistenza* and postcolonial formal features and ethical concerns. To date, the relationship between Somali Italian writings and the Italian literary tradition has been somewhat overlooked.

Initially, Italian studies predominantly scrutinized Italian authors through the lenses of gender, ethnicity and migration. It was only in a subsequent phase that a postcolonial perspective was introduced, with the specific objective of delving deeper into Italy's colonial history, its legacy and the representation of Italy as a former colonial power. Authors from Libya, Eritrea and Ethiopia, writing in Italian, began to be collectively examined due to shared thematic elements related to the retrieval of Italy's colonial past and shed light on present-day racist policies about migration and citizenship. This second phase heralded an increased focus on Somali Italian authors specifically, including figures such as Igiaba Scego, Cristina Ali Farah, Kaha Mohamed Aden, Garane Garane and Shirin Ramzanali Fazel (Proglio 2011; Brioni 2015; Gerrard 2016; Lori 2016; Di Maio 2017; Fotheringham 2019a).[15]

Overall, despite the notable contributions of scholars of Italian studies outside of Italy, who paid attention to the postcolonial Italian literary production and advocated for a transnational approach to Italian literature, scholars of *Italianistica* have shown a certain hesitancy to embrace this literary corpus fully. There still exists a reluctance to consider it as an integral part of the Italian literary tradition – if not ancillary or negligible (Comberiati and Mengozzi 2022, 11). This book, on the contrary, proposes that Somali authors have contributed to changing Italian literature and argues for the necessity to interrogate the canon and rethink the area of study of *Italianistica* from a transnational perspective, an approach recently proposed by some scholars of Italian studies (Bond 2014; Burns and Duncan 2020; Burdett, Havely and Polezzi 2020; Burdett 2022; Comberiati and Mengozzi 2022).

Somali authors writing in Italian, on the one hand, engage with the 'complex strategies of cultural identification and discursive address that function in the name of "the people" and "the nation" and make them the immanent subject' of their novels (Bhabha 2004, 201). In other words, they discuss the idea of nationhood after the historical event of the civil war, and they also negotiate their multiple belonging to the former metropole, Italy, and Somalia. On the other hand, Somali Italian authors challenge the supposed sameness of Italian society by placing themselves in dialogue with the Italian literary tradition and raising questions such as 'Who are the Italians?' and 'What does it mean to be Italian?' (Benvenuti 2012). In this sense, their novels work along transnational axes but simultaneously operate between and across local realities within the same literary space.

The comparison between the *Resistenza* and postcolonial Somali novels in Italian may appear far-fetched due to the cultural and historical distance between the events in question, post-Second World War and the 1990s. However, the attempt to reassess the concept of national identity after a civil war (Italian, between 1943 and 1945, and Somali, from 1991 to the present day) and dictatorship (Mussolini and Barre) strongly tie these two literatures. One further node of connection between these bodies of literature is the idea of *impegno*. Jennifer Burns (2001) thoroughly examines the development of this concept over time in Italian literary tradition. Loosely translated as 'political commitment' or 'engagement', *impegno* spans different literary landscapes and times, changing its aims and aesthetic manifestations. Burns meticulously shows how the post-war commitment to a political agenda (usually communist) during the 1950s and 1960s has become fragmented but is nonetheless present in later authors of the 1980s and 2000s. Building on her work on *impegno*, this book recovers its meaning – understood as a way of addressing sociopolitical issues through literature that directly engages with the reader – and aims to demonstrate how Scego's and Ali Farah's novels show a 'recuperation […] of ethics' and an 'ethical commitment' to address Italy's present-day environment (Burns 2001, 5). In doing so, they employ aesthetic features similar to those described by Calvino, thus building a bridge between past and present and between literatures and cultures.

A Route through the Book

The first chapter, 'Key Places in the Somali Diasporic Imaginary', investigates recurring and symbolically relevant sites in Mogadishu and Rome as represented in the novels by Nuruddin Farah, Afdhere Jama, Garane Garane, Ubax Cristina Ali Farah, Igiaba Scego and Shirin Ramzanali Fazel. The starting point of the analysis is that spatiality plays a fundamental role in shaping one's relationship with a given environment, as buildings, architecture, roads and monuments are not disconnected elements but parts of a larger framework of relationships (Cresswell 2015). This chapter, accordingly, encourages the critical exploration of specific fictionalized places that usually are included in the category of *non-lieux*. Each section of the chapter explores these key places, showing their significance in the diasporic imaginary: the airport of Mogadishu and Rome (in Farah's *Links* and *Crossbones*, Jama's *Liido Beach* and Garane's *Il latte è buono*), the Bakhaaraha and Tamarind Markets (Farah's *Crossbones*), and Stazione Termini in Rome (in Garane's *Il latte è buono*, Ali Farah's *Little Mother*, Fazel's *Far From Mogadishu*, Scego's *Oltre Babilonia* and *La mia casa è dove sono*). These places are strategic in the novels since they foster an analysis of the conflict between identity and belonging experienced by Somali diasporic characters who, strive to re-create local-based social bonds unrelated to *qabyaalad* (clannism). In Italy, too, they struggle to deal with the sense of estrangement of living in the capital city of the former metropole. While the analysis of the airports will show how the latter are locally shaped and deeply influenced by their locale, the investigation of the markets will demonstrate how their spatiality allows Farah and Ali Farah to look back at the cosmopolitan past of Mogadishu. Their examination of the pre-colonial and democratic periods serves to retrieve the lost urban ethos of Mogadishu and explain the present-day fragmentation.

Stazione Termini, Rome's central train station, is represented as the central node where several stories of immigration, racism and resilience unfurl. Its complex spatiality provides us with a perspective on the lives of Somali people living abroad and their attempt to reterritorialize the station to make it part of the Somali community. As the analysis will show, Termini plays a contradictory role, being a place where both a sense of home and exclusion can develop. Whereas the main critical approach considers these places as universal or atemporal, as the label of *non-lieux* by the French anthropologist Marc Augé suggests, novels by diasporic authors, on the contrary, will show how *non-lieux* are reshaped and reworked according to their context, without necessarily losing their global feature. This approach offers a focal point for understanding the way Somali writers resist Western-centric spatial relations and propose alternative visions of spatiality and space connections, which foster in their turn a cosmopolitan sense of nationhood.

Chapter 2, 'Literary Cartographies of Mogadishu', remains focused on spatiality but zooms out on the main topic of analysis to conduct a literary-oriented reading of Mogadishu's urbanscape. The chapter investigates the fictionalization of the capital city between the years soon after the end of the AFIS trusteeship (in the 1960s) and during the civil war (in the 1990s). Even though in ruins and with frail political authority, the capital city still holds its position as the centre of the 'lost' nation and, via its textual representation, becomes the source for understanding the recent historical development of the whole country. Though every writer has a distinctive cultural background, different linguistic education, generation and location (some of them were not born in Mogadishu), the fictionalization of Mogadishu seems to be one of the strands that bond diasporic authors and combines social and architectural aspects in ways that are reciprocally and inextricably formative. Diasporic novels become 'a kind of narrative map' of Mogadishu, 'where the heterogeneity and multitude of persons and places are somehow interconnected and made sensible' (Tally 2013, 88). The city represents, rephrasing Édouard Glissant, a *locus* where the past can be found; developing an archaeological notion of space and time, then, would allow us to retrieve the traces of the past that survive in both landscapes and language (1999). Drawing upon Glissant's idea, the chapter attempts to bring to the fore the social and historical complexity of everyday life in Mogadishu, thus providing an alternative to the simplified, a-historical and dehumanized representations presented in Western mass media. According to Glissant's 'archaeological approach', the chapter's first section focuses on the role played by map-making and imperial cartography in shaping Somali identities. It explores the tension between the enduring physical presence of Italian toponymy and the context of Somalia's post-independence. Garane's novella (*Il latte è buono*) and Jama's (*Liido Beach*), and Ali Farah's novels (*Le stazioni della luna* and *Madre piccola*) will be analysed together to highlight the bond between the architectural form and the identities of the protagonists. The importance placed on spatiality and cartography allows us to develop a comparative reading between a colonial guidebook from the 1930s, *Guida dell'Africa Orientale Italiana*, and the fictional descriptions of the city made in the novels. This comparison emphasizes how Italian colonial discourse was already present in the Liberal era (1861–22) and was not confined to the Fascist occupation. The last section of the chapter continues the analysis of Mogadishu but shifts to the 1990s, when the city was destroyed by the civil war. Here, the focus lies on Somali authors' strategies of narrating the conflict and their endeavors to envision a peaceful future for Somalia.

Chapter 3, 'Multilingualism in Farah's *Links* and *Crossbones*', keeps the focus on the Italian colonial legacy in Somalia and its importance in shaping Somalis' identities. The previous chapters have demonstrated the link between aesthetics and spatiality, so Chapter 3 moves from literary cartography and its representation to language, which plays relevant part too in shaping national and individual belongings. In doing so, the use of the Italian language becomes the *file rouge* that connects diasporic novels. For example, by analysing the use of Dante's quotations from *The Divine Comedy*, employed by Farah to make a comparison between Hell and Mogadishu, I aim to show how the poem is deeply constitutive of *Links*. The analysis then suggests that, on the one hand, intertextuality aims to address, represent and understand the civil war context of Mogadishu from the protagonist's point of view. On the other hand, it subverts and recontextualizes 'Inferno' to create new meanings and distance the novel from Dante's literary antecedent. This chapter, therefore, shows how through Dante and the use of Italian, Farah reconfigures both real and imaginary geographies. Following the analysis of intertextuality in Farah's *Links*, the chapter elaborates upon multilingualism as a tool to investigate the concepts of nation, Somaliness and belonging. For this purpose, the analysis explores the strategic use of the Italian language in Farah's English-written novels, *Links* and *Crossbones*, and the relationship between Italian, English and Somali. While there are some works on Farah's previous trilogies (Gorlier 1998; Vivan 1998; Weinberg 2013), little has been done about 'Past Imperfect', so electing *Links* and *Crossbones* as the main focus aims to fill a gap in the current scholarship.[16] Before close reading the novels, I suggest dwelling in Farah's linguistic background, so to consider the 'author's biography or the author as a historical figure' (Laachir, Marzagora and Orsini 2018, 304). Placing Farah in his context, in other words, will provide us with the socio-historical and literary environment in which he was born and raised, as it significantly shaped his works and his relationship with the English, Somali and Italian languages. Moreover, the chapter proposes that *Links* and *Crossbones* are helpful examples for raising the epistemological question of considering the choice of using a former colonial language for artistic purposes, as mere evidence of subjection and hegemony. In fact, by studying the use of Italian in *Links* and *Crossbones*, the chapter will show how the former colonial language undertakes a more nuanced role than the one ideologically laden due to colonialism. In the backdrop of the civil war, where allegiances and alliances change continually according to multiple and volatile factors, language rises as a marker of belonging or non-belonging according to the actors and contexts in which it is used. The Italian language provides Farah with a creative tool to explore the multiple belongings of his characters and the complexities of the civil war scenario, a context in which colonial cultural influences play a weaker role than clan affiliations.

Chapter 4, 'The Spoken Word Meets the Script: Somali, Italian and the Role of Orature', keeps the focus on multilingualism, expanding the analysis on the use of the Italian beyond Dante's *Comedy*. In doing so, it examines Garane's *Il latte è buono* with a specific focus of his 'indigenization' of the Italian language through specific discursive strategies and the intertextual use of Somali orature, resemanticized in the Italian linguistic framework of the novella (Zabus 2014). The chapter, therefore, explicitly challenges the idea of orature as mere aesthetic evidence of authenticity, retained by authors of African origin to validate their Africanness and cultural specificity. The analysis starts with a contextualization of *Il latte è buono* according to its multicultural influences to explore how languages and forms from different traditions reciprocally interact. As the analysis will show, the feature of being one of the first postcolonial Italian novels positions *Il latte è buono* in a specific creative space that allows us not only to connect it to the Italian literary tradition but also to retrieve a genealogical affiliation in terms of aesthetics to the early production of African Anglophone postcolonial writings of the 1960s and 1970s. Indeed, the almost unique presence of

Il latte è buono in the Italian literary tradition, which before its publication lacked examples of texts written in Italian by formerly colonized subjects living outside of Italy, encourages us to consider the novel as part of a broader multicultural production of literatures coming from the African continent.

Chapter 5, 'Resistance and *impegno*: Postcolonial Somali Novels in Italian and *Letteratura della Resistenza*', aims to analyse novels by Somali Italian writers – Igiaba Scego and Ubax Cristina Ali Farah – to trace their relationship with *Letteratura della Resistenza* (Resistance Literature or Literature of the Resistance). The chapter investigates how aesthetic principles and ethical commitments present in the Italian Resistance Literature – mainly defined by Italo Calvino in his preface to *The Path of the Spiders' Nests* – are analogous to some formal features and ideas of *impegno* employed by Scego and Ali Farah. This chapter is the first analysis that compares these two fictional outcomes and charts the significant yet critically neglected relation between postcolonial and post-war authors, thus challenging the idea that the former is 'extraneous' or artistically unrelated to the Italian literary tradition. On the contrary, the chapter shows the fluidity of the influences between these texts and how they present analogue strategies of representing and rewriting history. Indeed, the assumption underpinning my analysis is that, despite the differences in terms of space and time, the event of the civil war following the dictatorship puts in contact - in terms of the writer's commitment to represent society – these two literary productions, both aesthetically and ethically. The analysis also points out an aspect that has been overlooked, even though it emerges as the primary historical bond between Italy and Somalia: both nations underwent dictatorship (Benito Mussolini and Siyaad Barre as leaders of a one-party government) and civil war. The chapter investigates this connection through the analysis of the main rhetorical strategies concerning the historical event of the war and how the notion of *impegno* has been recovered and fruitfully used by postcolonial authors.

Notes

1   It should be noted that beyond prose and poetry, in the 1960s, the theatre gained importance and relevance as well. Dramas were written and performed in both verse and prose, with musical accompaniment (Andrzejewski 2011b, 85–6; Ali Farah 2018b, 27–8).
2   Similarly, historian Mohamed Haji Ingiriis points out that 'the word "Somalia" is heavily contested by some Somalis who consider it a term depicting a clan connotation' (2018, 62). According to this contention, 'Somalia was named after the Samaale clan, comprising the Hawiye, the Isaaq, and the Dir, together known as the Irir Samaale (the Daarood are not included in the Samaale as some scholars assumed)' (Ingiriis 2018, 62).
3   The Federal Government of Somalia (FGS) currently holds international recognition as the legitimate governing body of Somalia. Notably, it represents the first attempt to establish a centralized government in the aftermath of the civil war. In 2012, it succeeded the Transitional Federal Government (TFG) upon the promulgation of the

4   Constitution of Somalia, with Mogadishu serving as the designated capital.
4   I use the terms Anglophone and Italophone here, instead of 'English' and 'Italian', as they are more inclusive and implicitly suggest that languages are spoken and written differently according to geographic, historical, cultural and political contexts.
5   The Somali diaspora should be understood considering a two-decade-long dictatorship (1969–91) and the subsequent civil war (1991), events that led to the territorial fragmentation of the country, the dispersion of roughly 2 million Somali individuals worldwide and an enduring political crisis (Gerrard 2016, 1–2). Among its disastrous effects, this socio-historical and political turmoil prompted Somali authors and intellectuals to 'question seriously the very existence of the state and society over which the political struggle had been waged' in the past decades (Alpers 1995, 223).
6   Even though not all of the writers considered here have a direct experience of migration from Somalia (as in the case of Scego, who was born in Rome, and Cristina Ali Farah, who was born in Verona and moved to Somalia later before going back to Italy again), they demonstrate a deep relationship with 'the process of migrations itself', which indeed 'resound[s] across generations' and contributes significantly to defining the thematic core and literary horizon of their artistic production (McLeod 2018, XV).
7   For example, the Italian colonial discourse fashioned the invention of the Somali people as a community hierarchically divided into nomads (free men) and sedentary farmers (enslaved people) to maintain control by breaking the pre-existing concentration of power into pieces (Ahad 2019). The American media, on the other hand, have represented Somalia as a failed state and the Somali people as victims, pirates or terrorists (Myers 2011).
8   Instead of novels, the production of poems, both printed and online, may represent another starting point to look at the evolution of this genre across the diaspora and how it has endorsed the discussion about nationhood. Another perspective can take into consideration novels in the Somali language or other European languages (Dutch, German, Finnish or French, for example), thus stretching the multilingual and transnational analysis conducted here to an even more inclusive and broader comparison. Lidwien Kapteijns has looked at poems with the abovementioned approach (2010).
9   Farah affirms that 'I am conscious of my being Somali, my novels are basically Somali – all Somalis can see it, I can see it, everyone can see it' (Jussawalla and Dasenbrock 1992, 50).
10 'I am a city person. I write, I am cosmopolitan' (Jussawalla and Dasenbrock 1992, 50).
11 I am aware that 'space' and 'place' should not be used interchangeably and have been theoretically addressed in academic works. The difference between these two concepts has been discussed in human geography, sociology and anthropology, and it has become increasingly difficult to define them unequivocally. I will take advantage of this uncertainty and promote the slippage between space and place, which often appear in literary texts with a similar connotation. In this book, spatiality is generally preferred to both terms, as it underlines the connections between architecture and social relations. As Tim Creswell has noticed, the distinction between space and place has become somewhat confused with the introduction of spatiality and the idea of social space, which, 'in many ways, plays the same role as place' (2015, 17). The term

'place', for example, is used in this book for the generally adopted translation of *non-lieux* (non-places) and to specifically identify the supermodern sites of consumption and transfer identified by Marc Augé, such as stations, airports and shopping malls.

12 As we have seen, prose production survives and flourishes mainly outside the country in European languages, thus making the mentioned collective 'national' narrative more problematic. In the multicultural literary landscape of the diaspora, Anglophone writers of Somali origin or descent have a preponderant weight over Italian, Dutch and German productions, having gained international acclaim, a wider audience and academic attention over the years. However, since the growing body of novels by Somali writers comprises outcomes in different languages and from different countries, we can speak of contemporary Somali literature by embracing those texts written and published outside Somalia in European languages and Arabic. While, regrettably, novels in Somali struggle in terms of readership, translation and dissemination beyond Somalia due to factors such as the lack of a robust state infrastructure, a developed publishing system to foster and publicize them and a Western-dominated market, novels originating from the diaspora, conversely, possess an advantage in reaching a wider audience and circulating more effortlessly.

13 For example, migration and otherness (Gnisci 1998; Polezzi 2006), margins versus centre (Parati 2005), race and diaspora (Portelli 1999), and gender (Polezzi 2006; Coppola 2011; Marzagora 2015; Di Maio 2017). Only two monographs are dedicated to Somali Italian literary works: Laura Lori's *Inchiostro d'Africa* (2013) and Simone Brioni's *The Somali Within: Language, Race and Belonging in Minor Italian Literature* (2015).

14 Similarly, orality plays a less romantic and more problematic role in Nuruddin Farah's novels. Farah avoids enhancing the oral tradition similar to Ngũgĩ wa Thiong'o in *Matigari* or Ayi Kwei Armah in *Two Thousand Seasons* by showing 'how indigenous traditions, oral as well as domestic, have themselves been implicated in the new political tribulations and terrors of the independent state' (Wright 2002, 52).

15 Italo Calvino, though, has been studied in postcolonial terms in relation to Salman Rushdie, whose formal features developed from his reading of the Italian author (Giuliani 2007).

16 Lorenzo Mari's seminal work, *Forme dell'interregno. Past Imperfect di Nuruddin Farah tra letteratura post-coloniale e world literature* (2018), should be mentioned here as the only monograph about Farah written in Italian. It also represents an important starting point for this analysis, as it focuses on Farah's latest trilogy and the relationship between *Links* and Dante's *Divine Comedy*, which will be the subject of Chapter 3.

1

Key Places in the Somali Diasporic Imaginary

Introduction

A recurring trope in Somali diasporic novels is the representation of two cities: Mogadishu and Rome. On the one hand, the former features as the culprit and the epicentre of Somalia's sociopolitical crisis and the idea of a unified nation. On the other, it becomes a place of nostalgia, memories and loss due to the civil war and the following diaspora. Mogadishu is then both a real city, grounded in the history of the nation, and a textual, fictional urbanscape that survives in the memories and imagination of those who witnessed the civil war, those who stayed and those who received the account of its beauty and destruction from parents and relative who have transmitted their experience from one generation to the other.

Rome, too, frequently features in the novels by Italophone authors but is not limited to them. For a period, Rome served as a primary destination for Somali people departing the country due to Barre's dictatorship. It was not only a haven for Somalis fleeing the regime, such as Nuruddin Farah or Mohamed Aden Sheikh, but also a location for pursuing education or living after the civil war erupted, as in the case of Garane Garane, Ali Farah, Ali Mumin Ahad and Shirin Ramzanali Fazel. Their experience of the city, therefore, turns Rome into a space of resettlement or crossing, either occupied or traversed by Somalis of the diaspora. Due to colonialism and its symbolic and material prominence as the Empire's centre during Fascism, Rome holds strong ties with Somalia, so much so that it could be considered 'the natural Italian counterpart of the Somali capital' (Lori 2016, 77).

So, how does Somali fiction tackle these urbanscapes transnationally? More than looking at how Mogadishu and Rome are fictionalized in diasporic novels, this chapter investigates specific places that allow us to unravel the complexities around transnational formations that these places seem to prompt.[1] As Janine Dahinden suggests, 'in order to be able to *stay* mobile it is necessary [...] to develop some local ties and to be embedded in specific localities' (2010, 52). The following analysis, accordingly, aims to investigate these specific localities and their role in Somali diasporic novels, with particular attention towards the fictionalization of key spaces in Mogadishu and Rome that establish a strong connection within the literary community of the diaspora. The focus on the airport, market and train station also aims to shed light on 'sites within the continent, entry and exit points, not usually dwelt upon in research and public discourse, that defamiliarize common-sense readings' of Somalia (Mbembe and Nuttall 2004, 352). In other words, beyond being emblematically crucial in examining Somaliness and nationhood against the backdrop of diaspora, these sites also overturn predominant conceptions of Somalia and Italy. In this respect, I identified these 'entry and exit points' in the airport (in Mogadishu and Rome), the market (Bakhaaraha Market in Mogadishu) and the train station (Stazione Termini, in Rome). The starting point of the following analysis is that the representation of the two cities through specific sites of mobility and consumption is not limited to the material but involves social, relational and symbolical connections, and they can be understood as shaping factors in the 'mapping of' identity formations of Somali diasporic identity. This approach underlines the necessity of considering urban settings as cross cultural and glocal sites, serving as 'free spaces of meaning' and invention (Blum 2003, 34).

The novels I will consider for my analysis come from both Anglophone and Italophone authors but are not limited to them. *Links* (2005) and *Crossbones* (2012) by Nuruddin Farah and *Il latte è buono* (*Milk Is Good*, 2005) will be pivotal for the analysis of one key place, namely the airport. *Links* and *Crossbones* are part of a trilogy titled 'Past Imperfect', made up also by *Knots* (2006), which narrates the story of Cambara, a Toronto-based Somali woman who returns to Mogadishu to reclaim her family's estate. The 'Past Imperfect' cycle has been less studied than the previous trilogies, especially concerning the use of the Italian language and the pivotal importance of Mogadishu in the civil war context.[2] Before engaging critically with the representations of the three mentioned sites, it might be helpful to provide the novels' main settings and contexts.

Links and *Crossbones* can be read as two narrations of *nostoi*, since they both fictionalize the homecoming of Somali American Jeebleh in two different moments: in 1996, when *Links* is set, and in 2006, when the events in *Crossbones* take place.[3] The plot of *Links* unravels around the problematic return of Jeebleh to the ravaged capital city controlled by two warlords to visit his mother's grave. *Crossbones*, the last chapter of the trilogy, narrates the pursuit of Jeebleh's foster nephew, whom the terrorist group al-Shabaab has recruited during the ICU's rule.

Farah sets *Links* during the civil conflict in Somalia in the aftermath of Siyaad Barre's fall in 1991, when opposition groups began competing for influence in the power vacuum that followed. Armed factions clashed as each sought to exert authority over the capital city.[4] In *Links*, two rival warlords, whose real names are replaced by monikers (StrongmanNorth is Maxamed Faarax Xasan Caydiid and StrongmanSouth is Cali Mahdi Maxamed), fight for the control of Mogadishu, halved in two and controlled by armed militiamen. The city embodies the physical expression of the clan-driven system: fragmented, sectarian and surveilled by militias 'ready to kill, [...] to die until [their] ancestral territories are back in [their] hands' (Farah 2005, 27). Mogadishu, with the northern and southern districts controlled by warlords and divided into two areas of influence, seems to represent the 'bounded estate' where, to use Wole Soyinka's words, a ruinous 'lust of power' is at play, consuming urban services, social practice and any sense of community (2012, 14).

To further exacerbate the situation, UN forces led chiefly by the Americans attacked Somali guerrillas loyal to the warlords (until Maxamed Faarax Xasan Caydiid's eventual death in 1996). The foreign interventions fostered division in different factions and split the country, enhancing conflicts between Somalis of other clan affiliations. In this sense, Mogadishu mirrors the instability of the whole of Somalia, fragmented into territories (or clan-states) that, in turn, parallel the former areas of influence of pre-colonial state formations (Ingiriis 2018).

Crossbones, instead, is set in 2006 during the Ethiopian invasion of Somalia, in a Mogadishu ruled by the Islamic Courts Union (ICU), under the control of Sharia Law. Despite being set in different times, both novels present the protagonist Jeebleh immediately after his landing in Mogadishu (it should be noted that, in Farah's novels, the capital is always written using the Italian spelling, Mogadiscio, as if to emphasize through toponomy the influence and the material legacy of Italian colonialism). The fact that the incipit of both *Links* and *Crossbones* involves two scenes set in airports should not be overlooked. It is, indeed, the starting point of our analysis, as it marks a difference from the narrative that considers airports as atemporal and unrelational places.

Links and *Crossbones* will be compared to Afdhere Jama's *Liido Beach* (2018, Mogadishu-born author who lives in San Francisco), which will be a valuable addition to expand the analysis of airports as localized places where diasporic subjectivities and transnational belonging are tested. The novel follows the story of Farah, a young American Somali coming from London to Mogadishu for the first time, and seventeen-year-old Hanad, a Somali guy with a fascination for Italy who grew up in Mogadishu. Their unexpected and romantic relationship is set against the backdrop of a city on the verge of the civil war in the 1980s. Keeping the focus on airports, the analysis then moves to *Lontano da Mogadiscio* (*Far from Mogadishu*, 1996) and *Nuvole sull'equatore* (*Clouds over the Equator*, 2017b) by Shirin Ramzanali Fazel (born in Mogadishu, now lives between Italy and the UK), *Madre ramati* (*Little Mother*, 2007) and *Il comandante del fiume* (*The River Master*, 2014) by Ubax Cristina Ali Farah (born in Verona, grown up in Mogadishu and now based in Brussels), *Oltre Babilonia* (*Beyond Babilonia*, 2008) and *La mia casa è dove sono* (*Home Is Where I Am*, 2010) by Igiaba Scego (born in Rome), which will be instrumental in examining how diasporic subjects experience border crossing and multiple belongings.

Garane's novella *Il latte è buono*, too, will have primary space in the analysis, as it tells the coming-of-age story of a young Somali, Gashan, as he develops his Somali, Black and African consciousness while travelling from Somalia to Italy, France and the United States. Fadumo Korn's *Born in the Big Rains: A Memoir of Somalia and Survival* (2006, born in Somalia and resettled in Munich) and Ali Mumin Ahad's 'Da un emisfero e l'altro' ('From one Hemisphere to the Other', 2012), two autobiographical texts, will further strengthen the interliterary discussion around spatiality within the diaspora and provide a more nuanced understanding of Fiumicino airport in Rome, one of the key places considered here along with Termini and the airport in Mogadishu.

At the narrative level, airports, markets and stations can be considered significant *topoi* within the diaspora space, as they enable Somali authors to stage the tension between locality and mobility, and transnational identities and national belonging. By investigating their fictionalized spatiality, I aim to show how they are imbued with history and local dynamics instead of merely being epitomes of fluidity and consumerism. Implicitly, this chapter broadens and challenges the idea that stations and airports are transient, global and atemporal, and proposes that they function socially, historically and textually in the making of identities and local practices. Moreover, studying examples of Somali writing set in Mogadishu and Rome, filtered through the fictionalization of key places and the intertextual references within these texts, contributes to our growing understanding of how Somali diasporic subjectivities are shaped and discussed.

While the first part of the chapter focuses on airports and the Bakhaaraha Market, the second section shifts attention to Stazione Termini. The multilayered spatiality of Termini will be examined as the primary site where several stories of marginalization, exclusion and resettlement of Somali immigrants unfurl. It will be shown how it represents the site where Somalis struggle to build a sense of community in the host country, experiencing exclusion and ghettoization (Tembo 2017). Through the descriptions made by Garane, Scego, Ali Farah and Fazel, but also Farah, the section underlines the importance of spatiality for Somali characters of the diaspora to build themselves a home and retrieve a sense of community along national belonging. However, it also emphasizes the relevance of Termini across texts and languages within the diaspora.

'Anthropological' and 'Supermodern' Places

Anthropologist Marc Augé, in his renowned work *Non-places. Introduction to an Anthropology of Supermodernity* (1995), has notably labelled as *non-lieux* those places like motorways, hotel rooms, airports and shopping malls that, according to his reading of contemporary society, embody supermodernity (*supermodernité*). Since its first appearance, the term *non-lieux* has reached prominence across disciplines and has established itself as the epitome of postmodernity. Due to its semantic flexibility, it has been a prolific and equally debated term, at times used to denote a qualitatively negative aspect of a particular place. To read the supermodernity we live in, Augé proposes two kinds of places which coexist in the Western world: the anthropological and the supermodern. The former empowers people's identity with a sense of community, shared social references and aggregation. More importantly, in anthropological places, 'identities, relationships and a story can be made out' (Augé 2000, 8). On the other side of the spectrum, supermodern places are those of 'circulation, communication and consumption, where solitudes coexist without creating any social bond or even a social emotion' (Augé 1996, 178). In practical terms, anthropological places include historical villages or towns where a sense of history and community is made clear. They are associated with origin, identity, social relations and a strong connection to the past (Lee 2015, 197). The exemplary supermodern places are, instead, global places where subjects become users who rely on almost the same design and outline to provide consumers with a sense of familiarity and homeness.

Augé explains that by travelling to a foreign country, for example, the most familiar and therefore homely aspect of that country will be the non-place, as it reproduces a universalizing feature through architectural qualities, logos and international brands that are easily recognizable. The homogenizing aesthetics, to the detriment of specific cultural or social values, matches the similar universalization of social relations along the axis producer/consumer. In order words, *non-lieux* are built and organized without references to the *genius loci*, a sense of place that describes 'the assemblage of physical and symbolical values in the environment' (Cresswell 2015, 130).

However, Augé warns against strict separation between places and non-places, suggesting that they never exist in pure forms. Instead of being divergent polarities, 'the first is never completely erased, the second never totally completed; they are like palimpsests on which the game of identity and relations is ceaselessly rewritten' (Augé 1995, 78).[5] Augé's reference to spaces like the palimpsests evokes another connection, as proposed by Andreas Huyssen, who has described palimpsests as *texts* that 'imply voids, illegibilities, and erasures, but ... also offer a richness of traces and memories, restorations and new constructions' (2003, 84).

Somali novels, then, allow us to read spatial representations as complex configurations and intersections of histories, social relations, individual experiences, memories and identities. Airports, train stations and markets are, therefore, not only merely backdrops but specific nodes of the diaspora space that allow us to revisit the relationship between local and global because of their 'simultaneous enunciation of locatedness [...] and mobility' (Ilott, Mendes and Newns 2018, XXII). The concept of *non-lieux* itself, in fact, seems to find its antonym in diaspora narratives and diasporic identity formations, where coexisting aspects of mobility and locality highlight how transient spaces might be used in more than merely functional ways. In this regard, Termini clearly emerges as 'relational, historical' site, 'productive of identity' (Kirk 2015, 206). Displaced Somalis, once they arrived in Rome, transformed the station by importing social practices and small economic activities, so to rebuild a familiar relationship between culture and place in a form of reterritorialization (Deplano 2014; Brioni 2015, 2017; Giuliani 2021). Therefore, the idea that only anthropological places can produce stories is questioned in contemporary Somali literature. Rather than being two antithetical realities, anthropological and supermodern places overlap. They both can generate stories and engage with the 'scrambled game of identity and relations' without necessarily creating a third or a hybrid space (Augé 1995, 79). In the texts in question, non-places are mingled with history and informed by the specificity of their context; in the case of airports, for example, their very nature of being transient, fluid or globally familiar, is doubted, as they often become places where diasporic subjects are stuck, immobilized, questioned or detained. Airports arise as sites of intersection between local-bound practices and time-related dynamics and can capture the zeitgeist of their time. Therefore, the texts in question show a specific literary spatiality in which non-places may become anthropological and function as spatial forms that 'reflect the sociopolitical and economic realities of the country' (Ibitokun 1991, 415). Scholar Benedict M. Ibitokun theorized the concept of metonymic spatiality, which will be helpful here to describe those places that 'emphasize the spiritual ties that exist between the protagonist and the soil' (*ibid.*, 415). For example, in the case of Farah's *Links*, through the descriptions of the airport, he conveys the broader environment of Mogadishu and the spatial tension between the feeling of belonging and estrangement that Jeebleh experiences once he arrives in his motherland. In *Crossbones*, Farah also suggests, via the representation of the airport in Boosaaso, a similarity between Southern and Northern Somalia, against the narrative that describes the former as underdeveloped and riotous and the latter as safe and wealthy. This 'metaphoric essence of literary spatiality' (*ibid.*, 410) will be investigated here by analysing airports as key sites to interrogate the sociopolitical realities of a whole country.

The Airport: From *Non-lieux* to Metonymic Place

In her autobiographical account entitled *Looking for Transwonderland* (2012), London-based Nigerian author Noo Saro-Wiwa devotes the prologue to narrate the behaviours of her fellow citizens in the departure lounge at the Gatwick airport. Interestingly, she notices that 'only in Nigeria could you see machine guns, tuxedos, army fatigues and evening frocks together at the airport. The insane aesthetic summarised [the] country's vanities and bathos more clearly than anything else' (2012, 4). In the description, she implies that airports encompass the specificity of a particular society and country (as she remarks by using the adjective *only*) by accentuating the latter's prominent features through aesthetics.

Similarly, Farah's descriptions of airports convey a distinctive summation of Somalis' traits and set the tone of the whole novel. In *Links*, for example, the protagonist Jeebleh underscores the ethos of his fellow citizens by addressing them as an outsider:

> He knew that Somalis were of the habit of throwing *despedida* parties to bid their departing dear ones farewell, and of joyously and noisily welcoming them in droves at airports and bus depots when they returned from a trip.
>
> (Farah 2005, 3)

Farah's documentary tone distances Jeebleh from his fellows and confines Somalis in the realm of objects: he *knows* them, but he also emphasizes their extraneousness. This double process of othering is further developed in the following passage, where Jeebleh is at the passport check at the airport. Quite tellingly, Farah shows Jeebleh's dual and conflicting identity and the fluctuating use of 'we' and 'Somalis':

> Somalis never defer to the authority of a uniform in the way the Germans do, Jeebleh thought. We will defer only to the brute force of guns. Maybe the answer lies in the nation's history since the days of colonialism, and later in those of the Dictator, and more recently during the presence of U.S. troops: these treacherous times have disabused us of our faith in uniformed authorities – which have proven to be redundant, corrupt, clannish, insensitive, and unjust.
>
> (Farah 2005, 5)

The passport check also allows Jeebleh to zoom out from his present situation and look at Somalia's past, divided into colonialism, dictatorship and neocolonialism.[6] According to Jeebleh, these three phases hampered Somalis' attitude towards authority, epitomized here by the uniforms. Metonymically, this allusion can be understood as an implicit reference to the lack of an efficient central state, governmental regulations and public officials.

This glimpse into Somalia's geopolitical background opens a series of speculations about airports and allow us to examine further how, in the novels, they function as stylistic tools to describe the context in which the plot is inscribed.[7] In Farah's *Links* and *Crossbones*, through conveying images of disorder and brutality, airports offer insights into Somalia's 'diaspora space' and the sociopolitical situation of Mogadishu and the country itself. This attention to locating airports at the crossroads of history and individual events intersects the definition of anthropological places with the concept of non-places. Their spatiality, therefore, arises as one of the essential fragments for assembling a more holistic representation of Mogadishu, which allows us to contextualize the city within a specific physical and temporal frame: the initial stages of the civil war in *Links* and the ICU rule in *Crossbones*. We can notice this feature at work in the following passage of *Links*, in which Farah introduces the airport's time-space configuration through Jeebleh's internal focalization:

> He was in great discomfort that the Antonov had landed not at the city's main airport – retaken by a warlord after the hasty departure of the U.S. Marines – but at a desolate airstrip, recently reclaimed from the surrounding no-man's land between the sand dunes and the low desert shrubs, and the sea.
>
> (Farah 2005, 3)

The airport is here charged with the contingencies of time: the detail that it is a mere runway forty kilometres north of the capital reveals the singularity of the context in which the story is set, along with the presence of 'a warlord' (a term that has become an ill-defined marker for the Somalis), which introduces us in the second phase of the civil war. The departure of the Marines, indeed, signals the end of the UNOSOM II mission, the first United Nations intervention in Somalia (1993–5). After the withdrawal of the UN troops, a warlord has taken back control of the Mogadishu International Airport.

These details imply the several non-operational features of the city itself, which Jeebleh will experience later in the plot: like the city, chaos and lack of facilities prevail in the airport over order and security. The lack of a centralized government or political organization able to enforce rules recurs via the reference to uniforms, when Jeebleh asks himself:

> Who, then, were the men inside, since they had no uniforms? What authority did they represent, given that Somalia had had no central government for several years now, after the collapse of the military regime that had run the country to total ruin?
>
> (Farah 2005, 3)

In the description that follows Jeebleh's arrival, the overall condition of the airport, opposite to the supposed well-ordered atmosphere of such places, matches Mogadishu's prospective deficiency and degradation. For example, the repeated use of the verb 'to push', associated with the persistence of the noun 'crowd', anticipates the messy condition in which Jeebleh will find himself once in Mogadishu, where similar rowdy mobs of people are constantly 'pushing, shoving, and engaged in acrimonious dispute' (Farah 2005, 3). Before exiting the building, Jeebleh is confronted with hostile circumstances, markedly distinct from those he experienced in his youth, during peaceful times (Farah 2005, 16–17; 18–19).

Jeebleh's juvenile and nostalgic recollections, triggered by his arrival at the airport, build a bridge with his past and the pre-civil war Mogadishu, which are now lost. The stark temporal and spatial difference echoes Afdhere Jama's description of the airport in his *Liido Beach* (2018). Given its setting in the 1980s, the novel assumes significance as a pertinent fictional precedent for elucidating the temporal dimension of airports. In *Liido Beach*, a young Somali named Farah, arriving from London to Mogadishu for the first time, observes with astonishment the actions of 'eager Somali travellers already standing up in the aisles and opening the overhead compartments, as the plane taxis on the tarmac' (Jama 2018, 1). This recurring scene, previously depicted in *Links*, serves to delineate the distinctive and context-specific spatiality of the airport by highlighting the behaviour of Somali people. Moreover, through the eyes of his protagonist, Jama describes the airport as follows:

> Mogadishu's International Airport is in much better shape than Farah had imagined. It is bigger and cleaner. Despite the chaotic passengers, he and his mother are able to smoothly go through passport control. Soon they are picking up their bags and are sitting in a taxi.
> Somalia and its people have been independent for nearly thirty years. Although they had been living under a military dictatorship, which Farah notices through all of the posters of the president around them since they landed at the airport, the Mogadishans seemed a lot more cosmopolitan than what he had expected.
> (Jama 2018, 1–2)

In this case, the airport before the civil war appears neat and functional 'despite the chaotic passengers' (1). By showing the posters of Barre's propaganda, the Mogadishu's International reveals its place-based specificity and, simultaneously, points out the multi-ethnic feature of the city and its citizens. As we will see, the idea of cosmopolitanism, almost a synonym here to multiculturism, represents another shared aspect of Somali authors of the diaspora, who have designated the term as one of the key markers (and lost feature) to describe Mogadishu.

When reading Farah's and Jama's descriptions together, we draw a tie between two diaspora novels to ideally reimagine Mogadishu and Somalia's pre-civil war past. Jama's fictionalized account may arguably correspond to Jeebleh's memories of Mogadishu's airport before he departs for the United States, since he fled Somalia roughly in the mid-1970s or early 1980s, when *Liido Beach* is set. In *Links*, this memory of peacefulness and openness towards difference clashes with the reality of the new war-torn context, in which both the anthropic and natural environment bears the consequences of the civil war violence.

Animals such as 'sick-looking goats' and cows that cough 'like someone with a chest ailment' wander untended in the city and feed on pebbles, shoes and plastic bags; famished and emaciated dogs follow Jeebleh, hoping for scraps (Farah 2005, 96, 133). The persistent presence of wild animals, such as 'crows, marabous, and other carrion birds', who 'learned to show up as soon as they heard shots', knowing that there would be corpses, is telling of the endemic violence of the city (Farah 2005, 18). Death inhabits Mogadishu so that it is not 'abnormal to see scavengers of carrion at a four-star hotel, looking as though they are well placed to choose what they eat and where they go. They look better fed than humans' (Farah 2005, 66). Moreover, 'they are no longer afraid if you try to shoo them away [as] the crows and the vultures were so used to being on the ground foraging, [that] they were like tourist pigeons in a Florentine plaza' (Farah 2005, 65).

The animals roaming the city are not the only elements to emphasize how nature seems to have vanquished any human attempt at order: the occurrence of 'dust' and 'sand' further underlines this disruptiveness and unruliness, both metaphorically and literally, also building a bridge between *Links* and *Crossbones* (Farah 2005, 8–15 and in the following extracts). In *Links*, Jeebleh's first look at the city from a distance depicts it as 'a fine sea of sand billowing behind a minaret' (Farah 2005, 14), and this state of things resonances with the description made in *Crossbones*: the airport's spatiality appears similar in terms of keywords, even though this time is the Mogadishu International and not the desolate airstrip in Casillay:

> [...] billows of dust mixed with the midday heat and humidity whip up at him in an agitated vigour, the sea breeze from a mere half kilometre away hardly affecting the gooeyness of the amalgam. In addition, an irritating scrimmage of human traffic crowds the bottom of the stairway as posters squeeze through the descending passengers to their services.
>
> (Farah 2012, 11)

The details of the description convey a time-related specification and signal a change: whereas, in *Links,* the main airport was inoperable because of the civil war, in *Crossbones,* it came back to its original function, suggesting a return to the *status quo*. However, the recurrent presence of 'dust', already described as ominous in the civil war scenario of *Links*, disturbs this apparent normality.[8] The desert's spaciousness and the ocean's closeness contrast antithetically with the idea of order and tidiness that are usually connected to airports. The sand from the desert and the shoreline implies and anticipates the precarious conditions of the city; the airport itself, which lacks the elaborate and ordered network of procedures related to security protocols and document check, reveals Mogadishu's situation: sand and dust, in other words, connect the two periods described, 1996 and 2006, and the city's enduring degree of lawlessness.[9] Accordingly, later in *Crossbones*, Jeebleh states: 'Since his 1996 visit, most of the youths have grown beards and donned those white robes, save for the odd youth in military fatigues or an ill-matched uniform assembled from various post-collapse loyalties. The general collapse is still the same, though' (Farah 2012, 27).

It is helpful to point out another aspect connected to the airport's spatiality, as it provides an interesting connection with one of the main themes of *Links*, namely the use of language (which will be further investigated in Chapter 3). In the novel, the airport produces bewilderment in the protagonist because of the impossibility for him to grasp the meaning and the signs of what should be considered, instead, the universal language of such places. Later in the story, Jeebleh's friend, Bile, argues that 'In Somalia, the civil war was language', stressing a similar feeling of estrangement towards the new semantic of the civil war, which also led to a crisis of meaning and shattered the fabric of society ('I didn't speak the new language') (*Links*, 119). In this respect, the first line of the novel straightforwardly remarks on the airport's unusual and alarming atmosphere, later retrieved in the city too:

'GUNS LACK THE BODY OF HUMAN TRUTHS!'
Barely had his feet touched the ground in Mogadiscio, soon after landing at a sandy airstrip to the north of the city in a twin-engine plane from Nairobi, when Jeebleh heard a man make this curious statement. He felt rather flatfooted in the way he moved away from the man, who followed him. Jeebleh watched the passengers pushing one another to retrieve their baggage lined up on the dusty floor under the wings of the aircraft. Such was the chaos that fierce arguments erupted between passengers and several of the men offering their services as porters, men whom Jeebleh would not trust.

(Farah 2005, 3)

The scene discloses the war-torn scenario of disorder dominating Mogadishu, which has also damaged social relations and language. The word 'guns' emblematically draws attention to the ubiquitous presence of physical violence, as much as the 'fierce arguments' between passengers suggest an overall atmosphere of tension. Jeebleh reads this as the distinctive sign of a new semantic that he labels as 'civil war vocabulary' (Farah 2005, 4). Later in the story, Jeebleh remarks again upon the presence of war-related jargon when he explains the resemanticization of the expression 'house-sitting', meaning 'the taking possession of houses belonging to the members of clan families who had fled, by members who had stayed on' (13). In this context, in which truths are concealed, and language has been tampered with, so much to blur the difference between foes and friends and between victims and perpetrators, Jeebleh struggles to orient himself. His homeland appears to him like a gray area (*zona grigia*), as Primo Levi puts it, meaning a poorly defined area 'where the two camps of masters and servants both diverge and converge' (Chapters 3 and 5 will further investigate this matter) (2017, 31).

The airport, therefore, enables a reading of violence as normalized: the civil war has ignited a process through which behaviours that fall outside social norms are regarded as ordinary. This aspect is further stressed when Jeebleh experiences a traumatic event a few moments after his arrival. This event appears not to be out of place in the present-day situation. A ten-year-old child is shot dead while waiting with the mother for their flight; this unexpected accident stands out as appalling for Jeebleh, especially for the reaction (or lack thereof) of the onlookers: '[He] was shocked that no one in the crowd of people still milling about had been willing to confront the gunmen, to try to stop them from playing their deadly games' (Farah 2005, 17). This first-hand and close-to-death experience becomes even more daunting because of the general indifference. The killing extends its resonance through the whole novel, reaching *Crossbones,* too: soon after his second return to Mogadishu, Jeebleh still remembers with shock what happened ten years earlier: 'A boy not yet in his teens had been killed before Jeebleh even left the airport, as he and his mother boarded their Nairobi-bound flight' (Farah 2012, 15).

The astonishment in witnessing Somali people's lack of empathy remains etched in Jeebleh's after a decade, leading him to question his belonging and his role as a citizen (and human being) in war-torn Somalia. Such indifference surfaces again when Jeebleh, while walking around the city, notices a crowd gathered around a man who has suffered a seizure, doing nothing to help him. The crowd immediately look at Jeebleh with suspicion and his attempts to help result in reprimand: 'We do not bother with people we do not know!' (Farah 2005, 198–9). The overall lack of empathy recurs as problematic and tellingly explains the level of collective trauma that the city has suffered. This shakes Jeebleh's feeling of belonging and emphasizes the disconnection between himself and his homeland.[10]

In this sense, the novel attempts to negotiate Jeebleh's idea of Somaliness with the current society organization, which hampers his positioning and sense of belonging within the community. This friction is first disclosed at the airport, where he faces a challenging experience at the document check. Instead of using his American passport, Jeebleh presents his Somali document to 'a man neither in uniform nor bearing a gun', with twenty dollars in cash as a small bribe for the officer (*Links*, 9). However, Jeebleh's understandable choice to present his Somali passport triggers a puzzling misunderstanding because of the lack of a visa. Jeebleh himself remarks upon this Kafkaesque situation with a sarcastic comment: 'When has it become necessary for a Somali to require a visa to enter Mogadiscio?' (Farah 2005, 12). Only with the help of Af-Laawe, a mysterious and elusive figure who will escort Jeebleh through his trip to Mogadishu, can our protagonist pass the security check safely. In this regard, Ali A. Abdi suggests, describing these uncertain times, that while the aphorism *maxaad taqaannaa* (what do you know) regulates the lives of the inhabitants before the civil war, the more clan-oriented *yaad taqaanna* (whom do you know) replaced the former during the conflict (1998, 334–5).

This experience reminds him of the day when he left Mogadishu, twenty years before, during Barre's dictatorship. At that time, he was arrested and detained for years, until released and sent directly from jail to the airport. He remembers wearing a suit and the subtle ways the regime could dispose of those considered traitors by sending them away to Kenya, the United States or the USSR. Jeebleh compares the present of anarchy and the past of danger and censorship and shows, once again, that his sense of belonging is interrogated and his Somaliness mistrusted and questioned now as then.

As the following examples will show, airports represent at the narrative level key settings for staging the tension between the two polarities ingrained in the condition of diasporic subjects: the feeling of belonging, often deluded after the return and constantly questioned in the host country, and the sense of estrangement towards the new realities of the homeland. For example, the co-protagonist of *Crossbones*, Ahl (Malik's brother and Jeebleh's son-in-law), experiences the same estrangement when he arrives in Somalia to look for his stepson Taxiil, who has been recruited from Minnesota as a fighter for al-Shabaab. Farah uses the same keywords ('mob', 'sand', 'authority') to describe Ahl's arrival in the northern coastal city of Boosaaso in Puntland. Predictably, the airport arises as the metonymy for the whole country:

> The airstrip [...] has no barrier to fence it in; nothing to restrict unauthorised persons from walking straight onto the aircraft and mixing with the passengers as they land. A mob gathers at the foot of the stepladder, joining the man in yellow vest, flip-flops, and trousers with holes in them who guided the aircraft to its parking position.
>
> (Farah 2012, 92)

Also in this case, the airport enables a further understanding of the geopolitical situation of Somalia since it conveys a detailed image of the context. It should be noted here that Puntland leaders, at the time of the story, declared the territory a self-governing state, although internationally recognized as an autonomous region of Somalia. As of 2016, Somalia is divided into five Federal Member States (Puntland State, Southwest State, Jubbaland State, Galmudug State and Hirshabele State), excluding the secessionist region of Somaliland, which declared itself independent in 1991, with Hargeisa as the capital city (Ingiriis 2018, 58, 64, 69). In Boosaaso, the airport is presented as an airstrip, but Farah states with irony that 'airstrip is a misnomer for the sandy pit on which Ahl's plane lands' (Farah 2012, 91).

Though the description of Boosaaso's airport expresses a calmer situation than the one in Mogadishu, the overall atmosphere of shabbiness and precariousness discloses the subsequent representation of the city. When we compare the two airports, they hardly differ, as the following passage about the Mogadishu International shows:

> The airport opened to traffic only a few months earlier, for the first time in sixteen civil war years. The repair job on the hall is not quite done, the scaffolding criss-crossing and impeding one's movements, nor is the work on the archways anywhere complete. A rope is strung across the middle of the hall, separating arrivals and departures. In the departures area, some fifty or so cheap white plastic chairs are clustered in the corner, presumably for the use of passengers waiting to board their flights. [...] With no luggage carousels or carts, no trained personnel at Immigration and Customs, there is no knowing how things might pan out, not knowing what these robed, bearded men might or might not do.
>
> (Farah 2012, 13)

Farah connects here *Links* to *Crossbones* by starting the two novels with the two arrivals of Jeebleh in Mogadishu. At the stylistic level, negations denote the Mogadishu International Airport, which Farah filters through his protagonist's eyes to remark a deficiency from a standard. Ten years after the infernal look described in *Links*, Mogadishu is represented in *Crossbones* as 'featureless as a ground-down cog in a broken machine' (Farah 2012, 166). At the beginning of the novel, we can notice once again some similarities between the airport and the city, as they both present an overall condition of incompleteness; Jeebleh notes that 'the general collapse is still the same; houses with their insides caved in, with a Lego-like look to them, the floor below or the one above entirely missing' (Farah 2012, 27).

The presence of 'robed, bearded men' signals the new political situation, as the ICU now rules Mogadishu. Until the end of 2006, UIC governed most of southern Somalia, including the cities of Jowhaar, Kismaayo, Beletweeyne and the capital Mogadishu, run by the new warlord Yusuf 'Indho Ade' Mohamed Siad. The Northern regions (the self-declared autonomous Puntland and the self-declared independent state, Somaliland) and the furthest interior regions of the south were outside the ICU's control. On the eve of 2007, they abandoned Mogadishu, leaving the city in chaos and allowing the Transitional Federal Government (TFG) and Ethiopian troops to take over (Osman 2017, 8–9).

It is important here to notice that, in *Crossbones*, Farah expands the range of his usual setting, including Boosaaso in the plot. In doing so, he builds on the comparison between two regions of Somalia, probably giving the first-ever fictionalized account of the situation in Puntland. This double setting results in a geographical shift: one story is set in Mogadishu and deals with the invasion of Ethiopia, the constant presence of American drones and the violent censorship and repression by the ICU; the second story questions the misinterpreted piracy condition in Puntland, and tackles the issue of international terrorism (Jaggi 2012).[11] Accordingly, Mogadishu and Boosaaso are emblems of the geopolitical realities Farah seeks to capture, and airports represent key places to symbolically encapsulate these realities.

While, on the one hand, airports are places amalgamated with local practices, on the other hand, they function as sites that epitomize the troubles related to diasporic subjects. Through visas, passports, dual citizenship, immigration and anti-terrorism laws, airports have become the testing ground for diasporic identities moving to the Global North. In this sense, they are not just anywhere, but they embody the local framework in which they are inscribed, and the different social relations established within the same context. Even though they are modelled along anonymous commerce-related aesthetics that reproduces capitalist logic, airports are nonetheless influenced and domesticated by their localities and social relations. Also, they function at the narrative level as symbolical sites. More specifically, in the case of Farah and Jama, airports work as anterooms of their neighbouring cities. They emerge as microcosms that encompass the ethos of a people and where diasporic characters experience the hybridity of their transnational identity.

Somali novels in Italian also share this attention to airports, represented as sites where diasporic subjects are assessed but also as fictional places where characters can have preview of the city or the country where the airports are located. For example, in *Il latte è buono* (*Milk Is Good*, 2005) by Somali author Garane Garane, even though the circumstances are hugely different compared to Farah's novels, the scene a the airport has two essential points in common with both *Links* and *Crossbones*: the setting – Fiumicino, in Rome – and the passport check. In *Il latte è buono*, the protagonist of the novella, Gashan, leaves Somalia after Siyaad Barre's coup to study abroad in Rome and then moves to France and the United States to pursue his academic career after finally returning to Mogadishu during the civil war (Chapter 2 will focus on the representation of the war by showing similarities and differences in the texts by Garane, Farah and Ali Farah).

In *Il latte è buono*, too, Garane stages the document check scene of the protagonist not as merely uneventful. When Gashan is sent to Italy, the former motherland and a country he profoundly admires for its culture, food and music, he finally fulfils his longing. After years of colonial education, he embodies the mimic man, a line that scholar Homi Bhabha traces back 'through the works of Kipling, Forester, Orwell, and Naipaul' (1984, 128). The mimic man can be described as the colonial subject who, feeling inferior, enables strategies of identification with the colonizer by reproducing and mirroring colonial cultural practices.[12] As soon as Gashan lands in Rome, he abruptly comprehends the workings of colonial discourse and his position as a former colonial subject – marginalized, if not entirely non-existent, in society.

While in Farah's novels the protagonists struggle to be recognized as citizens of their own country even though being born there, for Gashan, the issue of belonging concerns ethnicity. Being Black and fluent in Italian shows Italian people's lack of awareness about Somalis as former colonial subjects. National belonging, strongly related to the idea of being white and Catholic, is depicted as predominant in the novella, and also suggests a complete amnesia of the colonial period. In the novella, Gashan is the subject of racist remarks and realizes that Italian people are ignorant about Somalia (Garane 2005, 67–8; 76–9). Garane further emphasizes this unawareness when Gashan reads for the first time *La Repubblica*, an Italian daily newspaper: after relating the title of the newspaper [republic] to the name of several African countries, he claims that *la Repubblica* was rich in information, but poor in African-related matters (Garane 2005, 76–9).

What is interesting in the experience of Gashan is that his first encounter with Italy at the Fiumicino airport already captures the complexity of Italy's relationship with its imperial past, the problematic absence of a collective memory about colonialism and the idea of Italianness built along the colour line. The scene at the airport stages the unfamiliarity, deeply rooted in the Italian society, towards the existence of former colonial subjects and the consequent racist attitude against Gashan. Indeed, after the war and the end of Fascism, 'there were neither trials nor anti-colonial wars of independence underway, and thus it was easier, but no less historically inexact, for the Italians to fashion themselves as *brava gente*' (good people) (Labanca 2005, 41). Consequently, the crimes perpetrated by Fascists in the African campaigns were easily self-absolved in the post-war period due to the lack of public condemnations, trials and the overall silence of intellectuals about the colonial period that, truthfully, had started in the 1870s and stretched after the Fascist period (1922–43) with the AFIS (*Amministrazione fiduciaria italiana della Somalia*, 1950–60). Besides, the absence of significant migrations from the colonies and the lack of extensive independence movements against Italy, able to exceed the borders of the former colonies and reach the motherland, prevented Italian society from becoming aware of the responsibilities of that historical period. Ignoring the colonial past in Africa – and dismissing it as lesser than the English and the French – has affected Italian culture, history and politics for decades and, at the same time, fostered Italian people to absolve themselves through a process of self-fashioning (Del Boca 1984). Ethiopia, Libya, Eritrea and Somalia, therefore, have been considered marginal to the history of Italy as if the colonies (and the relationship between colonized and colonizer) were uninfluential in the political agenda of nation-building in the post-war period and connected only to Fascism.[13]

This period of public amnesia, which started after the Second World War, lingered until the early 1990s, and made Italian society ill-equipped to face the arrival of the former colonial subjects (or, more broadly, Africans) within national borders (Lombardi-Diop and Romeo 2014, 14). Moreover, the lack of public discussion allowed fascist ideas about *razza* (race) to subtly persist in the media and political discourse, thus letting former colonial practices, such as fetishization, stigmatization and dehumanization, to survive and be (re)used to represent Black/African subjects. Garane describes this long history of colonial discourse when Gashan arrives at Fiumicino in the late 1980s. What strikes him most is that Italians seem to completely ignore Somalia's existence, while he feels to know everything about Italy. As the extract below shows, Garane uses irony to bring to the surface the protagonist's naïveté as soon as he lands in Fiumicino and, at the same time, hyperbolically addresses common stereotypes about African people to emphasize how the colonial mind, developed over the *longue durée* of the colonial experience, still lingers in the Italian national consciousness (Brioni 2015). Garane satirizes the metropole as the pinnacle of civilization by exposing the lie behind colonial education.

In illuminating this rupture between expectation and reality, Garane shows Gashan's disillusionment, but also debunks colonial discourse and subverts colonial strategies of representation by ironically describing Italians with the same Orientalist assumptions, stereotypes and aesthetic practices used for representing Somalis and African subjects (Garane 2005, 64–6). In other words, he mimics how Europeans represented Black/African subjects in colonial times 'as a mode of *knowing* them' (Ashcroft, Griffith and Tiffin 2000, 153). In *Il latte è buono*, it is the spatiality of the airport that enables these practices of subversion and demystification, allowing a reading of Italy in which both colonial discourse and the Italians' ideal self-portrait as *brava gente* are dismantled.[14] The spatiality of the airport, as in the case of Farah's novels, allows us to regard it as a metonymy of Italy itself:

> Di colpo, all'aeroporto [...] era africano. Era della stirpe dei nomadi. Sentiva come se sua nonna gli sussurrasse qualcosa:
> 'Sei un nobile. Sei Gareen.'
> Cominciò a camminare col passo svelto e in un modo pomposo.

'Sapranno chi sono', si diceva. 'Sono somalo, il più intelligente, il più bello in Africa e nel mondo. Siamo conosciutissimi.'

Per lui tutti gli italiani all'aeroporto si assomigliavano. Non riusciva a fare distinzioni. Era cresciuto in una società dove il multietnicismo era di norma: a Mogadiscio ce n'erano di tutti i colori, dall'indiano al cinese, dall'egiziano al siriano allo yemenita. Eppoi c'erano i cenci bianchi, gli italiani. C'erano, anche se in minor numero, americani, sovietici, canadesi, francesi.

Indho yar, indho weyn, san yar, san weyn, midgaan, gaal, gibil cad ... Erano tutti a Xamar Cadde. Ma qui era diverso: tutti avevano la pelle come quella degli arabi. Tutti uguali. Si sente che si è diversi, che si viene da un'altra galassia.

(Garane, 65)

Suddenly, at the airport [...], he was African. He belonged to the ancestry of the nomad people. He felt his grandmother whispering to him:

'You're a noble. You are Gareen.'

He started to walk with a quick and pretentious stride.

'They'll know who I am', he mutters to himself. 'I am Somali, the most intelligent, the most beautiful in Africa and the entire world. We are the most renowned.'

To him, all the Italians in the airport were similar. He could not make any distinction. He was raised where a multi-ethnic society was the norm: in Mogadishu, there were people of all colours, from the Indian to the Chinese, from the Egyptian to the Syrian and the Yemeni. And then there were the deathly pale: the Italians. There were also, even if fewer, Americans, Soviets, Canadians, and French.

Indho yar, indho weyn, san yar, san weyn, midgaan, gaal, gibil cad ...

All of them were in Xamar Cadde. However, here it was different: everybody's skin looked Arabic. All the same. One feels different, as if one is coming from another galaxy.

Garane ironically underlines the homogeneity of Italian society in terms of language, (Italian), religion (Catholic) and ethnicity (white), as opposed to the multi-ethnic fabric of his homeland, following Farah's idea of cosmopolitanism. The latter term will be further discussed in the analysis of the market, but in the case of Garane, we can argue that the presence of 'people of all colours' in Mogadishu represents a form of cosmopolitanism which shows 'a publicly visible diversity' (Gekas 2009, 102). Garane does not investigate the power relations between Somalis and foreigners, thus leaving aspects such as coexistence, integration and class unexplored. In the passage cited here, he seems more interested in reterritorializing Italy, as he compares Italians to Arabs, thus implying the proximity between the peninsula, North Africa and the Middle East. Italians' ethnicity is further complicated when Gashan explicitly describes them as white ('*cenci bianchi*'). This dialectic, flexible and contextual understanding of ethnicity strongly contrasts with the rigid, essentialist narrative of Italians as white and North European more than Mediterranean.

The dialogue between Gashan and the police officer flashes out this issue effectively. The meeting plunges both characters into a state of disbelief. On the one hand, by trusting to be recognized as Italian due to his deep affection for the metropole, Gashan is reluctant to show his passport as proof of his Italianness. On the other hand, the document, written in Italian, leaves the police officer sceptical, and Gashan's Florentine accent further fosters the officer's suspicion. Both are startled: the protagonist by the evident difference between reality and expectations; the police officer by the fact of having before him a Black, African subject who claims his belonging to Italy.

We can read Gashan's experience at the document check with the concept of the 'colonial uncanny'. Drawn from psychoanalysis, the term can be used here to aptly describe 'the feeling of the home-ly which morphs into the un-home-ly' (Leetsch 2021, 144). It might be helpful to define both the colonial subject's disillusion once the supposed welcoming metropole and the colonizers' feeling of bewilderment once confronted with the colonized. The 'uncanny' experience of Gashan occurs when he notices that Rome, and Italy too, allegedly as familiar in terms of cultural references, becomes unfamiliar and hostile. According to Garane, Gashan '*conosceva l'Italia attraverso i libri, i film, i nomi delle vie*' ('knew Italy though books, films, street names') (2005, 63). Likewise, the protagonist of Igiaba Scego's *Adua*, Zoppe, a Somali young man who works as a translator in Rome, states: 'I already pictured myself in Rome, a city I knew from books. In my head I recited the names of its streets and its squares [...] How wonderful!' (2019, 118).

However, due to their Black skins – considered as physical marker of extraneousness and non-belonging – Gashan and Zoppe are 'out of place' in the former metropole and forced to marginalization (Bhabha 2004). Gashan's exclusion appears even stronger considering how much he knows about the Italian culture, from music to football, from literature to history, compared to the total ignorance of the Italians towards Somalia. He experiences, to borrow Mia Fuller's words, a 'sense of out-of-place familiarity' (2007, 219).

At the same time, uncanny also defines the reaction of the colonizers once they face the sudden and unexpected appearance of former colonial subjects, who claim their belonging to the same culture and community as the colonizer by employing the same (spoken) language of the metropole and by exhibiting his belonging through the passport, printed in the same (written) language. What was supposed 'to remain secret, hidden away [...] has come into the open' through Gashan, an unexpected voice from the dismissed colonial memory, who now asks for recognition and inclusion (qtd. in Leetsch 2021, 144). The passport-check and the following misunderstanding trigger the relocation and the re-inscription of Gashan's identity, and the 'indeterminacy of [his] diasporic identity' (Bhabha 2004, 322), but also allow the colonial past to resurface.

In contrast to the experience of Gashan, we can analyse the first visit to Rome as described by Somali scholar and author Ali Mumin Ahad in his account '*Da un emisfero all'altro*' (2012). The airport again arises as one of the key places where Somali diasporic identities are confronted. Most importantly, this passage signals the interconnectedness between Somalia and Italy, but also between authors and the diverse narratives that inhabit the diaspora space. Accordingly, Brah suggests that 'it is within this confluence of narrativity that "diasporic community" is differently imagined under different historical circumstances' (Brah 1996, 183). Ali Mumin Ahad explicitly mentions Garane as a reference point to describe his experience:

> Sono contento che il mio primo incontro con Roma non sia stato qualcosa anche lontanamente somigliante all'arrivo all'aeroporto di Roma del personaggio-protagonista di *Il latte è buono* di Garane Garane. Né quella volta né di lì a un anno, nel 1988, di ritorno da Mogadiscio per quella che sarebbe stata l'ultima volta che vidi la Somalia. Gli agenti dell'aeroporto di Roma erano gentili e professionali.
>
> (Ahad 2012, 8)

> I am glad that my first encounter with Rome was not even remotely resembling the arrival of the character-protagonist of *Il latte è buono* at the airport in Rome. Neither that time, nor later in 1988, returning from Mogadishu to what would be the last time I saw Somalia. The police officers at the airport in Rome were kind and professional.

As expected, the encounter is different: the police officers are described as *gentili* (kind) and *professionali* (professional). There are no traces of misunderstandings about the relationship between colonizers and (former) colonial subjects, nor racist attitudes towards the author. Perhaps, the arrival of Gashan was reasonably meant to be more effective for the plot, emphasizing the lack of understanding between Italians and Somalis, as remarked in other episodes of the novel (Garane, 69–70; 76–7; 82–6).

Instead, the description of Fadumo Korn's arrival in Rome is similar to Gashan's. In one passage, quoted here from her autobiographical text *Born in the Big Rains* (*Geboren im großen Regen*, 2004), she lands in Fiumicino from Mogadishu. Once again, the airport rises as a significant geographical touchstone and a nexus connecting different texts within the diaspora. In her *memoirs*, Fadumo's first impression of the Italians resembles that of Gashan, as they both recognize the sameness of the Italian society in terms of ethnicity and skin colour: 'Millions of people seemed to be shouting, yelling, shrieking. And all of them looked like Signor Lavera' and, later, 'All of them – men, woman, children – were pale-skinned [...] I wondered if the colour would come off if I rubbed it' (Korn 2005, 82).

Fadumo, as well, more than describing the airport's physical appearance, focuses on the attitude of the Italians towards formerly colonized subjects and social imaginaries. The document check, once again, represents a key moment for diasporic Somalis:

> At customs, uniformed men looked at our passports. Some documents were handed right back with a nod, while others were retained and thoroughly thumbed through, observed with stern, tight expressions. My passport was among those carefully studied. Were they aware that a twelve-year-old Somali girl could not yet obtain a passport? Did they know that my uncle had had to print one for me in his shop?
>
> (Korn 2005, 82)

A certain degree of ignorance emerges here regarding the Italians, who seem sceptical about the document's authenticity, thus showing how racism is ingrained in institutional practice. While reaching the taxi stops outside the airport, Fadumo draws a parallel between Mogadishu and Rome: 'Here, too, streets were chaotic and noisy' (Korn 2005, 84), which resembles Gashan's description of the city as dirty, loud and full of traffic (Garane 2005, 75) and the previous description of Italians as 'shouting, yelling, shrieking' (Garane, 82). Korn experiences the same unwelcoming attitude presented in *Il latte è buono*, as she is the victim of overt racism when a man rubs his finger across her cheek after licking it (Korn 2005, 84). The narrator's expectations about the city are subverted, and she experiences, as Gashan, the clash between the real and the imagined Rome. While driving home, she remembers her aunt's comment about the Italians. The harsh remark brings to the fore the horror of the Fascist occupation and suggests that, in the 1970s, colonialism was still a fresh memory: 'When they were in Somalia, they paved the streets with Somalis so they wouldn't have to dirty their shoes' (Korn, 82). As in Gashan, this comment contrasts with 'the obliteration from the nation's collective memory of its colonial past' and openly denounces the atrocities committed during Fascism in the African territories (Lazzari 2023, 69).

Along with the same comparative approach, it is possible to consider one passage from the novel *Il comandante del fiume* (The River Master, 2014) by Somali Italian author Ubax Cristina Ali Farah. The protagonist, the eighteen-year-old Yabar, lives in Rome with his mother and sister and belongs to the so-called second generation (namely, the children of the first generation of immigrants). He does not have first-hand experience of dislocation, yet he struggles with the 'indeterminacy of the diasporic identity' (Bhabha 2004, 322). While returning from London, at the document check in Fiumicino, Yabar states:

> Potrei tatuarmi il passaporto italiano sul petto e non smetterebbero comunque di farmi a pezzi, la lingua da una parte, le mani e gli occhi dall'altra. Sentendo la parola «razzisti», i poliziotti hanno cominciato ad agitarsi e uno di loro, forse il più anziano, forse il più alto in carica, mi fa: «A regazzi', datte 'na calmata, ma 'o sai chi so' io?».
>
> (Ali Farah 2014, 101)

> I could tattoo my Italian passport on my chest, and this would not, in any case, stop them from tearing me apart, with the tongue on the one hand, and my hands and eyes on the other. After hearing the word «racist», the police officers got nervous, and one of them, perhaps the oldest, perhaps the one in chief, said: 'Chill out, sonny, don't you know who I am?'

This scene fictionalizes the suspicious behaviour of police officers towards the Italo Somali Yabar and the everyday racism that, even though it might not be consciously intended, results in daily violations against ethnic minorities. The incessant sense of being controlled and suspected fosters fear and anger in subjects like Yabar, who feel scrutinized and treated as second-class citizens. Yabar's black skin – in a country that 'firmly holds to the fiction of a national identity constructed on' Christian religion and white skins – leads the police officers to believe him to be a non-national (Coppola 2011, 123). Yabar's skin colour, being alien to the presumed monolithic whiteness of the Italian society, sparks the suspicion that he could be an illegal immigrant and, once again, the passport check suggests the discriminatory attitude of the Italian people towards Black/African subjects. Yabar, in other words, unconsciously prompts the stereotype often tied up with African people more broadly, namely illegality and criminality (Longhi 2023, 225). Despite the documents that legitimize their Italian citizenship, Yabar and Gashan's inclusion within the Italian borders is continuously questioned in the rituals for security purposes and never taken for granted (Dal Lago 2004, 20).

However, the similarities between Yabar and Gashan also suggest a clash between different temporalities and the *longue durée* of colonial discourse, whose legacy resurfaces in racist attitudes and unbalanced power relations. As noted, the stigmatization of Black subjects derives from the 'earlier removal and denial of the Italian colonial chapter', as Ponzanesi maintains (2005, 185), and the delay of Italian society to come to terms with its past and the failure to recognize any responsibility for the migration movements from the former colonies. Nuruddin Farah, in his article 'Citizen of Sorrow', emphasizes the same unfamiliarity towards Somali people in the Italian public sphere (and their invisibility) and explains this attitude with the lack of knowledge about the colonial past: 'For better or worse, Somalis did not earn a name for themselves in Italy until 1991, when their country fell apart' (2002, 10).

As the analysis has shown, a recurrent literary place useful to portray identity-related issues for Somali authors is the airport, which could be read as a textual *topos* with a metonymic value. Accordingly, airports form and shape identities but are shaped by global and local dynamics (Gordon 2008). As a metonymy for Mogadishu itself and the whole of Somalia, as well as for Rome and Italy, airports embody the ethos of society and are both modified and influenced by history and local relations. According to this perspective, the airports described here eschew too narrow definitions of non-places and show how fundamental human agency is in defining and shaping them (Cresswell 2015). In the experiences narrated by Garane, Farah, Ali Farah, Korn, Mumin Ahad and Jama, airports emerge as deeply relational places in which diasporic and formerly colonized subjects are confronted with the prejudices of the Western discourse, but also questioned about their identity and belonging, Somaliness or Italianness alike.

In this regard, Christopher Schaberg introduced the term 'culture of flights' to describe the dispersed sensibilities, personal feelings and collective moods circulating around airports (2012, 5). Schaberg quotes as examples of his concept the rigorous security checks in Israel and the 'ramshackle experience of commercial flights' in Russia, thus implying both a social and national influence concerning the airports (*ibid.*). In Farah and Garane's novels, the culture of flights emerges to relate to both Somalia and Italy: in a sort of infernal gateway, Jeebleh can glimpse anticipation of how the city will display itself, of its 'terrible misery' ravaged by 'futile violence' (Farah 2005, 20). In *Links*, the overall sense of anarchy and aggressiveness perceived at the airport is the same that goes with the reader during the trips of the protagonist throughout the city, a wasteland of chaos. In other words, the airport's metonymic spatiality captures Mogadishu's moral and social murkiness (Gagiano 2006, 263). In *Crossbones*, the description of the airport allows the reader to grasp the presence of eerie calm, concomitant to the unceasing feeling of being kept under surveillance by the panoptic logic of the ICU armed militiamen. At the same time, Farah has shown how airports depend on local sensibilities and aesthetics. He has described, along with Jama, the 'culture of flights' for Somali people (in particular, when they both described the habit of picking up the luggage on the airstrip or reaching the plane on their own by simply walking along the runway).

Moreover, the textual spatiality of the airport, essential to explore the struggle of diasporic identities and to epitomize the ethos of a people, plays a role at the textual level. The airport scenes are positioned, in Farah, at the very beginning of the story, in the first chapter of *Links*, and in the second of *Crossbones*; in *Il latte è buono*, the airport setting symbolically occupies the same initial position because the arrival in Fiumicino signals the starting point of Gashan's process of decolonization through Italy, France and the United States. However, more than their role as thresholds that allow the protagonists to begin their stories, airports function as physical and symbolic harbingers or anterooms and rise as key places in the diasporic texts of Somali writers. They are part of a transnational urban narrative that exposes unbalanced power relations and subverts monolithic assumptions of belonging and citizenship.

The Market: Local Spatiality and Cosmopolitanism

This section investigates another fictionalized spatiality, which Nuruddin Farah and Cristina Ali Farah envision as the embodiment of the fragmentation of Somali society. The spatiality of the Bakhaaraha and Tamarind Markets in Mogadishu allows us to explore the role they both play in recovering and tracing back the trajectories of Somalia's national formation (and fragmentation) from pre-colonial to colonial periods. They also provide an understanding of global dynamics and geopolitical influences involving Mogadishu, as *Crossbones* will show, during the period between the Transitional Federal Government (2004) and the Federal Government of Somalia (2012).

Following the infernal description of Mogadishu after ten years of absence, Jeebleh returns to his hometown in the last novel of the trilogy, *Crossbones*. Despite the destruction of the city that reminds him of his previous visit narrated in *Links*, a specific place seems to thrive in the surrounding aesthetics of dismay: the Bakhaaraha Market. Established in 1972, during Barre's regime in the Hawl-Wadag district, the Bakhaaraha is the largest market in the country, (*Crossbones*, 155). It is a vital source of income for Somalis across the Horn of Africa, especially for those living in Mogadishu and south-central Somalia. The market flourished during the US-led Unified Task Force intervention in the early 2000s, but before that, it was in decline due to the civil war (it was one of the areas where the Battle of Mogadishu was fought, in 1993) and a famine that hit the area in 1991–2. The market offers a variety of products, from medicine to electronic gadgets, often imported from India, Pakistan, Dubai and Kenya, including arms. After 9/11, several banks closed accused of supporting terrorism, and money transfers came under scrutiny, thus making it difficult to move capital from abroad to Somalia. However, goods could move freely, so the Bakhaaraha became a second-hand market of products bought in the Emirates and then shipped to Somalia. In the context of the prolonged political crisis, businesses have adapted and filled the regulatory void due to the lack of state regulations themselves, for example, 'maintaining close ties with warlords or in some cases by assuming warlord-like roles themselves, effectively blurring the boundary between the two' (Yusuf 2006, 478). When *Crossbones* is set, in 2006, the Courts received support with weapons and funds coming from the Bakhaaraha (Farah 2012, 155).

In terms of structure and organization, the market is divided into sections, each protected by security staff paid by the stores in the area. Its geography is conveyed when Malik (Jeebleh's stepson), who is visiting the market with his companions, Qasiir and Dajaal, arrives there looking for a computer and a colour laser printer (*Crossbones*, 153). The term 'market' itself is questioned, and before crossing the threshold, Farah emphasizes the distinctiveness of Bakhaaraha's spatiality through a detailed description:

> This market looks nothing like anyone's idea of an African market. It's more a mix of trading traditions, with stalls made of zinc sheets on one side, proper shops farther up, and low stands where women sell tomatoes and onions, all of it smack in the centre of what might once have been a thoroughfare. Then, to confound the visitor more, one sees all sorts of people mulling around, and many more gathered at corners, loitering, watching, gathered in groups, bantering, a few strolling about with whips in their hands and conversing with men bearing guns.
>
> (Farah 2012, 155)

The description suggests an overall atmosphere of frenetic activities where danger looms large. According to scholar Jamil A. Mubarak, who has studied how informal markets provide a functioning system for the economy, 'hundreds of small players [have continued to] trade in foreign currencies, goods and services openly and freely' after the political crisis (1997, 2030). The Bakhaaraha embodies this post-war informal economy, unregulated and unprotected by state legislations, where illicit practices occur, such as forging documents, smuggling medicines and trading weapons. However, Farah provides the Bakhaaraha market with a complex spatiality that engages with the urban planning of Mogadishu and the making of Somali national identity, thus shifting the focus from the present time to the past.

In an article (a sort of short personal essay) entitled 'Of Tamarind & Cosmopolitanism' (2010), Farah quite explicitly ascribes the loss of the cosmopolitan feature of Mogadishu to the closure of the Tamarind Market and the opening of the Bakhaaraha (2010, 12). Term cosmopolitanism, as used in Farah's novels, can be understood along with Kwame Anthony Appiah's definition, as an adjective that describes subjects coming from varying locations entering relationships of mutual respect and coexistence despite their different beliefs, backgrounds, language or belonging (1997, 617). Mogadishu's cosmopolitan and multi-ethnic feature reflects the presence of a dominant group (Somalis) in coexistence with minority groups (Africans, Arabs, Europeans). Ethnic distinctions or nationalities, therefore, are presumed to be of little account compared to being a member of the same nation-state or part of a welcoming and multicultural country. In Farah's terms, cosmopolitanism often appears as the alternative to clannism; it is not, however, in contrast with the 'local' but against forms of narrow parochialism derived from clan ideology. It should not be intended as a mere 'critique of views that suggest that identities are formed in specific places' but as a term that enables the negotiation between global and local practices at the cultural and social levels (Cresswell 2015, 81). Accordingly, scholar Lidwien Kapteijns has analysed the modern Mogadishu as described by Somali poets with the notion of *ilbaxnimo* (urbane civility). The latter term, like Farah's understanding of cosmopolitanism, denotes the 'sophistication of people living in urban communities made up of different kinds of people [...] aspiring to modern education and an ideal of gender relations' (Kapteijns 2010, 39).

To better understand Farah's use of the term, it may be helpful to compare the descriptions of the spatiality of the two markets, since they parallel the development of Somali society from (according to Farah) cosmopolitanism to ill-fated clannism:

Of the landmarks of Mogadiscio, I remember the Tamarind Market most. As is often the case, misnomers abound in a city with an ancient oral history and with a memory far more complex than the lives of the people currently residing in it. Try as you might to trace things to their origins, you will find that nobody has the slightest idea why the market, which isn't a market in the sense that we understand when we speak of an African market, was called Tamarind Market.

(Farah 2010, 10)

Even though both markets distinguished themselves from any other 'African market', sharp differences characterize the Tamarind and the Bakhaaraha Markets. Farah describes the former as the paradigmatic site of the city's cosmopolitanism, the buzzing centre of Mogadishu, and a microcosm of the urban life of the 1970s. The market is also described as a historical landmark because its existence connects the present to ancient times, when foreigners from Iran, India and Arabia migrated to Somalia in the tenth century (Farah 2002, 10). Mogadishu was then a powerful city in Somalia, a maritime gateway with economic and political importance. As noticed, also Cristina Ali Farah shares Farah's views, as 'for both writers the Tamarind Market is a marker of the cosmopolitan city they knew' (Dodgson-Katiyo 2020, 73).

This cross-historical tie between centuries is further developed when Farah compares the plunder of the city during the sixteenth century to the 1991 civil war: 'In both sackings, what took the cosmopolitan communities several hundred years to build was destroyed in a short time by the invading hordes of pastoralists and borderline city-dwellers, both groups being hostile to the cultural mélange of the city' (2010, 10). In doing so, Farah overtakes the binary partition of Somalia's history into colonial and postcolonial periods, thus grounding his analysis on a *longue durée* in which events that occurred during pre-colonial times can be read along with current events. The 'recourse to the effects of the *longue durée*' allows Farah to explain the paths taken by Somali society and history to 'account for contradictory contemporary phenomena' (Mbembe 2001, 6), such as the resurgence of *qabyaalad* to the detriment of *ilbaxnimo* and modern national affiliations and belongings. Farah deconstructs and re-constructs the pre-existing dialectical relationship between centre and periphery by placing it before colonial history, in an archaeological investigation that aims to make sense of the frictions within Somali society.

Interestingly, Farah also points out the responsibilities and the 'epistemic violence' of the Italian colonial rule in shaping Mogadishu's demography; Italians, indeed, recruited many Somalis into its army by bringing into the city a large number of people from other regions, other than those areas adjacent to the city. Over time, this migratory movement threw the city's demography off balance since, after the Second World War, Mogadishu became the only city in the country 'to find jobs, to be where the action was, where the industries were, where the only university was, and where you could consult an eye-doctor or a heart specialist' (Farah 2010, 11). The centralization of power in a city ill-prepared to host many inhabitants, therefore, resulted in vast peripheral areas dominated by neglect.

As the Tamarind Market was demolished, the city lost one of its cosmopolitan venues and the multicultural spirit it inhabited. The Bakhaaraha Market, built on the foundations of the old market, represents for Farah the symbol of Barre's regime and the current corruption and sociopolitical instability, exemplified by the 'militarized capitalism' (Farah 2002, 12). Farah's comment about this loss resonates with grief and delusion as he retells his visit to Mogadishu after the end of the regime and the civil war:

> For me, there was a cause to mourn: the murder of the cosmopolitan spirit of the Market. In its place, another market to serve the needs of a city now largely emptied of cosmopolitans has been created: the Bakhaaraha Market. At this newly established 'Market of Silos,' for that is how its name translates, market forces prevail, and 'the clan' reigns supreme. It is the height of a nation's tragedy when those who pillaged and therefore destroyed a city's way of life are allowed to turn murder into profit. Militarised capitalism is on the ascendancy, and the idea of cosmopolitanism is dead and buried.
>
> (Farah 2010, 12)

The silos are then juxtaposed with the tamarind seeds to emphasize the altered structure and function of the market. Farah's diachronic perspective points out both the economic importance of the market and its significance at the social and historical levels in Mogadishu's way of life and the whole of Somalia ('a nation's tragedy'). The clan ideology, successfully functioning and thriving in the Bakhaaraha, is negatively opposed to the cosmopolitanism of the Tamarind.

In *Crossbones*, the Bakhaaraha Market further enhances these ideas and fulfils a political role, too. Farah, on the one hand, remarks upon the local specificity of the market and its connections with Somalia's history; on the other, he compares the role the Bakhaaraha played during the civil war with the role the Casbah performed in the Algerian independence struggle against France (Farah 2012, 155). In a short and recent essay, Farah returns to this idea of the Bakhaaraha being 'the epicenter of resistance during the recent Ethiopian occupation' and 'the operations center of the militant Islamist group Shabab' (Pericoli 2014, 25). Accordingly, Malik's words echo the latter idea, as he thinks the market may be 'the centre for the insurgency after the invasion' (Farah 2012, 155-9). The invasion, specifically, is that of the Ethiopian troops, and the insurgency refers to the potential uprising against the Islamic Courts Union that controls Mogadishu.

In this complex scenario, different narratives inform the market's literary spatiality. First, the Bakaaraha Market exemplifies the end of the cosmopolitan era in Mogadishu, in favour of clan ideology, used by Barre as a political instrument to reinforce his power; second, it becomes the place *par excellence* where the informal economy thrives during the civil war but, also, an economic resource for the city as it 'offers immense profits' for the whole country (Farah 2012, 155). As shown, Mubarak noticed how the stigmatization of the informal economy as illegal, unethical and underground should be re-evaluated. Farah seems to agree with this view when he mentions that most informal workers employed in the market (such as the 'women [who] sell tomatoes and onions') are indeed trying to earn a living against great odds and contribute to both the community and their families (Farah 2012, 155). In this case, the description of the Bakhaaraha, seen from Malik's perspective, suggests accordingly that the market 'functions as an alternative to the state-imposed structures of economy and provides political brinksmanship to those opposing to the status quo' (Farah 2012, 155-6). However, the Bakhaaraha is also considered a surveilled place, where the Islamic Courts Union's propaganda recruits volunteers to fight against Ethiopia after an alleged imminent invasion. Later in the novel, Malik learns that a radio journalist, writing on *HornAfrik* against the Courts, has been shot dead inside the market's alleyways (Farah 2012, 333).

At the formal level, the Bakhaaraha description is pervaded by an eerie feeling of excitement, bestowed by the perilousness of the place. The market is a threatening 'labyrinth *cul-de-sac*' where 'danger is a neighbour', and death may emerge unexpectedly (*Crossbones*, 155, 157). The three characters are always vigilant; every movement is controlled and planned to avoid dangerous outcomes. According to Lorenzo Mari, two main reasons cause this feeling: first, because of the simmering conflict against Ethiopia, continuously evoked by the Islamic Courts Union, which aims to propagate an overall atmosphere of surveillance; second, the withdrawal of the climate of coexistence between cultures, ethnic groups and religions (that had characterized the Tamarind Market) has made the Bakhaaraha hostile to foreigners such as Malik (2018, 153). Farah reproduces this scenario by reiterating Malik's fear of imminent danger:

> In his mind he plays host to many scenarios, in each of which he entertains similar premonitions: of terrible things afoot, of death making the rounds, of airplanes bombing cities, of tanks rolling eastwards, of bullets, of lots of blood.
> (Farah 2012, 156)

Malik is hunted by the presence of death, being a freelance journalist visiting a country where censorship and intolerance towards any non-aligned voices can easily result in violence. The hostility emerges through the market description, accentuating the sense of exclusion and Malik's doubts about his ability to grasp the nuances of its networks. Malik himself voices his feeling of being othered when, later in the novel, he needs to return to the marker and misses 'a heavy exchange of gunfire' for a few moments' (Farah 2012, 333). He thinks that 'the geography of the Bakhaaraha and the casbah make sense only to a native' and that 'A stranger wouldn't know which alleys end in dead ends and which would lead them to safety' (Farah 2012, 333).

The feeling of danger and disorientation is also expressed in the description of the Bakhaaraha in Afdhere Jama's novel *Liido Beach*. Two characters, Hanad and Roti, arrive at the 'massive' market complex and notice that:

> It was the chaos hour. The day people were closing up while the night shift folks were just starting to arrive. Crisscrossing people, yelling people, and a lot of havoc in the air. The young man began looking for Cabdalle Shideeye, a guide to the black market [...]. They pretended to be tough, but to those who looked at their perfect skin knew they are just good kids. They also looked clueless. They asked around, and the people seemed to be suspicious of them.
>
> (Jama 2018, 50)

Jama's account resembles Farah's previous description of the market, focussed on the chaotic atmosphere and leery look of the people who work there. Like Malik, Hanad and Roti feel they do not belong, thus implicitly retrieving the idea that the Bakhaaraha is not a welcoming and cosmopolitan place but a bounded environment in which specific rules and forms of affiliation apply.

Farah makes the market both a labyrinth and a pit, like the circles of *Inferno* in which Dante the Pilgrim and Virgil progressively descend. Jama's *Liido Beach* also echoes this infernal feature in describing people as a *bolgia* ('Crisscrossing people, yelling people, and a lot of havoc in the air') and in mentioning a guide to help the protagonists orient themselves in the market. Farah further stresses the impression of descent by comparing the movement of Malik inside the market to a slope towards an underground centre, as if the physical structure of the market were that of a chasm: 'abyss', 'he moves in deeper', 'the deeper they walk into the market' (Farah 2012, 156–7; 331). Malik's feeling of plunging into a depth where darkness prevents any form of understanding and causes uneasiness is suggested when he himself senses his heart sicken 'the further he goes into the inner sanctums of the market complex' (Farah 2012, 331).

As in the case of the airport, Farah underlines how the market embodies the *genius loci* and provides the reader with socio-historical insights about Somalia's realities. In the case of the Bakhaaraha, it induces us to reflect on the events which have characterized Somalia's historical and political trajectories to investigate the palingenesis of the country as a nation. As shown, by considering the dismantlement of the Tamarind Market as the caesura between cosmopolitanism and clannism, Farah implies that the nation's political crisis does not coincide exclusively with the outbreak of the civil war. Instead, it should be backdated during Siyaad Barre's authoritarian regime. In doing so, Farah disturbs the linear Eurocentric historiography and connects the resurgence of clannism (as the dominant political formation) to the Italian colonial rule and the policies of Siyaad Barre, which have fostered greed-driven pulls within the Somali society. Moreover, Farah underscores the tension between centre and periphery within the national borders, ascribing the Somalis pastoralists for taking part in the destruction of Mogadishu.

In 'Of Tamarind and Cosmopolitanism', Farah describes the relationship between 'urbophiles' and 'urbophobic' (pastoralists) as conflictual. He affirms that 'the pastoralists that invaded Mogadishu did not trust the (pre-colonial, colonial and post-colonial) foreigners who settled in and built the city and were waiting for the day when they could regain control over their ancestral land' (Warah, Dirios and Osman 2012, 22). This dichotomy relates to spatiality as it opposes, on the one hand, the urbanscape of Mogadishu, inhabited by middle-class cosmopolitan Somalis, and on the other, the rural areas where pastoralist communities dwelled. The latter 'gradually accumulated hostility towards the city until they became intent on destroying it' (Farah 2010, 11). Garane Garane, too, seems to share this view in *Il latte è buono*, as it will be analysed in Chapter 4.

At this point, it should be noted that the permanence of the idea of the 'nation' in a moment of undeniable institutional fragility signals its importance in the present times of diaspora and disaggregation. The nation remains, for Farah, a privileged framework within which to consider and re-elaborate dynamics (such as those between the centre vs periphery, cosmopolitanism vs clannism, nationhood vs clannism) that explain the specificity of Somali history against generalizations about the failures of post-colonial history. Instead of supporting the idea that the nation's failure has been caused by colonial rule or dictatorship, Farah explores the social rigidities of the pre-colonial era and their further stiffening during Barre's regime, tracing back the tensions already at play within Somali society before the nation's formation.

In doing so, Farah exemplifies the dire present by representing the Bakhaaraha Market as a functioning state within a 'failed' state, a non-state-owned micro-economy in a country where public structures are missing or incapable of managing economic policies at the national level.

The Station: Termini between Physical and Linguistic Reterritorialization

The attention for a shared spatiality is a common trait of Somali novels in Italian, as they often fictionalize Termini, Rome's central train station. Scholars have investigated the recurrent presence of the station in several texts of migrant and second-generation writers, exploring the multiple ways in which Termini is represented and its complex, multifaceted roles in the narratives of resettlement and displacement. Simone Brioni has studied Stazione Termini in Italian films and texts, showing how it functions as a place 'that mirrors an idea of the nation as homogeneous, monolithic, and white' but that also 'as a space that marks otherness' (2017, 443; 448). Drawing on Michel Foucault's definition of heterotopia, Brioni also suggests that Termini differs from a non-place as it allows more complex social practices than those of consumption and transition. Similarly, the concept of non-place is critically addressed by Chiara Giuliani, who explored Termini's multifaceted role with specific attention to migrant writers. Interestingly, Giuliani maintains that:

> Termini [...] is a meeting point for several migrant communities who have turned it into a space to congregate with fellow compatriots, to speak one's own language, to eat traditional food and to, metaphorically, go back home.
>
> (2021, 28)

The idea of Termini as a 'key place of contact with and among immigrants' will be the starting point of the following analysis, which will look at how the station's spatiality is engaged with and expressed by Somali novels in Italian, which collectively construct an image of Termini that deals both its it materiality and architecture and its perception and connotation (Brioni 2017, 443; Giuliani 2021, 28). In the novels of Somali authors, who fictionalize the station to express the struggle of Somali immigrants to resettle in the host country but also their attempt to form a sense of community, language plays a fundamental role in conveying the multi-layered spatiality of the station and its manifold significance in their imaginary.

Termini, indeed, is at the same time a meeting point – full of home and filled with a sense of community – and a source of pain and nostalgia for the lost home, a ghetto where immigrants are confined and controlled. Graziella Parati has described Termini as a space of 'urban proximity', brimming with 'the anxieties and the tensions inherent in acts of appropriation between the native and the non-native' (2010, 433). Before analysing how this act of appropriation is fictionalized in Italophone novels and how this tension is conveyed, it is worth mentioning a passage from the Anglophone shore of the diaspora: in Nuruddin Farah's novel *Gifts* (1993), the protagonist, Duniya, thinks about the status of being a migrant reminiscing about her trip to Rome:

> Duniya remembered being shown such people in the environs of the Stazione Termini, the main railway station in Rome. Nearby there was a piazza called Independenza [sic], the Somalis' and the Eritrean's meeting-place in the Italian capital. Duniya wondered why it was that foreigners and the homeless congregated around departure- or arrival-points in their country of economic exile. There was no denying that expatriates living in Mogadiscio were prone to go to the airport at the slimmest pretext to welcome or bid farewell to their travelling compatriots. Somalis used to turn up in large numbers at Fiumicino, Rome's international airport, whenever a Somali Airlines flight arrived or departed.
>
> (Farah 1993a, 174)

Apart from showing once again the interliterary network of references between Somali diasporic authors and the dialectic engagement with spaces in the diasporic imaginary, Farah sheds light on the condition of exiles, migrants and expatriates in Italy, the former metropole. This aspect will be addressed later in relation to Scego's and Ali Farah's novels, so what is relevant here for our analysis is the idea of Termini as a 'meeting point'. The focus on this social aspect of the station has been pointed out by Simone Brioni, with direct reference to Marc Augé. Brioni argues that 'the representation of Termini as the hub of the migrants' togetherness contests its depiction as a space of alleged anonymity' (2017, 453). Garane's novella *Il latte è buono* transposes this togetherness, as it presents Stazione Termini as the gathering point for his fellow Somalis who fled the country. Whether Garane's description aims to trace a historical connection between Somalia and Italia, Farah emphasizes the role of the station for the diasporic Somali community of the late 1980s and early 1990s.[15]

> A Roma i suoi si riunivano nella «più grande stazione ferroviaria d'Europa», la Stazione Termini. [...] I suoi amavano questo monumento perché storicamente è come il parlamento di Mogadiscio. Furono entrambi costruiti dall'uomo grazie al quale erano finiti in quel posto. Gli africani vedevano questo posto come costruito da un vero uomo e non da questi mezzosangue, senza fibra, senza forza, che ti chiedevano se volevi un hotel, una donna, eccetera, cento volte al giorno! Tutto succedeva alla stazione, forse sotto lo sguardo benevolo del Duce. Si vendeva lì il *garbasar*, il *dirac*, il *rumay*, i biglietti aerei, i passaporti di un paese inesistente, dato che, per la proprietà transitiva, l'ambasciata non esisteva.
>
> (2005, 81)

> In Rome, his people [Somalis] gathered in the 'largest train station in Europe', Stazione Termini [...] His people loved this monument because historically is like the Parliament in Mogadishu. They both were built by the same man, thanks to whom they ended up there. Africans saw this building as made by a real man and not by those mixed-race people, without fibre, without strength, who asked you if you wanted a room to sleep in, a woman, etcetera, hundreds of times a day! Everything happened at the station, perhaps under the benevolent gaze of the Duce. *Garbasar, dirac, rumay*, flight tickets, and passports of an unreal country were sold there since, by the transitive property, the embassy didn't exist.

Garane clarifies the correspondence between Rome and Mogadishu by emphasizing the historical connection between the two cities. The parliament is then compared to the station, underlining the shared history of the two countries through the aesthetics of the building and another cross-historical connection: the presence of *il Duce*, Mussolini. In doing so, Garane recalls 'the mythical revival during Mussolini's imperial ambitions with the establishment of the *Africa Orientale Italiana*, or Italian East Africa' (Cantone 2016, 11). At the same time, he points out the Fascist project of envisioning Termini as the physical embodiment of Italianness, aimed at celebrating 'the memory of imperial Rome' (Brioni 2017, 445).

This connection allows us to consider the station as a place where 'spatial and temporal indicators are fused into one carefully thought-out, concrete whole' (Bakhtin 1981, 16). Mikhail Bakhtin's explanation describes the concept of the chronotope, namely the 'intrinsic connectedness of temporal and spatial relationships' and their representation (*ibid*). Bakhtin's theory implies that narrative texts are composed of a diegetic framework and a particular fictional world, the so-called chronotope. Since Bakhtin never offers a definitive definition of the concept, we can start from its indefiniteness and apply it to the case of Somali novels in Italian. The fictional description of Termini in the novels from diasporic authors arises as the chronotope that signals the displaced condition of Somali people.

In sum, Termini does not represent only a physical space but denotes the time of migration and resettlement in Somalia's history. Termini comes to define diasporic texts and turns out to be one of the centres of several diasporic trajectories. It also retrieves the legacy of colonialism, being the central station of the former metropole, Rome, which has been rarely described as such in Italian literature, thus never becoming, like London, 'the metonym for imperial power itself: its point of origin, the place where the empire was built and around which it revolved' (Ball 2004, 4). Only recently, thanks to postcolonial authors, Termini has gained a similar role as other landmarks such as, for example, Waterloo Station and Charing Cross, in the works of Sam Selvon and V. S. Naipaul (Ball 2004, 133, 150).

The station becomes a crossroad where to reinstate local practices and form networks across the nations. As Chiara Giuliani emphasized, 'Termini [...] is imbued with warm and familiar feelings which, along with the presence of other compatriots, make Termini a home space' (2021, 40). However, Termini is also a 'spatial compromise' (*ibid.*, 40). It is, indeed, both a centre (of the Roman Somali community) and a periphery, a global hub of connections and a site of local interactions; it occupies a marginalized place within the topography of the city but, at the same time, is the threshold to Rome, the *caput mundi*. It becomes the ecumene of Somali migrants and, as in the case of airports, it blurs the line between anthropological and supermodern *lieux*. Author Igiaba Scego explains that the city of Rome remained unknown for many Somalis who arrived there in the 1990s, as they remained in the station's surrounding area, where other fellow citizens settled before them. The station, therefore, can be read as the 'bridge between [Somalis'] new residence and home, a material and symbolic link with their distant homeland' (Curti 2007, 61). In *La mia casa è dove sono* (*Home Is Where I Am*, 2010), Scego stresses the same importance of the station and, like Garane, traces a hypothetical vicinity – or proximity, in Parati's terms – between Rome and Mogadishu, this time more geographical than temporal: 'Allora Termini dava loro l'impressione che Mogadiscio fosse dietro l'angolo. Bastava prendere un treno e volare via lungo i binari di un sogno' ('Then Termini gave them the impression that Mogadishu was just around the corner. It was enough to take a train and fly away along the tracks of a dream') (2010, 103).

Somali-Persian author Shirin Ramzanali Fazel, whose autobiography, as shown, is mentioned in Farah's *Links*, describes this in-betweenness as follows:

Roma, caput mundi. Sono alla stazione Termini [...] ovunque mi giro vedo volti somali. Donne belle, giovani e meno giovani, in sandali o tacchi a spillo, con chiome dai tagli moderni, vestite in jeans, gonne, pantaloni, magliette o con il tradizionale *dirac*; coperte da coloratissimi *garbasaar*, o modesti *hijabs*. Sempre in gruppo, come per esorcizzare la solitudine. Occhi perennemente in cerca di un volto amico di cui non si ha notizia da lungo tempo.

([1994] 2017, p. 52)

Rome, the capital of the world. I am at Stazione Termini [...]. Wherever I turn, I see many Somali faces. Beautiful women, young and older, wearing sandals or stilettos, with modern haircuts, in jeans, skirts, trousers, t-shirts o with the traditional *dirac*; their heads wrapped in colourful *garbasaar* or plain chadors. Always together, as to dispel solitude. Eyes perpetually looking for a friend you haven't had news of in a long time.

The symbolic bond with the motherland also becomes physical in the way displaced Somalis try to turn the station into a familiar place; at the same time, Termini becomes the link between the host country and home, 'an in-between place of arrival and departure' that can 'prompt nostalgia' and healing from loneliness and disillusionment (Ball 2004, 133). In the novel *Nuvole sull'Equatore* (*Clouds Over the Equator*, 2017b), Shirin Fazel tells the story of Giulia, a mixed girl (daughter of an Italian father and Somali mother) who lives her youth in Mogadishu and then moves to Italy, when Barre took control of the country. After some years in Rome and a degree in Political Science, Giulia wanders around the city to visit the *punti di ritrovo* (meeting points) of migrants, such as the Ethiopian restaurant and Termini.

She describes the station as follows:

Molte volte bastava andare alla stazione Termini e anche se non ci si conosceva risultava facile individuare i propri compaesani, dalla fisionomia e dalla parlata somala. Ti potevi avvicinare e iniziare a raccogliere notizie sulla Somalia, c'era continuamente qualcuna che era appena arrivato.

Questi incontri portavano sprazzi di energia nella mente di Gilia. Era il pentolone da cui attingere i sapori mai dimenticati di una terra che si stava lentamente sgretolando.

(Fazel Ramzanali 2017b, 203)

Many times, it was enough to go to Termini station and, even if you did not know each other, it was easy to recognise your fellow citizens, from the physiognomy and the Somali speech. You could get closer and start collecting news about Somalia; there was always someone who had just arrived.

These encounters were burst of energy for Gilia's mind. It was the cauldron from which to draw the never forgotten flavours of a land that was slowly crumbling.

Termini, in this case, is both a getaway of the transnational flows of several diasporic subjects and a homely place where news from home can be shared and even lost flavours can be retrieved. The station, therefore, mediates a feeling of proximity with Somalia, thanks to the flavours, the language and the physical appearance of other fellow migrants, and the spatial distance and separation between Italy and Somalia.

In a similar fashion, Scego describes the station as a centre for the migrants' transnational communities and shares with Fazel, Garane and Ali Farah a common vocabulary that enables Termini's deterritorialization. In *La mia casa è dove sono*, the narrator's questions directed to the reader present the station as a place where products related to Somalia can be purchased, expanding on the idea of the lost flavours mentioned by Fazel (cardamom for the spicy tea or drapes). The use of the second person ('Do you need?') prompts a particular intimacy between the reader and the narrator, but it also deterritorializes Termini by making it unfamiliar for the Italian-speaking reader. This double effect is further enabled by unglossed words, such as *rummay*, *goiabada*, *eenjera* and *zighinì*, which sound alien to any Italian-speaking reader and almost turn Termini, ironically, into an African*esque* market, playing with exotic cliché and references to colonial imaginary:

> La Stazione in questi ultimi anni è migliorata tantissimo. Da una parte ci sono stati i restauri del comune, dall'altra le varie comunità migranti si sono date da fare. Ci sono negozietti per tutti i gusti. Vuoi fare le extension? Vuoi un po' di cardamomo per i tè speziati delle tue parti? Vuoi un drappo con la storia della regina di Saba sulla parete di casa? A Termini trovi delle cose fantastiche: dai sari alla corteccia *rummay* per lavarti i denti, trovi anche la *goiabada* che i brasiliani mangiano con il formaggio [...] poi *eenjera* e *zighinì* a non finire.
>
> (Scego 2010, 106)

> The station has improved a lot in recent years. On the one hand, there have been the refurbishments done by the municipality, and on the other, the various migrant communities have done quite a job. There are little shops for every taste. Do you need to do extensions? Do you need some cardamom for the spicy teas of your country? Do you need a drape on the wall of your house with the story of the Queen of Sheba? At Termini, you can find fantastic things: from the saris to the *rummay* bark for brushing your teeth; you can also find the *goiabada* that Brazilians eat with cheese [...] then *eenjera* and *zighinì* galore.

Likewise, Cristina Ali Farah, in *Madre piccola* (*Little Mother,* 2007), represents the station as one of the principal assembly points for the expatriate Somalis, the place where a sense of community and familiarity may be rebuilt and maintained. One of the protagonists, Barni, who works as an obstetrician in Rome and fled Somalia because of the civil war, tells the story of her arrival in Italy and the importance of the station for her and other Somali migrants.

The term deterritorialization is useful again to broadly describe the re-establishment of aspects of Somali culture within a host place in the attempt to make the latter welcoming and familiar. Coined by French scholars Gilles Deleuze and Félix Guattari, deterritorialization describes the process by which social, cultural, economic and political practices, as well as languages, are altered. They produce a new, restructured and reconfigured territory in a process called reterritorialization (2013, 9, 72–3). Through Barni's eyes, we see how Somali people of the diaspora deterritorialize and reterritorialize Termini by rebuilding lost social practices and reproducing 'a sense of collective national identity' (Ball 2004, 102). As Vivian Gerrard has observed, this reconfiguration occurs at both the physical and symbolic level: on the one hand, diasporic subjects operate a Somalisation of a 'lived' Italian space such as Termini through commercial practices and social activities and, on the other hand, they transform the Italian language to represent their own experience of the station, thus refashioning the latter as fictional postcolonial space (2016, 164).

The fictionalization of Termini as a place of socialization takes place in Ali Farah's *Little Mother* through the practice of linguistic appropriation, as the following passage highlights:

> I don't think one can write about the Somali community in Rome without starting from the Roma Termini train station, the crossroads, and the scene of our longings. I even tried to convince myself for a while that it was a seedy place, only fit for tourists and refugees, a place where you had to hold on tight to your purse and gold chain. Preconceived ideas born out of my resentment. Who could not long for that buzz that hit you, in the central concourse, next to the train tracks, as soon as you got close to the café just like any other, the Somali café. Not that there was a sign outside, or that it was run by a Somali, but simply because there were always a whole lot of Somalis in that café. All you had to do was go to the Termini train station to meet the world. In those days, we went to the *draddorio* to eat rice with goat meat; we got a *defreddi* at the stand, and we bought *bajiiye* with fresh hot pepper and *rummay* from the young girls. People provided us with documents to rescue everyone, absolutely everyone, in our family.
>
> (Ali Farah 2011, 25–6)

Ali Farah makes calques of words to interweave Italian and Somali and perform a linguistic appropriation at the morphological and phonological levels. Whereas Somali authors reconfigure the Italian language in the sense of self-representation, in *Little Mother,* this aim is achieved with the act of appropriation of Italian words, such as *draddorio* as the vernacular transcription of *trattoria* (eating house), to intervene in the dominant discourse and decolonize the centre (Ashcroft, Griffith and Tiffin 2002, 37). Ali Farah tries to manipulate the language of the colonizers and to make it her own, as in *defreddi* (*tè freddo*, cold tea), *fasoleeti* (*fazzoletti*, handkerchief) or *kabushiini* (cappuccino), thus refusing to adhere to the concept of 'correct' or 'standard' Italian.

In the case of Ali Farah, Italian words are written according to Somali pronunciation to signify linguistic inclusion: vernacular transcription and unglossed words (such as *rummay*), more than showing a conflict, suggest a strategy of cohabitation in which words undergo a process of familiarization (Brioni 2015, 49). This linguistic appropriation of the Italian language to fictionalize the station parallels the physical reterritorialization of Termini, as in the case of the café or:

> Our places [...] Qamar's store, Xassan's Phone Centre, the *draddorio* and the area around it.
> Qamar's store: I can give you the address if you're interested. They sell everything a Somali woman could ever want. Brightly coloured *shaash*, *garbasaar* made of lightweight cotton stamped with flowers, *diric Jibuuti*, satin petticoats embroidered with pearls, long *goonooyin*, *guntiino* made of hand-spun raw fabric that once everyone turned their noses up at, but which today are back in fashion – the more an object is hard to come by, the more precious it become.
> (Ali Farah 2011, 27)

Barni's use of '*i nostri luoghi*' (our places) to refer to Xassan's phone centre and Qamar's shop emphasize a sense of belonging and familiarity, providing a well-defined alternative aesthetics and toponomy of the station itself. Similarly, in *La mia casa è dove sono* (*Home Is Where I Am*), Igiaba Scego mentions the same cafes and calls them '*luoghi di ritrovo*' (meeting places) and notices that they do not have signs outside and do not belong to the Somali people, but they represent places to meet and talk (2010, 109).

Apart from the textile products available at Termini, Barni mentions jewels (amber and silver), lotions, conditioners, oils and fragrances (27) and, especially, music. Her description of the station, once again, shows how the process of reterritorialization occurs at the small-scale level:

> And music, always more music, music, especially modern music. When they find something particularly special, or a woman brings a video of a wedding or an engagement, the young women gather together around the small television set to watch it, chat and pass comments.
> (Ali Farah 2011, 27)

Qamar's store and Xassan's phone centre, with their own distinctive spatiality, represent enclaves that re-house Somalis in Rome; these spaces are exclusionary territories, as much as the café previously mentioned; they are Somali strongholds, 'unfamiliar, unknown and unwelcoming' to white Italians (Procter 1998, 118). Small businesses such as the *draddoria*, the Ethiopian restaurant, Qamar's store and Xassan's phone centre become 'microcosmic colonies or outposts of cultural autonomy' (Ball 2004, 118).

At the formal level, Ali Farah's passage shows similarities with Fazel's, Scego's and Garane's extracts, as they share recurrent Somali words such as the *rummay* (a twig used as a toothbrush) and the attention to textile products as markers of Somaliness, such as the *garbasaar* (a woman's colourful shawl worn to cover head and shoulder). The references to the sensory field connected to food and scent appear shared traits in the description of the spatiality of Termini as a re-invented space (both physically and literally) and show the powerful sense of belonging to a home now distant and fragile.

However, reterritorialization and appropriation can be considered two sides of the same coin, as they are both in the making and, thus, imperfect, and incomplete. Cristina Ali Farah describes how Termini changed over time and how its spatiality influences her protagonist at the emotional level. Through Barni's perspective, Ali Farah does not shy away from acknowledging the condition of dispossession and unbelonging of Somali people in a city (Rome) and a country (Italy) that are unwelcoming and hostile towards migrants and African/Black people.

After the implementation of the Bossi-Fini Law (2002), a stricter law which introduced criminal sanctions and expulsion for persons caught entering the country illegally, Termini has become a place `pieno di dolore' (`so full of pain') (Ali Farah 2011, 26). Ali Farah enhances the complexity of the station, showing how the spatiality of Termini, once made up of small shops and friendly encounters between Somalis, has turned into a gentrified environment ruled by global brands, surveillance and migrants sent back due to the law. As the station changed its physiognomy, Italy became more reluctant and stricter regarding immigration policies. It is worth quoting the new description of Termini, 'loaded with nostalgia' (Brioni 2017, 452). Barni, with longing and sorrow, draws a comparison between migration flows and sheds light on the unwelcoming spatiality of the station:

> Now many things have changed: the central concourse has been refurbished with flashy shops, Benetton, Nike, Intimissimi, Levi's, Sisley; fast-food places, phone canters, pay-for-use public baths, automatic ticket machines, escalators, maxi screen with advertisements, updated train boards. A truly modern station. Those few remaining Somalis continue to meet in those places. Especially since they started arriving on those illegal boats [...] Before the Italian government started that business of fingerprinting, they all tried to go north or northwest. Toward one of those mythical countries that offer you a place to sleep and a plate of food. *Ingiriiska, Norwey, Holand, Swidish*. Even after they started that fingerprinting business, they still try anyway, trusting luck. Those who didn't make it are easy to recognize, the ones who were sent back. They roam around the station with a dirty backpack, a bundle filled with sorrow.
>
> (Ali Farah 2011, 26)

As described here, Termini has become a space of in-betweenness. The migrants who are sent back and are prevented from leaving due to the lack of documents are forced to immobility. This paradoxical condition, of being in a transient space but unable to leave, tellingly encapsulates the condition of contemporary African migrants who arrive via the Mediterranean to cross Italy and seek refuge in England, Norway, the Netherlands and Sweden. As Ali Farah implies, Termini metonymically represents the whole of Italy to remarks about the government's failure to protect refugees and welcome migrants. Carmen Concilio has observed that Italy is only a sort of waiting room, a sort of third space, not so much a third space of hybridity, but a purgatory between the hell of the civil war and the heaven of a future elsewhere, (2016, 122). It is interesting here to notice that, whereas for Fazel Somali people recognize one another because of the language and physiognomy, for Ali Farah it is the condition of migration itself that can be recognized in the new spatiality of the station ('They roam around the station with a dirty backpack, a bundle filled with sorrow').

These new spatiality and temporality are described in one passage of Scego's *La mia casa è dove sono* (*Home Is Where I Am*), which remarkably resembles Ali Farah's representation:

> Negli anni Settanta e Ottanta la stazione puzzava di piscio e non erano pochi gli angoli violenti. Ora invece è tutta ripulita, con negozi di tutti i tipi: Sisley, Etham, Calzedonia, Nike, Lindt, Benetton. È quasi piacevole farci una passeggiata.
>
> (Scego 2010, 104)

> In the Seventies and Eighties, the station smelled of piss, and there were many violent corners. Now it's all cleaned up, with shops of all kinds: Sisley, Etham, Calzedonia, Nike, Lindt, Benetton. It is almost pleasant to walk around there.

While Ali Farah underlines how the new station is unwelcoming for migrants and refugees, Scego also mentions the material improvement of Termini. However, in another passage, the same spatiality is negatively conveyed to emphasize the unhomeliness of Termini further, as personally experienced by Scego:

> Mi inquietava la stazione da piccola. Non ci andavo volentieri. Quando i miei volevano salutare un amico, mi ci trascinavano per forza. Spesso frignavo. Crescendo, il mio rapporto con la stazione non è migliorato. Non frignavo più, ma provavo fastidio. Per me Termini era un ghetto, una roba da sfigati. Non volevo metterci piedi. Non volevo essere travolta da quel puzzo di piscio, da quel puzzo di sconfitta.
>
> (Scego 2010, 104)

> The station worried me as a child. I didn't go there willingly. When my parents wanted to greet a friend, they dragged me there by force. I often whined. Growing up, my relationship with the station has not improved. I no longer whined, but I was annoyed. For me, Termini was a ghetto, something for losers. I didn't want to set foot in there. I didn't want to be overwhelmed by the stench of piddle, by that stench of defeat.

Scego dedicates a whole chapter to Stazione Termini and shows its importance in the experience of diasporic Somali people. Here she explains her ambivalent feelings towards Termini, of both attraction and repulsion: on the one hand, the station rises again as a meeting point for Somali migrants; on the other, it epitomizes the failure of inclusion and integration, turning into an ethnic enclave with limited connection with the rest of the city. Accordingly, Chiara Giuliani has pointed out that, in Scego's personal experience, Termini is also an 'obstacle towards her inclusion in Italian society' and 'a place of pain' (2021, 47). Being 'the spatial and metaphorical reminder of all the separations her family had suffered', Termini's ability to build a new home and a sense of community is slightly compromised (*ibid.*, 47).

Termini as a ghetto underlines, instead, how the presence of Somali people was subject to indifference by Italian institutions. However, Brioni has observed that the descriptions of 'Termini as an urban ghetto remove this space from the rest of the city and connect it to other national or transnational environments' (2017, 452). This idea of a 'transnational ghetto', is interesting here as it represents Termini as a space both self-contained and open beyond national borders. It is useful to emphasize, once again, that Termini symbolizes multiple tensions and it emerges as denoted by a flexible spatiality, deeply influenced by time and individual experiences.

In Shirin Ramzanali Fazel's previous account, the verb *esorcizzare* (to exorcise) is key to appreciating the importance of Termini as a nodal point of the city, able to banish loneliness. Scego, however, reflects on the limits of resettling and emphasizes the segregation and isolation of Somali people, unwelcomed in the former motherland:

Per molte persone della diaspora somala conoscere Roma non era la priorità [...]. Era lì il centro dei somali. Lì cominciava la vita vera. [...] Roma a molti non importava nemmeno.

(2010, 103–4)

For many people of the Somali diaspora, knowing Rome was not the priority. It was [Termini] the centre of the Somalis. There began the real life [...] Rome didn't even matter to many.

In this sense, Termini is a threshold marked by both mobility and immobility. It allows, at the same time, migrant Somalis to reach Italy, gather and open small businesses. However, it also prevents them from establishing strong relationships with the community of Italians – or the natives, in Parati's terms – and with Rome itself. Urban mobility is then limited and contained in a place which should be the embodiment of crossing and movement. The city, outside the borders of station, is unwelcoming and unknown. In this regard, Nick Tembo notes that Termini provides 'an interesting way of looking at how unsafe or haunting spaces', thus becoming 'a source of yet another form of migration for displaced bodies' (2017, 67). Indeed, diasporic places, like diasporic identities, are in constant negotiation between opposite polarities: movement and stability, visibility and invisibility, tradition, and transformation.

At the textual level, Stazione Termini turns out to be the defining chronotope of the Somali diaspora in Italy; it represents the impossibility for Somalis to feel at home and incorporated into Italian society, but also the place that triggers the processes of reterritorialization and reappropriation of the displaced subjects. The spatiality of the station embodies the feelings of both exclusion and inclusion experienced by diasporic characters, thus questioning fixed ideas of home and belonging.

Somali authors see Termini as a place where personal and collective identity and memory can be produced and interrogated. The station becomes the central node in the diasporic flow of the Somali people who fled their country due to the civil war and a powerful physical and literary site where diasporic consciousness is explored. Through recurring motifs and mutual references, Termini's fictional and physical spatiality is deeply anthropological, well-grounded in time and space, contrary to the idea that *non-lieux* 'offer little sense of where one stands in the world' (Lee 2018, 197). While they elaborate on the multilayered and contradictory spatiality of Stazione Termini, as a place where to rekindle lost relationships with fellow citizens to form a community and a *locus* of immobility, pain and suffering due to exclusion and displacement, Somali authors also expand the understanding of Rome; implicitly, the narrative of the city as a global *caput mundi* is questioned, as they show how Rome's unwelcoming attitude towards migrants marks it as exclusive for white Italians.

As in the case of Gashan, the protagonist of *Il latte è buono*, his sense of belonging to Italian society is given by the references to the Italian toponymy that sounds familiar to him. Therefore, in Mogadishu, he feels like an outsider in his native culture. The following chapter delves into the close relationship between colonial toponymy and identity by exploring the effect of the former on the making of colonial subjectivity. Moreover, it explores how, through the aesthetics of the civil war and the erased landscape of Mogadishu, Somali authors address the uncertainty for the future development of the nation but, at the same time, unsettle colonial and neocolonial ways of knowing, assumptions and concepts employed to produce knowledge about Somalis.

Conclusion

This chapter has focused on three key emblematic places, the airport, the market and the train station, which found a prominent discursive characterization in the Somali literary production of the diaspora. The analysis of their fictionalized spatiality has triggered a broader examination of their relevance in terms of nation-making and identity. With their temporal and spatial specificity, airports have shown how their descriptions achieve two main goals: first, from the narrative point of view, they metonymically showcase the society to which they belong and, broadly speaking, the country in which they are located. They are helpful settings, or narrative anterooms, for emphasizing the ethos of a whole society and disclosing or sketching key features of their related cities, namely Mogadishu and Rome. Second, instead of being non-places, where human subjects are reduced to buyers or passengers, and personal identities are nullified, they emerge instead as spaces of conflict and trauma. This latter aspect has been examined in relation to *Links* and *Il latte il buono*. While, in the former, Farah narrates the occurrence of a shocking event that eventually traumatized the protagonist, the latter describes the problematic experience of Gashan, as a former colonial subject, to be recognized as Italian at the passport check.

Similarly, I have shown how the Stazione Termini emerges as an anthropological place where Somali people have tried to reconstruct a sense of community. Through spatial and linguistic reterritorialization, I have shown how Somali Italian authors have described the process of refamiliarization and transformation of the station according to their cultural and social practices. In doing so, they also try to resist marginalization and ghettoization, as Italy reveals itself as an unwelcoming country, ill-equipped to host African migrants, especially those coming from the former colonies.

The following chapter carries on the analysis around the idea of nationhood by analysing, instead of specific spaces, the role played by Mogadishu itself in shaping Somali identities (both individual, as in the case of Garane, and national, as in Jeebleh's experience). Furthermore, to obtain a more holistic understanding of Somalia, the chapter provides a comparative and diachronic analysis of Mogadishu's spatiality grounded in the different representations of the urbanscape given by Somali authors over time. They all foreground a dynamic fictionalization of the city against the dominant Western narrative that defines Mogadishu as ground zero and associates it with a battleground ravaged by warlords and armed militia.

Notes

1   Even though referring to spatiality as a social construct in which space and society are mutually embedded, I will use here the term 'place(s)' instead of 'space(s)' for airports, stations and markets according to the translation of *non-lieux* as non-places and not 'non-spaces'.
2   The two other trilogies are: 'Variations on the Theme of an African Dictatorship' (*Sweet and Sour Milk*, 1979; *Sardines*, 1981; *Close Sesame*, 1983) and 'Blood in the Sun' (*Maps*, 1986; *Gifts*, 1993; *Secrets*, 1998).
3   Even though, in *Links*, Farah does not mention the exact time of the events he narrates, it is possible to retrieve the time-setting by using an explicit reference made in *Crossbones*, where Farah writes: 'Since his [of Jeebleh] 1996 visit' (2012, 27). This reassesses Carbonieri's previous dating of the novel: '[...] the story mentions that Dajaal's granddaughter was injured by the fall of a helicopter during the confrontations on 3 October 1993, when she was barely one year old. At a certain moment during his visit, Jeebleh goes to see her: «How old is she?» «Almost five and a half» (Farah, 2005, 273)', leading her to think that the novel was set in 1997 (Carbonieri 2014, 84).
4   'Only one route linked the northern part of Mogadiscio, once under the control of the warlord Aideed's faction, to the south, formerly under the control of warlord Ali Mahdi' (Farah 2008, 13).
5   Despite this ambiguity, Augé's definition presents another drawback: is this binary, yet ambivalent, configuration of places suitable for the West only? Is supermodernity confined to the Western episteme? In which paradigm of modernity may the African contexts be included? These questions arise because the meta-categorization of supermodernity seems to exclude the postcolonial world. More broadly, the concept of modernity – from its origins in sixteenth- and seventeenth-century Europe – has been troublesome when describing African contexts (Enwezor 2010). Western

societies have appropriated and accommodated the project of modernity as associated with the power of science and technology, secularization or laicization, economic growth, industrialization, urbanization and nation formation. This theorization, established and defined by European philosophers within the framework of rationalism, is at the heart of the dispute about understanding modernity in non-Western countries. This set of manifestations or modes of thought have clashed against different practices and historical trajectories experienced, for example, by African countries, which reclaim their own modernity; in doing so, they revise general principles and formulations according to their own cultural, political, economic and social agenda. To understand the African debate on modernity is, to a great extent, to pinpoint how the concept has circulated in Africa, with the different constructions and numerous realities it conceals. Forms of appropriation, opposition and resistance have shaped the concept, but also expectations concerning the understanding of the term. The question regarding the genealogy of the concept of modernity and its different forms, from its initial appearance to its deployment and subsequent debates, lies outside this analysis's scope. Instead, Okwui Enwezor coined the term 'aftermodern' to define the contemporary state of Africa. He theorized four types of modernity: the first, 'supermodernity', applies to the West, namely Europe and the United States, as the expression of the Enlightenment, the belief in rationality, empiricism and freedom. The second is 'andromodernity', which describes the amalgam of Asia; the third is 'speciousmodernity', as in the rise of Islamic theocracies and the anti-Islamic movements with it. The last type is 'aftermodernity', namely Africa, whose narratives are asserted on an encounter of antagonism (Enwezor 2010).

6 Mogadishu airport was established in 1928 with the official name of Aeroporto Petrella di Mogadiscio (Caprotti 2011a). The first facility to be opened in the Horn of Africa, the airport began offering civilian and commercial flights in the mid-1930s. After a period of continental flights, in 1936, Ala Littoria launched an intercontinental connection between Mogadishu-Asmara-Khartoum-Tripoli and Rome, the metropole (Caprotti 2011b).

7 Accordingly, Martin KiMani, in his 'Airport Theatre, African Villain', describes how African people who move abroad inevitably clash with the Western paranoia for security and illegal immigration. He ends his story asserting that, after the frustrating events occurred at the document check, 'This airport show is not divorced from the world'. KiMani emphasizes, in opposition to the idea of non-places, that airports cannot be considered as unrelated to both the environment and the time-setting; space and time both play a role in shaping them, so to allow us to read them as literary places, with their symbols and meanings (2011, 29).

8 'The clouds of dust stirred up by successive armies of destruction eventually settled back to earth, finer than when they went up' (Farah 2005, 15). Also: 'Outside, there was a faint whirling of sand. And there was life as Jeebleh might have imagined it in its continuous rebirth, earth to dust, dust to earth, wherein death was avenged' (Farah 2005, 22).

9 The presence of dust as the signpost of the new context can be compared to the description of the city that Farah makes in his personal account of his days in Mogadishu, during his youth. In that period of peace, dust appears as a typical feature of the city, but its presence is natural more than ominous: 'There was an epic dustiness to the pre-monsoon storms, as the sea raged and the minarets blared, praying for rain'

(Farah, 2008). In Farah's case, the potential referent is the Joycean symbolism of decay and lifelessness. However, the symbolic weight connected to 'dust' is here physically recontextualized in a waste land that emerges as real, rather than allegorical; the Joycean paralysis in the case of Farah is not caused merely by the lack of movement or by stagnation, but by destruction and desolation (Brown 2008, Andindilile 2014).

10 Later in the novel, he calls his fellow people schizophrenic. The question of Jeebleh's identity and his Somaliness, which surfaces here, will be analysed in depth in Chapter 3, especially in relation to language.

11 'Nobody wants to talk about illegal fishing or the destruction of the environment – the marine life and coral reefs. What we talk about is the consequences of this destruction. There's enough UN information about nuclear and chemical waste dumped on the shores of Somalia – the tsunami unearthed it. Entire communities in Puntland have children born with deformities' (Jaggi 2012).

12 This aspect and the reading in Fanonian terms of *Il latte è buono* are examined in the next chapter, in relation to toponymy.

13 Recent studies are instead retrieving the narrative of colonialism since its first inception in the Italian political agenda, namely the end of nineteenth century (Tomasello 2004; Morone 2011; Lombardi-Diop and Romeo 2014).

14 Simone Brioni also notices that 'Gashan interrogates the essentialist terms through which Italians define immigrants as a homogeneous group. [...] In addition, Gashan compares Italy to Africa and often represents Italians as Africans, challenging and reversing the dominant stereotypical and racist representations of immigrants as well as the Fascist idea of Italian ethnic purity' (2015, 65).

15 Somali scholar Ali Mumin Ahad, who arrived in Italy in 1988, considers Termini a pivotal place for aggregation in his autobiographical account: '*Col tempo, in coincidenza con la caduta del regime e la guerra civile in Somalia, la stazione divenne il punto di ritrovo e di riferimento per la crescente popolazione di profughi somali dalla guerra civile. Era inevitabile recarvisi per una ragione o per un'altra. Una delle ragioni era anche la presenza della SIP nei sotterranei della stazione. Tutti, senza eccezione, dovevano recarsi lì per telefonare a casa, in Somalia*' (After some time, along with the end of the regime and the civil war in Somalia, the station became the gathering and reference point for the growing population of Somali refugees from the civil war. One inevitably ended up there for one reason or another. One of the reasons was also the presence of the SIP (telephone company) in the underground part of the station. Everyone, with no exception, had to go there to call home, in Somalia) (2012, 10).

2

Literary Cartographies of Mogadishu

Introduction

This chapter aims to investigate, through the fictional representations of Mogadishu, how Somali diasporic novels – not programmatically but collectively – designate the capital city as a focal urbanscape for the manifestation of their 'critical engagement with colonialism's aftereffects and its constructions of knowledge' (Radcliffe 1997, 1331). By fictionalizing the material remnants of the Italian colonialism in Mogadishu, through specific attention towards toponymy and architecture, these novels concurrently articulate narratives surrounding the far-reaching repercussions of colonial urban plans on the societal framework of the entire nation. While Chapter 1 concentrated on key sites within the diasporic imaginary, interweaving literary connections across cities and texts within the diaspora space, this chapter broadens the previous geocritical perspective to scrutinize Mogadishu itself.

In describing Mogadishu, Somali authors fictionalize, on the one hand, the so-called 'post-colonial event', namely 'the sum of events experienced by the native peoples after independence [as] witnesses, actors and sometimes victims' (Triulzi 1996, 79). On the other hand, through the pressure of diaspora, where families and nations are spread apart, and against the backdrop of the civil war, which demolished the nation-state, they address questions of belonging and identity, both individual and national (Lee 2015, 198). In doing so, Somali authors connect different historical layers to the city's development to make sense of the national crisis. Mogadishu becomes a metonym of the nation as it 'denied its inherited function of a capital city to embody the contradictory interests of the clustering diverse warlords' (Coquery-Vidrovitch 2005, XIX). From the diaspora, Somali authors then look at Mogadishu as the epicentre of the political disaster and as the starting point of the national downfall. The authors' nostalgic recollections of the city that once was are juxtaposed to a more pragmatic assessment of the idea of the nation as a multi-ethnic and cosmopolitan construction, thereby focusing their attention beyond the material and symbolical borders of the city.

Accordingly, this chapter offers a diachronic exploration of Mogadishu through its fictionalization, aiming to comprehensively assess its significance in confronting historical legacies and participating in current constructions of both collective and individual identities. The analysis brings to the forefront the inherent tension between the notions of home and belonging, as encapsulated in the representation of Mogadishu. The city is rendered as a complex symbol within the diasporic narrative – a lost city evoking nostalgia and memories, yet simultaneously a tangible site of destruction where, nonetheless, a little hope for a more promising future can be seen. Mogadishu is, therefore, what Pierre Nora identifies as *lieu de mémoire*, a 'significant entity, whether material or nonmaterial in nature, which by dint of human will or the work of time has become a symbolic element of the memorial heritage of any community' (1996, XVII; Kapteijns and Richters 2010, 35). This twofold feature of the city, both material and nonmaterial, yet equally powerful, will be the driving principle of this chapter, along with Édouard Glissant's concept of landscape as intractably linked to that of time. As he affirms, 'Landscape retains the memory of time past' (1999, 150). According to Glissant, the past is embedded in material objects, able to reveal their latent meanings only through imaginative engagement. He posits that the past manifests in traces and languages, constituting distinct realms of reality that collectively serve as repositories of history. Writing about the Caribbeans and their encounter with Western colonialism, Glissant maintains that:

> The past, to which we were subjected, which has not yet emerged as history for us, is, however, obsessively present. The duty of the writer is to explore this obsession, to show its relevance in a continuous fashion to the immediate present.
> (Glissant 1999, 64)

According to Glissant's idea that the past leaves traces on both language and landscape, the structure of this chapter ideally parallels the process of 'digging deep' into history and memory, in this instance Mogadishu's past and its recollections, 'to reconstituting its tormented chronology' (Glissant 1999, 65). The following analysis then starts from the years soon after the end of the AFIS trusteeship (1960s), through Garane's *Il latte è buono*, moving to the civil war (1990s), through's Farah's *Links*, Garane's *Il latte è buono* and Cristina Ali Farah's *Little Mother*, and ending with the Islamic Courts Union administration (2000–2007), a period described in Farah's *Crossbones*.[1] This diachronic and comparative approach, which does not engage with colonialism alone but traces the ways in which Somali fictions interpret the violence of the civil war in light of pre-colonial sociopolitical formations, is set against established approaches that label the city as a ground zero. The discursive dimension of Mogadishu's spatiality, scrutinized through a transnational and multilingual analysis, allows us to underscore how the capital city formed personal and national identities and how they evolved over time. More specifically, looking at the socio-historical evolution of the city and at the relationships between characters and places allows us to notice that Somali diasporic authors connect the violence of the civil war to a broader timeline (pre-colonial, colonial and post-independence period) and contrasting ideologies (clan, cosmopolitanism, modernity and traditions) that need a reconfiguration process (Gagiano 2006, 263).

To this aim, the following analysis considers the city as a complex urban reality shaped by historical layers, spanning from its pre-colonial past to the most recent global and neocolonial dynamics. In doing so, it will look at maps, archives and novels and how they all contribute to the reflection on Somalia's past and actively engage with 'the quarrel with history', as Glissant puts it (1999, 65). Mogadishu, indeed, was founded more than ten centuries ago and has a long history as a gateway city since Medieval times, until it became the capital city of Italian Somaliland from 1905 to 1943, and of the independent Somali Republic in 1960 (Eno 2005, 366). It witnessed the birth of the first freedom movements and Somali political parties in the late 1940s, under the British administration and, like several other cities in Asia and Africa after the break-up of colonial rule, it became 'the site where regional, national, international and globalizing forces intersected' (Eade 210, 108). Ultimately, it experienced a long-lasting civil war, which reduced it to ruins. This rich history of interoceanic influences has also been shaped by the Europeans (Portuguese, British, Italian) and the Arabs, which have imprinted a cosmopolitan feature and left their traces at the spatial level, in terms of architecture, toponymy and urban plans. As Mohamed Ahmad explains:

> Many features of Mogadishu, particularly its urban morphology, illustrate the influences of the different periods. The old, original urban centers, Hamarweyne and Shingaani, still stand on Mogadishu's initial site; however, they became extensively damaged during these years of civil war. Shingaani suffered the most damage of the city itself. Arab influence in architecture is widespread. The Italians were the first to formulate and effect urban planning in their area of residence in Mogadishu. Before the collapse in 1990, it was the dominant national urban center in terms of governmental activities and military positions.
>
> (2012)

The recurrent incidence of the city in the novels from the diaspora should not be explained *only* considering this prominent role or because it represents the centre of the individual experiences of several authors. What should be noticed is that Mogadishu, instead of being a scenery, left unnoticed in the background, is represented, reinvented and reconfigured as much as the protagonists of the novels in question. Once again, the concept of landscape might be useful here if associated with that of *urban*scape, as they both embody material entities where the past can be found. Glissant describes how this function of landscape to retrieve the past should be enacted:

> The relationship with the land [...] becomes so fundamental in this discourse that landscape in the work stops being merely decorative or supportive and emerges as a full character. Describing the landscape is not enough. The individual, the community, the land are inextricable in the process of creating history. Landscape is a character in this process. Its deepest meanings need to be understood.
>
> (1999, 105–6)

These strategies of turning Mogadishu into a character to make it part of the process of creating history – a history threatened to be erased by colonialism first, and the Civil War later – are key for Somali diasporic authors. They allow them to demystify the monolithic portrayal of Mogadishu as a city outside history that, in Western accounts, has sanctioned the failure of any military and humanitarian international intervention.

The current narrative, mainly American, further nurtures this stigmatization of Mogadishu, which since the 1990s has become the epitome of violence, corruption and devastation and, from the 2000s, the quintessence of terrorism and ruinous diplomacy (Besteman 1999, 4–5; Myers 2011, 138–9, 144). This harmful standpoint has prevailed over a more diachronic approach and overlooked Mogadishu's past, its cosmopolitanism and global connectivity and, most importantly, its role in the making of Somali national identity. Especially during and after the civil war, reportages, articles, pictures and documentaries have recorded the harsh reality of Mogadishu by emphasizing its disfigured urban spatiality (Draper 2009, 71). In particular, after the military intervention part of the 'Operation Gothic Serpent' that led to the Battle of Mogadishu, fought between 3 and 4 October 1993 (when eighteen US soldiers died, two American helicopters were downed, and between 800 and as many as 1,000 Somalis were killed), the city has become 'a space outside the norms of social order' (Myers 2011, 138–40).[2] Due to this narrative of violence, the historical, cultural and political layers of Mogadishu have been removed from media representations, which have encouraged the idea of the city as pathologically incoherent and uncontrollable, in line with a narrative of African urban realities reduced 'to negative generalized stereotypes' (Falola and ter Harr 2010, 1).

The inhabitants of Mogadishu, too, have been stigmatized as mere victims or represented as accomplices of inter-clan fights.[3] The media representation usually ignores them whether they elude the role of victims or terrorists frequently ascribed to them (Markovitz 1995, 22). In the accounts and chronicles about Mogadishu, their agency is almost invisible or related to terrorist attacks and piracy. Despite obvious practical problems related to a war-torn environment, the residents of Mogadishu also face a less visible and only apparently less critical issue: the fight for their representation. In this case, it can be useful to stress the polysemic nature of the word 'representation' and its double meaning of both 'portrayal' and 'delegation'. The inhabitants of Mogadishu, as well as many Somalis, struggle to overturn the generalized logic that depicts them with a polarizing perspective, turning them into terrorists/pirates or passive victims. As noticed, the lack of positive representations of Somalia, its culture and society, is not merely an issue for those Somalis who have resettled abroad, but it also presents a problem for those who remained and see themselves as the objects of a negative imagery (Gerrard 2015, 22). In fictionalizing the war through the eyes of Somali characters, diasporic authors tackle both dehumanization and objectification and produce a more nuanced representation of their country, too-often seen through stereotypes.

Diasporic novels, then, provide a counter-discourse to the dominant Western narrative as they rework and challenge the prevailing representation of terror and destruction.[4] Nuruddin Farah explicitly addressed this issue in one article, stating that:

> What I would like to do, instead, is to give another kind of testimony in times when the notion of truth suffers unimaginable abuse at the hands of an entire community or a group of professionals and when truth is compromised. I am referring here to the commentaries and other forms of reporting by journalists, writers or political analysts, who offer us misguided testimony regarding Somalia,

when they should know better. My argument is that much of the commentary on the Somali civil war is based on a false premise in the form of a cliché, an easy peg on which to hang a misguided theory.

(2010, 9)

This reappropriation of the truth finds its place in the complex textual spatiality of the capital city, which retrieves, besides violence and war, a cosmopolitan past and suggests that the inhabitants' daily-life stories of both suffering and regeneration are worth telling.[5] A starting point of the re-envisioning process is to turn Somalis from objects to subjects and place them at the centre of the narratives about their country.[6] Mogadishu, too, is not seen merely as the main site of the nation's downfall, but as a lived space in which identities (national, communal and individual) can be negotiated and where local histories can be unravelled through the eyes of its citizens (Liberatore 2017, 53). In this sense, Mogadishu can be considered the fulcrum of these changes, being 'directly exposed to all the major political, social and global economic trends' (Guglielmo 2013, 11). The atemporality of the city and its chronic condition of war are then challenged by counterpoising the representation of historical layers that had bundled up over time and have influenced and shaped urban physiognomy and its social practices.[7]

This chapter aims, accordingly, to investigate the fictionalization of Mogadishu and its prominent role in the poetics of Somali diasporic authors. All the writers considered here, such as Igiaba Scego, Garane Garane, Ubax Cristina Ali Farah and Shirin Ramzanali Fazel, are interested in fictionalizing the materiality and symbolical weight of Mogadishu, suggesting that even 'the most wounded city might be constructive of alternative modes' of representation (Myers 2011, 140).[8] Even though the practices of representing the city vary according to each author, the ways in which the city prominently figures in their narratives present some similarities. For example, as the analysis will show, instead of fostering a clan-based narrative, Somali diasporic authors inscribe their texts within a national framework, where Somalia still possesses a unitary feature, with Mogadishu as its capital city. The characters' relationship of love/hate with the city finds its fulfilment in the complex and unique affiliation with its spatiality, namely with its physical features and the social relations established between fellow citizens. In this regard, little academic work has been done on the role of Mogadishu in the prose of the diaspora;[9] even less has been done about the colonial toponymy when connected with Somali cityscape or landscape. Apart from Mia Fuller's work *Moderns Abroad* (2007), which nevertheless deals mainly with Libya, Eritrea and Ethiopia, there are no comprehensive geocritical studies about Mogadishu across different languages. Iman Mohamed's useful work about the city which, as the following analysis, relies on maps and archive as useful resources to investigate Mogadishu over time, does not include creative works as part of the analysis.

The purpose of this chapter, therefore, is to prove how the fictionalization of urban spatiality is fundamental from the diaspora to discuss the historical events that led to the civil war and the lingering effects that the conflict had on Somaliness, without losing sight of the legacy of colonialism on the social fabric. Moreover, it aims to show how Mogadishu's urbanscape, creatively reinvented in the novels, plays a key role through its symbolic, cultural and historical connotations, thus shaping a specific poetics.

The 1960s: The Legacy of Colonial Spatiality

The second chapter of *Il latte è buono* (2005), entitled '*Mogadiscio la noiosa*' (Boring Mogadishu), is set in an indeterminate timeframe, loosely spanning from the conclusion of the AFIS (1950–60) to the beginning of Siyaad Barre's regime in 1969. Garane describes Mogadishu through two contrasting and conflicting viewpoints, which are personified in the characters of Gashan (the protagonist, an *alter ego* of the author) and Shakhlan (Queen of the Ajuran and Gashan's putative grandmother). This bifocal perspective on Mogadishu not only offers a literary account of the post-independence period but also enables an exploration of the multiple, often conflicting trajectories inherent in the process of nation-building and the construction of the Somali identity.[10]

It should be noted that Somalia achieved independence and national sovereignty via a particular historical-political process. Where, for example, former colonies such as Mozambique, Algeria and Angola freed themselves from colonialism through armed national liberation struggles, Somalia achieved political, cultural and economic independence through negotiations (Guglielmo 2013, 21). Instead of being the result of anti-colonial fighting and protracted, often violent, processes of decolonization, the independence of Somalia had been the outcome of diplomacy (Ahmed 1996, 36; Mohamed 2013, 2). The Italian administration guided Somalia to independence and allowed Somali people to gain experience in political education and self-governance. However, this coexistence of Italian and Somali political practices was shadowed by the considerable presence of former Fascists, who held institutional positions (Del Boca 1993; Morone 2011; Naletto 2011). This problematic cooperation between the former colonial power and the ex-colony, highly contested by the Somali Youth League, 'hindered the creation of a modern Somali nationalism by repressing any radical progress in the fields of economy and education' (Calchi Novati 2005, 65).[11]

The novella delves into the post-independence period characterized by political and cultural Somalization – the progressive replacement of Italian functionaries with Somali ones to minimize the country's dependence from the former metropole – during which the conceptualization of nationhood underwent conflicting trends and paradigmatic oppositions (Morone 2011, 154–5). These oppositions manifested in the tension between the endeavour to dismantle the colonial apparatus and the persistence of sociopolitical formations grounded in clan affiliations. This process of Somalization, as Iman Mohamed has noticed, also involved space:

> At independence, colonial sites were appropriated and nationalized – streets honouring Italian figures were renamed to honour Somalis; colonial buildings became national buildings. With these transformations, the colonial past became almost invisible.
>
> (2013, 3)

Garane's novella, however, shows how the invisibility of colonialism remains superficial, as Mogadishu, at that time, was still imbued with Italian toponymy, which played a fundamental role in shaping the protagonist's identity. Garane reads this period as a conflict between two nations in the same country, epitomized by the two protagonists, Gashan and Shakhlan, who coexist in the text as symbols of post-independence and pre-colonial times, respectively.

In this context, architecture emerged as 'a way for the country to assert its identity' after the Fascist urban plans of the 1920s and 1930s (Ali and Cross 2016, 10). Architect Rashid Ali suggests that architecture itself 'tells the story of Somalia's journey from traditional African nation, via colonization and post-colonialism, to emergent independent state' (2016, 10). The urban transformation of the post-independence period, as well as the Italian plans of the 1930s, provides a specific visual identity of the city, which can be explored through its literary representation. *Il latte è buono* reveals how colonial discourse involved urban planning, architecture and, more broadly, the organization of space as a way of controlling colonial subjects. Inevitably, the impact of 'colonial spatiality was not confined to the built form' but influenced 'local cultural practices' too (Ali and Cross 2016, 15). Italian colonialism, indeed, involved education, politics, architecture, urban planning and, most importantly, a reconfiguration of space as a way of exerting control over colonial subjects.

These two aspects coexist in *Il latte è buono*, as the novella pays close attention to spatiality and toponymy in relation to the personal geographies of the characters and their relationships with the city and its social fabric. As they stroll through the streets of Mogadishu, Gashan and Shakhlan observe and remark upon the ongoing urban transformations, expressing their distinct perspectives on the uncertainty inherent in that intermediate period for Somalia, wherein the nation was transitioning from being a former colony to an independent state.

The specific attention of Garane for the material presence of colonialism allows us to examine his novella by comparing it to colonial texts; this comparison will provide us with a panoramic view of the impact that colonialism had on both society and space. In particular, I will use a popular leisure guidebook from the Fascist period called *Guida dell'Africa Orientale Italiana* (1938) and a map created by the Italian Geographic Society. This map displays the urban plan that the Italian government of the Liberal era (1861–1922) implemented in the 1910s to transform Mogadishu. These transformations were operative prior to the advent of Fascism, thus showing the long-running enterprise of Italian colonization, too often dismissed as fleeting or circumscribed to the short-lived period of the *Impero Italiano* (1936–41). By analysing these different texts together, we can gain a deeper understanding of the *longue durée* of colonialism and hopefully facilitate a productive conversation between sources that have not previously been examined together.[12]

Before looking at the novella and the maps comparatively, it is worth addressing another effect of the new political system and Somalization. In terms of society, the newly autonomous country experienced a dichotomizing process that saw *qabiil* versus socialism; agrarian versus urban communities; oral (poetry) versus written (newspaper, novels, plays) culture and, finally, emblems of the past (colonial architecture) versus new planning (modernism). These aspects are condensed in Mogadishu, as Garane describes it as a city where the clan-based system has vanished, at least on the surface.

The character Shakhlan observes that Mogadishu is the centre of a new nation and the 'cradle of a moderate nationalism' (Garane 2005, 43), where Somali people show their 'good side' ('*lato buono*'). Shakhlan notes, 'No tribalism, not even the neighbour's clan was known, at least officially. The doors were never closed, and sometimes there was only a slim and thin veil as a door' ('*Niente tribalismo, non si conosceva neanche il clan del vicino, almeno ufficialmente. Le porte non erano mai chiuse e a volte c'era solo un tenue e sottile velo come porta*') (Garane 2005, 43).

Somalis live together in the urban environment without knowing their clan affiliation, in what seem to be a secularized, Westernized and modern society. They play *kalscio* ('football', a loanword from the Italian *calcio*) and like spending their free time eating and strolling. Once again, it is through Shakhlan's eyes that this transformation is described:

> A Mogadiscio guardava dappertutto, studiava tutto con la bocca aperta! Si guardava attorno. Vedeva solo donne con monili d'oro, con le mani, le gambe, i capelli pieni di henné. Vedeva case dove nel pomeriggio si mangiavano biscotti e tè. Vedeva bambini giocare, con bambini di diversi clan, ad uno strano sport chiamato *kalscio*, con una cosa rotonda chiamata *balloni*.
>
> (Garane 2005, 44)

> In Mogadishu, she looked everywhere with her mouth open, studying everything! She looked around. She only saw women with gold jewellery, with hands, legs, and hair covered in henna. She saw houses where biscuits were eaten with tea in the afternoon. She saw children playing with children of different clans a strange sport called *kalscio*, with a round thing called *balloni*.

Along Via Roma (a street in the city centre, in the historical Xamar Weyne district), there are clothing stores and ice cream shops. The 'long, wide thoroughfares previously used for ceremonial marches', like Viale del Littorio or Corso Vittorio Emanuele, are 'appropriated for new local forms of social, economic and cultural practices' (Ali and Cross 2016, 10). However, before being renamed and Somalized (Viale del Littorio became Viale della Repubblica and Corso Vittorio Emanuele III was renamed Corso Somalia), toponymy remained Italian until the 1970s, thereby marking off the legacy of the urban plan started during the 1930s aimed at 'celebrating the triumph of the Fascist state' (Ali and Cross 2016, 15). Cinema Centrale, Cinema Missione and Via Roma represent some of the landmarks that characterize Mogadishu at the time of *Il latte è buono*, a city where 'the café culture, cuisine (pasta become a staple of the Somali diet) and the unhurried Mediterranean tradition of evening strolling to shop, see and be seen' were embraced as cultural and social urban practices (Ali and Cross 2016, 13). These practices are effectively described in the novella, as the following passage shows:

> Mogadiscio era una «Little Italy». Le vie, i negozi, le scuole, i cinema erano all'italiana. Molti nuovi nomi erano diventati parte della cultura somala: via Roma, Corso Italia, Cinema Centrale, Liceo Scientifico Leonardo da Vinci ... Garibaldi era più importante dell'Imam, anche se tutti e due avevano avuto la stessa ideologia

di tutti i capi. Shakhlan Iman intravedeva il futuro, pieno di morte e di catastrofe. A Mogadiscio, ogni casa, ogni filo elettrico, ogni persona, ogni albero faceva parte di un linguaggio, di un popolo, che riportava Shakhlan alla gloria del passato.

La differenza stava nel fatto che qui, a Mogadiscio, agli antenati si erano aggiunte le luci elettriche, il chiasso delle Fiat e il *climatiseur*: la pelle nera voleva trasformarsi in pelle bianca, l'africano in europeo. Vedeva facce imbiancate con una maschera nera.

(Garane 2005, 45)

Mogadishu was a «Little Italy». The streets, the shops, the schools and the cinemas were Italian-like. Many new names had become part of the Somali culture: via Roma, Corso Italia, Cinema Centrale, Liceo Scientifico Leonardo da Vinci ... Garibaldi was more important than the Imam, even though both had the same ideology as all leaders. Shakhlan Iman glimpsed the future, full of death and catastrophe. In Mogadishu, every house, every electric wire, every person, and every tree was part of a shared language of one people, which took back Shakhlan to the glorious past.

The difference was that, in Mogadishu, electric lights, Fiat cars' noise and the *climatiseur* joined in with ancestors: the black skin wanted to turn white, the African into European. She saw whitened faces with a black mask.

As Shakhlan Iman gazes upon the bustling city, she feels a sense of what scholar Harry Garuba defines as 'postcolonial alienation'. He uses this concept to explain 'the alienation that results from *the wholesale transference of rural norms into the space of the city*' (Garuba 2008, 181). Accordingly, Shakhlan Iman, the ancient Queen of the Ajuran who magically survived up to the AFIS and the independence period, notices that the first fracture within Somali society consists of a dualism between rural and urban norms. She casts a suspicious eye upon the newly configured Somalia, articulating her perplexity as follows:

Da guerrieri I somali si erano trasformati in operai, architetti, professori ... Ma lei, saggia, intravedeva un bagliore che le diceva tutto su questi nuovi somali: l'ambiente era diverso, ma la mentalità era la stessa, clanica e settaria, che aspettava soltanto il momento opportuno per plasmare Mogadiscio e la costa all'immagine dell'interno, all'immagine della boscaglia.

(Garane, 45)

The Somalis had turned from warriors into workers, architects, professors ... But she, wise, glimpsed a glimmer that told her everything about these new Somalis: the context was different, but the mentality was the same, clan-based and sectarian, waiting only for the convenient moment to mould Mogadishu and the coast into the image of the interior, into the image of the bush.

This narrative of Somalia, built on the dualism between rural and urban people, echoes the words of an unnamed character in Nuruddin Farah's *Links*, who confesses to the protagonist that 'Our people are restless nomads in search of city-based fulfilment'

(2005, 330). Even though Jeebleh, the protagonist of *Links*, partially dismisses this idea, Farah seems to enforce it, as already analysed in the previous chapter. This fracture at the societal level also marks two different spatialities, rural (nomad pastoralist) and urban (sedentary), which were still blurred at the time of the story. Their coexistence in the urbanscape of Mogadishu causes a sense of bewilderment in the Somali people who have lived as nomads outside the city, as shown in the passage below, from 'Of Tamarind and Cosmopolitanism':

> The pastoralist Somalis, who are by nature urbophobics, saw the city as alien and parasitic, and because it occupied an ambiguous space in their hearts and minds, they gradually accumulated hostility towards the city until they became intent on destroying it.
>
> (Farah 2010, 11)

This aspect is also present in another novel by Farah, *From a Crooked Rib* (1970), a coming-of-age story in which Ebla, an eighteen-year-old orphan, runs away from her nomadic and rural environment and escapes to Mogadishu hoping for a better future. Once resettled in the city, she finds herself as dependent on men as she was before, because she finds herself unable to navigate urban life. A short passage from the novel clarifies Ebla's confusion and her attempt to understand the city with references coming from her previous nomadic life. Another character explains her the difference:

> 'Did you hear about the Government?'
> 'No. Another tribe?'
> 'No. No. No. In towns, we don't talk in terms of tribes. We talk in terms of societies. You see, in this town, there are many different tribes who live together.'
>
> (Farah 2003, 66)

Igiaba Scego, in her novel *Adua* (2015), addresses the same issue: one of the protagonists, Zoppe, who lives in a village of fishermen, expresses his uneasiness in visiting the capital city during the late 1930s. He 'loathed Mogadishu' and that 'in Mogadishu he felt like a foreigner. Someone from down south, a yokel [...] whom the residents looked at snobbishly and even with a certain pity' (2019, 161).

In *Il latte è buono*, Garane illustrates the same contrast and the overall confusion towards the city. At the formal level, in the passage mentioned above, this is reproduced by the juxtaposition of Garibaldi (an emblem of the colonial foreign culture) and the Imam (a symbol of the social and religious local structure) (Garane 2005, 45). Moreover, while the first paragraph includes the recent and operating Italian influence, the second underlines the veiled persistence of Somali tradition in an apposition that unfolds in the final paragraph, where Garane makes the contradiction manifest by bringing to the surface conflicting but concomitant elements, such as how cult of the ancestors dwells alongside Fiat cars and air-conditioners. In the extract, three other aspects are worth mentioning. First, the alarming allusion to the imminent civil war – right in the middle of the two paragraphs, as an imaginary glimpse of the future between past and present – is foreseen by Shakhlan. For her, the war is the result of the unsolved social contradictions of that time. Second, the reference to Frantz Fanon's famous work *Black Skin, White Masks*, is slightly distorted into 'whitened skin, black masks' to underline the epistemic violence of colonialism in the making of colonial subjects' identities.[13] Last, the manifest presence of Italian toponymy marks both a sense of belonging (conveyed through Gashan) and estrangement (conveyed through Shakhlan).

Using Italian place names to refer to specific buildings implies a problematic continuity of colonialism on the road to Somalia's democratic state (1960–9). It highlights how the iconography and geography of imperial power still loom large and that 'Mogadishu remained culturally, economically, and politically closely tied to Italy after independence' (Mohamed 2023, 19). This continuity and the idea that the colonial past has not been fully addressed and resolved parallel the title of Farah's last trilogy, *Past Imperfect*.[14] Diasporic authors, then, reflect on spatiality with a double aim: on the one hand, they break the Italian amnesia about a period too quickly removed from history and from collective conscience after the Second World War; on the other hand, it prompts an investigation into Somalia's colonial past and colonialism's ubiquitous presence during both the democratic (1960–9) and totalitarian (1969–91) periods. In her novel *Le stazioni della luna* (2021), Cristina Ali Farah sets her story in Mogadishu in the 1950s, at the very beginning of the AFIS. In the ten years of Italian co-administration of the country, political parties and discussions around nationhood increasingly grew, especially in Mogadishu. The novel addresses the nationalist political discourse tangentially and, in doing so, overtly mentions toponymy to explain the tension between the Italian colonial presence and the new, democratic nation that was about to develop from the AFIS.

The plot of *Le stazioni della luna* revolves around two characters, Ebla and Clara. The former, an explicit intertextual reference to Nuruddin Farah's protagonist of *From a Crooked Rib*, grows up in the Somali hinterland with her elderly father, who set her up in an arranged marriage. To escape, she finds herself in Mogadishu in the 1930s, where she will have two children with Gacaliye, a poet and truck driver. Ebla's story is intertwined with Clara's, a girl born from Italian parents living in Mogadishu. Forced when barely a teenager to leave the country with her mother and brother, Enrico, Clara later returns to her hometown in the early 1950s as a young teacher at the beginning of the Italian trusteeship. Through the close relationship between Ebla and her children, Clara will be involved in Somalia's independence struggles.

In one passage of the novel, Ebla and Clara discuss the idea of renaming the Italian toponymy with Somali place names. Their discussion revolves around the publication of a letter in the Italian newspaper, *Il Corriere della Somalia*, from the Somali Youth League – the first political party in Somalia that also opposed the restoration of Italian rule – where they propose that the remaining traces of Italian presence be removed to allow Somalis to know their history and their leading figures.[15] Upon *Il Corriere*'s reply to this letter, saying that retaining the place names would facilitate maintaining friendly relations with Italy, given its assistance in Somalia's development, Clara and Ebla discuss this topic from a spatial perspective:

> 'Ma di quale sviluppo parlano? Sviluppo?' ripeté Ebla basita.
>
> 'Esattamente così! E precisano che, a proposito delle strade, sono i somali a doversene occupare, mentre per i nomi di città e villaggi è più difficile perché sono riportati sulle carte geografiche e circolano in tutto il mondo. Tu cosa ne pensi?'
>
> Per la maggior parte della sua vita, Ebla aveva fatto conto soprattutto sul cielo e non aveva dunque mai immaginato che occorressero nomi su mappe e cartine per ricordare la propria storia.
>
> 'Piccola, sai bene che tra noi nessuno direbbe incontriamoci in corso Italia, ma piuttosto davanti a un negozio, alla moschea, all'angolo di un incrocio. Tuttavia, questa rimane una questione importante. I nomi sono sempre stati nostri. Occorre riappropriarsene. Per esempio, ora abbiamo appena attraversato quella che gli italiani conoscono come la piazza del mercato ma per noi è solo Afar Irdood.'
>
> (Ali Farah 2021, 105)

> 'But what development are they talking about? Development?' repeated Ebla, stunned.
>
> 'Exactly like that! And they also point out that, regarding roads, it is the Somalis who must take care of that, while for the names of cities and villages, it is more difficult, because they are shown on maps and circulate all over the world. What do you think about that?'
>
> For most of her life, Ebla had relied above all on the sky and had, therefore, never imagined that names on maps were needed to remember one's history.
>
> 'Little one, you know very well that among us no one would say let us meet in Corso Italia, but rather in front of a shop, at the mosque, at the corner of a crossroad. However, this remains an important issue. The names have always been ours. It is necessary to reappropriate them. For example, we have now just gone through what the Italians know as a market square, but to us, it is just Afar Irdood.'

As the dialogue shows, the legacy of the Italian rule and how to deal with the colonial process of 'textualizing the spatial reality of the other, naming or, in almost all cases, renaming spaces in a symbolic and literal act of mastery and control' (Ashcroft, Griffith and Tiffin 2000, 28). Ebla shows a degree of resistance to that form of control, opposing the prescriptive and Eurocentric use of maps with a form of geographical knowledge that relies on the stars. It might be interesting here to report a letter to the periodical *Somalia d'Oggi*, written by Abdullahi Elmi Barcadle in 1956. Iman Mohamed quoted the same extract in their article, as it emphasizes the urge to properly renamed Italian toponymy to decolonize the city and reclaim the land. In our case, Abdullahi Elmi Barcadle's letter is useful as it remarks upon Ebla's idea that Somali people have different system to orient themselves in space and do not rely on the Italian planimetry. Barcadle affirms that:

the streets and squares carry names of famous and illustrious people, but who are in effect foreign and unknown to the Somali public. These names, as guides, are useful only to Italians. Somalis, to orient themselves, resort to other directions.
(Barcadle 1956, 56, qtd. in Mohamed 2023, 17)

Indeed, the struggle to reclaim the urban spatiality, both physically and symbolically, which was expunged by the colonialist act of mapping, is a significant aspect of Somalization. Italian occupation, as in the case of British and French colonialism, effectively erased the prior knowledge and understanding of the land to impose its own inscriptions. In Ali Farah's and Garane's novels, the complex textualities of Mogadishu are then retrieved, reappropriated and devalued in relation to colonial modes of representation. It is fruitful then to further investigate the colonial act of mapping and renaming. In doing so, the following analysis considers a popular guidebook, titled *Guida dell'Africa Orientale Italiana* (Guide to Italian East Africa), which shows maps of Mogadishu during the 1920s and 1930s, interesting to retrieve the role played by Italian colonialism in shaping Somalia. The comparison of Ali Farah's and Garane's novels and the guidebook, which allows us to connect colonial with postcolonial texts, both formally and thematically, clarifies the epistemic violence of colonial discourse and reveals the enduring influence of the Italians' ethnographic descriptions in shaping Somalis people. My reading aims to emphasize the effects of the colonial encounter but also to bring to the fore the strategies of Western colonial discourse enabled through texts and spatiality to reinscribe and overwrite the colonized land, so that 'the names and languages of the indigenes are replaced by new names or are corrupted into new and Europeanized forms' (Ashcroft, Griffiths and Tiffin 2000, 28). The *Guida dell'Africa Orientale Italiana* is a useful source to exhume the practices of colonial knowledge production through the mapping of conquered territories and the stigmatization of the colonial subjects via ethnographic observations.

Published in 1938 by the *Consociazione Turistica Italiana*, the name given to the Touring Club after the Fascist regulation regarding the Italianization of foreign names, *Guida* is a document 'of the ambitions of a Fascist state determined to impose its authority and its model of modernity onto the territories it had conquered', but also 'a prescient recognition of the economic potential of mass tourism' (Fotheringham 2019b, 52). Indeed, the *Guida*, which aimed to lead Italian tourists through the towns and landscapes of the colonies in Italian East Africa (Italian: *Africa Orientale Italiana* or AOI), employs maps, preset itineraries, detailed spatial descriptions, calculations of distances and an ethnographic analysis of the 'indigenous' people. Somalis, in the 'discourse of scientific measurement and written texts that cartography implies [...] have no voice or even presence that can be heard', as they appear more as objects than subjects, foreigners in their own land (Ashcroft, Griffiths and Tiffin 2000, 29). The guide warns against any potentially threatening behaviour of the local populations and sketches out the typical traits of Somalis, Eritreans and Ethiopians to help readers familiarize themselves with the environment. For example, Somalis are described as 'generally smart [and] generous, but also very often indolent and dissembler' (*Guida* 1938, 20). The guidebook aimed to control and domesticate the foreign land and its inhabitants in line with those stigmatizations and generalizations functional to the colonial agenda. By 'making the world intelligible as a systematic order', the *Guida* transformed the former colonial territory into a 'hierarchically ordered whole' (Gregory 1994, 36).

The following extract from the *Guida dell'Africa Orientale Italiana* is a valuable resource to examine the colonial configurations of space during the 1930s. It sheds light on how Italian urban plans shaped the cityscape of Mogadishu and affected Somali society. As Christopher Fotheringham has observed, the guide has a twofold aim: it 'contributes to writing the colony into existence as a textual entity' and, at the same time, it functions 'as a manual for colonisation and settlement' for 'the would-be settlers and investors' (2019b, 54). Leaving aside for the moment the ethnographic approach and the objectifying Western gaze, it is interesting to notice that some of the spatial references in the *Guida* are similar to those found in *Il latte è buono*. This recurrence highlights how the planimetry and toponymy of the city remained unchanged at least until the 1960s, when the story takes place:

> Dalla piazza Giama, per la tortuosa e stretta *via Roma*, ci s'interna nel vecchio quartiere Amaruíni, pittoresco dedalo di viuzze senza nome, piazzette e sottopassaggi tra alte, massicce case.
>
> Nelle viuzze laterali, spesso si osservano ancora i tessitori *Rer Hamàr*, emergenti dalla cintola in su dalla buca nella quale si accovacciano innanzi ai loro telai primitivi, da cui escono le policrome «fute (marò) Benádir» anticam. Rinomate in tutto l'Oriente.
>
> La via Roma, fiancheggiata da numerosi piccoli negozi di arabi, indiani, ebrei e somali (assai poco rimane della produzione locale), discende sulla *via Principe di Piemonte*, che collega il *viale Federazioni* al *Corso Vittorio Emanuele III*.
>
> (Guida 1938, 570)

> From Piazza Giama, through the curvy and narrow *Via Roma*, one enters the old Amaruini district, a picturesque maze of tiny streets with no names, little squares and underpasses between high and thick houses.
>
> Along the tiny secondary streets, one can still notice the *Rer Hamàr* weavers rising above the belt from the dip where they crouch before their primitive looms, which produce the polychrome «fouta (marò) Benádir», once renowned in the whole Orient.
>
> Via Roma, lined by numerous small shops of Arabs, Indians, Jews, and Somalis (truly little remains of local production), descends *via Principe di Piemonte*, which links *Viale Federazioni* to *Corso Vittorio Emanuele III*.

At the formal level, the language is emblematic of how colonial discourse operates: the adjective *pittoresco* (picturesque) is widely used in the whole of the *Guida* to describe the local settlements. Similarly, diminutive forms (*viuzze* or *piazzette*) are employed to denote ancient buildings and have the effect of downgrading colonial subjects and reiterate their believed ontological inferiority. Consistent with this approach, the use of the adjective 'primitive' and the remarks on the lack of native toponomy (e.g. 'tiny streets with no names') further contribute to a process of lateralization and infantilization. Geographer Emanuela Moreschi has noticed that foreign territories were often classified either as nobody's empty lands (*terra nullius*) or 'as exotic, picturesque and primitive' (1998, 272). In this context, *Guida* presents no exception, as it conforms to this pattern by incorporating these discursive practices to describe Mogadishu.

The street-level description of the city is enhanced and complemented by detailed maps, meant to be valuable tools for tourists and Italian settlers who needed to navigate their way around unfamiliar urban settings. In the *Guida*, then, cartography plays a comparable role to that of language, as it partakes in those discursive strategies enabled by the Italian colonizers to control and to inscribe Somali subjects within a Western-centric system of knowledge. As scholar J. Brian Harley and Yi-Fu Tuan suggest, maps are always ideological, encompassing their time's cultural, social, economic and political milieu (Tuan 1977, 178; Harley 1992, 244). Maps represent a 'spatial panopticon' through which land and people can be controlled and subjugated, since maps physically and symbolically reorganize the space without allowing colonial subjects to take part in this process (Harley 1992, 244). In other words, maps have been complicit in serving the colonial political agenda. Similarly, Harry Garuba affirms that 'physical containment was necessary to circumscribe the natural mobility of the body (in space) and discursive containment served to define the limits of the cultural (identity) mobility available to the subject' (2002, 87). As the *Guida* shows, both cartography and ethnographic commentary estrange colonial subjects from their own land and limit their movements and agency both physically and symbolically. A passage of the *Guide*, however, also emphasizes another aspect. It says:

> In generale, tutti coloro che sono venuti in contatto con gl'Italiani riconoscono la nostra superiorità e i vantaggi della nostra civiltà; e soprattutto i giovani accolgono con gioia le novità che l'Italia porta dovunque, imparano con sorprendente rapidità l'italiano e sono pronti a lavorare e progredire. Gli Italiani, con il loro carattere umanissimo e con l'istintiva penetrazione psicologica, hanno già stabilito un equilibrio nei rapporti con gl'indigeni: non altezzosità e separazione assoluta, ma superiorità e comprensione.
>
> (1938, 20)

In general, all those who come into contact with the Italians recognise our superiority and the advantages of our civilisation; above all, the young people joyfully welcome the innovations that Italy carries everywhere, [and] they learn Italian surprisingly fast and are ready to work and develop. The Italians, with their very compassionate character and instinctive psychological understanding, have established a balance in their relations with the natives: neither arrogance nor absolute separation, but superiority and compassion.

The *Guida* celebrates the conquest of Africa and promotes the idea that Italian people are *brava gente* (good people), a phrase that endured long after the end of the short-lived Italian Empire and has been used in the public discourse to self-absolve Italians from the crimes committed during colonialism. The idea of the civilizing mission is fully endorsed here, embodied by the Italians, who are at the same time superior and compassionate. Besides, the civilizing mission is justified by the moral and intellectual superiority of the Europeans, and the territory of the colony, accordingly, becomes a 'hierarchically organized space' in which civilization can be materially displayed through roadmaking, infrastructures and works of engineering (Gupta and Ferguson 1992, 8).

By analysing the map in the *Guida dell'Africa Orientale Italiana*, then, we can shed light on how power relations were established and how colonial architecture was instrumental in glorifying the *genius italicus*. Following the description of the itineraries across the city, the guidebook presents a supporting map (Figure 2.2) in which it is possible to recognize the colonizer's aim of controlling and containing colonized subjects (*Guida* 1938, 570). By altering and reordering the spatial structure of the urbanscape, the Fascist cartographic practice seems to consist of two main approaches: segregation and separation. Accordingly, the scholar Safia Aidid has underlined that 'the presence of a large Italian community in Mogadishu [...] circumscribed the mobility of urban Somalis through enforced practices of segregation, which prevented native access to certain neighbourhoods, restaurants, theatres and even sidewalks' (2011, 107). It is worth also looking at a previous map (Figure 2.1), supplied by the Italian Geographical Society, as a demonstrative plan of the new constructions prepared in 1912, to highlight how colonial practices were at work in Somalia even during the Italian Liberal era (1861–1922). This comparative analysis seeks to underscore the preexisting operation of colonial discourse preceding Fascism. The examination of cartography and map-making serves to accentuate the continuity of this discourse, thereby challenging the prevailing narrative that frequently characterizes colonialism as solely a Fascist enterprise (Calchi Novati 2011; Finaldi 2017).

The first map (Figure 2.1) dates back to the early colonization of Somalia, when Mogadishu, which had become the capital in 1908, was ruled by the Italian governor of Somaliland Giacomo De Martino (1910–16). The second map (Figure 2.2) was drawn after the plans started in 1928 under Cesare Maria De Vecchi (1923–8), the first Fascist governor of Somalia, and later protracted by Guido Corni (1928–31), thus marking the beginning of the Fascist urban planning period (Fuller 1994; McLaren 2008). During this period, famous architects of that time, such as Carlo Enrico Rava, Antonio Vandone and Cesare Biscarra, participated in the new project to rebuild Mogadishu.

The demonstrative map, as Iman Mohamed noticed, 'exhibited some continuity and significant changes to the existing fabric of the city' (2023, 6). The toponymy of the pre-existing districts of Xamar Weyne and Shangaani in the old historical centre of Mogadishu, indeed, highlights the process of linguistic appropriation, as the two districts are Italianized as Amaruíni and Scingani to typographically match their pronunciation. The rational effort to split Italian colonizers and Somali residents is already clear, since the map marks the two indigenous historical quarters with a

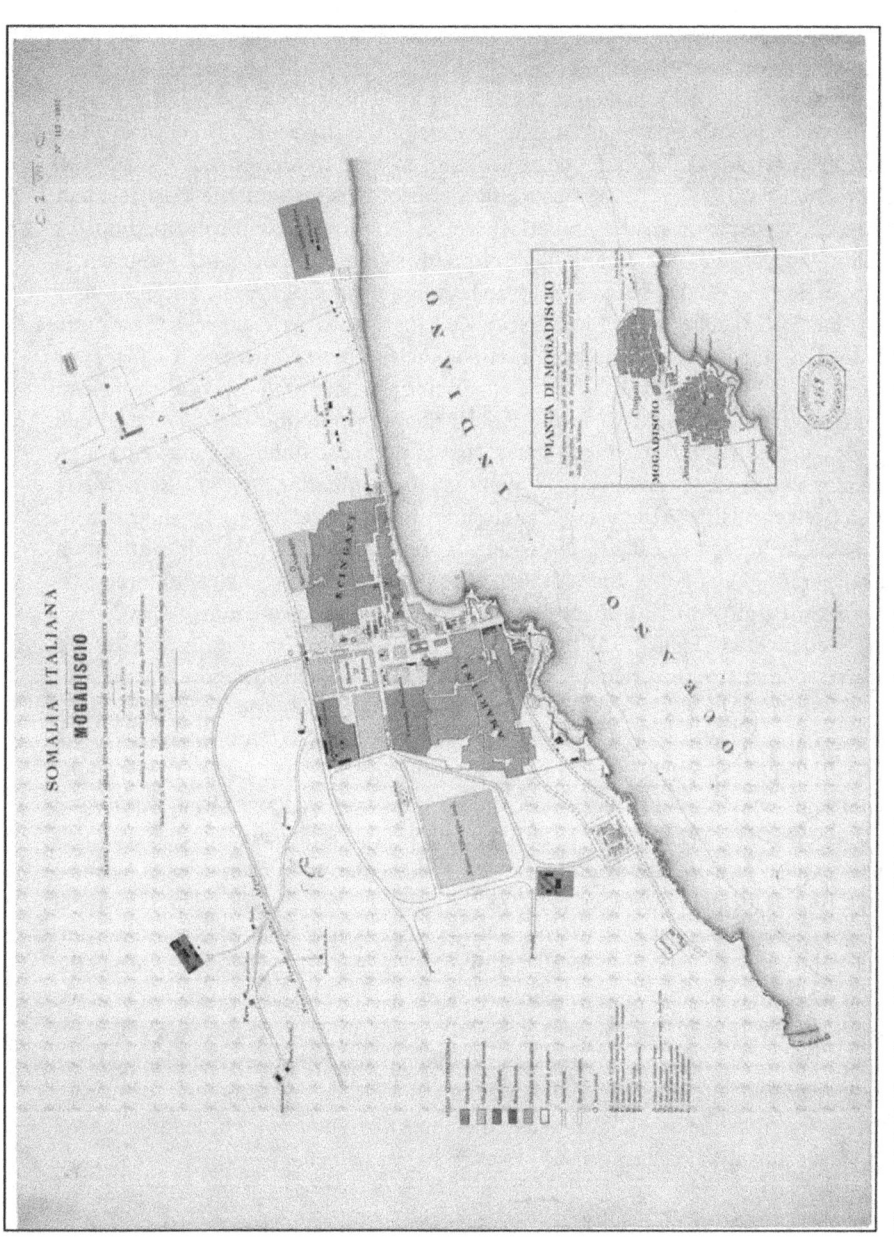

Figure 2.1 Italian Somaliland: Mogadishu, demonstrative plan of the new constructions carried out and started on 1 October 1912. *Società Geografica Italiana.*

distinct colour and flags them as *fabbricati esistenti* (constructions already existing). Furthermore, on the northeast side of the map, far from the arbitrary borders of Mogadishu, is the military camp of the Eritrean *askari*, native soldiers serving in the Italian colonial army in Africa. In a similar isolated and far-off position, at the opposite side of the *askari*'s camp is the jail. While Italian offices and headquarters were built in the ancient city (A to F in Figure 2.2's legend), the new indigenous villages were supposed to occupy the space outside the borders of the city centre. Borders, as Brah noticed, 'are territories to be patrolled against those whom they construct as outsiders, aliens, the Others' (1996, 198). Accordingly, the exclusion and the displacement of indigenous people from the 'Italian' centre can be understood as a method for controlling and physically enabling hierarchies of power. In this regard, in the article 'Citizens of Sorrow' (2002), Nuruddin Farah highlights this long-term ghettoization by writing that 'Italian colonists in Mogadiscio lived apart from their subjects, in far more sumptuous circumstances. There were non-channels of communication, no places or occasions for encounter' (*ibid.*, 10). It is worth noting that Farah draws a parallelism – in terms of spatiality – between the Fascist ghettoization and the current Somali diasporic condition of those living in Italy: 'Things are not so different today. Although the Italians ceded their territory in Somalia at independence, in 1960, somewhere between twelve and fifteen thousand Somalis now live in Italy today […]. Until recently, all Africans in Italy were called *Marocchini*, Moroccans' (*ibid.*, 10). This segregation already operating during the liberal Italian state period reduced Somalis to foreigners or, to borrow Farah's words, 'indigenous noncitizens in their own country' (2002, 10).

The second map (Figure 2.2) points out a recrudescence of the disjunctive and segregated spatiality of the urban plan of the early 1910s and, furthermore, emphasizes the utter result of the process of making by naming. According to De Vecchi, as he himself explains in a chapter of his work, *Orizzonti d'Impero* (1935), the new urban plan, and the whole colony, 'pushed by the powerful, vivifying blow of Fascism' ('*spint[o] dal pontente soffio animatore del Fascismo*'), should have removed any physical traces of Somali people (1935, 345). In 1924, he enacted a decree that established the demolition of 'many unhealthy and crumbling native houses' ('*molte case indigene malsane e cadenti*') to make rooms for new buildings (such as the Cathedral and the Roman Triumphal Arch), *piazzas* and avenues (De Vecchi 1935, 343; Mohamed 2023, 8). Accordingly, in the map, the toponymy of the Somali districts was relegated to the background (the previous labels of Amaruíni and Scingani are barely detectable), leaving no traces of the natives' presence. In doing so, the map erases the specificity of the two areas and ignores the *genius loci*.[16] Thus, the map resembles any other city built in the metropole under the Fascist legislation. This homogenization matches the colonial map's inherent regulatory purpose to exclude 'the others' and delete their specificity to ensure order and control (Casti Moreschi 1998, 281). As Iman Mohamed has explained,

> With the advent of fascism, however, there was new emphasis placed on the prohibition of racial mixing in the colonies and a concern about Italian men's sexual and social relations with colonized subjects.
>
> (2023, 10)

Literary Cartographies of Mogadishu 87

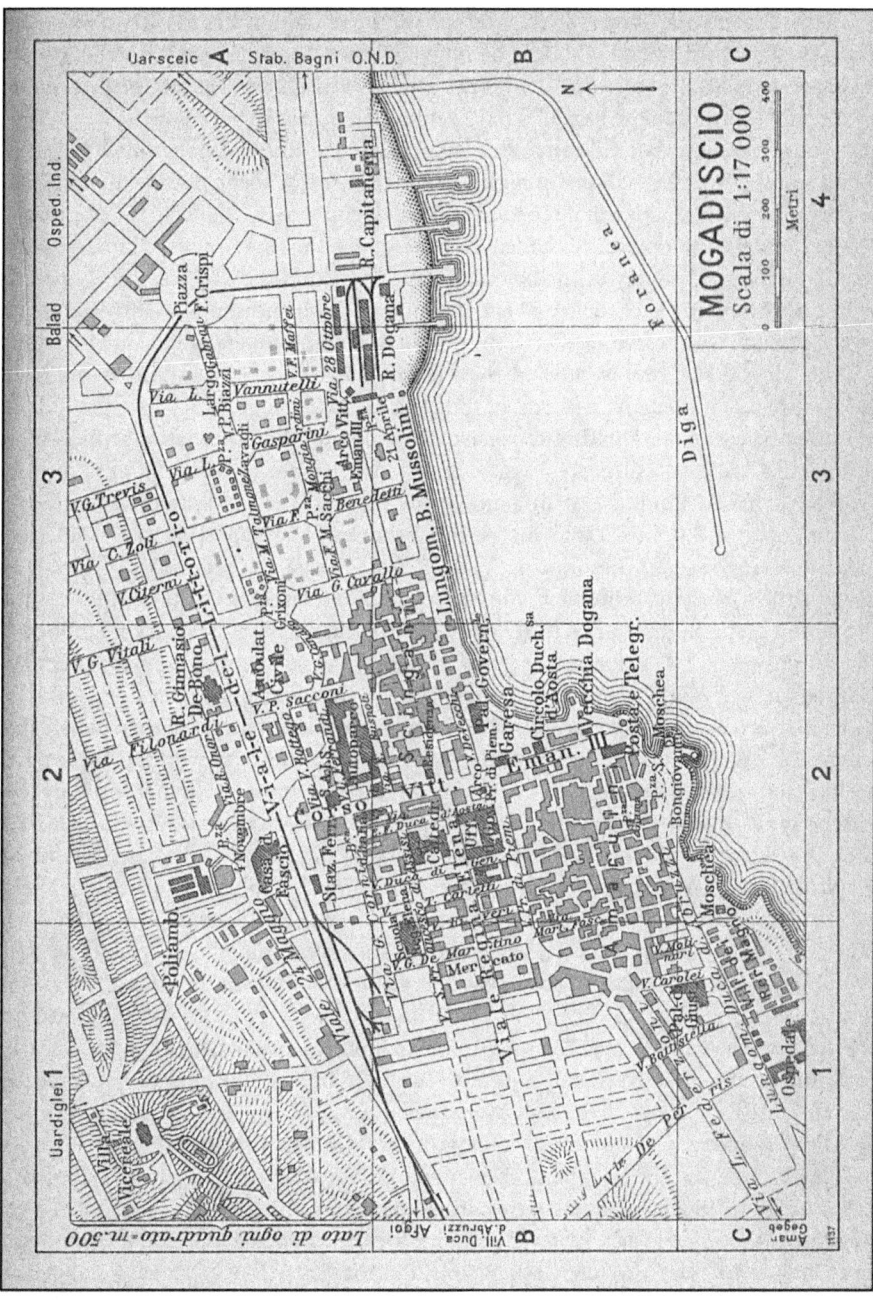

Figure 2.2 Map of Mogadiscio, 1938. From the *Guida dell'Africa Orientale Italiana*.

In this second map, however, the presence of the notations that mark two mosques along the Southern coastline should be noted (sectors B2 and C2). Although they are incorporated into the colonial framework and deprived of their names, they stand out as the only ruptures in the overall Italianization of the city conveyed by the map. They stand out as two unexpected forms of resistance or, according to scholar Jose Rabasa, as 'blind spots' (1985, 2). Graham Huggan, who reuses the concept, defines 'blind spots' as previous configurations that represent a form of counter-discourse to Eurocentrism (2008, 118–19). Their presence challenges and eschews the superimposed homogeneity and the Italian toponymy of the colonial map. Therefore, the physical and symbolic reproduction of an exact replica of the Italian city in Mogadishu is slightly hindered by the presence of the two mosques, the only remaining markers of the native space.

The Mogadishu represented in the map of the 1930s, similarly to Asmara or Addis Ababa, underpins a form of 'coherence of cartographic discourse, [...] historically associated with the desire to stabilize the foundations of a self-privileging Western culture' (Huggan 2008, 118). Imperial Mogadishu is indeed crossed by roads imbued with names drawn from Fascist rhetoric and with references to the political and historical context of the 1930s, such as Viale del Littorio, Lungomare Mussolini or Viale Regina Elena. Street names, triumphal arcs, statues, *piazze*, cinemas, theatres and advertisements all enforced and promoted colonial discourse. In *Il latte è buono*, the protagonist Gashan embodies the functions of both architecture and map-making in shaping Somali's identity. Garane describes the protagonist's relation to the places he likes to attend in Mogadishu, called *luoghi prediletti* (favourite places). These places physically exemplify his sense of belonging to the Italian culture, which he himself describes as 'like flying', when he 'passes close to the Somali Parliament, told to be built by the Fascist with special stones carried on purpose from Italy, because it was believed that the Duce would have visited Mogadishu' ('*Era come se volasse, passando vicino al Parlamento somalo, si dice costruito dai fascisti con pietre speciali portate apposta dall'Italia, perché si credeva che il Duce si sarebbe fermato a Mogadiscio*') (Garane 2005, 61). It is worth mentioning, however, that the so-called Somali Parliament was an imposing building of red bricks, known as Casa del Fascio, with a 30-metre-high tower called Torre Littoria. Built in 1938 and inaugurated the following year, Casa del Fascio later became, in the trusteeship period, the location of the first National Assembly until it hosted the post-independence Parliament (De Napoli 2018, 354; Mohamed 2023, 17).

These references to colonial buildings make Gashan imagine Mogadishu as a calque of Rome, but the references also emphasize Somalia's problematic passage from colonialism to independence, as the urbanscape was changed and reinvented but, nonetheless, still acted as a 'place of memory for the colonized' (Çelik 2002, 144, qtd. in Mohamed 2023, 16). While Gashan considers the native Mogadishu as a 'jungle' or a 'sandy land of dunes' inhabited by 'barbarians' (*boscagliosi*), he looks at the colonial architecture with awe and admiration, as shown in the following passage.

Questi erano i suoi luoghi prediletti, perché portavano nomi gloriosi: Sacro Cuore, Liceo Scientifico, Scuola Elementare, Stadio Coni, Fiat ... Lo Stadio Coni gli ricordava il calcio italiano, gli ricordava Facchetti, Mazzola, Gianni Rivera, Boninsegna, Gigi Riva ... Non pensava a Said Duale, a Killer, a Garille, a Scott, a Geilani ...

(Garane 2005, 61)

These were his favourite places, because they held glorious names: Sacro Cuore, Liceo Scientifico, Scuola Elementare, Stato Coni, Fiat ... Stadio Coni reminded him of Italian football; it reminded him of Facchetti, Mazzola, Gianni Rivera Boninsegna, Gigi Riva ... He did not think about Said Duale, Killer, Garille, Scott, Geilani ...

The attention to football players, singers and food (*cappuccino* and Italian pastries) implies, as Brioni has conveniently noticed, 'not merely a corporeal but also [a] cultural nutrition of colonialism' (2015, 49). In the case of Gashan, colonialism has produced within him an identity that aligns with an imagined 'Italianness' and views his fellow Somalis as alien. At the time when Gashan, as well as other Somali refugees or exiled Somalis, arrived in Italy, he felt a confident sense of intimacy with the former metropole, conferred by the names of the places he was accustomed to in Mogadishu, such as Via Roma, *licei* and *scuole*, demonstrated in the below passage:

Andava a piedi dappertutto. Da Wardhigley a Shangani, passando per Via Somalia. Andava al Liceo Scientifico Leonardo da Vinci, passando di fronte alla Scuola Elementare Guglielmo Marconi. Ne guardava le mura con gli occhi pieni di ammirazione [...] Passava vicino al Sacro Cuore, dove giocava a calcio. Poi davanti alla Fiat e allo Stadio Coni, gli altri due centri della passeggiata attraverso la 'giungla' di Mogadiscio.

(Garane, 60)

He walked everywhere. From Wardhigley to Shangani, passing through via Via Somalia. He walked to the Liceo Leonardo da Vinci, passing in front of Guglielmo Marconi Elementary School. He looked at its walls with eyes full of admiration [...] He passed near the Sacro Cuore church, where he played football. Then, he passed in front of the Fiat workshop and the Coni Stadium, the other two centres of his walk through the 'jungle' of Mogadishu.

As Gashan effectively shows, from the early twentieth century to the post-independence period, Italians played a dominant role in shaping Somali's identity. Garane marks the continuity and legacy of Italian rule by emphasizing the importance of Italian toponymy to his protagonist, whose affection for the colonizer's culture plays well with the urbanscape. Corso (or Via) Somalia is what was known as the Corso Vittorio Emanuele II during the Fascist era (B2 in Figure 2.2); the Coni Stadium, later renamed Benádir Stadium and built on the same ground as the small stadium erected in the 1930s (Sauli 1954), is among the places along with hotel Croce del Sud, Scuola Guglielmo Marconi and the restaurant *Cappuccetto nero* that actively contribute to making Gashan view Italy as his inner homeland.[17]

It is only later in the novel, after living abroad and looking at Somalia from an outward perspective, that Gashan has the chance to rework his idea of home. Through experience (his travels), learning (he attended university in Italy and France) and several meetings (with other exiled Somalis and with Thomas Sankara, the Marxist revolutionary and Pan-Africanist who guided Burkina Faso from 1983 to 1987), Gashan comes to understand that Italian colonialism is one of the forces that ruined his country, along with dictatorship and clan ideology. The development of Gashan's consciousness corresponds to the conflictual relationship between colonial discourse and intellectuals that the French West Indian psychiatrist Frantz Fanon described in his *The Wretched of the Earth* (1961).

Fanon theorized decolonization as a three-stage process (2001, 166–98). In the first stage, the colonized self-prove that they have assimilated the colonizer's culture by mimicking colonial cultural practices. It is a period of integral assimilation, and in *Il latte è buono*, this incorporation of Italian colonial practices is highlighted by the disregard that Gashan shows his fellow Somalis.[18] In the second stage, rejection of colonial practices prevails, enhanced by the memory of the past or, in this case, by Gashan's outside perspective, which allows him to feel exclusion and displacement. By encountering non-Western and anti-colonial intellectuals and experiencing harsh resettlement in a racist and indifferent Italy, Gashan reassesses his 'Somaliness' and his 'Africanness'. Finally, in the third stage, the colonized subject returns to his/her own culture, trying to find a form of authenticity that is free from the bonds of colonial discourse.[19]

While this third stage will be analysed in the following section, I will now emphasize another important aesthetic and spatial connection between Garane's novella and Shirin Ramzanali Fazel's memoir *Lontano da Mogadiscio*. As Christopher Fotheringham suggests, for Fazel, and for Farah too: 'Mogadishu was the site of the strongest Italian influence in Somalia and became in many ways just that, a province of Italy' (2019a, 121; Farah 1992a, 129). As we have seen, colonial urban plans produced this idea of Mogadishu as an Italian 'province' both symbolically and spatially, with the removal of the original sites of the city via renaming and the replacement of the native neighbourhoods with new Italian buildings.

Cristina Ali Farah also stresses this close relationship between architecture and the sense of Italianness of the Somali urbanscape; in her *Little Mother*, one of the protagonists, the Somali expatriate Taageere, recounts his fascination with the Italian language and a place in Mogadishu in particular, the Italian Cultural Centre. He says:

> I remember when I joined the Italian Cultural Center in Mogadishu. My book was bought with lots of shillings, a thick package of wastepaper. To learn Italian! Going around like a student, with my notebook and the pen in my pants pocket. What use was Italian to me? It was the idea that attracted me; the fact that it was spoken by proper gentlemen, with good jobs at the ministry, in a school, in the army. All

classy man, fluent in Italian, so fluent that it pops up here and there when they speak Somali. Here and there, often. I want to speak like that as well, every third word an Italian one, I thought. It's elegant. Will it come so naturally to me too? I never found out, war made me give it up.

(Ali Farah 2011, 73)

This importance conferred on the Italian building also emerges in Afdhere Jama's novel, *Liido Beach*. In one chapter, the two protagonists are having lunch in a restaurant tellingly named *Mama Roma*. One of them, Farah, a Somali man who lives in London and has returned to Mogadishu, reiterates colonial ideas by stating that '[the Italians] built beautiful buildings here, old arches and churches, and they even [have a] train system' (Jama 2018, 16). His friend (and future lover) Hanad, born to Somali parents who met and married in Italy, listens to Franco Battiato and Renato Carosone, swears using Italian curse words and has an Italian flag hanging outside his window (Jama 2018, 7, 11, 32, 84). His relationship with the former colonial culture is comparable to that of Gashan, as Italian music and language become part of his cultural horizon, but there is also the idea that architecture can convey and develop a sense of place that overlooks the local and reaches for the former metropole, which becomes the idealized, putative home of the colonized. It is the Italianness of Mogadishu that nourishes Hanad's, Taageere's and Gashan's senses of belonging. Hanad states: 'I longed to follow my parents back to Italy. I spent my first six years there and still dreamt in Italian. Somalia was home, but it was dirty, corrupt and dysfunctional' (Jama 2018, 6). His feelings towards Mogadishu, the city of his everyday life, conflict with his ideal image of Rome, a city he describes with a colonial flavour:

He wondered what it would be like to walk around the city of his birth again and see all the beautiful places he had read about. He wondered what it would be like to visit all the landmarks he had seen in those movies.

(Jama, 130)

Jama's novel addresses, as does Garane's novella, the contamination of Somalia with the Italian culture and language and the latter's potential to shape Hanad's and Gashan's identities. After studying the long-lasting influence of Italian colonialism on architecture and social practices, the following section investigates the period of the civil war, marked by the annihilation of the multilayered spatiality of the city. The analysis will focus on the early and most violent phase of the civil war and how it is represented in Somali novels and poems.

The 1990s and the Poetics of War

Scholar Lidwien Kapteijns has analysed how popular songs and poetry are mediations of civil war violence in Somalia that accompanied and followed the state collapse, especially the campaign of clan cleansing from 1991 to 1992 (2013, 21–70). In following this path, this section aims to broaden the scope of analysis to the prose works of Somali diasporic authors to show how the narrative strategies they adopt disclose the attention that they give to the spatiality of emptiness. Through this shared aesthetic practice, Somali authors try to understand through writing the magnitude of violence and the vacuum created by the civil war to understand how the whole nation could come to terms with its present destruction and aim for a future of peaceful coexistence.

For example, in *Il latte è buono*, the protagonist Gashan, after leaving Mogadishu to study in Italy, France and the United States, returns to his hometown after decades away. The novel shows that he has followed quite a similar path to Jeebleh, the protagonist of Farah's *Links*: they have both studied abroad, Gashan in Florence and Jeebleh in Padua and Rome, they both have a strong tie to the Italian language through Dante and his *Divine Comedy* and they both have become teachers in the United States (Gashan in the fictional city of Devil and Jeebleh in New York). It is useful here to compare the descriptions of the war-ravaged Mogadishu in each story to emphasize their shared narrative strategies. The novel *Little Mother* by Ubax Cristina Ali Farah will also be analysed, as it reproduces the spatiality of emptiness that can be felt in *Links* and *Il latte è buono*, but it also draws upon another intertextual reference with the poem 'Mogadishu, You Have Been Violated' ('*Xamar waa lagu xumeeyeyeey*'). This poem was written and performed by Axmed Naaji Sacad, 'perhaps Somalia's most accomplished and versatile songwriter, singer, musician, and musical entrepreneur' (Kapteijns 2013, 28).

Garane describes Gashan's return to Mogadishu after twenty-five years of exile in the last chapter of the novella, emblematically entitled '*La morte*' ('The Death'). Once in his hometown, Gashan finds it a desolate place, almost unrecognizable. The spirit of his ancestor, Shakhlan Iman, appears to guide him through the ruins. As she directs Gashan through the ruined city, Shakhlan parallels the role of the ancient Roman poet Virgil in Dante's *Divine Comedy*, thus creating a further connection with Farah's *Links*, where Mogadishu is figuratively compared to Dante's Hell (as Chapter 3 will show) and with Farah's *Crossbones* too. Indeed, during Jeebleh's second visit to the city in *Links*, he notices that Mogadishu is still in ruins and feels puzzled:

> [Jeebleh] cannot tell where they are in relation to the apartment, disoriented by fresh ruins from the latest confrontation between the warlords and the Courts three months ago. One loses one's sense of direction in a city that has suffered civil war savageries; one is, at the best of times, in want of the guidance of those who have continued to live in it.
>
> (Farah 2012, 27)

This idea of needing a guide in the city reinforces the intertextual links between the three texts and further shapes the aesthetics of the void used to represent the civil war scenario. Both Shakhlan and Virgil are non-physical entities that appear to guide the protagonists through the spatiality of Mogadishu and Hell, respectively, but also through grim times of loss and dismay (the Dantean *smarrimento*). Their transcendence, however, bestows on them a symbolic status: Shakhlan and Virgil embody the consciousness of the past and the bond with tradition.

While in the second chapter of *Il latte è buono*, 'Boring Mogadishu', previously analysed, Gashan's grandmother and nephew were strolling through the bustling, independent and cosmopolitan city, in the last chapter, they wander through the city, witnessing the decay caused by the violence of the civil war. In this context, Shakhlan appears as the spiritual mentor, being the ancestor of Gashan's clan lineage, and suggests to Gashan how to rebuild the city and the country from what is left. Different to Farah, who never mentions clan names and openly opposes clan ideology as the basis for nationhood, Garane seems to remark upon their ambivalent importance within the Somali tradition, along with Islam and Western culture, and their role in both the formation of the nation and its collapse ('It's time to rebuild the clan, then Somalia', Garane 2005, 114). Clannism is understood as an unsolved issue of Somali society and national development, and Garane shows ambiguous approaches towards this national and self-identity issue, as Simone Brioni noticed: although Gashan argues that clans produce a never-ending process of violence, Garane's description of clannism is problematic (Brioni 2015, 115; Garane 2005, 84). For instance, Garane places clans and political parties side by side, equating an elective system with a hereditary one (Garane 2005, 77).

However, it is also interesting to note that two more interlocutors appear for Gashan, namely, Somalia and Mogadishu. In the closing chapter of *Il latte è buono*, Garane anthropomorphizes both the nation and the city, silent but evocative of the overall spatiality of emptiness that surrounds Gashan (exemplified by the following quotes: 'Mogadishu, rise up and walk!', 115; 'Speak to me, Somalia!' and 'Somalia was in front of him, lying down, breathing irregularly. Like a patient waiting to be put down', 125). Similarly, in *Links*, another guide, the unreliable and sly Af-Laawe, who goes along with Jeebleh after his arrival, describes the city by personifying it: 'Some of us think of the cities we know very well and where we've lived as intimate friends' (Farah 2005, 6).

These multiple intertextual layers between Farah, Dante and Garane are further emphasized in *Il latte è buono* when Gashan witnesses how both space and social relations have been violated during the civil war fighting while walking in the bleakness of the infernal war-ravaged city, which is evident in the following passage:

> Camminava per le strade di Mogadiscio. Strade senza nomi, senza destinazioni. Quando era partito dalla sua terra c'era tutto, insieme: la cultura somala, la cultura occidentale, i semafori, le strade, i cammelli, gli asini ... Adesso non c'era più niente. Niente nomi. Niente cultura. Niente popolo. Solo lui e la sua coscienza e le sue domande.
>
> Il popolo non esisteva più. Il potere non esisteva più. I semafori non esistevano più. I cammelli non c'erano più a Mogadiscio. Gli asini erano stati mangiati dalla gente e dalle mitragliatrici. Non c'era più niente. Niente di niente.
>
> (Garane 2005, 120)

> He walked through the streets of Mogadishu. Streets without names, without destinations. When he had left his homeland, there was everything, all together: Somali culture, Western culture, traffic lights, roads, camels, donkeys ... Now there was nothing. No names. No culture. No people. Himself alone with his conscience and questions.
> The people didn't exist anymore. Power didn't exist anymore. Traffic lights didn't exist anymore. There weren't any camels in Mogadishu anymore. The donkeys had been eaten by the people and by the rifles. There was nothing. Nothing at all.

The streets are nameless, and the houses are left empty as if no invaders or losers, foreigners or residents could claim the properties. Both modernist and colonial buildings have been turned into ruins, and 'most public symbols [have] lost their status as places and merely cluttered up [the] space' (Tuan 1977, 164). Gashan struggles to retrieve the sense of familiarity with his *luoghi prediletti*, since these, too, have been erased, thus turning his 'home' into an unrecognizable and unwelcoming place. Along with the physical destruction, the idea of nationhood seems lost, too. The absence of any spatial reference and the emptiness of such a wasteland parallel the vanished idea of cosmopolitanism and national unity, and the fact that the civil war has left a power vacuum that has been filled by hatred between Somalis.

It is important here to recall the development of Gashan's consciousness mentioned in the previous section to explain the role of the civil war as a rupture of his *Bildung* (formation). The last stage of decolonization, when colonized subjects should return to their own culture to find a form of authenticity apart from colonialism, seems to be hindered for Gashan. Indeed, Garane conveys the impossibility of completely fulfilling this process by showing the destruction of Somalia and the consequent collapse of the idea of nationhood. While Gashan walks through the ruined city, Garane suggests some unclear and ambivalent solutions to build the new Somalia. For example, Garane implies that the starting point should be the emptiness in which the nation currently lies. As the previous passage shows, the physical destruction parallels the cultural and political dismay ('Now there was nothing. No names. No culture. No people', 120). This idea, however, echoes the Western notion of colonial territories as *terrae nullius* (no man's lands) to take over and create from them 'a new world out of nothing' (Garane, 121). Simone Brioni also notices that Garane probably takes this image from Fanon too, as in *The Wretched of the Earth* 'decolonization is problematically described as a new beginning from a *tabula rasa*' (Brioni 2015, 144).

This emptiness, either a *terra nullius* or *tabula rasa* (lit. a blank slate), is reproduced at the stylistic level in *Il latte è buono* through negations which also convey Gashan's opposing feelings and doubts about the future of the nation. For example:

> Gashan camminava con tanti perché senza risposte. Era frastornato tra il clan, il ragionamento e il Corano [...] Domande e domande ancora. Domande senza risposte.
>
> (Garane 2005, 118)

Gashan was walking and wondering without answers. He was dazed because of the clans, his thoughts, the Quran [...] Questions, and more questions. Questions without answers.

Like Farah did in *Links*, Garane reflects on Gashan's feelings regarding Somalia by showing Gashan's destructive thoughts about dismantling any idea of a homeland and rejecting cognate notions such as nation, state or community. In *Links*, the city is portrayed using a similar wording:

The roads had no names. No flags flew anywhere near where the car was now parked, and there were no sheds, however ramshackle, to mark the spot.
(Farah 2005, 76)

This passage resembles Garane's description of the city, as both authors employ the same image of nameless streets that lead nowhere. In *Links*, Jeebleh labels Mogadishu as 'the city of death', 'the city exploded into anarchy', 'a place vandalised' and, again, a 'place of sorrow' (Farah 2005, 5, 20, 35, 70). The frequent occurrence of vultures, which share the urban space with the inhabitants, further reinforces the portrayal of Mogadishu as a place of lifelessness and decay. As death is an all-pervading presence in the city, scavenging birds maliciously wander around, waiting for a chance to feed themselves. In *Crossbones*, this perception is further emphasized when Jeebleh himself compares his 1996 visit to his return ten years later:

The general collapse is still the same, though; houses with their insides caved in, with a Lego-like look to them, the floor below or the one above entirely missing.
(Farah 2012, 27)

The aesthetic of void, made up of images of emptiness conveyed through words belonging to the semantic field of decay and destruction, goes hand in hand with the annihilation of the sense of community and nationhood during the post-independence period.[20] The following passage from *Crossbones* suitably points out the relation between physical destruction and social collapse, as well as the relation between ruined buildings and the loss of national unity.[21] The all-pervading devastation instils in Jeebleh a nostalgic longing for a peaceful Mogadishu, which contrasts with the sense of hopelessness and ethical decay of the city's inhabitants. The passage reads:

He is deeply disturbed that it is no longer the metropolis with which he is familiar, its current residents imported to raise a fighting force. Everywhere he looks, destitute men, women and children in near rags wearily trudge by, many of them emaciated, their bellies swollen with undiagnosed illnesses, their eyes host to swarms of roaming flies. They seem exhausted, inarticulate with fear and vigilance, which imposes a further formlessness.
(Farah 2012, 167)

Death surfaces through subtle references ('emaciated', 'undiagnosed illnesses', 'exhausted' and 'roaming flies') but also emerges as deeply entrenched in Mogadishu and its residents. It is interesting to compare this description with Farah's own recollections of his days in Mogadishu, which foreground both the cosmopolitan feature and the spatial 'layeredness' of the city. He says:

> When I first arrived in Mogadiscio, I loved the labyrinthine networks of the city's alleyways; I loved the mélange of its cultures –an eleventh-century minaret cheek to jowl with a glass house. Mogadishans spoke every language in an idiom of their own manufacture. I loved the contrasts on display at every turn, from the monument raised in memory of Mussolini to the palace in which the city's Zanzibari sovereign defines the city's cosmopolite.
>
> (Farah 2008, 8)

As the extract underlines, the reference to a past of coexistence, released from clan ideology, explicitly evokes the link between peaceful times and cosmopolitanism. According to Farah, by eschewing *qabiil*, which led to the scramble for power and the violence that surrounds fratricide, this long-lost coexistence could be achieved again with a secularized state, freed from what Farah considers artificial creations (such as clans), and the re-establishment of forms of solidarity and affiliation unconnected to blood lineage. More specifically, Farah refers to the term *tol*, a Somali word meaning both 'kinship' and 'to stitch together', as a viable alternative to *qabiil* (2008, 10).

Like Jeebleh, Gashan remains uncertain about the forthcoming development of both the city and the nation but, where the ruins may be the ashes of rebirth for the latter (an ambiguous resurgence of both clans and Somalia), for the former, the destruction conveys a prevalent feeling of hopelessness towards the inhabitants of Mogadishu, who Jeebleh sees as 'wicked and murderous through and through' (Farah 2005, 201). In *Links*, this view is further highlighted through Jeebleh's eyes, as he notes:

> Many houses have no roofs, and bullets scarred nearly every wall […] The streets were eerily, ominously quiet. They saw no pedestrians on the roads and met no other vehicles. Jeebleh felt a tremor, imagining that the residents had been slaughtered 'in one another's blood', as Virgil had it. He would like to know whether, in this civil war, both those violated and the violators suffered from a huge deficiency – the inability to remain in touch with their inner selves or to remember who they were before the slaughter began.
>
> (Farah 2005, 70)

This imagery of bullets and collapsed houses draws another intertextual link with the poem 'Disaster' ('*Masiibo*'), authored by Mustafa Sheekh Cilmi in the early 1990s. The poet goes into detail about the violence committed in the first stages of the civil war. While he describes the perpetrators as people 'with no sense of religious injunction or ethical principle' (Kapteijns 2013, 24), he also pays attention to urbanscape and asks himself:

How many tall houses were reduced to rubble, how many multi-storied houses brought down and burned.
How many mat-and-mud houses were blown high into the sky.
How many cannons were let loose on us without interruption.
How many bullets did they shower down on us like rain.

(Kapteijns 2013, 24)[22]

As the civil war emptied houses and buildings, it also emptied the essence of nationhood and people's ability to 'remain in touch with their inner selves' (Farah 2005, 70). However, while Farah blurs the line between perpetrators and victims, Mustafa Sheekh Cilmi seems to more directly point out who is to blame for the destruction. Cilmi's poem refers to a group of young men known as the , brought in from the countryside, who gained notoriety in Mogadishu (Marchal 1993; Mohamed-Abdi 2001). The poet describes them as ruthless and violent youngsters who did 'the dirty work of the more powerful and power-hungry men who incited them from behind the scenes' (Kapteijns 2013, 25).

Ali Farah's novel *Little Mother* further highlights the convergence in the representation of the civil war scenario across diasporic texts via intertextual and intermedial connections. In a chapter of *Little Mother* dedicated to the decay of Mogadishu – set in January 1991 and titled 'Interlude' – the ancient cosmopolitan city is directly invoked and once again personified. The following passage, a litany that unveils the account of the war as witnessed by Taageere, one of *Little Mother's* protagonists, stresses the same nostalgia for the peaceful past of the post-independence period as shown in *In latte è buono* and *Links*. The passage goes:

Xamar waa lagu xumeeyay, Xamar they have ruined you. Who will pay for the sins committed? City of mine, city where they buried my umbilical cord. City where everyone lived in peace and harmony, safety and freedom. Magnificent city on the African coast. My brothers, parents, and cousins all lived there. But because of the blood and strife these same brothers are fighting among themselves.

Xamar waa lagu xumeeyay, Xamar they have defiled you. Filled you with bullets, destroyed and burned you, devastated your neighbourhoods, sacked your treasures. The respected families fled across the borders. The just and honest people liberated the country from criminals and foreigners. Today all of them lie buried. Nobody cares anymore about the wisdom of the elders.

(Ali Farah 2011, 127)

The sentence '*Xamar waa lagu xumeeyay*' (Oh Mogadishu, you have been terribly wronged) is a line from the song 'Mogadishu, You Have Been Violated' (*Xamar waa lagu xumeeyeyeey*), written and performed by Somali songwriter Axmed Naaji Sacad. As in the song, Ali Farah's repetitions in his novel form a refrain that can be considered an adaptation of the poem. Taageere's account is a loose rewriting of 'Mogadishu, You Have Been Violated', aiming for an anthropomorphization of the city Xamar by comparing it to a woman who was raped (Ali Farah 2018a). Axmed Naaji, similarly to Somali authors, asks himself how to restore the lost honour, 'especially when its violators are the very men who should have protected it' (Kapteijns 2013, 28). In line with Farah and Ali Farah, Naaji Sacad condemns clan logic and advocates for a sense of kinship that goes beyond blood lineage (*ibid.*).

In Taageere's narrative, the city emerges as 'filled with bullets, destroyed and burned', similar to the aesthetics shown in Garane's and Farah's texts. In the previous passage, any coherent accounts of the war are rejected, favouring a fragmented retelling that is syntactically rendered via broken sentences. The feature of being a peaceful and beautiful coastal town, built upon layers of cultural influences and trade routes, is set against the current destruction, as is shown in Naaji Sacad's song:

> With furious force, they obliterated your neighbourhoods
> – Mogadishu, you have been violated –
> Snatching away your beauty all at once.
> We used to reside in you calmly, safely and freely.
> Mogadishu, you have been violated; who will restore your honour?
> (Kapteijns 2013, 28)[23]

The fratricide conflict between fellow citizens, as well as the loss of historical consciousness and the beautiful physical features of the city, is connected to the visions of Farah, Ali Farah and Naaji Sacad, according to whom clannism has taken a wrong turn in Somalia's political development. Even though the future of the country is disputed, as various diasporic authors have shown a different understanding of the forthcoming developments, the authors' opinions converge when they show their disdain for clannism (or what clannism has become) and its logic of power, which pitted Somalis against each other and undermined the unity of the nation and the peaceful coexistence of different communities.[24] The poems and the novels attempt to bring Somalis together instead of reigniting hatred based on clan affiliations, thus presenting the idea of a unifying nation as the solution (Kapteijns 2013, 44). More specifically, the novels do not seem to attempt to identify who is to blame for the civil war or mention clans explicitly. Even in the case of *Il latte è buono*, which might be considered the text that is most interested in exploring clan formations and responsibilities, Garane names colonialism and European countries, religious leaders and Barre as mainly responsible for Somalia's condition (2005, 117, 119, 121). Moreover, Garane refrains from explicitly naming any clans or individuals involved in the incidents he writes about. Instead, he chooses to focus on the broader themes and underlying societal issues at play, reusing the imagery of Mogadishu as a woman who has been violated. In a passage of the novella, when Gashan learns about the civil war when he is in Italy, he considers Somalia's history:

> 'La storia della Somalia,' pensava Gashan, 'è la storia della violenza dei pastori guerrieri. Ma Mogadiscio fu stuprata, violentata, distrutta dai guerrieri sedentari.

Perché hanno violentato la parte più pacifica e più storica della Somalia? Anche i *Reer Xamar* diventeranno violenti. Come dicono i somali, dopo che le cavallette se ne saranno andate, il danno rimarrà. Nessuno sarà come prima.'

(Garane 2005, 84)

'The history of Somalia,' thought Gashan, 'is the history of the violence of the warrior shepherds. But Mogadishu was violated, raped, and destroyed by the sedentary warriors. Why did they rape the most peaceful and historic part of Somalia? The *Reer Xamar* [inhabitants of Mogadishu] will also become violent. As the Somalis say, after the grasshoppers are gone, the damage will remain. No one will be the same as before.'

Even though there are intertwined discourses in the texts of diasporic authors – clannism, nomads/agriculturalists, city/countryside, colonialism and dictatorship – the reference to Somalia as the singular name for a singular entity is not merely understood as a geographical space or a name on the map, but as a community that still seeks to be a sovereign state. It is still a nation with Mogadishu as its capital instead of a failed country split into independent or autonomous territories. The civil war, then, becomes a shared setting of time and place among Somali authors of the diaspora and also dictates the distinctive aesthetics of their novels; it emerges as the expedient that enables the negotiation between personal and national experiences. Moreover, it pushes Somali authors to review the past and investigate the causes of this intestine conflict.

Conclusion

This chapter has investigated a feature shared among Somali diasporic novels, namely 'the element of imagining the city from an individual and collective perspective, but also of constructing images' of Mogadishu. Drawing upon Glissant's notion of *landscape* as the physical *locus* where the past can be retrieved, this analysis explored how Somali authors addressed the material legacy of colonialism, which protracted during the AFIS period and Somalia's independence, and the destruction caused by the civil war. Focusing on distinctive historical moments, the comparative reading has emphasized the city's significance in forming the self-identities and national identities of Somalis. To 'give greater credence to diverse voices, different mediums of representation, and, therefore, different perspectives on the city', this chapter has suggested that a wider range of works focused on Mogadishu's urbanscape should be considered (Forbes 2008, 46).

In *Il latte è buono*, for example, the analysis showed how Garane highlighted the importance of colonial architecture and toponymy in shaping Gashan's identity and how the presence of colonial toponymy hindered Somalia's process of institutional and symbolic decolonization. Through Gashan's affection for his *luoghi prediletti*, he embodies the concept of the mimic man. His decolonization process can be explained through the three stages theorized by Frantz Fanon in *The Wretched of the Earth*. The connection between space and identity has fostered a comparison with colonial textual and figurative sources, showing how colonialism shaped Somalis' national and individual identities through mapping and specific discursive strategies aimed to control and marginalize colonial subjects. As the comparative reading between the two maps from the colonial guidebook and the descriptions of Mogadishu in the novella has shown, Somalia after independence was a nation where colonialism – though in a different form – still played a fundamental role at the social, political and economic levels. The analysis then revealed that Italian urban plans were not limited to the 1920s and 1930s but dated back to the Liberal era (1861–1922) when the colonial spatial practices later reinforced during Fascism were already at work. In highlighting this *long durée*, the importance of colonial legacy and its influence on self-identity and nationhood even during the post-independence period is underscored.

In this context of lingering colonial practices, short-lived independence and new nationalist and authoritarian forces that exacerbated clan affiliations, the traumatic event of the civil war erupted. This represented a massive shift in Somalia's history, and its consequences and reach have not yet been fully comprehended. One of the discursive strategies employed by Somali diasporic authors to represent civil-war violence is the depiction of Mogadishu – as the emblem of the whole nation – as ruinous and devasted. The poetics of destruction, as shown, arises as a shared feature of stories by Somali novelists and poets who, in their attempt to make sense of the annihilation of the capital and the whole nation-state, rely upon this common narrative practice to convey the suffering of their fellow citizens and the role that clan solidarity and affiliation played in the civil war. This analysis presented how Somali authors, instead of explicitly mentioning perpetrators and clan names, avoided deepening the communal hatred between Somalis and instead articulated their discourse through the lost idea of nationhood, kinship and *tol*.

Even though these authors proposed different solutions for the future of Somalia as a nation, they share a common sociopolitical framework that considers clannism a problematic practice in Somali post-independence history and do not shy away from discursively engaging with the large-scale clan-based violence that caused the collapse of the nation-state through writing. Whereas Chapter 1 presented spatiality as a way to address diasporic identities and belonging, especially for those Somalis who moved abroad and returned, Chapter 2 explored the violence of the civil war and the long-lasting effects of colonialism as shown through Somali texts. In this investigation, the novel emerged as a polyphonic form in which multiple voices can find a space to confront and negotiate various positions. Instead of reinforcing narratives of clan hatred, Somali authors emphasize the communal destruction and the need to re-establish social relationships across past divides. In doing so, rather than proposing a single, collective and authoritative truth and signposting clans and perpetrators, Somali writers 'bring out a plurality of interpretations of the past that […] are all in need of critical engagement' (Kapteijns 2013, 237). In other words, in their novels, the memories of individual experiences aim to undermine the authoritativeness of the self-serving truths constructed by clan narratives.

The following chapters will push the idea of polyphony further, connecting spatiality and language. Specifically, Chapters 3 and 4 will show how diasporic authors engage with multilingualism. These authors show a more nuanced use of the former colonial language, as Italian gradually lost its conflictual connotations during Barre's dictatorship. In particular, the analysis will explain how multilingualism shaped the identity of the protagonist of *Links*, Jeebleh, and how, through Dantean intertextual references, the Italian language emerges as a means to reterritorialize Somalia from a peripheral context to global relevance. In other words, *The Divine Comedy* allows Farah to compare medieval Florence, which has become well-known globally due to Dante's works, and Mogadishu, two cities that have been through civil wars. The *Comedy* provides the lens through which the war-torn setting of Mogadishu, and Somalia as a whole, is portrayed in *Links*, and it also rises as a powerful diegetic device to support the protagonist's opinion of the civil war violence and emphasize the need for a moral repair and social reconstruction to bring Somalis back together. As in the case of the representation of spatiality, the following chapter aims to show how, through the form of the novel, the issues of nationhood, Somali identity and clan logic are interconnected within the discursive strategies used to represent the civil war.

Notes

1   The AFIS (*Amministrazione Fiduciaria Italiana della Somalia*) was a United Nations Trust Territory administered by Italy from 1950 to 1960, with Mogadishu as the capital. Following the dissolution of the former Italian Somaliland, Italy was designated to rule its former colony until independence.
2   In this regard, the theorization of the concept of the 'Mogadishu line' is telling because it highlights how the city has been prescribed a new meaning related to the impossibility of any military intervention by international actors due to the fear of high human costs. 'Formally, the concept of "the Mogadishu line" refers to the point where a foreign power abandons a pure peacekeeping mission in a particular country and begins combat operations instead, often with the aim of bringing about regime change' (Larcom, Sarr and Willems 2018, 8).
3   This is shown in two articles, both with telling titles, 'A Dangerous Place', by Mark Doyle and Binaifer Nowrojee and 'Anarchy Rules' by Peter Biles. More recently, in contrast with the mere narrative of violence, the article by Jason Florio, 'Facing Mogadishu', explores the ordinary life of Mogadishu through poignant portraits of its inhabitants.
4   The same attempt to resist deconstruction and restore the memories of the past by linking the individual to the collective can be found in two recent photographic books, both focused on Mogadishu: *Mogadishu Then and Now* (2012) by the photojournalist and writer Rasna Warah (with the contribution of Mohamud Dirios and Ismail Osman), and *Mogadishu Lost Moderns* (2014), edited by the architect Rashid Ali and the photographer Andrew Cross. Both these books trace the recent history of Mogadishu. While *Mogadishu Then and Now* deploys frequent quotations by Nuruddin Farah and directly engages the misrepresentation by the media using

literary texts and films (above all, the unfair *Black Hawk Down* by Ridley Scott), *Mogadishu Lost Moderns* relies on images (colonial and contemporary pictures) and texts, including a short story written by Ubax Cristina Ali Farah, with the aim of documenting the eerie destruction of the city and suggesting the possibility of a future reborn.

5   In her article about the Mogadishu Book Fair, Nanjala Nyabola maintains that Somali people are often associated with war and seen as numbers more than people (Nyabola 2018). Likewise, online publications of Somali authors support this manifold vision of the city and, more broadly, of the Somali people. Independent literary online journals such as *The Maandeeq* and *Warscapes* aimed to address '[the] need to move past a void within mainstream culture in the depiction of people and places experiencing staggering violence and the literature they produce. The magazine is [also] a tool for understanding complex political crises in various regions and serves as an alternative to compromised representations of those issues.' This statement can be retrieved from the online page of the journal at http://www.warscapes.com/about.

6   In an interview for the magazine *Cityscape*, Maxamed Nuur, mayor of Mogadishu during the post-war reconstruction (2010–14), accordingly observes that the citizens of Mogadishu were starting to think about their condition of instability and conflict as ordinary. To illustrate his aim of solving this situation, Nuur used the telling expression: 'fighting a battle of mind', so 'to change the mentality of the people of the city' (Warah 2012).

7   While Lidwien Kapteijns has studied the representation and importance of Mogadishu in the poems of Somali authors, Giulia Liberatore collected the accounts and testimonies of women who lived in the city during the 1970s (Liberatore 2017).

8   Several articles and interviews by Nuruddin Farah have Mogadishu as their primary object of interest. In this study, three autobiographical reports will be taken into consideration: Farah (2002), Farah (2008) and Farah (2010).

9   As already mentioned, the works of Liberatore and Kapteijns looked at, respectively, direct testimonies and poems. Only one section of Kapteijns' book, *Clan Cleansing in Somalia*, analyses the novels of two Somali authors, Abdirrazak Y. Osman's English-language *In the Name of the Fathers* (1996) and Faysal Axmed Xasan's Somali-language *Maandeeq* (2000). Even though the two authors, unlike those considered here, 'are also not afraid to "speak clan" and mention specific clan names throughout their narratives', they also both consider clan affiliations as a dangerous and imposing framework in which to inscribe the idea of the nation.

10 Garane's fictionalization of Mogadishu is quite relevant because the presence of the city in that period is not frequent in works of fiction. Regarding the AFIS and the following independence period, there is mostly reportage, journal articles and personal accounts, but a few literary works, such as *A Naked Needle* (1976), the first novel by Farah entirely based in Mogadishu, and Ali Farah's *Le stazioni della luna* (2021), described the post-revolutionary Somali life in the mid-1970s. For historical and journalistic accounts of that period, see Sheikh Aden (1994), Omar (1993), Petrucci (1993) and Cappelli (2011).

11 Italian remained the official language from 1950 to 1960, and the Somali national anthem was the same as that of the metropole, 'Inno di Mameli' (Del Boca 1993; Morone 2011; Naletto 2011; Pandolfo 2013).

12 It is reasonable to consider the *Guide to Italian East Africa* as a widespread publication, since 500,000 copies of the first edition were printed and sent to just as many Italian families between 1938 and 1939.
13 In this case (and in many other passages of the novels), Garane gives a critical perspective of Italian colonialism that, according to historians such as Del Boca, Naletto and Labanca, has been unsystematic, brutal and tending towards a particular inclination to practice without organization and competence. Italian colonialism changed the very reality of the Somalis, forcing them towards disintegration, the erasure of clan hierarchies, internal order and the promotion of differences between nomads and farmers.
14 This novel connects Farah's other novels, as it echoes his production of his first trilogy, *Variations on the Theme of an African Dictatorship,* and his second, *Blood in the Sun*, which are set, respectively, in the Mogadishu of the 1970s and of the 1980s. In *Sweet and Sour Milk* (1979), for example, two characters, Loyaan and Margaritta, dine at the *Capocetto Nero* [*sic*] and visit the De Martini hospital (Farah 1992a, 129; 143). At the end of *Gifts* (1993), a scene is set at the restaurant and hotel *Croce del Sud* (Farah 1993a, 235). In *Close Sesame*, the protagonist walks 'in the direction of Via Roma, with Mirwaas Mosque to his left and Super Cinema and the Indian-owned shops to his right' (Farah 1992b, 106), and *Ufficio del Governo e Baar Novecento* also appears in the Italian-related landmarks of Mogadishu (1992b, 96–7). Farah also refers directly to the 1920s and '30s Fascist occupation in *Close Sesame*, a novel set in the 1980s in which the main characters are deeply entwined in the waking nightmare of a police state. A particular passage reads:

> … pacify a 30,000 population of indigenous extraction so that 300 Italians could live as masters (in 1930, there were 300 Italians in Mogadishu of whom 40 were women, 230 men and 30 children; of these, 84 worked for private business, 70 in the army, and 78 in the civil service; the Somalis of Mogadiscio: 30,000). History (in the 1920s, the years of the Fascist rule) gave to Mogadiscio '*tre buoni ristoranti e tre alberghi così così; tre circoli con ampie sale da ballo*,' two cafes, one cinema hall and six hundred motorcars.
>
> (Farah 1992b, 96)

15 For a more detailed history of the Somali Youth League and the formations of political parties in Somalia, see Morone (2011), Calchi Novati (2011), Guglielmo (2013), Trunji (2015), Samatar (2016) and Urbano (2016).
16 In the novel *In the Name of Our Fathers*, the author brings to the fore the spatiality of the Hamar Weyne (Amaurini) district, which is described as a distinctive and historic economically prominent area of Mogadishu, as is shown in the following passage:

> Hamaris were the people who lived in the very oldest stone-build part of the city called Hamarweyne. They were not involved in politics and were not known for their fighting spirit like the rest of the Somalis. They hated violence.… They were well-known for business. Most of them, if not all of them, were engaged in commercial activity. They owned most of the shoe shows, sweet shops, and tailoring businesses in the city. They were light-skinned and could easily be recognised, if not by their complexion, then by their dialect.
>
> (Osman 1996, 75–6)

17 The hotel *Croce del Sud*, an emblematic place that stresses the presence of the Italians, also appears in Ubax Cristina Ali Farah's, *Madre piccola* (143), Farah's *Gifts* (235) and Scego's *La mia casa è dove sono* (30). Moreover, the *Scuola Guglielmo Marconi* recurs in Scego's *La mia casa è dove sono*: 'The Guglielmo Marconi was my elementary school. Later, with the dictatorship of Siad Barre, they called it Yaasin Cusman' (28–29).
18 Gashan often calls Somalis *boscagliosi*, a depreciative term to label bushmen 'morons, ugly mugs and savages who adore camels' (Garane, 57).
19 Gashan's 'noble' status remains present in the novel, thus implying his multiple belongings. He feels Italian when he speaks the language fluently and knows Dante's and Petrarca's poems by heart, but, at the same time, he distances himself from most Italians, viewing them as racist and uncultured. Concerning the Somali culture, he situates himself as a noble who is 'different in terms of class and lineage from other Somalis' (Brioni 2015, 119).
20 In a description of the city, Farah uses 'devastation' and 'destruction' five times in the same paragraph (*Links*, 79). Moreover, in Farah's personal account of his visit to Mogadishu, he states:

> We walked eastward… into a zone of total grief. I had never seen so much devastation in my life. What I saw called to mind wartime images of humans with their eye sockets emptied, their noses removed, [their] heads bashed in until they were featureless and couldn't be recognized as humans anymore.
>
> (Farah 2008, 14)

21 In a short passage of the novel *Knots*, the second novel of the *Past Imperfect* trilogy, Farah stresses this physical destruction. The passage reads:

> Within an hour, soon after a shower, she joined him in the kitchenette and right away noticed the tell-tale disfigurements in body and soul, which she would see more of when she met other Somalis who had just come from Mogadiscio: trauma born of desolation.
>
> (Farah 2007, 26)

22 For the original, Somali text of 'Masiibo' see Hassan (1998, 98–102). For the full text translated into English, see Kapteijns (2013, 24–8)
23 For the full text translated into English see Kapteijns (2013, 28–9).
24 In Igiaba Scego's *Adua*, money is blamed for the failure of Somalia, more so than quarrelsome social behaviours: '*Business è diventata l'idea fissa di tutti i somali*' (Business has become the fixed idea of every Somali) (2015, 11). This idea echoes a line from *Links*; according to Bile, 'money was the engine that ran Somalia's civil war' (Farah 2003, 331).

3

Multilingualism in Farah's *Links* and *Crossbones*

Introduction

The previous chapter has shown how the civil war in Somali diasporic literature is fictionalized through aesthetic devices that aim to convey both the physical and symbolic destruction of Mogadishu and the whole nation. The representation of Somalia as a nation marked by internal discord and of Somalis as lacking empathy and communal solidarity is symbolically carried out through the descriptions of the dilapidated materiality of buildings, streets and ruins. The physical destruction serves as a reflection of the deterioration of social structures, exerting a profound influence on the protagonists' sense of belonging, as they feel left out – if not rejected – from the clan-centric logic that rules the country (Norridge 2012).

In the void of empty streets and pierced walls, different visions of the future have emerged, too: the city itself, *Xamar* (as it is known by its residents), turns into a character while the protagonists try to make sense of the destruction and reflect on possible ways to rebuild the nation. A shared trait, however, distinguishes different authors, namely the silence regarding the identification of clans as perpetrators. This deliberate and consistent omission of attributing blame to specific clans can be understood as an attempt to reinforce and reproduce a national discourse, alternative to sectarian ideologies. Besides, it serves the purpose of averting the reproduction of a narrative steeped in hostility, rancour and hate-laden relationships among Somali people (Kapteijns 2013, 51). This aporia, as called by Kapteijns, emerges as a distinctive literary trope in Somali novels, which seek to circumvent particularisms and avoid replicating the same logic and violence that led to the civil war (2013, 52).

This chapter will further investigate the close relationship between material and symbolic aspects, physical destruction and social degradation. It starts from the aesthetic of void analysed in the previous section to delve into Nuruddin Farah's *Links* and his reading of the civil war through *The Divine Comedy*. Dante's poem, indeed, appears as the primary reference to describe and explain the Somali political and social context, as its *cantos* become a significant constitutive intertextual reference of *Links*. The intestine conflict in Florence in the fourteenth century, between Dante's party, the White Guelphs (*Guelfi Bianchi*) and the Black Guelphs (*Guelfi Neri*), figuratively mirrors the factions within Somali society. The author does not suggest either a perfect correspondence or a comprehensive explanation of the period of the civil war, but uses Dante's view as a powerful and evocative interliterary source with the aim of 'deterritorializing Somalia as a national project, and reterritorializing it as a place that belongs with the world' (Myers 2011, 146). Indeed, this historical and literary antecedent reframes Somalia not only in the Italian Middle Ages, but in the well-known infernal imaginary of Dante's Hell, showing affinities and similarities between different contexts. The civil war, more than a local and parochial conflict, becomes deeply human, as universal as themes of love or death.

This idea will be further explored in the last chapter, which will place Somali's writings about the civil war along with the Italian literary production of the post-war period, when literature assumed the task to fictionalize the fights between Fascists and *partigiani*. In doing so, the chapter ideally continues what Farah creatively undertook in *Links* and analytically explores neglected similarities between Italy and Somalia, two countries that experienced civil war contexts and produced a literature about this historical, political and social event trying to make sense of the collective and personal trauma. In this sense, Somali authors connect diverse cultural traditions to envision an idea of Somalia that transcends the country's characterization as an isolated case outside of history and geography.

The presence of Dante, however, is not only relevant in Farah's *Links*, but emerges as a node that ties diasporic authors, especially those who use the Italian language as their preferred creative medium. As the following analysis will show, Dante is part of Garane's *Il latte è buono* and is mentioned by Igiaba Scego as the embodiment of Italianness. However, Somali diasporic writers often use in their novels more than one language, thereby making multilingualism a pivotal feature across the diaspora. Its significance extends beyond aesthetics, as it functions as a political tool, too. The use of multiple languages serves the purpose of revisiting the colonial narrative, challenging the normative dominance of former colonial languages (Italian *in primis*) and, crucially, embracing the transnational voices that define the contemporary diasporic experience. Multilingualism rises as a strategic means to reach a broader audience and surpass national-linguistic borders, thus effecting a reterritorialization of Somalia from a peripheral and marginalized context to a global position.

The second part of this chapter, accordingly, investigates multilingualism beyond Dante and investigates how English, Somali and Italian creatively interact in the novels *Links* and *Crossbones*, part of the 'Past Imperfect' trilogy. Chapter 4 will further explore this linguistic 'interaction' and how Italian and Somali relate in *Il latte è buono*, ideally building upon the analytical groundwork initiated in Chapter 1, wherein Cristina Ali Farah's representation of Stazione Termini in *Little Mother* was examined through the lenses of linguistic reterritorialization.

Before looking at the novels, however, an introductory section about Farah's linguistic background will hopefully help contextualize his approach to the English, Somali and Italian languages. In doing so, I argue that multilingualism features in his latest production in opposition to well-defined concepts based on linguistic hierarchies or grounded in the superior status of former colonial languages (English and Italian). Farah's use of Italian, if analysed in relation to English and Somali, prompts a revaluation of the prevailing paradigm about the use of former colonial languages in postcolonial writings, muddling and complicating concepts based on linguistic agency and (colonial) power dynamics. Specifically, *Links* and *Crossbones* confront the core idea of 'colonial' as an overarching term for domination and superiority. Instead, the novels suggest a more context-specific relationship between language and former colonial subjects, advocating for a reconsideration of the understanding of the relationship between language and those subjected to colonial influences.

Nuruddin Farah's Linguistic Background

This section delves into Farah's individual linguistic education to elucidate how his background shaped his approach to writing in the context of multilingualism. Born in Baydhabo in 1945, a city situated in the former Italian Somaliland, a hundred miles from Mogadishu, Farah's formative years were marked by an enriching linguistic exposure. He pursued his education in Qalaafe, a town under Ethiopian dominion in the Ogaadeen territory, an experience that made him, in his own words, 'virtually an Ethiopian citizen' (Jussawalla and Dasenbrock 1992, 47). During this period, he acquired proficiency in English, Amharic and Arabic from an early age. Since he could not pursue his academic education there, he moved abroad, selecting India as his destination. After a degree in philosophy, literature and sociology at Panjab University in Chandigarh, he returned to Mogadishu to work as a teacher (*ibid.*). At that time, in the mid-1970s, he wrote a novel in Somali entitled *Tolow Waa Talee, Ma!*, serialized in *Xiddigta Oktobaar* (the official government newspaper) but then discontinued due to the censorship of Siyaad Barre's regime (Mari 2018, 51). Censorship also halted a play he wrote, a satire of the cosmopolitan Somali élite of that period, akin to Edward Albee's *Who's Afraid of Virginia Woolf?* (Jussawalla and Dasenbrock 1992, 49). He then moved to the UK, where he enrolled in an MA in theatre at Essex University (1975–6) and wrote his first novel in English, *A Naked Needle* (1976). Due to the novel's alleged mockery of the dictator and its representation of the government as corrupted, while in Rome, Farah was deemed *persona non grata* and an enemy of the revolution by the Somali ambassador in 1977. In a strategic decision to evade a thirty-year prison sentence in his home country on charges of treason, Farah opted to remain in Italy. It is interesting here to note Italy's influence on Farah's work:

> I was in Italy from 1976 until October, or November 1979, working on the trilogy. […] *Sardines* underwent a great deal of change. At one point, one of the versions was wholly set in Milan.
>
> (Alden and Tremaine 2002, 43)

Farah's first trilogy, 'Variations on the Theme of an African Dictatorship', indeed shows a strong relationship with Italy and the Italian language, as extensively documented (Gorlier 1998; Vivan 1998). After a brief period between Milan and Rome, Farah relocated to Nigeria, West Germany, then to Sudan, and Uganda, finally returning to his country only for a visit in 1996, after twenty years of exile (Jussawalla and Dasenbrock 1992, 62). He then moved to Minneapolis and, settled in Cape Town, where he currently resides.

Farah's trajectory to becoming an Anglophone writer, as delineated in his biography, has been shaped by a confluence of personal decisions and circumstantial factors. Censorship, resettlement abroad, exile, university studies and the intrinsic transformation of the Somali language, which underwent transliteration into the Latin alphabet in 1972, collectively influenced his linguistic journey. Farah himself emphasizes his multilingual and cosmopolitan framework:

> AS: 'I would assume that besides Somali and English, you still think in other languages such as Arabic ... ?'
> NF: 'Arabic, and Italian, and I read French, and I read a little German, not much, and then I also have an attachment to the literatures of India because I went to university there.'
>
> (Samatar 2001, 89)

It is in this framework that we can locate the notion of 'democratic drift', Farah puts it. The term explains that, in his narrative, language functions as a tool to express ideas, themes and the protagonists' points of view (1993b, 64). Accordingly, Patricia Alden and Louis Tremaine have studied at length how the English language in Farah's novel does not aim at any 'psychological verisimilitude' or realism, but rather wishes to express the character's thoughts, and political views, and articulate their perspective, thus avoiding a singular authorial way of telling a story (1999, 157–61). Each character expresses their ideas analytically, regardless of education, psychology, age. For example, the eight-year-old daughter of Medina in *Sardines*, Ubax, gives voice to her thoughts using a well-educated adult's fluency and linguistic competence (Farah 1992, 13–14; Alden and Tremaine 1999, 161–2). In *Links*, an armed member of the militia in Mogadishu, who responds to the title of Major, and his driver, accompany the protagonist Jeebleh to his hotel. Along the way, they engage in a dialogue with him about politics, history, and identity, quoting Voltaire and mocking the supposed superiority of American modernity over Somali primitiveness (2005, 21–2).

Therefore, English may be understood as a creative tool for representing Somalia from both and outside and inside perspective, as it allows Somali characters to express themselves through a shared medium, which defines them more than the psychological insight or the verisimilitude of their social, linguistic and cultural background. In other words, English emerges as a literary language that does not aim to provide a mimetic representation of Somalis' way of speaking or Somalia's linguistic context. It suits Farah's highly erudite and analytical style to create a fictional country that for a long time has existed only in his imagination, during his exile (Alden and Tremaine 1999, 162).

When asked about the choice of English and its relation to colonialism, Farah often reiterates the idea of languages as tools to express concepts, rather than being carriers of culture. Quite remarkably, he notes that English was not *his* colonial language

(Samatar 2001, 93; NCLA 2015; Radical Books Collective 2023). For Farah, the 'ideas that carry the book' are crucial in the writing process, so the main aim of his narrative appears to be the representation of the multiple views of the protagonists. Farah's well-defined and self-aware opinion on the creative and literary use of language marks his distance from the debate on African languages that have seen authors Chinua Achebe and Ngũgĩ wa Thiong'o as foremost representatives.

It should be noted here that Farah's works always had a position somehow tangential to the main themes and aesthetics present in the novels and plays of the established triumvirate of post-independence African authors, Chinua Achebe (1930–2013), Wole Soyinka (1934–) and Ngũgĩ wa Thiong'o (1938–). Accordingly, Simon Gikandi has pointed out how Farah's literary works 'have never been imprisoned [...] by the foundational moments of African literature' (1998, 753). This is evident, for example, in Farah's departure from the thematic preferences of contemporaries like Achebe, Soyinka and Thiong'o: Thiong'o, who, in the 1970s, were inclined towards exploring post-colonial narratives through the perspective of male subjects in the aftermath of independence. Farah offered instead *From a Crooked Rib* (1970), the coming-of-age story of Ebla, a nomad girl, and her turmoil in adapting to Mogadishu's lifestyle from the countryside (Gikandi 1998, 753). At the formal level, in contrast to the prevailing trend of realism to narrate post-independence African contexts, Farah exhibited a closer affinity to the Anglo-Irish modernism as exemplified by Joyce, Beckett and Yeats (*ibid.*, 754). This departure, following Gikandi, signals Farah's distinctive literary trajectory and his willingness to engage with narrative approaches and thematic concerns beyond well-established paradigms of African contemporary authors and novels.

Regarding language, Farah shows a certain reluctance to engage with the dispute about colonial and indigenous languages, and an attempt to distance himself from it, thereby making clear his supposed non-involvement in the debate:

> NIEMI: You have very often been asked why you write in English and not in Somali. But as we know, there are strong reasons behind your decision to write mainly in English. First of all, you wrote your first novella [...] before the Somali language had a script. After the Somali orthography was established in 1972, you wrote a novel in Somali, but you ran into trouble with this novel and switched back to English. This question of English vs indigenous African languages evokes the language disputes first discussed on a larger scale [...] in Makerere in 1962. Since then, for instance, Chinua Achebe and Ngũgĩ wa Thiong'o have openly disagreed on the language question, i.e. whether African authors should or should not feel free to use former colonial languages, particularly English, in their writing. I am wondering what is at stake today in the decision to write in English rather than in Somali or another indigenous African language.
>
> FARAH: My position is obviously not taking sides. What matters in fact is not often the language, but the content of what one writes. Obviously, language matters in determining the nature of the content, but I think in the current situation in Africa sometimes it would be very, very difficult to write in

indigenous languages and remain neutral in political questions. And the reason is because, in a multi-ethnic, multi-language country like Kenya, somebody speaking a different language from Ngũgĩ might think, 'Well, are he and I of the same mental mould?' And the other thing is that there is a great deal of jingoism and national jingoism in local languages. Which obviously does not necessarily happen when you are writing in European languages.

(Niemi 2012, 330)

In fact, despite Farah's assertion of impartiality in the debate and his concerns about the supposed 'neutrality' of African languages, there appears to be an implicit concurrence with Achebe's viewpoint. Farah tacitly acknowledges that a language does not inherently encapsulate its own ethos. He implies instead that a language can function as a versatile tool, capable of representing any foreign culture, as exemplified by using English to portray Igbo culture in Achebe's novels. In his answer, Farah seems to challenge the idea of uniqueness and authenticity, supporting instead the concept of 'function' as presented by Achebe in his book of essays, *Morning Yet on Creation Day* (1975, 61–2). Function should be understood as the ability that a language possesses to adapt to the context, which depends on how the writer approaches the use of that specific language. The latter, therefore, is not considered as the bearer of a whole culture, but as an instrument the writer may use to convey cultural specificity (Ashcroft 2008, 109).

Farah's approach to language can then be understood through his biography, highlighting that his choice to use English was shaped by socio-historical and personal circumstances rather than by British colonial education like in the case of Achebe and Thiong'o. As his life shows, he attended schools in a region that, geographically, was located at the crossroad of cultures and he started writing before Somali became a written language. This latter fact implied, for Farah, the fundamental impossibility of writing in a language that had no official alphabet until 1972.[1] In this scenario, the English language, as Michael Andindilile points out, has become the foremost 'vehicle for bringing together diverse linguistic, literary, cultural and religious expressions into a genre that facilitates transnational discourse' (2014, 256). In the diaspora space, English further enhances the possibility for Farah's works to circulate globally and reach a wider audience. Nevertheless, as Gikandi has rightly noticed, 'Farah's political referent is local (his novels rarely go beyond the politics of his native Somalia); but [...] it is through intertextuality that he extends his literary and philosophical referent to make postcolonial Somali culture part of a cosmopolitan discourse' (1998, 758). As in the case of spatiality, Farah and the other diasporic authors inscribe Somalia in a global framework of literary connectivity without losing focus on the local and the national. Accordingly, the following section will explain how the Italian language, as used in *Links* and *Crossbones*, and the intertextual use of Dante's *Divine Comedy*, supports Farah's 'cosmopolitan discourse' and reterritorialize Somalia on a global position.

Speaking with an Accent: 'Inferno' and *Links*

In *Links*, the epigraph section is exceptionally rich, comprising twelve quotations by four authors. The quotations establish a complex relationship between the plot, its protagonist and the intertext, namely the source of the epigraphs. In *Links*, the latter role is played by Dante Alighieri's *Divine Comedy*, which establishes several intertextual resonances with the novel and the protagonist. This section then proposes an investigation of how Farah's intertextual practices work between *Links* and the *Comedy* to shed light on the specificity of Farah's understanding and employment of 'Inferno' but, also, to examine how the 'process of indigenization' of Dante helps draw a cross-cultural and cross-historical parallel between 1990s Mogadishu and Medieval Florence (De Luca 2020, 28).

In his poem, the Florentine poet recounts in first-person narration his allegorical journey through the three realms, to which he commits three canticles: 'Inferno' (Hell), 'Purgatorio' (Purgatory) and 'Paradiso' (Paradise). By employing the interlocking three-line rhyme scheme called *terza rima*, the *Comedy* provides a comprehensive overview of the knowledge of the Middle Ages, but also offers an understanding of Dante's worldview and vast erudition about literature, politics and religion. Born in Florence in 1265 and expelled from his city due to political reasons, Dante spent his life in exile until he died in 1321, after years of wandering and unceasing writing; in exile, he conceived most of his literary production, including his preeminent work, *The Divine Comedy* (1308–20).[2]

Fiona Moolla has rightly noticed that *Links* overturns the grounding premise of the *Comedy*: 'Dante the Pilgrim descends into Hell and discovers that it looks remarkably like his native Florence. Jeebleh, by contrast, returns to his native Mogadiscio and discovers that it looks remarkably much like Hell' (2014, 158). Moolla's comment on the two texts clearly shows that Farah does not aim to rewrite the *Comedy*. Accordingly, there are no systematic correspondences, for example, between the poem and the novel in terms of structure: while the *Comedy* is divided into three canticles consisting of thirty-three *Cantos* (34 in 'Inferno'), *Links* is made up of four parts and an epilogue, for a total of thirty-one chapters. The plot itself does not reflect Dante's symbolic journey through the three realms of the dead, nor does it embrace its allegorical scope. Ultimately, Farah jettisons several of the pivotal assumptions grounded in Dante's medieval ethos, drawn upon Christian theology and Thomistic philosophy, such as the ubiquitous role of God, the divine and rational order of the afterworld and the logic of *contrapasso*, namely the principle by which punishments are assigned.

Despite these differences, the *Comedy* emerges as the primary literary antecedent for *Links* and as a powerful source of intertextuality. According to Gérard Genette, intertextuality does not represent only 'a relationship of co-presence of one text within another', but it engages with a series of different practices within the variable system of textual analysis and interpretation (1997a, 1). In the case of *Links*, as Lorenzo Mari maintains, Farah employs intertextuality as a means to build a metaphorical-metonymic conversation between the poem and the novel through some extra-textual elements, such as the epigraphs, which are significant for its in-depth interpretation (2018, 103). The focus of this section is to show that the complex intertextual network should certainly be investigated, as Mari indicates, as a dialogue between the novel and the poem, but from the protagonist's point of view. More specifically, the *Comedy* provides the lenses through which Farah and Jeebleh address the war-torn setting of Mogadishu and Somalia, and it also represents a powerful diegetic device to support the protagonist's point of view, the latter being a Dante scholar. Indeed, Jeebleh looks at 'Inferno' as his principal source to unravel the complex skein of Somalia's reality, to grasp the events he witnessed and to describe the characters he met during his journey.

This process occurs at two levels, namely that of the author and that of the protagonist. On the one hand, Farah supports his protagonist's analytical understanding of Mogadishu's civil war by fostering a parallel between the latter and medieval Florence, thus reading the civil war scenario in Somalia with Dante's distinctive visual and narrative skills. On the other hand, he implies a degree of incommensurability between his novel and the poem by suggesting the limits of Jeebleh's perspective based on Dante's references. This practice can be retrieved in the *Comedy* as well: in the poem, even though the author is the protagonist, Dante the Poet distances himself from the character; in *Links*, this distance is paralleled (or recalled) by Farah's attitude towards his protagonist both to underscore the latter's limited perspective and to endow him 'with sufficient voice to express an understanding, particular to [him], of what it means to be human and to play roles in human communities' (Alden and Tremaine 1999, 161). In other words, the tercets from 'Inferno' aim to give, from the protagonist's point of view, 'shape and significance to the immense panorama […] of anarchy' into which Mogadishu and Jeebleh are plunged (Eliot 1923, 483). Drawing upon the imaginative richness of Dante's poem, the protagonist deciphers and interprets his experience in the city. Farah fosters this view by weaving a multifaceted thread of intratextual and intertextual connections, either allusive or explicit. At the same time, I argue that Farah also disturbs the rationale behind Jeebleh's interpretation: he prompts the readers to place his novel against the backdrop of Dante's poem, by using the latter as the primary literary resource to structure *Links* and Jeebleh's mental universe, but he also distances himself from the *Comedy*, thus attesting its insufficiency to represent present-day Somalia's condition.

The following analysis will show how this double strategy occurs, and how Farah both articulates similarities and parallels with 'Inferno', but also unsettles his protagonist's understanding by implying his one-sidedness. Specifically, Farah reveals that Dante's view is partially incomplete and inadequate to understand the realities of Somalia unless one employs different practices of intertextuality, such as subversion, simplification and recontextualization, which can be considered as key practices to elucidate the relationship between the *Comedy* and *Links*. At this point, the choice of the *Comedy* as the primary intertext could appear unclear due to the apparent differences and the necessity to modify and adapt it. However, I argue that Farah's choice to draw on Dante's poem relies on its ability to cross time, space and language through its eschatological scope and universal claim. As I will show, Farah seems interested in the political aspect of Dante's poetics and his evocative representation of Hell as the after-life equivalent of Florence.

Farah uses the *Comedy* to his advantage to represent Somalia's specific context. In 'Inferno' he finds a rich set of imaginative resources and visionary images that support his representation, dramatizing and understanding of Somalia's present-day condition, which resembles an infernal experience. In the case of *Links*, Farah looks at Dante's poem in relation to its ability to intertwine universal aspects with the local framework of medieval Florence. By invoking a universal and human condition of suffering, Farah resolves the separation between the two texts and fosters their intertextual link. Hence, the following intertextual analysis aims to stress 'interpretation rather than [...] the establishment of particular facts' between the poem and the novel, to retrieve and examine 'the cultural codes which are r (and contested) in texts' (Frow 1990, 46). Farah does not closely read the poem, denoting a lack of philological interest in retrieving the exact historical context of Dante's times (Mari 2018, 102). Likewise, instead of reclaiming the *Comedy*'s theological, teleological and allegorical scope, Farah shows interest in Dante's fictionalizations of the relationship between humans in an ill-fated time of grief and sorrow and dire political contexts.

Before examining Farah's interpretative process of the *Comedy*, I wish to highlight three aspects of the novel concerning the theme of exile, the narrator and the edition of the poem used by Farah. Concerning the first aspect, Jeebleh shares with Dante (and Farah) the same condition of exile, as Moolla has noticed (2014, 158). However, as the analysis will clarify, the quotations from Dante's poem never refer to this biographical connection, thus leaving the shared feature of exile in the background. Farah suggests, on the one hand, by presenting the Somali civil war as a modern-day Hell along with the paired comparison between Dante's Florence and 'Inferno', a profound interconnection between past and present, but also between Italy and Somalia, along with cross-cultural and cross-historical analogies. On the other hand, Farah emphasizes the need for a recontextualization, suggesting that Dante's intertext is also partly inadequate for wholly describing Somalia's contemporary reality.

This latter aspect surfaces due to the high degree of recontextualization and in a network of intertextual links encompassing several other references to Somali folktales, American television news, newspapers, films, Irish fables and the Koran. In other words, 'Although Dante's "Inferno" constitutes a prominent literary intertext of *Links*, the latter also integrates references to media representations of the war, in a way deploying them as another subtext' (Mzali 2010, 95). While the protagonist recognizes in Mogadishu an earthly Hell drawn upon Dante's description of the netherworld, Farah implies that this perspective is confined to Jeebleh's point of view. Indeed, other characters may have engaged different representations and understandings of Mogadishu and the civil war, derived from their own beliefs and cultural background. For example, in a dialogue of the novel, Farah explores three different ideas of Hell according to Jeebleh, Bile and their friend Seamus (2005, 57). The first, as shown, shares Dante's imaginative creation unfolded in 'Inferno', building a bridge between the representational level of the fictional character and the paratextual element supplied by the author. The second, Bile, draws his interpretation from the Koran, which enables a relationship between 'Hell' and 'fire' while, lastly, Seamus argues that Hell should be considered 'a state of mind' by telling an Irish fable (57).

This example, along with the limited third-person narrator, who provides the reader with the thoughts and actions of the protagonist alone, further supports the understanding of the novel as primarily focused on Jeebleh's point of view. He is the focal character and always appears on the scene so that the events of the plot are described through his perception; the reader, then, comes to know about the offstage actions when and if other characters tell them to Jeebleh once they have happened. The *Comedy* surfaces as a bridge between the 'mental universe' of Jeebleh and that of the reader, via intertextual and intratextual practices (Moolla 2014, 158). The reader, in turn, plays an active role in unravelling this multi-layered intertextuality made up of recontextualization, allusions and subversions.

An example of how the *Comedy* occupies the mental universe of Jeebleh may be found in the passage of the novel, also pointed out by John Masterson, when the protagonist himself states: 'I recited a verse from Dante's *Inferno*, in which enslaved Somalia was a home of grief, a ship with no master that was floundering in a windstorm' (Farah 2005, 193; Materson 2013, 153).[3] Farah analogizes Somalia to Italy via the metaphorical use of the 'home of grief', and the ship left adrift to deconstruct the concept of a 'failed nation' and the idea that it can be applied only to Somalia. This trans-historical analogy supports the argument that Farah employs the *Comedy* as a source that allows him to develop a universalizing process: by drawing a parallel between thirteenth-century Italy and contemporary Somalia, Farah points out the joint historical trajectories occurred by both the metropole and the so-called colonial periphery.

Finally, the third aspect concerns the issue of language. Farah used Allen Mandelbaum's English translation of the *Comedy*, instead of the original Italian version, as he acknowledged in the final 'Author's note' (335). This choice of relying on the translation, despite the familiarity with the Italian language by both Farah and the protagonist, seems to overshadow the role of Dante as a former colonial author. The latter term, in this case, should be understood as a reference to the Italian canonical authors who were employed in the 'colonial' education in Somalia since 1907 (Italian Dante Alighieri Society), as well as during the AFIS (1950–60) (Abdi 1998, 331). However, in *Links*, Farah minimizes this scholastic role of Dante by avoiding any specific reference to the Tuscan poet's presence in the colonial educational system, as instead explicitly highlighted by other Somali authors, such as Garane in *Il latte è buono* (47).

More than a colonial author imposed by the former Italian cultural supremacy in Somalia, Dante appears as a transnational model to represent human suffering, along with an extensive tradition of authors who have re-actualized and re-interpreted the *Comedy*, such as James Joyce, T. S. Eliot, Primo Levi, Osip Mandelstam and Derek Walcott. This universalizing feature of the poem is then the shared starting point to trigger the following intertextual analysis, focused on the particular and personal approach employed by Farah to adapt the *Comedy* for his purpose, as he focuses his attention on how the poem exemplifies Jeebleh's affiliation to the Italian culture, and how it represents a diegetic device to provide the symbolic background through which the protagonist experiences Mogadishu.

Concerning the epigraph, Gérard Genette defines it as 'a quotation placed *en exergue*, generally at the head of a work or a section of a work' (1997b, 144). In *Links*, the corpus of quotations of the epigraph section may be divided into two groups according to the source, location and function. Farah places three quotations from different authors before the title and after the dedication.

> If you don't want to be a monster, you've got to be like your fellow creatures, in conformity with the species, the image of your relations. Or else have progeny that makes you the first link in the chain of a new species. For monsters do not reproduce.
> MICHAEL TOURNIER

> The individual leads, in actual fact, a double life, one in which he is an end to himself and another in which he is a link in a chain which he serves against his will or at least independently of his will.
> SIGMUND FREUD

> A dog starved at his master's gate
> Predicts the ruin of the state!
> WILLIAM BLAKE

Tournier, Freud and Blake's epigraph's function 'is one of commenting – sometimes authoritatively– and thus of elucidating and thereby justifying not the text but the title' (Genette 1997b, 156). Also, they disclose the identity struggle of the protagonist, but they do not reappear as intratextual references, and they do not seem to belong to the imaginative universe of the characters. Even though interesting, they are beyond the scope of this analysis and, thus, they will not be discussed here in-depth. The quotations with a higher 'illocutionary force' are, in fact, those from Dante, which represent the primary subject of this analysis (Genette 1997b, 1). They are all taken from 'Inferno', and they share the same position, being located before each of the four parts and the epilogue.

Looking at the first four epigraphs from 'Inferno' placed before Part 1 might help us to examine the practices of subversion, simplification, allusions and recontextualization at work in the novel. The first epigraph is made up of lines 1–3 of *Canto* III:

> THROUGH ME THE WAY INTO THE SUFFERING CITY,
> THROUGH ME THE WAY TO THE ETERNAL PAIN,
> THROUGH ME THE WAY THAT RUNS AMONG THE LOST.

These words appear to Dante the pilgrim and his trustworthy guide, the Latin poet Virgil, as engraved on the gate of Hell before they cross the threshold that would allow them to enter the dark realm. Jeebleh's quotation of Dantean Hell as a 'suffering city', as explored in the first chapter, is also used to connote Mogadishu, described as 'a place of sorrow' and as 'the city of death', with clear reference to Dante's tercet (Farah

2005, 5,7). In this case, the intratextual reference between the paratext and the text via Jeebleh allows Farah to establish the literary framework in which both his protagonist and the novel are inscribed.

Accordingly, another example of the Dantean framework is the less explicit allusion that Jeebleh makes between Virgil and Af-Laawe. The latter, a suspicious character who offers to escort Jeebleh throughout the city soon after he has landed, appears in the novel as a shadow, like Virgil in the first meeting with Dante (Farah 2005, 4; Moolla 2014, 158). Jeebleh himself endorses this parallel by noticing that Af-Laawe's name means 'the one with no mouth' and that, 'to a Dante scholar', it 'might allude to the *Inferno*' (Farah 2005, 123).[4] Nonetheless, the allusion remains unclear, as there are no explicit mentions of characters or sinners lacking mouths in 'Inferno'. As in the case of the metaphors of the ship and the house, Jeebleh (and Farah) loosely employs Dante's images without precise references but as a productive and evocative reservoir that matches with the war-torn and hellish setting of *Links*. The overall vagueness and creative reuse of Dante's poem support the idea that Farah is not interested in a philological and accurate rewriting of the *Comedy*, but in reproducing the poem's ability to represent human suffering with relevant images for the Somali context.

This attention placed on the human aspect, rather than on the dogmatic features that underpin the poem, is retrieved in the second epigraphic quotation, taken from *Canto* III (lines 16–18), while the last epigraphs, from *Canto* XXIII (line 144), further buttresses the novel's cloak-and-dagger background:

> For we have reached the place …
> where you will see miserable people,
> those who have lost the good of the intellect.
> (*Canto* III)

> They said he was a liar and father of lies.
> (*Canto* XXIII)

With the latter single line, Dante describes Lucifer but Farah, discarding the context of the *Canto*, borrows the periphrasis to refer to the former dictator Siyaad Barre. As well as Lucifer, who is not mentioned in that line, Barre in the novel is present *in absentia*, and his role and ruinous legacy are only implied (Mari 2018, 104). However, Farah's reuse of the *Comedy* is anything but straightforward and it complicates our reading of *Links*. While Jeebleh explicitly foregrounds betrayal, distrust and lies as the primary factors (one could say 'sins', to retain Dante's vocabulary) responsible for Somalia's current state, he himself does not seem to be unaffected by them. For example, he tells half-truths to his wife in New York regarding his business in Mogadishu (*Links*, 178); Caloosha, the antagonist, repeatedly calls him a liar and implies that Jeebleh's mother may have died thinking him a traitor (101, 237); finally, he admits that he 'wouldn't hesitate to lie if he believed that, by doing so, he might serve a higher purpose' (48). In the end, this latter idea leads him to justify violence for justice (332). Farah dramatizes how Jeebleh becomes progressively involved in the social and moral codes of the civil war, so that, 'paradoxically, the quest for justice draws him closer and closer to the Devil' (Moolla 2014, 123). In stark contrast with *Links*, the *Comedy* does not imply that Dante's gradual descent to the icy pit of Hell parallels the pilgrim's corresponding moral corruption; quite the contrary, the sighting of Lucifer and the following departure from him represent Dante's transitioning point towards God, in line with the poem allegoric arch, which allows 'the pilgrim [to] move on and transit out' (Barolini 2018d, para. 38).

The lines from *Canto* III, instead, recontextualize the lost souls of Hell as the inhabitants of Mogadishu, thus acquiring the function of 'commenting on the text, whose meaning it indirectly specifies or emphasises' (Genette 1997b, 157). Rephrasing Dante's words, Jeebleh describes his fellow Somalis as 'dwelling in terrible misery' and as people who have lost their ability to 'remain in touch with their inner selves' (15, 70). This description, besides linking the novel and the epigraphs *intra*textually, paraphrases the word 'intellect', thus distancing it from Dante's meaning: while, in the tercet, 'intellect' means God or the Supreme Good, in the novel, it denotes the capacity to choose between right or wrong, good or evil (Sapegno 1981, 31). The harsh judgement made by Jeebleh about Mogadishu's citizens further reduces them into non-human beings who, 'living in such vile conditions, [are] bound to lose touch with their own humanity' (Farah 2005, 201). Due to the cruelty of the civil war, the spectrum of human feelings is decreased, and the inhabitants turned into 'brutes' (*Canto* XXVI, 118–20).

The third quotation of Part 1 remarks upon this condition by further developing a symbolic association between Inferno's sinners and the people of Mogadishu:

Your accent makes it clear that you belong
among the natives of the noble city … '
My guide – his hands encouraging and quick-
thrust me between the sepulchers toward him,
saying … 'Who were your ancestors?

Farah assembled the tercets himself by accurately choosing more appropriate lines from *Canto* X (25–6; 37–9; 42) to highlight Jeebleh's struggle with his belonging and the chiasm between individual and collective identity. To better elucidate this effective intertextual relation, the discursive structure of *Canto* X should be briefly clarified. In the *Comedy*, Dante and Virgil stand in the sixth circle, surrounded by open tombs engulfed by flames. Here lay the heretics, meaning by heresy the 'self-separation from' that with which we should be connected (city, God, family, friends) (Barolini 2018b, para. 56). This explanation echoes Jeebleh's statement about the inhabitants of Mogadishu, who lost the ability to live according to the rules of the society, and 'showed little or no kindness to one another' (Farah 2005, 201). In the epigraph, Farah relies on the translation 'noble city' for '*nobil patria*' (noble fatherland), thus making Dante's allusion to Florence an explicit reference to the urban context. Mogadishu's inhabitants, having restored ill-fated clan logic based on blood affiliation, are like Dante's heretics in the sense that they have become unable to either recognize or understand their fellows' sorrow, caring 'little about one another' (Farah 2005, 237).

In *Canto* X, Dante stages this self-separation through a meeting with Farinata degli Uberti and Cavalcante de' Cavalcanti, two souls described as self-centred and ignorant of each other's suffering (Musa 1995, 85). In the epigraph, the 'him' in the second to last line refers exactly to Farinata, a member of a noble family and a military leader of the Ghibellines. The meeting between him and Dante allows the poet to stage his affection for his place of origin, doomed by the struggle between the factions of White and Black Guelphs, the former supporting the Pope and the latter opposed to his influence. Following the defeat of the Ghibellines over the Guelphs at the Battle of Campaldino and at Vicopisano (1289), the Guelphs began infighting. By the turn of the century, the Florentine Guelphs underwent a schism, delineating themselves into the factions of Black and White Guelphs. The Black Guelphs continued to lend support to the Pope, while the White Guelphs opposed Papal authority, specifically contesting the influence wielded by Pope Boniface VIII. Dante aligned himself with the White Guelphs and, consequently, faced exile in 1302 when the Black Guelphs took control of Florence. Farah subtly recontextualizes the conflict between Black and White Guelphs showing Jeebleh's affliction towards the destruction of the city due to fratricidal conflicts. More specifically, Farah relocates the meeting between Dante and Farinata into the new context to draw a parallel between Florence and Mogadishu (2005, 14, 35).

Another crucial point of contact between the novel and the poem is the word 'accent'. In the *Comedy*, Farinata recognizes Dante the pilgrim thanks to his *loquela* (accent), a term that allows us to introduce a primary theme in *Links*, namely language. Both in *Canto* X and in the novel, language may be considered a 'weapon of choice' that can prevent any form of dialogue and hinder any real possibility of conversation (Barolini 2018b, para. 22). This negative feature of language stands out in the novel since Jeebleh often finds himself being misunderstood, misinterpreted or not listened to, as analysed in the previous section. Accordingly, the most suitable example to illustrate the relationship between 'accent' and 'belonging' can be retrieved in the words of Bile, Jeebleh's oldest friend:

> In Somalia the civil war then was language [...] At one point, a couple of armed men flagged me down, and one of them asked, '*Yaad tahay*?' I hadn't realized that the old way of answering the question 'Who are you?' was no longer valid. Now the answer universally given to 'Who are you?' referred to the identity of your clan family, your bloody identity!
>
> (Farah 2005, 119)

After experiencing seven years of imprisonment because of his opposition to Barre's dictatorship, Bile's statement builds a cross-cultural and multilingual link between the question in the last line of the epigraph: '*Chi fuor li maggior tui?*' ('Who were your ancestors?') and the Somali sentence '*Yaad tahay?*' (Who are you?) as referred to clan belonging.

This question, as bewildering as the resulting strenuous quest for a proper answer, distillates the subject of clannism as tackled by Somali diasporic authors. Farah has extensively explored this issue in his literary production and *Links* is no exception. In the case of Bile, concerning this issue, he:

> [...] found the correct responses in the flourish of the tongue, found them in the fresh idiom, the new argot. I was all right. I was a good mimic, able to speak in the correct Somali accent, nodding when my questioner mentioned the right acronym.
>
> (Farah 2005, 119)

Jeebleh, on the other hand, seems less keen to compromise, openly showing his hostility towards clan logics, having 'no clan-based loyalty himself – in fact, the whole idea revolted and angered him' (Farah 2005, 11). Nonetheless, he cannot avoid being questioned about his origin by other characters, such as Major, Af-Laawe, his antagonist Caloosha, and by clan elders (Mari 2018, 105). In his only consultation with the elders, Jeebleh explicitly clarifies his opinion 'of distrust of clan', continuously reiterated throughout the novel, feeling insulted by 'the way in which [they] formulated [his] identity' (128).

As mentioned, clan association is a theme not only connected to Farah. In a passage of the novel *In the Name of Our Fathers* (1996) by Abdirazak Y. Osman, the word 'accent' performs a similar role as is almost equally fictionalized. The novel unfolds the story of the seventeen-year-old Ali using a first-person narrator that immerses the reader in the first-hand experiences of the traumatic events that ultimately sparked the civil war. Ali is part of the Hawiye clan, and his father holds a prominent position as one of the co-founders of the United Somali Congress (USC), a key rebel organization in late 1980s Somalia. Established in 1989 in Rome as a response to Siyaad Barre's retaliation against the Hawiye, the USC had a pivotal role in the removal of the government in 1991, only to later fracture into various factions.

Ali is often described while roaming the streets of Mogadishu, a city on the brink of destruction, where he, nevertheless, loves to roam and spend time with his friends. When he is unwillingly involved in the armed fighting, in an attempt to run away from the violence, he meets a soldier of the militia ready to shoot him. The passage reads:

> 'Speak up!' The voice repeated. 'Who the hell are you?'
>
> The question Who are you? meant To which tribe do you belong? That was the way the question was put since the government was supposed to be against the use of tribes and tribalism.
>
> 'We are all brothers!' I yelled, just like my companion, using his dialect and courage. 'Don't you see that!'
>
> (Osman 1996, 83)

Thanks to his ability to mimic another clan's accent (Isaaq), the young Ali, as much as Bile, can escape and avoid being recognized as a Hawiye, an antagonist of the Darood during the war. Even though Abdirazak Osman does not conceal the names of the clans involved in the infighting as Farah, he shares with the latter the same distrust, as the call for brotherhood shows. In the novel, Ali is described as unconcerned about clan affiliation, but he inevitably finds himself involved in the civil war. The duplicity and ambiguity of Siyaad Barre's government towards clannism (or tribalism, as in the passage) are also highlighted. As Lorenzo Mari and Teresa Solis explains:

> Siad Barre's political action, initially inspired by the secular principles of scientific socialism, was officially based on the motto, 'Socialism unites, tribalism divides', but his regime eventually turned out to be supported by a specific inter-clan faction called 'MOD', from the initials of the three clans composing both Barre's family and government (Mareehaan, Ogaden and Dulbahante).
>
> (2017, 235)

During the early years of dictatorship, Barre adopted a socialist ideology to discourage clan associations, fostering affiliations connected, at least on the façade, to national bonds. But as his dictatorial regime became gradually more contested, he relied increasingly on his Darood clan to hold on power, and specifically on his Mareehaan sub-clan. When, in 1991, Barre managed to escape in Kenya, his forces faced defeat by the Hawiye clan. Following this defeat, Mareehaan and members of the broader Darood clan fled from Mogadishu. However, the Hawiye found it difficult to reach a consensus on power-sharing, leading to the continuation of the civil war, which saw mainly two sub-clans of the Hawiye fighting over the control of the city. As shown in the first chapter, this conflict led to the division of Mogadishu into northern and southern zones (Tripodi 1999, 138; Muthuma 2007).

Jeebleh's repulsion for clan logic isolates him from the community and causes him trouble to relate to his fellow Somalis. This generational aspect is also present in *In the Name of Our Fathers*. The protagonist Ali, throughout the novel, witnesses the negative effects of tribalism on Somali society, starting from the distancing between his generation and his father's. As he puts it:

> Young people could make fun of each other's tribe without any hard feelings at all. Actually one of my friends was called Saeed and we have him the nickname Saeed 'Marrehan' because he was the only one of our group who belonged to the Marrehan tribe. But to older people it was different. Very difference. They could kill each other for less.
>
> (Osman 1996, 69)

The gap between generations, due to clan belongings, is evident also in *Links*; in his only consultation with the elders of his clan, Jeebleh explicitly clarifies his opinion of distrust towards clan genealogy (Farah 2005, 127–8; Dodgson-Katiyo 2016, 70). Jeebleh's isolation, resulted from his feelings of unbelonging and incompatibility with social dynamics based on clans, is further emphasized through the presence of mobs. Farah represents his protagonist as the only one who stands out. As Dante the Pilgrim is the only living body among the souls, who often gather in groups or flocks, Jeebleh is excluded from his fellow inhabitants' gathering and, ironically, recognized as an outsider (Farah 2005, 16, 96, 117, 130, 135, 195–200). This is explicitly displayed in the novel, in one passage in particular: 'What distinguished [Jeebleh] from the men in the crowd, apart from the fact that he had neither a club nor a firearm, was that they were all wearing sarongs. He had on trousers' (Farah 2005, 196). The protagonist's name, too, seems to imply his distinctiveness, meaning 'the one with pockets' (95). This feature, which marks Jeebleh's position of extraneousness within fellow Mogadishans, allusively foreshadows the incommunicability reiterated throughout the novel, as it will be analysed in the following sections.

The recurrent presence of crowds leads us to another Dantean reference and to the first quotation of Part 2. Assembled by Farah himself, the epigraph combines lines 16, 19–20, 22–3 and 26 from *Canto* XIV:

O vengeance of the Lord ...
I saw so many flocks of naked souls,
all weeping miserably ...
Some lay upon the ground, flat on their backs;
some huddled in a crouch, and there they sat
... supine in punishment.

(Farah 2005, 147)

Once again, this quotation shows Farah's refusal to reassert the moral judgement placed upon the souls in Hell, as the original reference to the sins is removed. Rather than on the divine *contrappasso*, the emphasis is placed instead on the image of people suffering. In the *Comedy*, Dante and Virgil are in the third ring of the seventh circle, and the groups of souls gathered in flocks are those guilty of the three kinds of violence against God: the blasphemers, who lie on their backs; the usurers, who are crouching, and the sodomites, omitted in the quotations, who ceaselessly wander (Musa 1995, 119).

Similarly, the other quotation before Part 2, taken from *Canto* XXIV (lines 88–93), underlines a condition of suffering with more attention to the geopolitical context of the novel:

With all of Ethiopia
or all the land that borders the Red Sea –
so many, such malignant, pestilences.
Among this cruel and depressing swarm,
ran people who were naked, terrified,
with no hope of a refuge or a curse.

(Farah 2005, 147)

In *Canto* XXIV, Dante the pilgrim reaches a narrow and deep trench, where thieves are punished. The reference to Ethiopia here points to the abundant presence of serpents in the seventh *bolgia*, surpassing even the quantity of snakes found in the Ethiopian desert, conventionally considered as the place with the highest number of serpents, as Dante's source, Lucan's epic poem *Pharsalia*, attests (Barolini 2018c, para. 31). Farah omits this orientalist flavoured hyperbole and manipulates the tercet to point up the novel's geopolitical framework, with a possible reference to those displaced Somali fleeing the civil war or those who were exiled because of the war with Ethiopia (1977–8). Farah emphasizes this recontextualization by modifying the original last line, which is: 'With no hope of a hole or heliotrope', the magical stone which could supposedly heal from snake's venom and give invisibility (Sapegno 1981, 270). Thus, the 'land that borders the Red Sea' can be understood, instead of Arabia, as Somalia, which engaged with Ethiopia in an abiding territorial and political dispute over the Ogaadeen region, a territory comprising the eastern portion of Ethiopia predominantly populated by Somalis. The 'people who were naked, terrified' represent, rather than Dantean thieves, the countless displaced people of that region, who have been experiencing war for decades and have 'no hope of a refuge' and are further threatened by the civil war. While removing snakes and magical stones, Farah also aims for a more pragmatic, and less symbolical, reterritorialization of the Ogaadeen region, thus subverting the orientalizing feature that informs Dante's description (Chiavacci Leonardi 1991, 718).

While this example showcases Farah's recontextualization of 'Inferno' via paratextual elements, it might be worth noting that the transition between Part 2 and 3 occurs through an intertextual allusion unrelated to the epigraphs but strongly linked to Dante. The closing lines of Part 2 are a rephrasing of Dante's *Canto V*, as shown below:

Io venni men così com'io morisse
E caddi come corpo morto cade.

And I fell as a dead body falls
I fainted, as if I had met my death.
(*Canto* V, 141–2)

Finally he fell, forehead first, as though he were dead.
(Farah 2005, 241)

It should also be noted that Jeebleh often faints, much like Dante the Pilgrim during his journey through Hell. In the case of 'Inferno', Dante relates the loss of consciousness as a response to terrifying, distressing or overwhelming situations. This shared physiological response between Jeebleh and Dante the Pilgrim can be read as Farah's attempt to deflate the sensationalism of the representations of war as conveyed by the mass media (Mzali 2010, 93–8; Mari 2018, 100–11). As Ines Mzali has noticed, the whole novel attempts to counter the media representation of the civil war, and the military intervention from the UN and the United States, by mediating and deferring the direct spectacle of violence (2010). Hence, the recurring theme of fainting within the larger intertextual network of references should be seen as way, for

Farah, to highlighting human qualities of the protagonist and offering a reflection on the traumatizing impact of violence within a non-sensationalist approach.

The epigraph before Part 3, after the mentioned Dantean allusion, opens the third part of the novel with another reference to the inhabitants of Mogadishu. By quoting the lines from *Canto* XI (37–8; 40–1; 52–4), Farah suggests to the reader an investigation into Somaliness that underpins Jeebleh's experience:

> … Murderers and those who strike in malice,
> as well as plunderers and robbers …
> A man can set violent hands against
> himself or his belongings …
> Now fraud, which eats away at every conscience,
> is practiced by a man against another
> who trusts in him, or one who has no trust.
>
> (Farah 2005, 243)

The fact that Farah himself – once again – assembled the tercets, allowing the choice of the more relevant images to suit the novel's thematic spectrum, further supports the creative use of the *Comedy* and Farah's open process of recontextualization. In the case of *Canto* XI, Virgil exposes the structure of Hell and the different punishments, but the enumeration in the epigraph seems to suggest another all-embracing and evocative description of Mogadishans without relating them to sins and *contrappasso*.

The word 'belongings' acquires particular importance concerning the role of private property in *Links*. As Farah highlights, private houses represent a critical problem in Mogadishu, where brutal expropriations and unlawful dispossession are means to establish control over an urban area or district. In terms of this perspective, the place that Bile and Seamus call 'The Refuge' in *Links* (a self-made medical clinic as the abode for those Somalis who seek shelter) gains a symbolical value, becoming an object, or a *bene* (a material good), which needs protection from depredation and violence.[5]

Whether the quotation mentioned above refers metaphorically to the inhabitants of Mogadishu as described throughout the novel, the other quote of Part 3, from *Canto* XXVIII (lines 1–6), may be read via a specific intratextual reference. *Links*, as well as the *Canto*, is committed to unfolding the issue of how to describe and portray horror (Sapegno 1981, 308). In other words, *Links*' chapter engages with how Western neocolonial knowledge production informs the representation of Somali people.

> Who, even with untrammeled words and many
> attempts at telling, ever could recount
> in full the blood and wounds that I now saw?
> Each tongue that tried would certainly fall short
> because the shallowness of both our speech
> and intellect cannot contain so much.
>
> (Farah 2005, 243)

The acknowledgement of being unable to fully describe 'the blood and wounds' forms a common bond between Jeebleh and Dante the Pilgrim, both 'overwhelmed by the sight of mutilated, bloody shades' (Musa 1995, XXIX). Correspondingly, we encounter one of the most brutal events in the novel: the story of the 1993 American military intervention, which reached its peak in the Battle of Mogadishu. This battle resulted in the downing of two helicopters and a considerable number of casualties. Farah provides a Somali perspective on the incident, serving as a counter-narrative to the prevailing American account and offering an alternative representation that challenges the one-sided and sensationalist portrayal often found in the media (Mzali 2010, 96–8; Myers 2011, 138–9; Bystrom 2014, 413).

The lines in the epigraph, which appear at the beginning of the *Canto*, resonate in the very last part of the chapter. Jeebleh assumes the role of the listener, much like Dante when the souls in Hell share their stories, as he lets two eyewitnesses recount the terrifying incident when two Black Hawk helicopters were downed (Farah 2005, 275). Among the witnesses, a five-and-a-half-year-old girl suffered from damaged hearing because of the deafening noise of the helicopter, also making her unable to speak. The mother tells the story to Jeebleh, who reimagines the scene as she describes it. The rotating blades and their razor-sharp noise resemble the 'blade of the devil's sword' described in *Canto* XXVIII. Farah portrays Jeebleh in the act of envisioning the episode in the attempt to become a first-hand witness himself ('Jeebleh imagined'; 'Jeebleh was able to imagine' and he 'could hear the sound in his own mind', 275). However, Farah also deflates the sensationalism of the baleful account by showing Jeebleh's inability to fully fathom it ('Jeebleh stared, dumbfounded, unable to imagine the terror', 275). In this case, therefore, the epigraph underscores the diegetic bond that connects Jeebleh to Dante, with both sharing the inability to fully represent the horror.

The Epilogue further highlights this analogy between them, as Jeebleh draws his conclusion upon the political view that underpins the *Comedy* and states that 'his own story lay in a tarry of other's people tales, each with its own Dantean complexity' (331). This analogy reinforces the comparison between Mogadishu and Florence, both ravaged by a civil war fought between factions who share the same religion, Islam and Catholicism respectively, the same language and territory. Dante perceived both the pope and the Church members as morally corrupt, striving for temporal power, thus failing to fulfil the Church's sole mission of taking care of religious matters rather than secular ones. Similarly, political leaders focused on their interests, neglecting the needs of their subjects. He observed a time when both the emperor and the pope failed in their responsibilities, leading to the moral and political chaos he witnessed. In Florence and Mogadishu, the split between the two parties occurred along family lines at first; later, ideological differences arose based on contrasting views in politics and religion, with the Blacks supporting the Pope and the Whites craving more freedom from Rome. Specifically, Jeebleh's ideas recall Dante's political view as expressed in *De Monarchia* (a Latin political treatise on secular and religious power written between 1312 and 1313). With this text, Dante intervened in one of the most controversial subjects of his period: the relationship between secular authority (represented by the Holy Roman Emperor) and religious authority (represented by the Pope). In the third book, Dante condemns the theocratic conception of the power elaborated by the Roman Church, which assigned all power to the Pope, making his authority superior to that of the Emperor: this meant that the Pope could legitimately intervene in matters usually regarded as secular (Musa 1995, 162). As Dante regards unity and concord as the utmost political virtues, their opposites, division and discord, inevitably result in conflict and political instability (Barolini 2018a, para. 6).

Jeebleh seems to embrace this overall interpretation of Dante, since religion and politics are accountable for the current hard reality of Somalia. By considering religious leaders among the actors who ignited the civil war, *Links* proposes a universalizing comparison between two usually antithetical cultural systems. The faults that Dante ascribes to the religious leaders of Christianity are re-centred onto the religious leaders of Islam, who share with the former the same longing for temporal power to the detriment of transcendental, or spiritual, concerns. Religious and clan elders are to be blamed for the collapse of the state and the betrayal of their fellow Muslim Somalis, as he thoroughly explains:

> Jeebleh thought of how the country had been buried under the rubble of political ruin, and how Somalis woke to be betrayed by the religious men and the clan elders who were in cahoots with a cabal of warlords to share the gain they could make out of ordinary people's miseries. The clan elders got their reward in corrupt gifts of cash; the religious elders, turning themselves into cabaret artists, conned the rest of the populace, as they carved an earthly kingdom for themselves.
>
> (Farah 2005, 331)

Jeebleh's understanding of the Somali context regarding religious and political power is then drawn upon Dante's idea, and supported in the Epilogue, when he explicitly refers to Dante to read Mogadishu's dire reality. However, when *Links* concludes, the plot lacks a proper denouement, thus suggesting a difference between the poem and the novel. The story's main events – the kidnapping, the following release of Bile's niece and the death of his arch-enemy Caloosha – happen without Jeebleh being present. Furthermore, he looks less resolute than after his arrival, in a sort of inverse trajectory to that of Dante the pilgrim. Accordingly, the line that rapidly closes the last epigraph of the novel, from *Canto* XX (124–6; 130), pairs the quickness of Jeebleh's departure from Mogadishu, as shown below:

> But let us go; Cain with his thorns already
> is at the border of both hemispheres
> and there, below Seville, touches the sea.
> … Meanwhile we journeyed.
>
> (Farah 2005, 334)

> Jeebleh quit Mogadiscio the following morning, without changing his clothes. […] He left before the mist in his mind cleared, afraid that he might alienate his friends, to whom he owned his life. He left as soon as he sensed the sun intruding on the horizon of his mind.
>
> (Farah 2005, 334)

The final lines of the novel rework Dante's extensive astronomical periphrasis that expresses the moment of sunrise, when the moon reaches the horizon and is about to descend, at 6 am, the times of Jeebleh's departure. After days spent in Mogadishu, Jeebleh leaves as he senses the sun intruding his mind, a symbolical connotation that might relate to insight and understanding. The enigmatic closing lines mark the distinctive indeterminacy of the novel and deflate the 'classic denouncement [...] where the narrative ascribes deeds to doers' (Mzali 2010, 100). At the end of the story, Jeebleh appears confused and insecure, as Dante's pilgrim at the start of his journey. In this sense, Farah subverts the beginning of the *Comedy* by representing his protagonist as 'lost, unable or unwilling to decide which road to follow' (as the pilgrim who 'had lost the path that does not stray') (333). It seems that, in the end, Jeebleh requires a guide, a role that this time Dajaal performs, offering to accompany him, holding him by the elbow and showing him the way. Like Dante the Pilgrim with Virgil, during his first steps in the unknown territory of the afterlife, Jeebleh cannot but 'silently follow' his guide (333).

The recurring use of lines from 'Inferno' to depict Mogadishu suggests that Dante's *Comedy* emerges as a powerful meta-textual reference that links and encompasses experiences, languages and traditions coming from distinct cultural and historical backgrounds. The importance of the Italian poet, as shown in the case of Farah, also emerges in other Somali authors of the diaspora. Even though less extensively and less constructively than Farah's intertextual network, they employ the *Comedy* as an evocative parallel that might sound immediately familiar to Italian readers.

Igiaba Scego, for example, in her novel *La mia casa è dove sono* (*Home Is Where I Am*) quotes Dante to describe the sense of the protagonist for a neighbourhood of Mogadishu:

> I liked via Roma with its little shops, I liked the livestock market in Wardhingleey, and I liked that sort of circle of Dante's *Inferno* that was Buur-Karoole in Xamar Ja-jab, a place where it was easy to bump into alcoholics drunk.
>
> (2010, 29)

Likewise, in *Adua*, Scego refers to Italian as 'Dante's language' ('la lingua di Dante') and the Florentine poet himself is quoted explicitly by one of the protagonists, Mohamed Ali Zoppe, who repeats by heart the lines that appear on the threshold of Hell in 'Inferno' (2019, 16, 41). In Garane's *Il latte è buono*, the *selva oscura* (shadowed forest) recurs as a leitmotiv that can be read as 'a poetic illustration of Gashan's disorientation during the coup-d'état in Mogadishu' and of his alienation during his time in the United States (De Luca 2020, 35). As analysed in the previous chapter, however, Gashan also experiences a sense of confusion and bewilderment when he returns to Mogadishu and feels a sense of 'spatial perplexity' in front of the ruins of his hometown (Tally 2013, 1). In the following chapters, these references to Dante will be further explored, with specific attention to *Adua* and *Il latte è buono*.

As in Farah's *Links*, but with less punctual references and details, 'Inferno' and Dante the Poet/Pilgrim are part of how characters and narrators describe Somalia and their personal relationship to it, especially concerning the altered spatiality of the capital city. Dante's presence in their novels, therefore, both through his personal experience of exile and his vast and evocative imaginary of sorrow and desolation as depicted in 'Inferno' become part of a strong intertextual network that connects authors and texts within the diaspora. Despite Dante's embodiment of Italianness and being the epitome of the Italian literary tradition, Somali authors appropriate his literary work and make him 'a fellow witness to the divisiveness of human life everywhere' (De Luca 2020, 44). In this regard, the following chapter aims to explore how Garane recontextualizes Dante and the Italian language and places them in dialogue within a network of intertextual references made of Somali language and orature.

The Italian Language in *Links* and *Crossbones*

Being an author who predominantly writes in English, Farah has been overlooked by scholars of *Italianistica*, even though his contribution to the enrichment of Italian (postcolonial) literature has been – and still is – crucial. Due to his way of recovering and dramatizing the Italian colonial past and its legacy in Somalia, he should be included in the conversation around the problematic definition of Italianness that, with respect to the African occupation, is still defined in the public sphere according to the idea of *brava gente*. In fact, as Claudio Gorlier observed, Farah's narrative endeavours extend beyond the fictionalization of Italy's colonial history. In *Sardines*, he directly engages with the Italian *Sessantotto* (Sixty-eight), a period marked by youth and student-led protests advocating for the working class and guided by Marxist-Leninist ideology (1998, 784). A few studies, however, have addressed the Italian presence in Farah's novels (Gorlier 1998; Vivan 1998; Weinberg 2013). Their contribution, though fundamental, is limited to the trilogy 'Variations on the Theme of an African Dictatorship' (1979–83), except for Christopher Fotheringham's recent work (2019a) that, however, is more focused on the receptions of Farah's *oeuvre* through translations over time.

The influence of the abovementioned scholars has been essential in the Italian studies since they have raised the issue of the legacy of the Italian colonial past through the literary work of an author who does not belong to the canon of Italian literature. One shared key topic of their articles is the complex role that the Italian language played in the making of Somali identity and its ambivalence of being both the tool of colonial domination and of cultural empowerment for the Somali urban middle-class of the 1960s and 1970s. Their works reflect on Farah's employment of Italian words and expressions, which informs Somalia's 'unusual relation to the culture of colonialism' and 'the multiplicity of its cultural and historical influences' (Gikandi 1998, 753). For instance, Claudio Gorlier surveys the Italian words in Farah's early production to highlight his linguistic approach towards the former colonial language. Itala Vivan suggests an intriguing intertextual relationship between *Sweet and Sour Milk* (1979) and Leonardo Sciascia's novels, which Farah arguably used as narrative models for structuring the plot and outlining the main theme, namely the 'useless quest for truth' in a context of dictatorship and censorship (1998, 789). Grazia S. Weinberg, through Homi Bhabha's concepts of hybridity and liminality, investigates the relationship between the protagonist of *Sardines* (1981), Medina, and her multiple belongings. Weinberg maintains that Medina 'identifies neither with the colonized nor with the colonizer', thus occupying an in-between position between the two (2013, 41).

Nevertheless, even though these scholars have contributed to expanding Italian literary studies beyond national borders, the analysis of the Italian language in Farah's novels has been neither revised nor updated, thus overlooking if and how his use of Italian has changed over time. To reassess the previous critical debate around this subject, this section proposes a new investigation on the role of the Italian language in Farah's late production and, particularly, in the novels *Links* and *Crossbones*, part of the 'Past Imperfect' trilogy. In doing so, it aims to question the dichotomy between colonial and local languages, since Farah questions general theories and concepts fashioned by postcolonial scholars regarding the use of a colonial language. As the analysis will show, Farah systematically employs words and expressions in Italian in the same way African writers employed their native language *against* the colonial language, such as with the use of italics and untranslated words, in novels such as *Things Fall Apart* (1954) by Chinua Achebe or *The Voice* (1968) by Gabriel Okara. The main point here is that, in the case of *Links* and *Crossbones*, and according to the multilingual context of Somalia and Farah's biography, the opposition between colonial and native languages is not binary, as more than two 'colonial' languages come into play.

Since Farah writes in English, he employs unglossed or untranslated words in both Italian *and* Somali, thus upsetting fixed categories and blurring the line between colonial and postcolonial linguistic strategies. In doing so, in his late production, Farah does not underscore the idea of Italian as a former colonial language but proposes a more nuanced approach that prompts questions of belonging and identity along a different axis than the one between colonizers and colonized. As the analysis will show, in *Links* and *Crossbones*, the Italian language shifts from being the cause of inclusion-exclusion as in *Sardines* (1981) to a *lingua franca*.[6] In this regard, if we consider the 'Variations on the Theme of an African Dictatorship' trilogy (1979–83), Italian has an ambiguous role – a love-hate relationship – being considered as both a remnant of the colonial past and a means to cultural and social enrichment (Gorlier 1998, 783; Vivan 1998, 786).

In the 'Past Imperfect' trilogy (2003–12), the use of Italian turns out to be peripheral – but not incidental – in the setting of the 1990s and early 2000s. After the 1970s, Somalia witnessed a decrease in its 'linguistic links with Italian' due to endogenous factors, such as the status of the official national language acquired by *Af Soomaali* (Somali language) after Siyaad Barre's linguistic policies (Gorlier 1998, 783). Regarding the former Italian-ruled territories in the South, colonial education supported the main aims of exploitation and suppression of colonized subjects since its inception in Somalia. If we consider the first period of the Italian occupation, at the beginning of the twentieth century, it must be noted that the Dante Alighieri Society opened the first school to teach Somali children the Italian language in 1907. However, the highest scholastic level set for Somalis was grade 7, thus preventing them from attaining the same instruction as the Italians. Naturally, this type of education was functional to the purposes of imperialism, which aimed to train low-level cultured locals to perform simple tasks, thus preventing them to achieve the same level of education of the Italians (Hussein 1988).

During Fascism and following the promulgation of the *Leggi Razziali* (Racial Laws, 1938–43), Somalis faced exclusion from the educational system and were physically barred from 'white' spaces (Abdi 1998; Duale 2004). While Italian governors were interested in training Somalis to become farmers or unskilled workers, the British in the North needed Somalis who could help in the colonial administration to maintain law and order. Due to the Italian policies of land exploitations, the number of Somali people who had the opportunity to receive a proper education was then minimal in the South (Hoben 1988, 404). To further complicate the scenario, according to geopolitical influences, every Somali region adopted a different language for its own educational system. At the time of independence, in July 1960, there were three main languages taught in schools: Italian, English and Arabic, the latter being used in Qur'anic *madrasas*. Further complicating the educational effort was that Somali became a written language only after 1972. Before that period, in 1954 – during the AFIS – the Italian government cooperated with Somali institutions in building a university system, so that in 1969 The Somali National University (in Italian: *Università Nazionale Somala*), based in Mogadishu, was born, as part of a project of the Italian Ministry of Foreign Affairs (MAE). Italian was chosen as the primary language of instruction, before introducing Somali and English as additional languages of teaching. From 1973 onward, during the first years of Barre's regime, Somali language courses sprang up throughout the country while English and Italian started to be uprooted. The language of instruction in primary and secondary schools also became Somali, trying to balance out the system all over the country in the name of Somalization (Hussein 1988).

In the wake of the civil war, university courses were suspended due to the rising difficulties of holding classes and acquiring books. The same fate occurred to the entire educational system, which dissolved during the civil war. The lack of a well-established Italian educational system contributed to dim the influence of Italian in Somalia, to the advantage of English, which was already spoken in British Somaliland. Accordingly, in *Links*, set during the civil war, the presence of the Italian language marks this decrease. Italian, instead of playing the role of the colonial language, thus splitting the identity of the colonized into two conflicting selves, serves to contextualize the cultural boundaries inhabited by the main characters, two well-educated Somalis who had the chance to study in Italy. Other factors, more relevant than the Italian language and cultural reference, impact the protagonists' struggle to assess their idea of Somaliness in the new civil war context.

To investigate this issue and read the decline of the Italian presence against a sociopolitical and historical backdrop, I analyse the ways in which Italian informs *Links* and *Crossbones*. Farah uses unglossed Italian words and expressions which can be grouped into three main categories. For practical reasons, it could be useful to list them, in what could be considered an attempt to draw up an Italian catalogue of *Links* (see Appendix). The first category comprises single words and short expressions usually emphasized in italics and never translated; the second includes mostly proper names; the third involves sentences that generally refer to Italy or Italian culture. I decided not to focus only on the Italian words in the narrow sense, but rather to embrace any references to the Italian background to better understand the multidirectional relationship between language, characters and the latter's cultural milieu.[7]

If we compare this list to the previous catalogue that Claudio Gorlier drafted in relation to the Italian words present in *A Naked Needle* and in the 'Variations on the Theme of an African Dictatorship' novels, one first observation is that the Italian words recur less frequently (1998, 782–3). The presence of fewer Italian references in the context of Somalia during the civil war marks a historical turning point in Somalia as they underline a gap between the present-day generation (born in the post-independence period) and the old one, namely the one of the main Somali characters, Jeebleh and Bile, who witnessed the AFIS and the democratic period. Both Jeebleh and Bile studied in Italy, when the latter was elected to conduct Somalia to independence and was seen as a valuable destination to study and have a working career. Ambiguity denoted the AFIS period, since Italy revealed both its interest in guiding Somalia towards its independence following the UN agenda and a nostalgic attachment to colonial practices. It kept managing and controlling Somalia's economy and running the administration of the country, thus preventing Somalis from taking sovereignty in governing their newborn nation (Del Boca 1984; Calchi Novati 1999, 2011; Tripodi 1999). After the AFIS, the relations between Somalia and Italy did not cease, thereby allowing Somalis to study in Italian universities, such as those of Padua or Rome. These two academic institutions were deeply involved in developing a higher education system in Somalia at that time. Italian, however, started to lose its relevance as the main medium of education, despite the presence of the university:

> After 1960 the Ministry of Education sought to turn all elementary schools into four-year programs, followed by four years each of intermediate and secondary schooling. It was decided that English should eventually replace Italian as the medium of instruction in the third year of primary school.
> (Cassanelli and Abdikadir 2008, 97)

In the different context of civil war Somalia, with the erasure of any educational systems and institutions, the presence of Italian survives in the older generation, as present-day Somalis are not directly affected by colonialism or its legacy. On the contrary, the generation of Jeebleh, and his lifelong friend Bile – but also his mother Hagarr – grew 'following a custom which has seen many Somalis […] furthering their studies in Italian institutions' (Weinberg 2013, 31).

In *Links*, the narrator informs the reader about this cultural link mentioning explicitly that they all attended university in Padua and Rome (Farah 2005, 170). However, the list of Italian words also shows that the remnants of colonialism do not surface only in education, but also in bureaucracy and food (see Group 3 in the Appendix). Besides signalling a shift in the sociopolitical context of Somalia, Italian words such as *arrivederci*, cultural references such as *Fellini's 8 ½*, Fiat cars and the tower of Pisa, or interjections, such as *Che maledizione!* (see Groups 1 and 2 in the Appendix), provide contextual specificity for Jeebleh, Seamus and Bile, who are distinguishable from other characters because of 'the formulas and conventions of the particular [...] language' they all know (Alden and Tremaine 1999, 161). The fact that they could speak Italian locates them in a different position from, for example, Caloosha, the antagonist of the novel, or Af-Laawe, Jeebleh's malevolent and sly guide through Mogadishu. In other words, whether Farah uses English to describe the intellectual debate in his novels, he also aims to give his characters 'psychological verisimilitude' through the Italian language (Alden and Tremaine 1999, 160). These two tendencies coexist in *Links* and while Farah continues, on the one hand, to organize his novels following a narrative of inclusiveness (given by the English language), on the other hand, by using Italian he pays attention to convey a precise sociocultural characterization of the protagonists (Wright 1990, 17).

In relation to the connection between language and identity, Italian words also mark a shift. Whereas in the previous trilogies Italy showed its influence as the former colonial power through toponymy and cultural affiliation, in *Links* and *Crossbones* the United States appears as the latest emblem of the neocolonial global dynamics. If, after the AFIS, Italy was one of the superpowers in a dominant position along with the United States, the UK and the USSR, in the 1970s and 1980s it progressively lost its role and influence. The primary cultural references for the young Somalis of the 1990s and the 2000s, as shown in the novels, are definitively global, coming from American movies, Bollywood, the internet, such as from YouTube videos, and international magazines (*Links*, 274, 294; *Crossbones*, 8, 9, 21, 127).

In *Links*, Jeebleh recalls his youth spent in Italy with bittersweet nostalgia, as a period of hopes and promising expectations, both for him and Somali people (see Group 3 in the Appendix). Against the unfortunate turn of events in his own country, Jeebleh depicts his life in Italy as bohemian, and reminisces anecdotes from his university years (*Links*, 82). When the protagonists' memories and recollections are connected to Italy, an overall tone of wistfulness denotes them (Farah 2005, 80-7, 191). In *Crossbones*, Farah succinctly encapsulates this feeling: 'Jeebleh is back now to the remote past, where he pays a nostalgic visit to his and Bile's childhood and revisits his student day in Italy' (Farah 2012, 82).

A true enthusiast of *spaghetti all'amatriciana*, the protagonist's association with the Italian language emerges as marked neither by the engagement with nor by the burden of colonialism. In *Links*, the latter remains implicit and is not met by Jeebleh with the same internal conflict as Medina faces in *Sardines*. In her case, her relationship to Italian culture and language is not characterized by assimilation, as in the case of Gashan in *Il latte è buono*, but by an in-between state of both inclusion and exclusion (Weinberg 2013, 38). It does represent, a *lingua franca* or the common ground where Jeebleh's friendship with Bile and Seamus is sustained. Tellingly, Jeebleh describes their friendship as 'a country – spacious, giving, and generous' and it can be argued that the prominent language spoken in this imagined country is Italian, as Jeebleh himself remembers that 'the last time they met they used Italian' (*Links*, 57, 185).[8]

It should be noticed, then, that Farah's use of the Italian language has followed the thematic shift in his works, from the concerns about dictatorship to the post-independence configuration of nationhood and the national collapse. From 'Variations on the Theme of an African Dictatorship' (1979–83) to 'Blood in the Sun' (1986–98), Farah has moved the thematic centres of his novels from 'the problematics of decolonisation and nationalism to [...] those of self-rule' (Wright 1990, 122). This shift accompanies a different discursive practice, particularly towards Italian, to mirror Somalia's changed geopolitical situation. This does not mean that a clear line separates different periods, but rather that they are interconnected, unsolved and blended, as the adjective 'imperfect' of the title's trilogy implies (Mari 2018, 15).

The shift between the earlier and the later works is more visible if we compare the experiences of Jeebleh to that of Medina, the protagonist of *Sardines*. Both pursued their academic careers in Italy and returned to Somalia after their studies abroad. However, while Medina inhabits the so-called 'third space' theorized by Homi Bhabha, namely the displacement induced by the feeling of being both a native and an outsider due to the familiarity with the former colonial language and culture, Jeebleh does not feel the same uncertainty related to identity, in spite of a similar experience towards Italy (Bhabha 2004, 55; Farah 2005, 53–6). Medina's in-between condition differs from Jeebleh's position, which results from neocolonial dynamics in which the United States and his American affiliation play the leading role. In this sense, *Links* questions and fictionalizes the power of a dominant culture, the American one, in creating, controlling and distributing knowledge and images of Somalia. As the previous section has examined, Farah directly engages with the Operation Gothic Serpent (3–4 October 1993) and challenges the dominant narrative about the military intervention produced by the American media, in direct conversation with the Academy Award-winning film *Black Hawk Down* (2001) and Mark Bowden's non-fiction book of the same name (Myers 2011, 138–9).

Jeebleh's problematic process of identification and belonging to different cultures is played out in the domain of language. Rather than Jeebleh's fluency in Italian or his knowledge of Dante, his Somali language, passport and American citizenship trigger his identity-related turmoil and his exclusion from the clan-based community (Farah 2005, 9, 32–6). Whereas Medina finds herself split between her Somali heritage and her acquaintance with Italy, Jeebleh struggles with his American nationality. For example, he repeatedly asks himself how to express his feelings about the United States, concluding that he cannot say he loves his host country, being only 'engaged with America' (Farah 2005, 42). Even though he considers New York as his home, he doubts he 'would use the word "happy" to describe [his] state of mind there' (266). Similarly, the novel makes no references to his life in the United States, and almost nothing is revealed about his family, job, house or everyday life. Jeebleh seems to embody the idea that diasporic subjects 'have little or no mixing with their country of adoption' (Bradatan, Popan and Melton 2010, 176–7). It may be considered diasporic towards America, since his emotional life appears more connected with Somalia than his host country (Bradatan, Popan and Melton 2010, 169–78). At the same time, his relationship towards Italy seems closer and more emotional, even though, at the time of the story, it is linked to the past.

As the presence of the words and references to Italy show, Farah gives the reader more information about the time spent by Jeebleh in Padua and Rome, decades earlier, than about his current life in New York, which randomly surfaces about his wife and daughter (mostly absent from the novel if not for a very few allusions). Also, instead of negotiating his belonging between his Italian and Somali identities, Jeebleh struggles with his affiliation to clan ideology and the traditional culture it endorses, dubbed as backward (*dhaqan hiddo*). As the whole third chapter of *Links* shows, Jeebleh experiences the condition of being constantly interrogated about his Somali and American belongings, both by Somalis in Mogadishu, and by Americans in New York, who assume that he has arrived recently as a refugee. As Jeebleh himself states, his relationship with the adopted country is far from serene and more troubling than his connection to the former metropole: 'I was fed up being asked by Americans whether I belonged to this or that clan' and, similarly, he remarks that it is 'irritating to be asked by people at the supermarket which clan I belong to' (*Links*, 36).

As analysed in the first chapter, at the beginning of the novel, Jeebleh has trouble with his identity at the airport when the police officer does not recognize his Somali passport at the documents check. According to Dodgson-Katiyo, 'characters who return to Somalia from the West do not necessarily move from "the comfort zone" into "a chaotic situation", since they have problems in the comfort zone' too (2016, 72).[9] In these movements across countries and cultures, language poses its own problems, inciting Jeebleh's feelings of displacement and misunderstanding. Bile as well, who never left, affirms that in 'Somalia the civil war then was language', addressing his exclusion from the new order imposed by the civil war ('[...] only I didn't speak the new language') (Farah 2005, 119). Similarly, Jeebleh often finds himself in the condition of being misinterpreted: he has difficulties in translating Somali expressions into English, as in the case of *dagaalka sokeeye* (civil war) (Farah 2005, 137–8). As Lorenzo Mari has noticed, Jeebleh struggles with the use of Somali pronouns, trapped in the uncertainty between 'we' and 'they' to mean Somalis in general or the clans, respectively (Farah 2005, 12, 41, 219; Mari 2018, 53, 85–7). He recognizes that the civil war has created its own vocabulary and has accordingly shaped the language, as examined regarding the airport spatiality and the traumatic event that Jeebleh experiences once he lands in Somalia (Farah 2005, 4–5).

All the linguistic barriers that Jeebleh faces are not caused by the Italian language: English and Somali, instead, function as a means of exclusion and inclusion, and work in parallel with his multiple belongings. *Links* seems to portray the challenging issue of diasporic identities, in which both 'language and gesture need to adapt to a different context' without being completely accepted, either at home or abroad (Bradatan, Popan and Melton 2010, 176). To be identified as a Somali, Jeebleh must practise his Somaliness and understand that the civil war context requires a new set of actions and behaviours according to the social actors involved. *Links*, in this sense, encompasses all the nuanced identity-related possibilities of someone who, like Jeebleh, feels alienated and displaced more than being comfortable with more nationalities (Niemi 2012, 336).

The sense of displacement that Medina feels in *Sardines* presents a crucial difference from the one described in *Links* about Jeebleh: on the one hand, Medina's in-between situation is brought on by the dichotomy of having acquired the culture of the colonizers and being a colonized subject, while simultaneously being neither of those things. The Italian language, in Medina's case, represents the emblem of her cultural hybridity and, in terms of identity, shapes her liminal position across two nations that have been in hierarchical positions (metropole: colony). On the other hand, Jeebleh's uprootedness does not result from his experience in the former colonial country, because, in his case, Italian 'functions […] as an identity-grounding home under a condition of displacement' (Bammer 1994, 15). Jeebleh's relationship with language has upset old power dynamics, introducing a third element into the equation, the United States as the most predominant neocolonial power, along with his problematic relationship with the clan-based system, which makes him feel like a stranger in his own country. As shown, the Italian language embodies a *lingua franca* through which his friendship with Bile and Seamus developed, and the language of his studies and of Dante's *Comedy*, which he uses as a literary referent to make sense of the national collapse.

However, Farah does not hesitate to underscore Italy's illegal activities in Somalia and its role as a neocolonial power. In *Crossbones*, set almost ten years after *Links*, Farah seems more focused on the legacy of the Italian government's involvement with Barre than on retrieving colonial history. Accordingly, at the linguist level, *Crossbones* marks a further decrease of Italian words, so that the only references to the Italian language are the spelling of Mogadishu ('Mogadiscio'), proper names such as Padre Colombo, Brigate Rosse or Istituto Universitario L'Orientale di Napoli, and the interjection '*Basta!*' ('Enough!') (*Crossbones*, 59, 319, 314, 273). This reduction emphasizes the marginal position that now Italy has in relation to Somalia, explicitly showing that the socio-cultural influence of the former metropole from colonialism to the 1970s has vanished in the 2000s. According to the changed geopolitical dynamics that witnessed the diminished influence of Italy, Farah makes clear that the civil war, along with the buildings, has erased the capital city's past and its cosmopolitan features:

> In Mogadiscio the cathedral was razed to the ground in the general mayhem at the start of the civil war, but here in Djibouti the synagogue stands as testimony to peace. One of the first victims of the Somali strife was an Italian, Padre Salvatore Colombo, who lived in Mogadiscio for nearly thirty years as the head of the Catholic Church-funded orphanage, one of the oldest institutions in the city. More recently, a Shabaab operative desecrated the Italian cemeteries, digging up the bones and scattering them around. To Ahl, the presence of a synagogue in a country with a Muslim majority is a healthy thing: cities, to qualify as cosmopolitan, must show tolerance towards communities different from their own. Intolerance has killed Mogadiscio.
>
> (Farah 2012, 59)

It is interesting to notice here that the cathedral, built by Italian colonial authorities in the late 1920s, defined for a long period Mogadishu's cityscape and was 'the most prominent monumental legacy of De Vecchi's governorship' and the emblem of Italy's civilizing mission in Somala (Mohamed 2023, 8–9). Padre Salvatore Colombo, the last Bishop of the Diocese of Mogadishu, was murdered in the cathedral by an unknown assassin in 1989 and this event symbolically marked the beginning of that period of violent chaos from which Somalia has yet to fully recover. At the time of *Crossbones*, in the early 2000s, the cathedral has not been used for decades. In Jeebleh's view, its ruins, a few standing walls with no roof, exemplify the intolerance for other cultures and religions. A parallel is suggested between Somalia and Djibouti, where this intolerance seems to be weaker, as shown by the presence of a synagogue (even though Jeebleh finds out later that the place is abandoned and not used as a place of worship anymore, 60).

In Mogadishu, with the old building destroyed, the toponymy once dominated by Italian references has been erased and, language, too, has undergone the same destruction, disappearing in the new scenario. The collapse of the nation-state and the neocolonial order in which Somalia is embroiled have changed the relations of power. Islam now plays a more substantial role than before and appears, in Farah's writing too, as 'a self-evident, and integral part of the Somali' present (Kapteijns 2013, 43). According to the mimetic stylistic use of the language we have seen in *Links*, Farah shifts his use of Italian to reflect the historical moment in which the novels are set. Indeed, once again Italian surfaces only in the old generation of Somali people who grew up when the former colony was still influential at cultural, political and economic levels. As the civil war made a *tabula rasa* both of Mogadishu and Somalia, the memory of the (Italian) past has been collectively lost and it survives at the individual level, in the recollections of the old generation who witnessed those times.

One example is Dhoorre, a secondary character who dreams about Vittorio De Sica's *Shoeshine* (1946) and recalls, nostalgically, the 'mesmerizing beauty of the camera work as it captured the two boys riding a horse through Rome' (48). The beauty of his memory is then overshadowed by the tragic reality of Mogadishu, 'a city with no innocence', where 'every resident [...] is guilty, even if no one admits being a culprit' (48). This idea echoes Jeebleh's view of the civil war, as the previous section has shown, via Dante's *Comedy*.

The other character who marks the Italian presence in *Crossbones* is Kala-Saar, a professor with a doctorate from Orientale University in Naples who 'has the habit of peppering his Somali with foreign terms in Italian, Arabic or English' (Farah 2012, 314).[10] About Kala-Saar, who represents the old generation of Somalis who studied abroad during the AFIS or in the early post-independence days like Jeebleh, it is noteworthy that Farah introduces him using an ironic tone, to encourage a parody of a know-it-all professor, as in the following:

> A no-cooking bachelor, Kala-Sarra appreciate good tables; he is the rounder of guests at tables, invited whenever there aren't interesting men, or when a single woman is visiting town and there is no other man to invite.
>
> (*Crossbones*, 314)

It should be noticed, however, that while in *Sweet and Sour Milk* Farah compares Siyaad Barre to Benito Mussolini, stressing the continuity between the colonial dynamics and their equivalent in Somalia's dictatorship, in *Crossbones*, Professor Kala-Saar draws another comparison that foregrounds similarities between Italy and Somalia.

> Kala-Saar chews awkwardly, as though his front teeth are wobbly and of little use. He speaks with his mouth half-full and spits bits of food in all directions. 'I might approve of Shabaab if their actions were likely to bring about change – a change towards a better society. They are not. They are good at disrupting, not at constructing anything. Like the Brigate Rosse. I lived in Italy when they terrorized that country. I do not approve of destructive methods.
>
> (Farah 2012, 318–19)

Al-Shabaab is equated, not without problems, to the Italian far-left armed group Brigate Rosse (Red Brigades). Operating as a terrorist and guerrilla group, they were responsible for several violent incidents, including the abduction and murder of former Prime Minister Aldo Moro in 1978. According to him, what these groups have in common is that they fight for sectional interests and not for national ones. Even though this comparison sounds far-fetched and is implicitly downplayed by the overall description of Kala-Saar as a pontificating conceit, it nonetheless emphasizes the presence of Italy in the cultural horizons of a certain generation of Somali people.

Conclusion

Through an analysis of the relationship between language and characters, narrative strategies and historical contexts, this chapter has addressed the nuanced discursive practices of *Links* and *Crossbones*. Farah's novels, indeed, disclose a connection between Somali and Italian culture beyond the colonial influence. By incorporating Italian words, distinctively set apart in italics within the English text, Farah reproduces different verbal levels and prevents the homogenization of the multilingual Somali context. Furthermore, the analysis has interpreted Farah's discursive strategy as a marker of sociopolitical and historical shifts in Somalia: Italy progressively lost its influence on the former colony and has become relevant only to generations of Somali who lived through the AFIS, the democratic period and the early revolutionary period. For them, Italy still represented a springboard for the aspirations of young intellectuals or urban bourgeoises. As Claudio Gorlier has noticed by analysing the Farah's first trilogy, 'Somalia's linguistic links with Italian are being severed' (1998, 783). This gradual disconnection from Italian influence is perceptible in both *Links* and, more markedly, in *Crossbones*. In these novels, Italian is telescoped into a solid English linguistic framework, serving as a more artistic and impartial tool to connect characters from different nationalities and languages (Jeebleh, Bile and Seamus).

By focusing on the character of Jeebleh and drawing comparisons with Medina, protagonist of *Sardines* (1981), the analysis has shown how Italian does not play a significant part in the struggle for belonging as it did during the 1960s and 1970s. In the mid-1990s, Jeebleh is questioned about his American citizenship and Farah, accordingly, fictionalizes this problematic interplay not between Jeebleh and his Italian affiliation, but between Jeebleh's cosmopolitan idea of identity and clan ideology. In this struggle for belonging played on the ground of language, however, Dante's *Divine Comedy* assumes significance, serving as a literary intermediary connecting historically distinct yet symbolically analogous realities. Because of the thematic and structural intertextual references, Farah's novel can be considered 'an allegorical rewriting of […] and a commentary on Dante's *Inferno*' (Dodgson-Katiyo 2016, 71). The poem, however, more than being considered as the Italian text *par excellence* and the cultural epitome of Italian colonial education, emerges as a fruitful literary intermediary and intertextual source. Indeed, the extensive use of the *Comedy*, and of 'Inferno' in particular, occurs in the English translation and not in the original, thus showing Farah's clear intent to engage with the poem as a global, more than Italian, text. Accordingly, Farah recontextualizes and deterritorializes the poem, omitting any references to its allegorical, historical, cultural and theological specificity to show its universality and global scope. This approach allows him to move Somalia away from a provincial or marginal position and place it on the global stage, framing the Somali civil war as a human and universal fight more than a parochial one.

With a particular attention to formal and thematic aspects, the chapter has shown how the recontextualization of the *Comedy* has produced a fruitful dialogue between different historical contexts. The Somali civil war and the hell-like scenario of the 1990s Mogadishu trigger a comparison with both the representation of the suffering sinners in Hell, as imagined by Dante, and the strife-ridden Florence of the fourteenth century. This symbolic connection between the poem and the novel, as shown, opens avenues to several interpretations and further comparative readings, due to the breadth of allusions, references and images drawn into the novel from the *Comedy*. Among them, the chapter has focused on the relationship between the narrator and character, as well as between text and paratext, the latter being the main locus for enabling the intertextual links between *Links* and the *Comedy*.

The *Comedy*'s magnitude and universal scope are then retrieved and recreated to position local Somali infighting on a wider cultural scale. However, the transcultural and transnational dialogue between the two texts, as shown, is also disturbed, as Farah implies the need for adapting and recontextualizing the poem. Accordingly, he assembles several tercets from 'Inferno' by himself, as to underscore the considerable influence of Dante's poem but, at the same time, to point out its incommensurability.

In the following chapter, Dante's influence on diasporic authors will be further analysed, as well as the role of the Italian language in shaping Somalis' identity. By examining Garane's multilingualism in *Il latte è buono*, the discussion will delve into how the novel challenges the normativity of the former colonial language (Italian) and retrieves some fundamental aspects of orature. Beyond being a mere aesthetic proof of authenticity or Africanness, supposedly employed by authors of African origin to state their cultural specificity in opposition to written Western literary forms, orature undertakes in *Il latte è buono* a deeply constitutive role. Thus, the analysis will show how orature should be specifically related to the Somali contexts, as the novel represents one of the first examples, in Italian literature, of a text that employs the former colonial language to give voice to colonized subjects. Owing to these reasons, the chapter provides a new methodology for studying the relationship between written and oral forms.

Notes

1. Farah, in an interview with Kenyan author Binyavanga Wainaina, ironically explained that the practical reason which prevented him from writing in Somali and Amharic was the absence of a typewriter with Somali fonts (Rift Valley Institute, 2013, 25:20).
2. The presence of exile emerges as an apparent association between Dante and the protagonist of *Links*, the diasporic Somali Jeebleh, who fled Mogadishu at the outbreak of the civil war to settle in the United States. Moreover, it recalls Farah's life, as he began an exile that would last for twenty-two years after being warned by the Somali government that he would be arrested over the content of his novel, *A Naked Needle* (1976). In *Links*, however, Farah does not uphold this association explicitly, thus leaving the shared biographical aspect of exile in the background. *Links*, in fact, is a novel about homecoming and describes the experience of Jeebleh's return home, rather than his life in New York as an expatriate.
3. To be precise, these metaphors have a different source: while 'a home of grief' is the translation of 'doloroso ospizio' in 'Inferno' (*Canto* V, 16), the image of the ship is taken from 'Purgatory' (*Canto* VI, 77) and translates the line: '*Nave senza nocchiere in gran tempesta*' [ship without a helmsman in harsh seas].
4. Af-Laawe might represent the 'negative parody' of Virgil and that his name refers to Siyaad Barre, whose sobriquet was *Af-Wayne* (Big Mouth) (Abdullahi 2001, 32; Mari 2018, 104). However, starting from this interpretation, a reader familiar with the poem may spot another similarity: Af-Laawe and Charon, the mythological boatman who ferries the souls across the river Acheron. As in the *Comedy*, Af-Laawe does not drive Jeebleh to the city, and he only manages to organize a lift for him, like Charon's role as psychopomp, who withholds from Dante, being a living body, a trip in his boat. In the poem, the crossing of the river Acheron is left undescribed, since Dante faints, waking up on the other side, at the beginning of the following *Canto*. The comparison between the mythological ferryman and Af-Laawe is also reinforced, as the latter is described while being busy with carrying away a boy's corpse (a ten-year-old boy senselessly murdered at the airport, as described in Chapter 1) with his funeral vehicle (12). The same uncanny resemblance and degree of uncertainty also affect the analogy with Virgil, who has no direct counterpart in *Links*. Since no one can be trusted, because 'distrust was the order of the day, and everyone was suspicious of everybody else' (51), Jeebleh cannot be wisely guided through Mogadishu. The ubiquitous presence of conspiracies and machinations suggests one of the causes at the heart of the civil war: 'the betrayal of one Somali by another' (Moolla 2014, 159).
5. Afterwards, Dante mentions fraud, which he relates to reason because of its

premeditation and purpose to betray both friends and strangers. As already highlighted, during his stay in Mogadishu, Jeebleh seems to be surrounded by fraudulent sinners, as described in last two lines of the quotation. Due to an overall situation of fraud, betrayal and half-truths, everyone should be looked at with suspicion, thus fostering the presence through the whole novel of a leitmotiv of mistrust.

6   The presence of the Italian language in Somalia has been studied by Hoben (1988), Abdi (1998), Duale (2004), Cassanelli and Abdikadir (2008) and Ahad (2017).
7   Ashcroft *et al.* underline a similar practice in the case of Hindi words used in V. S. Naipaul's story 'One out of many' (1971) and Ibo words in Chinua Achebe's *No Longer at Ease* (1963) (Ashcroft, Griffith and Tiffin 2002, 64–5).
8   As already noticed, Italian is also one of the links between the Somali people across the globe, as suggested in the episode when Jeebleh talks about the book by Shirin Ramzanali Fazel who, while in exile in Italy, wrote her autobiography *Lontano da Mogadiscio* (Farah 2005, 226).
9   This is also evident in Farah's *Crossbones*, which shows the treatment of Somali characters who underwent a process of stigmatization and brutalization after 9/11.
10 Regarding Kala-Saar, who represents the old generation of Somalis who studied abroad during the AFIS or in the early post-independence days, it is noteworthy that Farah introduces that character using an ironic tone, to encourage a parody of a know-it-all professor (*Crossbones*, 314–15, 318, 321).

4

The Spoken Word Meets the Script

Somali, Italian and the Role of Orature

Introduction

In this chapter, we will delve deeper into the literary practice of multilingualism, carrying on the previous discussion on the role and use of the Italian language in diasporic novels. As we have seen, Italian plays the role of a *lingua franca* for the protagonist of Farah's *Links*, Jeebleh, who also draws upon Dante' *Comedy* as way of understanding Somalia's national collapse. The previous chapter systematically examined the Italian linguistic dimension in *Links* and *Crossbones*, revealing its role in accentuating a transformative shift in Somalia towards the formal colonial language. The decrease in the use of Italian vocabulary at the textual level in Farah's last trilogy mirrors the socio-historical evolution of Somalia, which has come out from the cultural and linguistic authority of its former metropole and has now given way to contemporary neocolonial influences from, for example, the United States.

With this in mind, we will shift our attention to another text, written in Italian, in which multilingualism is once again employed creatively to fictionalize the relationship between the main character, Gashan, and his multiple belongings. In this case, however, the Italian language plays a relevant role in shaping Gashan's identity during the AFIS (1950–60) and the democratic (1960–9) period, characterized by the material and cultural legacy of Italian colonialism. Accordingly, as Claudio Gorlier (1998) and Itala Vivan (1998) observed, in Farah's first trilogy, set in the 1970s, Italian has a prominent role, as the considerable number of Italian words present in the novels show.

Building upon the work laid in Chapter 2, which examined the significance of spatiality in the making of the postcolonial self, this chapter will extend this investigation by showing how Garane's novella underscores the importance of Dante's language as a 'passport to civilisation' ('*un passaporto verso la civilizzazione*', Garane 2005, 47). However, as we delve deeper into the formal aspects and the use of the Italian language, we will also observe how Garane's novella negotiates the coexistence between the former colonial language – the chosen language to write the novella – with Somali orature, which surfaces as a key textual presence, not only formally, but as deeply constitutive of Somali people's identity and culture.

In doing so, the analysis challenges the idea of orature as a mere aesthetic validation of Africanness that certifies African authors' authenticity and cultural specificity in opposition to written Western literary forms. As recent – albeit limited in number – academic publications have shown, orature is often associated, in written practice, with an aesthetic purpose, as a signifier of the polyphonic and dialogic feature of a text, implying that the latter is derived from or influenced by a presumed 'African' oral tradition (Benvenuti 2011, 253; Coppola 2011 132; Lori 2013, 71). Addressing this issue, Maria Grazia Negro has correctly noticed that his approach might lead to replicating Orientalist methods of analysis that considers orature as congenital to the African continent. Negro contends that 'it should therefore be necessary to point out from time to time the link with the oral tradition of the country' in question and the analysed text (2013, 58). Such an acknowledgement is essential for understanding and contextualizing the use of orature as a narrative strategy in the works of postcolonial writers who are situated within or draw upon one or more literary traditions and not on vague 'African' references. Aligned with this objective, the following section wishes to examine Garane's *Il latte è buono* with specific and contextual focus on the role of Somali orature beyond its relevance at the formal level and not only according to its relationship with the written form and the Italian language.

Before proceeding with the analysis, we should contextualize *Il latte è buono* according to its multicultural influences. As Armando Gnisci claims in the back cover of the book, Garane's novella can be considered the first Italian postcolonial text, since it departs from the distinctive features of the *letteratura della migrazione* (literature of migration or migrant literature): the autobiographical plot, the presence of an Italian co-author, the first-person narrator and the main themes of migration and resettlement. Indeed, *Il latte è buono* is a work of fiction, and even though the events of the novel resemble some aspects of Garane's life, the author is consistently concealed under the protagonist's actions and thoughts, which are never presented with the first-person narrator. Besides, it is not co-authored as most of the writings included in the *letteratura della migrazione* and while the protagonist's migration undoubtedly involves Italy, it also includes France and the United States. Above all, in the case of Garane, Italy represents the former metropole and is not only a host country.[1] This last detail marks a fundamental difference from *letteratura della migrazione*, because it informs how the author employs Italian not as a *lingua franca*, but as a device for decolonization. In this regard, Garane is 'writing back', but not in the sense of rewriting canonical texts, but rather using the former colonial language to give voice to (formerly) colonized subjects.

Therefore, Garane's novella holds a somewhat distinct position in comparison to the works of Igiaba Scego and Ali Farah who, were inherently exposed to the Italian language from birth. In contrast, Garane's acquaintance with the Italian language is rooted in his educational experience, given his status as a Somali born and raised in Mogadishu. This detail of being the first postcolonial Somali novel in Italian, neither written by a second-generation author nor co-authored, does not constitute a mere chronological datum, nor suggest superimposing biographical elements onto the interpretation of the text. It implies a different association with the Italian language than other authors such as Scego, who were raised and born in Italy, or Ali Farah, who relocated to Somalia before subsequently returning to Italy. The presence of *Il latte è buono* in the Italian literary tradition, therefore, encourages us to consider the novella as part of a multicultural and multilingual framework in which both Italian and Somali literary influences play a pivotal role. Beyond investigating the relationship between these two traditions through orature, the analysis also suggests a possible connection between the novella and the early production of Anglophone postcolonial authors from the 1960s and 1970s. For example, as I will show, Garane employs Italian as his privileged creative tool to describe a pre-colonial context – the eighteenth-century Azania – in which the linguistic framework was mainly non-Western, and culture and religion were influenced by Islam and the contacts with the Arabic Peninsula (Mukhtar 1995). In doing so, Garane establishes a correlation between different belief systems via the former colonial language. This stylistic and transcultural process can be described as indigenization. Chantal Zabus employs the latter term to explain how:

> writers from formerly colonized countries have sought to convey concepts, thought patterns, and even linguistic features of their mother tongues or first languages in the European languages.
>
> (2014, 32)

Indigenization is conveyed in *Il latte è buono* through various formal features, which will be the focal points of the analysis and serve as the primary connections to compare the novella, at the formal level, with African literary outcomes of the post-independence period. Garane, can be argued, positions his novella within the debate on language and identity in the 1970s African context, incidentally placing himself in a role akin to the one held by Chinua Achebe in the same dispute. As Chapter 3 has underscored, Achebe perceives language not merely as a 'carrier of culture', as posited by Ngũgĩ wa Thiong'o, but rather as a creative instrument with the capacity to flexibly adapt to diverse settings and circumstances (Achebe 1975; wa Thiong'o 1986, 13). Among the several strategies used by postcolonial writers to adapt and transform the colonial language 'according to the needs of their source culture', Garane employs the insertion of unglossed words or sentences, translated and untranslated, and references to the Somali culture through a process of code-switching (Ashcroft 2014, 24). I argue that the novella's multilingual framework, by mixing literary language (Italian) with vernacular words and syntax, engages with practices of contextualization, cushioning, relexification and 'transfer of context', key concepts that will be expounded upon in the following close reading of *Il latte è buono*.

Italian and Somali in *Il latte è buono*

The originality of *Il latte è buono*, in terms of language and content, becomes evident from the first chapter, '*Nascita di una regina*' (A Queen's Birth), characterized by a narrative tone reminiscent of a fairy tale. The plot develops *in medias res* in an unspecified, past (approximately the eighteenth century), set in a region referred to as Azania. This toponym has been historically associated with various geographical areas of southeastern tropical Africa, possibly aligning, in this instance, with southern Somalia (Galadeta 2006). The term Azania, then, accentuates the ambiguity of the temporal framework, imbuing the narrative with a mythological resonance.[2]

The chapter describes the ascendancy of the Ajuran, a sub-clan of the Hawiye, over this territory, establishing a community where political and religious authority is consolidated and centralized in the authoritative figure of the Imam. The Imam assumes the leadership of the sultanate, laying claim to a robust linkage between the clan and the lineage of Prophet Muhammad (Mansur 1995, 117; Mukhtar 2003, 35). Historically, the Ajuran held sway over the central-southern regions of contemporary Somalia from the mid-thirteenth to the late seventeenth century, eventually succumbing to internal schisms. Western colonial expansion did not reach the Somali coast until the Ajuran-Portuguese conflict, which took place in the first half of the sixteenth century (Mukhtar 2003, 35).

The historical elusiveness of the setting and the overall mythical tone inform the novella and strengthen the fantastical aura of the plot, as the following passage suggests:

Shakhlan Iman era nata dopo ventiquattro mesi vissuti nel grembo di sua madre. Era lei che aveva fatto la scelta, perché voleva formarsi all'interno di una donna, di sua madre, in una terra dove gli uomini facevano il bello e il brutto tempo. All'interno di sua madre aveva ascoltato le discussioni all'esterno del grembo. Sapeva tutto su tutti e su tutto, ma loro non sapevano che c'era una femmina nel corpo di una donna che non parlava quasi mai. Il grembo le diceva tutto. Sapeva tutto sul reame che un giorno lei avrebbe diretto.

(Garane 2005, 5)

Shakhlan Iman was born after twenty-four months spent inside her mother's womb. She chose this because she wanted to develop inside a woman, her mother, in a land where men ruled the roost. Inside her mother, she listened to the discussions outside of the womb. She knew everything about everything and everyone, but they did not know that there was a girl inside the body of a woman who hardly ever spoke. The womb told her everything. She knew everything about the kingdom she would rule someday.

As is clear from the first lines, the prose combines the historical setting with supernatural elements ('Shakhlan Iman was born after twenty-four months'), as well as idiomatic phrases ('men ruled the roost'), hyperboles (as 'She knew everything about everything and everyone') and allusions to a land she would rule over someday. The etiological narrative tone allows Garane to connect the past with the present, thereby establishing a link between the events occurred in the eighteenth century and the making of Somalia as a nation. As delineated in Chapter 2, this continuity is evident as the past resurfaces in the ghostly form of Shakhlan Iman walking across the streets of the post-independence Mogadishu. Her manifestation, as shown, inquisitively bears witness to the transformations Somalia experienced in the aftermath of colonial rule.

In the first chapter, Shakhlan Iman is still a baby and Gashan's ancestors gather to decide and discuss the future of their people. The third-person narrator plays the role of an unreliable voice and informs the overall polyphony of the chapter. In analysing the novella, Simone Brioni rightly notes that '*Il latte è buono* shows the oratorical and rhetorical ability of Somalis, which is a significant trait of this cultural tradition' (2015, 114). Accordingly, the chapter – unhampered either by actions or events – is shaped as a dialogic tale dominated by different perspectives revolving around a central dilemma: the choice between an elective and a dynastic filiation. Can a female heir (Shakhlan Iman) be justified and accepted within the patriarchal, non-secularized custom of the Ajuran?

The narrator presents their opinion with brief comments while the characters express their thoughts and views concerning the role of the future queen. Hence, given that Garane's first chapter predominantly centres on dialogic exchanges between characters, language assumes a pivotal role at both the diegetic and non-diegetic levels. In '*Nascita di una regina*', sentences and dialogues in Italian are juxtaposed with words and clauses in Somali; in this regard, Garane employs a formal approach that features two distinct strategies of indigenization: the Somali words are not provided with a translation, as in the case of *cilaan* in the sentence: '*Respirò profondamente e cominciò a toccarsi la barba piena di* cilaan' ('He breathed deeply and began to touch his beard full of *cilaan*') (Garane, 8). In other cases, a translation is implied in an informative way, as in: '*Era come ascoltare il* mocallim, *l'insegnante del* dugsi, *la scuola coranica*' ('It was like listening to the *mocallim*, the teacher of the *dugsi*, the koranic school') (*ibid.*). In the latter case, the use of cushioning, involving the addition of an explicative translation or explanation following the vernacular word, serves to convey the original meaning while establishing a linguistic bridge between the two languages. Also, implicitly, these strategies suggest the inherent limitations of the Italian language to comprehensively 'colonize' and superimpose itself on Somali as an exhaustive literary tool to represent formerly colonized subjects.

This aspect is further emphasized in the case of entire untranslated sentences, as in: '*Naag la'an yaa noolaan karaa?*' or '*Waxaan weydisanayaa in dabadooda nadiif ay ahaato sidii dabada daanyeerada!*' The non-Somali-speaking reader can only attempt to understand their meaning according to the context (*ibid.*, 5, 10). This process of contextualization, which intentionally involves and relies on the reader, emerges as a more enigmatic formal device: usually, Garane places the untranslated sentences in proximity to their supposed loose translation, giving the impression of a process of multilingual paraphrasing. In this regard, Ashcroft argues that 'the absence of an explanation [as a] sign of distinctiveness also ensures that meaning is not a matter of definition but an active engagement' (2014, 26). As, for example, in the following extract:

> La tradizione era come il letto dove Shakhlan era seduta. Il suo *jimbaar* era fatto della pelle di cammello. Era duro, diritto, né il sudore, né la pioggia, niente poteva cambiare il colore del suo *jimbaar*.
>
> (Garane, 16)

Tradition was like the bed where Shakhlan was sitting. Her *jimbaar* was made of camel skin. It was hard, straight; nothing, neither sweat nor rain could have changed the colour of her *jimbaar*.

Readers unfamiliar with the Somali language might find themselves excluded from reaching a complete understanding of the passage. This multilingual strategy, however, may envision the presence of both Somali and Italian readers, rather than Italian readers only, thus placing the texts in direct conversations with the wider context of the diaspora (Brioni 2015, 35).

On other occasions, Garane translates Somali proverbs into Italian, introducing them with repeated locutions such as '*Non dice forse*' or '*Non dice d'altronde*' ('Isn't it said that'), followed by the translated proverb.[3] This 'process of embedding proverbs into the very texture of the novel' is called relexification and aims to 'simulate the indigenous tongue' by not giving a verbatim translation, but by adapting it, in this case, to the Italian pattern (Zabus 2014, 34). Within the Somali oral tradition, proverbs are regarded as a 'grammar of values', serving as a 'frame of reference for the deeds of the hero' and simultaneously acting to 'cut short all discussion on any subjects' (Ahmed 1996, 41). In the novella, correspondingly, the narrator employs proverbs to succinctly encapsulate pivotal points or offer commentary on the characters, especially about Shakhlan (Garane 2005, 32–3). However, relexification does not function only at the syntactic level, as it concurrently operates semantically. The semantic relexification is accomplished by imparting the original meaning in accordance with the norms of the Italian language, thereby familiarizing Italian readers with the culture of the Ajuran. Despite the non-immediacy of the processes involved in retrieving the Somali proverb and comparing the translation with the original syntax, Garane systematically engages in semantic relexification by transposing the meaning of the proverbs from one language to another.

As Chantal Zabus has noticed, these three different practices (contextualization, cushioning and relexification) create both estrangement and understanding in Western readers and are common in several English-language novels by Igbo authors of the post-independence period, such as Onuora Nzekwu's *Blade among the Boys* (1962), Nkem Nwankwo's *Danda* (1964) and Chinua Achebe's *Things Fall Apart* (1958) and *Arrow of God* (1964) (2014, 34–47). Garane's novella, similarly, uses the same stylistic and rhetorical devices to achieve the same double effects, familiarizing Italian readers to a foreign context and, at the same time, disorienting – or, in Zabus's terms, 'frustrating' – them (2014, 44). The latter aim is achieved with the lack of translation of Somali words, neither in the text nor in a glossary, that precludes a straightforward understanding of the meaning of the unglossed words.

The affinity between Garane and the authors of the post-independence period is also highlighted by the shared feature of being one of the first authors to appropriate and 'indigenize' a European language (Italian) to fictionalize an African context (Somalia). In the case of Somalia, however, the starting point of this appropriation does not fall in the post-independence period (1960s), but needs to be postponed until the 2000s or, according to scholar Armando Gnisci, until 2005, when *Il latte è buono* was published. For this reason, even though the ignition of the linguistic decolonization for a Somali-born author marks a discrepancy of almost five decades if compared to Nigerian or Kenyan experiences, the aesthetic strategies underpinning the process of appropriation persist with notable similarity. This aesthetic affinity, I think, might be understood as an attempt to provide readers with an unfamiliar context. In other words, due to the delay in processing postcolonial novels, the Italian public of the 1990s and 2000s can be compared to the early English readers of Achebe's or Nzekwu's novels in the 1960s. In this regard, Zabus notes that 'time has not come yet when the African novelists can insert an African word or refer to an African cultural event in the same manner as European novelists can throw into their text German, English, or Latin locutions and refers to Jupiter, Mozart, and Nietzsche without any explanation' (2014, 35). Accordingly, *Il latte è buono* shows this vernacular resonance only towards Somali, while the novella is also set in France and the United States. The presence of French and English words, indeed, is almost absent, as if to mark the specific role of Italian as the former colonial language.[4]

The use of these strategies positions Garane's novella differently from, for example, Ubax Cristina Ali Farah's novel *Little Mother*, which enacts an alternative appropriation practice in her work. As explained in Chapter 1, Ali Farah chooses to create calques of words, establishing a linguistic connection, if not a dependence, between Somali and Italian. As we have seen, she reconfigures the Italian language in the sense of self-representation, emphasizing the legacy of colonialism but also staging a subversion of the colonial language, challenging 'the notion of a monolingual standard language and homogenous national culture' (Brioni 2015, 58). In *Little Mother*, this linguistic counter-discourse is achieved with the appropriation of Italian words, as in the case of *draddorio* as the loanword for *trattoria* (an eating house), or *defreddi*, which is the voiced phonetic calque of *tè freddo* (cold tea). Ali Farah tries to manipulate the colonizers' language and make it her own, suggesting a strategy of cohabitation more than conflict (Brioni 2015). In essence, Italian words are turned into Somali to signify the attempt at linguistic inclusion. Cristina Ali Farah herself states:

> Bending Italian (my mother's tongue, but also the very language of the coloniser) to the rhythms of Somali, I was trying to interlock the two countries' histories, to put together two worlds that apparently were separated.
>
> (2017)

In Garane's novella, however, the aesthetic device of leaving words untranslated becomes 'a political act, because while translation is not inadmissible in itself, glossing gives the translated word the higher status' (Ashcroft, Griffith and Tiffin 2002, 35). In this regard, it might be useful here to introduce the concept of 'transfer of context'. Understood as 'the transfer of those cultural patterns which are absent or different in those cultures where English is used as a first language', transfer of context focuses more on the semantic perspective of linguistic strategies such as relexification or cushioning (Kachru 1983, 131; Srivastava 2008, 146). In the case of Garane, proverbs transfer the references of the oral tradition into Italian not only via an aesthetic process but also according to the ethical concerns of Somali poetry, which aims to emphasize relevant themes, promoting mnemonic capacity and focusing on specific values (Ahmed 1996, 41). Naturally, the mnemonic function and the use of alliteration, pivotal structural devices of Somali poems to reiterate the moral of the story, are lost in the novella, but proverbs nonetheless maintain the main aim they have in the oral tradition, namely allowing the 'narrator to depicts a bond which holds the communalist ethos of the society together' (*ibid.*).

This argument has been overlooked in the studies about orature in Somali postcolonial and diasporic novels, thus nourishing the idea that proverbs, dialogism and supernatural elements were the only markers of the oral influence on the script or its Africanness.[5] Another feature often related to the 'African' oral influence is the use of repetitions, as they stylistically reproduce the spoken language. However, if we look closely at *Il latte è buono*, repetitions are in fact sentences in Italian and not in Somali, such as Dante's line: '*Nel mezzo del cammin di nostra vita*' ('Midway upon the journey of our life'), which links Garane's novella to one of the most renowned (written) works of the Italian literature, *The Divine Comedy*, and not to the Somali oral influence. Thus, the argument that the novel is related to orature via the repetitive pattern of sentences, words or proverbs sounds somewhat misplaced.

Indeed, *Il latte è buono* retrieves oral practices in a manner akin to other Western or African novels, employing techniques such as repetitions, proverbs, a dialogic form and a non-linear structure featuring ellipses. These features, typical of any oral narratives, do not prove *Il latte è buono* to be influenced by Somali orature because, I contend, the specificity of Somali orature emerges in the novel at a different level: through the reprise of the sociopolitical role of poetry and the use of a set of metaphors belonging to orature.[6]

This approach, which allows us to analyse orature from a different angle, enables the reader to point out the oral features that are *definitively* Somali.[7] As I will show, the term 'Somali' itself, as related to a homogeneous literary tradition, is fraught with complexities, thus encouraging the argument that any allusion to an even more nebulous African tradition is untenable. The starting point to develop the following approach is identifying genres, themes and styles of the Somali oral tradition that are intertextually referenced or adapted in the novella. To underline which characteristics are preserved or inevitably lost between the oral form and the script, this last section analyses how *Il latte è buono* negotiates stylistic features and ethical aims of the Somali oral tradition.

Somali Orature and in *Il latte è buono*

According to Garane himself, his novella (not only the first chapter) can be considered a *gabay* (Galadeta 2006).[8] The latter is an epic and long (30 to 150 lines) oral form composed according to rigid prosody, required alliteration and the use of archaic poetic diction (Abdullahi 2001, 75–7; Moolla 2012, 439). It can convey solemn themes, encompassing praise, philosophical reflections and satires, which are presented to the community during social or public events. Similar to Garane's approach, political issues constitute primary subjects in the *gabay*, given their perceived significance for the community and the imperative to address and disseminate them. Poetry, then, 'is not only a classic expression but it is also the daily journal which makes the masses aware of the issues which concern their world' (Adan 1981, 115; Andrzejewski, Piłaszewicz and Tyloch 1985, 340). The specificity of the *gabay*, being a predominantly male poetic form focused on political subjects, renders Garane's assertion of representing Somalia inherently problematic.

In other words, the *gabay* is just one of the forms of *maanso* (poetry), and it has been mainly employed by nomadic clans. Scholar Ali Jimale Ahmed has addressed the troublesome shift of understanding *gabay* as the universal expression of Somali oral tradition, while being instead a specific genre of the traditional pastoralist societies (1996b, 13–14).[9] Similarly, Didier Morin has stated that: '*Le conflit interclanique passant par un échange poétique, le* gabay [...] *il est devenu synonyme de 'poésie classique somalie(nne)',* gabay hooyaaleedka Soomaaliyeed' (The interclan conflict through a poetic exchange, the *gabay* [...] has become synonymous of 'classical Somali poetry', *gabay hooyaaleedka soomaaliyeed*) (1997, 5).[10]

Regarding *Il latte è buono*, on the one hand, Garane contaminates the *gabay*'s traditional form and themes, but it also regards it as a synonym for Somali poetry. As Ali Jimale Ahmed has claimed, by universalizing the *gabay*, 'Somali poetry has been robbed of its most salient contour: engaging dialogue with tradition and sub-cultures' (1996b, 14). Even though I agree with Ahmed's suggestion that the *gabay* is indeed a sectarian form of poetry that questionably came to represent Somali poetry altogether, I also aim to explore Garane's attempt to foster a negotiation between different traditions within Somali culture and orature, and with Western forms. So, focusing on the novella's filiation with the *gabay* and the latter's role as a specific genre in Somalia's literary and political history should not prevent us from considering the text according to its multiple influences and cross-cultural references.

Garane disentangles the *gabay* from its specific sociopolitical context and aims instead for a more inclusive and hybrid ambit. As it will be clear after the analysis, I also contend that this goal is partially achieved and that a many-voiced and more comprehensive representation of Somali history and society is not entirely fulfilled. In terms of the hybridity of forms and syncretism, for example, Garane challenges any definition of the genre as rigid by playing with both Western and African literary forms. Garane himself explicitly suggests analogies between the two while describing Italians' habits:

> Si esce dal caffè e ci si ferma alla fermata d'obbligo, dal giornalaio, dove si compra il proprio giornale, secondo l'affiliazione tribale, democristiana, socialista ... Il giornale dell'italiano è come la cultura orale, parla, racconta tutto, ma è fedele alla persona che lo compera, giacché ha le sue stesse idee politiche, religiose.
>
> (Garane 2005, 77)

After leaving the coffee shop, the obligatory stop must be at the newsagent to buy the appropriate newspaper according to the tribal affiliation, Christian Democrat, socialist ... The newspaper of the Italians is like the oral tradition: it tells everything, but is loyal to the one who buys it, because it shares the same political and religious ideas.

This parallel is reinforced when Garane compares Italian political parties (socialists, communists, Christian Democrats) to African tribes and clans. At the same time, Garane employs metaphorical references that are well-established in the Somali oral tradition. Three main symbols appear to be at the core of the novella, all of them referring to Somali orature: *latte*, *cammello* and *asino* (milk, camel and donkey). These references inform Garane's attempt to negotiate a sense of community beyond the factional logic and specific historical-political trajectories of the Ajuran clan. Despite taking a different path from Farah and Ali Farah, who disregard clan lineage and explicitly line up again clan ideology, Garane tries to achieve the same goal of making sense of the nation-state collapse by exploring the cognate concepts of identity (Who are the Somalis?) and nation (What is Somalia?) in relation to pre-colonial societal formations.

In this process, the importance of milk (*caano*) emerges from the title and the opening line as one of the main key elements around which Somali customs and society seem to be built. With a possible connection or tribute to Nuruddin Farah's novel *Sweet Sour Milk* (1979), the recurrence of milk is persistent if we consider the number of times it refers to Somalia by peering into sociological, political and literary studies or academic publications (Brioni 2015, 113). As has been already observed, it is strictly connected to the etymology of the names *soo-maal* (in the north) and *sa-maal* (in the south), as if milk could be read as the identity cypher of Somali people.[11] The oral tradition has narrates the virtues of milk and its beneficial and nurturing properties, thus attributing a positive connotation to it. *Caano* is indeed regarded as the archetype of life: nomadic populations relied on camel milk as a vital source of livelihood (Abokor 1987). However, in the novel, milk becomes an almost universal and transnational element able to signify different cultures; it is a flexible and adaptable symbol that Garane uses to reflect on Gashan's feelings towards specific situations inside and outside Somalia. For example, in the United States, the milk is 'good and burning', in reference to his experience in the country where he feels alienated and undergoes 'the experience of *becoming Black*' (De Luca 2020, 34). Before leaving Mogadishu for Rome, the milk becomes cappuccino, suggesting Gashan's expectations towards Italy (Garane, 72). While in Rome, the same cappuccino turns to be sour, as if to reflect the overall atmosphere of racism that Gashan experiences in the capital and his disillusionment after discovering the reality behind the 'mythologized status' and *grandeur* that Rome holds (Burns 2013, 151). Milk, in contrast, is always good in times of peace – 'Milk is good' is the opening line of the novella – but is 'complicated to drink', 'bloody', 'dusty' and 'bitter' during the civil war (116, 124, 127).

The semantic flexibility of milk as a symbol of Gashan's feelings towards Somalia expands the specificity of the *caano* and questions its positive connotation. It also stands in contrast with the quite specific meaning held by the camel and the donkey. For example, the prominence of the camel arises in orature due to its importance in nomadic everyday life, being a powerful animal capable of crossing arid and desert areas, especially in the northern regions. In the past, tamed camels were useful in providing all kinds of necessities: milk and meat for nourishment, strength and resistance to heat and thirst for transport and travel (Mansur 1995, 108). Besides, the camel (and the she-camel, called *Maandeeq*) emerged as the emblem of the nation's independence in the oral poems of the mid-twentieth century, when the first anti-colonial movements sprung all over Somalia (Abokor 1987; Mansur 1995, 111–12; Ahad 2007). Garane incorporates this intertextual reference but does not identify the camel solely as a unifying symbol of the nation; rather, it is regarded as one of the two primary elements within Somali society. Thus, the donkey figures as the other animal that Garane employs to represent the southern part of the country, crossed by few rivers with a constant water supply throughout the year (Davies 1987, 208). The soil conditions in the southern regions create a fertile plain favourable to the growth of a farming population. This starkly contrasts with the semi-desert plain along the Gulf of Aden coast in the north, where limited rainfall permits the growth of shrubs, sufficient only for the pastures of nomadic populations. The camel in these northern territories was considered superior to any other grazing animal, and it also established its owner's social role.[12]

Garane himself explains the symbolic value of these two animals in relation to national identity in an interview for the magazine *El Ghibli*:

> Volevo rappresentare i due poli della cultura somala: ho usato l'asino per certe tribù sedentarie del sud [...] Mentre ho usato il cammello per le tribù del nord e dell'occidente somalo. I somali sono discendenti dei nomadi e il nomade glorifica il cammello: se una donna è bella dicono che assomiglia a un cammello. La Somalia è stata vittima dello scontro del cammello e dell'asino: c'è stata una guerra civile e il cammello rappresenta i nomadi che si sono insediati nelle città che gli asini non volevano, perché erano portatori di una cultura clanica.
>
> (Galadeta 2006)

> I wanted to represent the two poles of Somali culture: I used the donkey for certain sedentary tribes of the South [...] while I used the camel for the tribes of the North and the West. Somalis descend from nomads and nomads worship the camel: if a woman is beautiful, they say she looks like a camel. Somalia has been the victim of the clash between camels and donkeys: there has been a civil war, and the camel represents the nomads who set themselves up in the city against the donkeys' will because they were bearers of a clannish culture.

The recovery of this imagery from the oral tradition allows Garane to represent two polarities in the history of Somalia according to both geographical position and the traditional structure of the kinship lineage. Even though Garane broadens the spectrum of the representation of historical Somali communities by mentioning the sedentary culture of the South (donkey), he maintains the nomadic of the North as the dominant one (camel) (Brioni 2015). In this sense, Garane reinforces the idea of a binary system in making Somali society and supports the dichotomy between nomads and sedentary people in shaping the ethnic development of 'the Somali-speaking people' (Markovitz 1995, 64). Accordingly, when Gashan visits Mogadishu after his exile, finding the city demolished (as examined in Chapter 2), he explains the civil war as follows:

> Una città distrutta, rasa al suolo dagli asini e dai cammelli [...] I due si erano conosciuti di fronte ai semafori avidi di giustizia. Si erano fermati alla luce rossa dei semafori, si erano guardati e avevano cominciato a odiarsi. Un odio che si era assopito per anni. Un odio storico. L'asino, sempre portatore, più piccolo del cammello, odiava quest'ultimo che aveva lasciato le sue distese per venire da lui. E per di più, il cammello aveva cominciato a guidare macchine, a costruire le sue proprie ville, i suoi semafori. Il cammello aveva tutto il disprezzo per questo piccolo asinello di provincia, che non aveva nessuna cultura.
> (Garane 2005, 115)

> A destroyed city, razed to the ground by donkeys and camels [...] The two had met in front of traffic lights eager for justice. They had stopped at the red light of the traffic lights; they had looked at each other, and they had begun to hate each other. A hatred that had been dormant for years. A historical hate. The donkey, always a bearer, smaller than the camel, hated the latter who had left its plains to come to him. And what's more, the camel had begun to drive cars, build his own villas, his own traffic lights. The camel had all the contempt for this little provincial donkey with no culture.

The duality between nomadic and sedentary, as well as the geographic opposition between North and South, echoes the Western understanding of Somali people as an ethnic community hierarchically divided into nomads (free men) and farmers (slaves) (Ahad 2019). In this sense, Garane seems to rely on the double partitions made by European explorers and later buttressed by colonial anthropologists about Somali society. According to this division, the noble Somalis were those nomads of the North devoted to pastoralism, while the agriculturalists of the South were non-noble (Ahad 2008, 438, 465). This division, besides, seems to suggest that ethnic minorities are not part of the sociopolitical and historical development of the nation, as they are excluded from framework of the novella. Yibir, Bantu and Gosha/Jarer, which are distinct from the nomadic culture, are thus silenced, being effectively 'removed from the social boundaries of Somaliness' (Kusow 2004, 4). Without addressing the role of farmers and coastal cultures, the novella risks reproducing the colonial narrative of superimposing the traditional pastoralist structures on them.

At the same time, however, *Il latte è buono* may be read as a forum where different perspectives and opinions converge and coexist. If oral poems are understood as means to 'excite controversy [which] were answered by other poems', then in the novella, dialogues –more than actions – decide the future of the people of Azania and have the power to influence the choices that the Ajuran would face in the future (Andrzejewski, Piłaszewicz and Tyloch 1985, 340). I argue that the presence of orature results in the use of dialogism not only as a stylistic trait or form of political commitment, but also as a didactical device. This effect is also achieved in the oral form via the omniscient third-person narrator, who 'makes both subtle and overt remarks about both the attitudes and actions of the characters' (Ahmed 1996, 48).

The intrusive narrator, then, plays the role of the *abwaan* (the gifted poet) of the Somali literary tradition, since they 'speak in the collective tongue of the group' (Afrax 2009, 3). However, as shown, the narrator does so not in Somali but in Italian, thus building an intertextual, cultural and linguistic bridge between two literary traditions. The Italian language, used in the wake of colonialism for anthropological and ethnographic accounts about Somali-speaking people, is appropriated by formerly colonized subjects in the novella to reclaim their history before colonization.

In *Il latte è buono*, Garane directs his attention to a specific moment in the Ajuran's historical context, a juncture situated between the pre-colonial and colonial periods; his novella aims to inscribe the clan's development in relation to the broader scenario of Somali nationhood and almost suggests a filiation from the Ajuran Sultanate to modern Somalia. When, in the end, queen Shakhlan decides to move to the coast, she explains that 'a people called "Somali" is taking shape' there, who speak the same language, but with an accent, as the Ajuran defeated them (Garane 40). This seems to refer to the beginning of nationalism and colonialism, but in Garane's account, history is condensed and distorted, mixed with historical facts and myths. Simone Brioni, in this regard, notices that this 'division between a real historic present and a dreamlike golden age recalls a Eurocentric chronology which identifies the beginning of history in Africa with colonialism' (2015, 114). However, it seems that the structure of the novella – and the first chapter, in particular – can be read in opposition to the Western partition of time in Western society. The lack of actions, the structure based upon dialogues and the indefinite setting of the first chapter show that the plot is not organized along a linear axis and that, above all, 'history' started far before European colonization. Whereas in '*Nascita di una regina*' (A Queen's Birth) the time hastens, slows down and finally broadens, and the main corpus of events is condensed into the dialogic form, the rest of the novella, too, lacks precise references regarding the time-setting. The reader grasps that the plot stretches from Siyaad Barre's coup in 1969 to his death in 1991, but these two dates are never made clear. Moreover, the narrator is always vague concerning Gashan's life, whose movements between continents resemble 'the journey motif common to Somali folktales' (Moolla 2012, 453). The reader can hardly understand how long he stayed in each country or when he moved from Rome to Florence, then from France to the United States. Gashan's life flows from one paragraph to another with recurrent ellipses and the repetitions of '*Il latte è buono* ... ' ('Milk is good ... ').

Above all, it is the presence of Shakhlan that highlights the non-linearity of time and the lack of 'strict organisation and partition of time in Western society' throughout the novel (Brioni 2015, 114). Her presence, spanning from the eighteenth century to the post-independence period in the 1960s and again amidst the civil war in the early 1990s, underscores that the formation of the post-independence Somali nation is perpetually contingent on the negotiation process between past and present, pre-colonial and postcolonial history, and traditional sociopolitical structures and modern nationalist currents. In this sense, the fictionalized history of the Ajuran represents *one* of the trajectories followed by Somali clans at the end of the eighteenth century. It possibly exemplifies the decision-making of other clans before the colonial period and, at the same time, it questions the enigmatic origin of Somali clans and their mythological descent. About this latter aspect, Garane emphasizes how religion and traditions play both a cohesive and a divisive role in shaping Somalia's national identity. Scholar Mukhtar and Kusow, accordingly, explain the ambiguity of the origin and history of the Somali people noting that 'some claim that their ancestors migrated from Arabia, but do not know the date or place of arrival. Others will tell stories about their past, about antiquity and about phir'onic civilizations itself having been originated by Somalis in Puntland' (1995, 19; Kusow 1995, 106).

Garane stages this syncretism and, in the attempt to portray the pre-colonial past, he aims, to paraphrase Chinua Achebe, to 'look back and try and find out where [Somalis] went wrong, where the rain began to beat [them]' (1975, 43). The effort to image a putative lineage or a shared history among Somalis places Garane in the ongoing debate on genealogy that underpins the works of Somali historians and intellectuals who consider the origin of Somali people as an open question. As Mohamed Trunji notes, 'The existing literature on this important historical period is scanty, shallow and incomplete by nature; it is a work by foreign writers, and consequently does not provide a comprehensive or clear picture of major events' (2015, XXIII). In the novella, the lack of a coherent narrative of the history of the Somali nation and the often-incoherent relations of the protagonist towards the clan-based system leave the issue of the past unsolved or, in Farah's terms, 'imperfect' (Brioni 2015, 15).

However, the account of the 'dreamlike golden age' of the first chapter is nonetheless an effort to relocate the beginning of Somali history before colonialism and investigate a period that rarely figures in the novels of the diaspora. At the time of the story, the Ajuran people are facing a dilemma resulting from the birth of a female heir, Shakhlan Iman, namely whether to choose between an elective or a dynastic descent or, in other words, between tradition and change. Throughout the chapter, the third-person narrator reports the opinions of several characters about Allah, the Quran, infibulation and legitimacy under the leaves of the sacred tree, a *quarac*, an acacia (Mahoney 1990, 32). In doing so, Garane deploys several points of view, such as those of Kana, the wise older man on which the decision-making confidence lies, and of secondary characters, whose role is to express doubts about the future and the gender issue in relation to having a queen. In this dialogic decision-making process, Garane shows who were the active subjects in the Ajuran society and both reinforces and challenges normative roles. For example, even though the main protagonist is Shakhlan, the only characters allowed to speak are men, thus supporting the patriarchal structure of the Ajuran Sultanate (Brioni 2015, 116). In this regard, the novel may be connected firmly to the *gabay* because the story is told by men and is *mostly* about men.[13] Shakhlan, indeed, does not appear as a speaking protagonist, since the narrator tells her story while she is still silent, in the womb, and overlooks her reign as the queen of the Ajuran. She remains a listener for the whole chapter, until the last pages, when she suggests moving to the coast, and later, when she wanders around Mogadishu to interact with Gashan. Shakhlan's mother, as well, is described as silent and obedient. Their role in the clan is side-lined and questioned, even though they are Iman Omar's wife and her daughter, the future queen. Their womanhood, in a land ruled by men, is also subjected to scrutiny; for instance, Shakhlan is compelled to undergo infibulation to 'emasculate [her] woman's body' (Brioni 2015, 116). Hence, male characters, exemplified by Kana and Gashan, persist as the holders of the historical narrative that Garane traces back to the ancient Land of Punt – an entity situated in the region encompassing North Somalia, Djibouti and the Red Sea coast of Eritrea (2005, 37).

However, it should be noted that in staging the *shir* (the meeting under the sacred tree), Garane displays one of the primary roles of orature, an aspect covered rarely in the analyses of *Il latte è buono*: to allow children to know their culture. As Ali Jimale Ahmed puts it, 'Oral literatures [...] apart from their aesthetic quality and the experiential wisdom inherent in them, ensured the survival of tradition in the minds of the young' (2018). The creative gimmick Garane uses to retain this feature is to make Shakhlan part of the discussion about her future even though she is still in her mother's womb. In this way, she is introduced to the rites, values, history and the whole dense symbolic lore of her clan. Shakhlan embodies, before birth, a character situated in a historical moment of transition: she is destined to occupy a male role as the leader of the Ajuran before the arrival of the first Europeans. Shakhlan interrupts the patriarchal system and breaks the net roles as encoded within the clan. Garane, nevertheless, includes in the plot the representation of subjects who confront the homogeneity and the hierarchical roles of the clan, incorporating them in the narrative as to mirror a public discussion. Even though he does not completely subvert power relations, he allows a certain degree of flexibility within the Ajuran clan.

In this regard, the character of Dirir (meaning 'warrior') can be introduced as the embodiment of the marginalized subject who is allowed some room to talk back. His position lies in-between acceptance and rejection, as there is no mutual understanding of how to consider him within the clan hierarchies. For example, when he tries to share his opinion about the dynastic issue by standing up, one of the young warriors asks him to sit down (Garane, 23). He is granted the right to speak thanks to Kana, who, nevertheless, looks at Dirir as an outsider. Garane presents him as the emblem of difference in a land where nomads and male warriors are the norm:

> Nella terra dei nomadi e dei guerrieri, Dirir non aveva uno statuto ben definito: assomigliava ad un uomo, aveva la voce femminile, non era sposato, non parlava tanto con le donne, non si indirizzava agli uomini … Ma era un guerriero e Kana lo sapeva. Sapeva che nessuno poteva dire a un guerriero di sedersi.
>
> (Garane 2005, 23)

> In the land of nomads and warriors, Dirir did not have a well-established status: he looked like a man, he had a feminine voice, he was not married, he did not speak much with women, he did not address men ... But he was a warrior, and Kana knew it. He knew that nobody could tell a warrior to sit down.

In this passage, Garane depicts the perceived ambiguity of Dirir in respect of a supposed heteronormative Black masculinity as he shifts between masculine and feminine features. At times, Dirir's descriptions denote a fluidity in terms of gender roles, while other times they explicitly target his sexual orientation (Garane 2005, 15, 27). In one passage, Garane explains that 'Dirir knew that everyone was wondering if he was Adam, Eve, or ... ' (27), while Shakhlan remarks upon the fact that 'there is no difference between Dirir and me. We both escape rules' (23).

At a stylistic level, Dirir's description seems to be characterized by a ineffability. Using the three suspension dots gives space to a certain degree of uncertainty, either to avoid mentioning the reality of Dirir's situation or to emphasize the lack of words that can identify him unequivocally. Once again, in telling the tale of the Ajuran, the narrator seems to require the participation of the reader, implicitly asking them to fill in the blanks. This uncertainty towards Dirir is quite telling, given the literary context in which the Ajuran social reality is described, in detail, in both Somali and Italian. In this regard, the dialogue of a man belonging to the Maale group in southern Ethiopia comes to mind. Questioning his sexual orientation, he describes himself like a *wobo*, 'crooked'. He continues with phrasing similar to Dirir's description: 'If I had been a man, I could have taken a wife and a begotten child. If I was a woman, I could have married and borne children. But I am a *wobo*; I can do neither' (Murray and Roscoe 1998, 23–4). In *Il latte è buono*, this idea of being both is not expressed through negations as in *wobo*, but with the coexistence of male and female and the Somali word *labeeb*, explained as '*un maschio e una femmina*' (a male and a female') (Garane 2005, 12).

The hierarchical scale of values, which places the figure of the warrior at the apex of the social pyramid, guarantees him a role within the clan: being a warrior assures him the status needed not to be an outcast. Dirir is aware of representing the exception within the heteronormativity of the group he is part of. At the same level is Shakhlan, as she must perform a male role to be the leader of the Ajuran.

With these references to non-heteronormative characters, Garane questions the supposed stillness and homogeneity that colonial discourse relates to indigenous culture, thus creating a microcosm grounded in cultural syncretism and flexible social structures. At the same time, the novella pushes back against claims made by some African leaders that queerness is a Western import (Murray and Roscoe 1998, XV). In addition, Shakhlan's ambivalence is the same as his father, and to stress that changes do occur within the clan. Garane describes him as follows:

> [...] era un grande capo, grazie al suo coraggio, alla conoscenza del carattere dei suoi sudditi, e alla sua eloquenza che gli permetteva di improvvisare delle poesie per eccitare i nomadi di cui era il capo. Era, insomma, un vero Gareen. Aveva l'istinto pastorale e l'istinto del sedentario.
>
> (Garane 2005, 38)

[…] he was a great chief, thanks to his courage, his knowledge of the nature of his subjects and his eloquence that allowed him to improvise poems to inspire the nomads he led. He was, indeed, a true Gareen. He had the pastoral and the sedentary instinct.

In this concise description emerges the importance attributed to knowledge and the value given to orature, as the ability to compose poetry appears as a form of personal superiority at the social level. Garane also suggests the need for a compromise to reconcile the dichotomy he envisions in the very structure of the Somali nation, namely the antagonism between nomadic and sedentary people. In doing so, he moves along multiple axes, in which the Sultanate, clans, nomads, sedentary people and the Somali nation appear as categories of a pyramidal structure in which the hierarchies are never fixed but questioned over time. As we have seen, in the pre-colonial period, clan and sub-clan formations were described as the dominant sociopolitical organizations, with the power centralized in the religious-warrior (Imam), the head of the state. During the post-independence period, political parties replaced previous clan leaders, as well as the figure of the president took the lead of the new democratic nation. Lastly, the regime of Siyaad Barre, perpetuating an ambiguous behaviour about clannism, re-established previous hierarchies of power, thus allowing clan leaders to become front-runners of political parties.[14]

The chapter concludes with an imminent catastrophe for the Ajuran, foreshadowing the novella's end, when Somalia plunges into a civil war. By a rapid temporal leap in which decades of events are accustomed to each other, the narrator touches upon events that would change the Horn of Africa, if not the entire continent: the first incursion of the English in 1840, of the Italians in 1888 and the rule of Ethiopia on the Somali territories of Haud and Ogaadeen in 1897. The narrative flows with a discursive tone and the events of a century are summarized in a few paragraphs, which are worth mentioning in full because they link the Ajuran's pre-colonial history to colonialism and, specifically, the Italian occupation:

I bianchi arrivarono sulle coste africane. Olol andò da loro e diventò loro amico. Ai bianchi conveniva un tipo del genere: volevano creare i loro propri nobili. Quando l'*eeb* Olol Dinle prese i nemici italiani come amici, il Re dei Re e il Sultano dei Sultani, il Cristiano e il Musulmano, si riunirono per battersi contro l'invasore italiano. Di fronte alla saggezza africana, c'erano i cannoni. Olol Dinle credeva che tutto sarebbe andato bene e che sarebbe stato nominato, come tanti africani, re degli invasori, senza tenere conto delle norme e della tradizione degli avi. Ma gli italiani persero una guerra memorabile ad Adua. Olol fu ucciso. Ebbe una sola consolazione: […] l'Occidente fece di un *eeb* un sultano, di un pretoriano un capo. Lui si era nominato sultano: sultano Olol Dinle. Nobili si nasce, non si diventa. È un titolo che non si compera, come fanno sovente in Occidente. E soprattutto non lo si impone a un continente! La sua nobiltà nacque e morì con lui. Che effimero titolo! Un titolo che sprofondò con l'effimera velleità coloniale italiana. Povera Africa e povera Italia!

(38–39)

White people arrived on the African coasts. Olol went to them and became their friend. Such a character was useful to them: they wanted to create their own noblemen.

When *eeb* Olol Dinle took Italian enemies as friends, the Kings of Kings and the Sultan of the Sultans, the Christian and the Muslim, gathered to fight against the Italian invaders. Against African wisdom, there were cannons. Olol Dinle believed everything would go well and that, like many Africans, he would be named king of the invaders, without considering the ancestors' norms and tradition. However, the Italians lost a great war at Adwa. Olol was killed. He had only one consolation: [...] the West made an *eeb* into a sultan, a praetorian into a chief. He had been named Sultan: Sultan Olol Dinle. Nobles are born, not made. It is not a title that can be bought, as often happens in the West. And above all, it is not imposed on a continent! His nobility was born and died with him. What an ephemeral title! A title that collapsed with the ephemeral Italian colonial fantasy. Poor Africa and poor Italy!

This brief account of Olol Dinle, superfluous for the main events of the plot and incorporated in an imprecise chronological context (Olon was not killed in the Battle of Adua, 1896, but was allegedly executed during the early 1960s), is instead illustrative if viewed from a symbolic perspective. Olol Dinle could be seen as the embodiment of the damage that colonialism caused in the relationship among Somalis and not just within the Ajuran clan. Besides, Garane's tale blurs the boundaries between the pre-colonial and the colonial era and sidelines colonialism in the clan's history. European colonialism is seen as a contingent event to be added to the internal evolution of the Ajuran people, which were already facing a change – the election of a woman as heir – and whose sultan would eventually align himself with the Italian authorities.

Indeed, there are several trajectories in the same chapter, each of which could have yielded different outcomes had it not been for the arrival of the Italians. In other words, Shakhlan's decision to leave the Azania region will decide if the Ajuran perish or survive, beyond the importance attributed to the 'cannibal Europeans' and their coming (Garane, 40). Once again, Garane's narrative moves along multiple axes. In describing this complex evolution, he describes the Ajuran (and the House of Gareen, the ruling hereditary dynasty of the sultanate) as a functioning state, dominant in Somalia during the eighteenth century and places them among the noble warriors who have the rights to rule in the new country (Somalia as a democratic nation). However, he shows how this sultanate should not be considered as a static entity (such as nation) with a precise territory (the idea of Azania suggests this inconsistency), but as a community able to negotiate its traditions. In doing so, the author of *Il latte è buono* aims to retrieve the historical development of Somalia's political formation, from a pre-colonial clan-based state to the post-independence secularized nation-state. In the end, when Gashan frantically wanders in the destroyed Mogadishu, Garane expresses his struggle to find a way of coexistence and unity between clan ideology, Western influences and Islam, but also between orature, as the privileged form of communication and the carrier of a Somali ethos, and the written language. After his years spent in exile, Gashan understands that he is part of 'the culture of donkeys, camels and Dante' and that he is the result of this syncretism, 'a hybrid' and the 'sum of all cultures, like the Supreme Poet [Dante]' (Garane 2005, 115, 121, 122). This awareness allows him to understand that the starting point to preserve Somalia's history should be the written form. This consideration, which downplays the role of orature, seems also to reflect Garane's decision to write a novella as the preferred form to represent Somalia. Gashan's words towards the end look as if they echo this idea: 'It is necessary to transfer everything from orality to writing. So Somalia will not be denied, lost' ('*Bisogna trasportare tutto dall'oralità alla scrittura. Così la Somalia non sarà negata, persa*') (Garane, 124). In this sense, Nuruddin Farah's words resonate at the end of Gashan's journey, when he states his aim of keeping Somalia 'alive by writing about it' (Jaggi 2012).

Conclusion

This chapter focused on multilingualism with specific attention towards the strategies of indigenization of the Italian language. In the case of Farah, Italian serves as a means for Somali characters to elucidate the national collapse through the lens of Dante's *Divine Comedy*. In the work of Garane, Italian functions as the primary tool for depicting a pre-colonial reality. Both Farah and Garane, however, share the need to address the past to make sense of the present, investigating pre-colonial formations to identify the reasons behind the civil war.

The use of the former colonial language to represent the eighteenth century establishes a parallel between Garane and the post-independence generation of African authors. Accordingly, the chapter stressed the relation between Garane's novella and the aesthetic practices employed by the first Anglophone African writers of the 1960s. It showed how contextualization, cushioning, relexification and 'transfer of context' can be read considering the Italian literary context of the 2000s, in which *Il latte è buono* emerged as one of the first postcolonial texts. These strategies have been compared to Cristina Ali Farah's deterritorialization of Italian as a creative tool, as already analysed in Chapter 1, which might be explained due to the different proximity with the Italian language than Garane.

After closely reading the novella to scrutinize the main strategies that Garane uses towards Italian to represent Somali people, the last section of the chapter presented a methodological framework for engaging with Somali orature and its intertextual influence on *Il latte è buono*. By contextualizing the oral tradition and focusing on three metaphors, Garane reproduces some traits of the oral form and retrieves the political relevance of oral poetry. Against the generally accepted reading of orature as a marker of authenticity and Africanness or as an aesthetic trait, the chapter explained why, to investigate its impact on prose, orature should be understood contextually, avoiding generalization and narrowly shaped categories.

Also, this chapter has shown how, in Italian postcolonial studies, the presence of the Somali oral tradition has never been discussed or studied properly. *Il latte è buono*, instead, is a key example to demonstrate that Somali orature is far from a simple aesthetic device that affects dialogues and syntax. On the contrary, its presence in Garane's novella has been analysed according to the specific tradition of Somali oral poems, which cannot be labelled as broadly African.[15] The first chapter in particular, 'Nascita di una regina', has been understood as a forum in which different voices, sometimes conflicting, debate and confront each other. As in the *gabay*, the chapter raises political and social issues and the controversy surrounding a matter of dynasty, trying to reproduce the didactic role of poetry and its feature of presenting and discussing a theme within the community. By means of three key symbols (the camel, the donkey and the milk), the novella problematizes, without necessarily resolving them, the tension between identity and belonging of the protagonist towards Somalia.

The following chapter aims to delve deeper in the Italian side of the Somali diaspora, focusing on the novels by Somali Italian authors (Igiaba Scego and Cristina Ali Farah) and their relationship with Italian canonical authors of the post-war period. More specifically, their novels will be analysed along with some texts about *la Resistenza* (the partisan struggle during the war and against the Fascist state and the Nazi occupation) to retrieve shared aesthetic and ethical principles between postcolonial and post-war and anti-fascist writings. According to the grounding principle of this thesis, namely the cross-cultural and multilingual feature of Somali writings, Scego's and Ali Farah's novels will be analysed from their 'Italian' side, with particular attention to the Italian literary tradition, often neglected in favour of a more Anglo-centred postcolonial approach.

Notes

1. One could argue that the first literary work to be written by an immigrant writer without the help of an Italian co-author is *Lontano da Mogadiscio* (*Far from Mogadishu*) by Shirin Ramzanali Fazel (2017a). However, even though it is now a milestone of Italian postcolonial literature, it is not a work of fiction but an autobiographical account. It should also be mentioned the extensive and unfortunately forgotten literary production by Alessandro Spina (1927–2013). Darf Publishers recently translated his Italian novels into English (Spina 2016; Spina 2018; Vimercati 2018).
2. The first attestation of the word 'Azania' dates to the anonymous work entitled *Periplus of The Erythraean Sea* (AD 40–70), a travelogue that describes navigation and trading opportunities from Roman Egypt to the towns on the coast of the Red Sea along the Horn of Africa and the Arabic peninsula to the Indian Ocean (Mukhtar 1995, 11).
3. It is the case of '*Non si dice d'altronde nella terra dei nomadi che non ti si chiami donna, se prima non hai visto la polenta in tempo di carestia e si sia vista la tua pudicizia e la tua pazienza?*' ('Isn't it said in the land of the nomads that you do not call yourself a woman, if you have not seen the polenta in times of famine and have seen your modesty and your patience?') (Garane 2005, 32).
4. In *Il latte è buono*, the words *minority* (Garane 2005, 107) and *reservations* (102) are the only English recurrences; French words are *climatiseur* ('air conditioner', 45)

s'il vous plait ('please', 89), *somaliens* (90) and *boum* ('party', 93). In each case, no translation is provided, as to imply the familiarity of the Italian reader with these foreign words.

5   This approach appears to be misleading, as it unveils how orality is seen from a Euro-American perspective. To point out this issue with an example, I suggest considering the novella *Heart of Darkness* (1899) by Joseph Conrad. This well-known story is told by the protagonist-narrator Marlow, who recounts to his fellow sailors the events that led him to the expedition in Congo. Another narrator, who appears only at the beginning and in the end, listens while Marlow is telling his story and reports his words to the reader. This narrative structure of the frame story allows us to consider the protagonist as the storyteller and the readers, as well as the unnamed second narrator, as listeners. The novella references sea tales, like the venture of the *Erebus* and *Terror*, unglossed words in foreign language (French, Latin) and sentences which sound proverbial ('In the tropics one must before everything keep calm'). However, scholars have rightly overlooked *Heart of Darkness* as an example of traditional European style of storytelling. Western novels may retrieve oral forms or proverbs and show a strong commitment to dialogism or storytelling as well (as in the case of *Il latte è buono*) but are hardly considered as influenced by a supposed Western orality.

6   For example, if we consider proverbs in African texts, they are usually looked at as the most evident traces of an 'African oral tradition' and they are rarely addressed with the same approach about their specific context as when they are employed in Western texts, such as those of Tolkien, Melville or Dickens, to name a few (Bryan and Mieder 1997; Hayes 1999; Trokhimenko 2003). In these cases, proverbs are never considered as overarching markers of European or American cultural traditions. Besides, in *Il latte è buono*, their presence is limited if compared to their recurrence in other Somali authors, such Faarax M. J. Cawl or Xuseen Sheekh Biixi (Orwin 2007).

7   I borrowed this expression from Elleke Boehmer's *Postcolonial Poetics*, which explores how poetics shapes the reading practices of postcolonial writings. Boehmer's attention is thus directed to underscore the aesthetic principles that make a poetics which might be called '*definitively* postcolonial' (2018, 11).

8   For the description of the *gabay* see Gadhweyne (2009, 93), Abdullahi (2001, 75–7) and (Brioni, 114).

9   Also Said Samatar suggests a possible metonymic use of the word *gabay* to identify Somali poetry as a whole (1980, 451).

10 Didier Morin studied the role of the *gabay* and its evolution as a national genre in the nation-building period. '*Le genre* gabay [...] n'a pas de thématique assignée. Son recueil qui cite une trentaine de poètes, comparé à ceux de Lewis et Andrzejewski (1964, 1993), Samatar (1982), Antinucci et "Idaajaa" (1986) ne coïncide que pour les partisans des Derviches. Ce "noyau", central dans l'histoire de la littérature politique, qui ne traduit en aucun cas la diversité d'inspiration du gabay et de la création poétique en général, se signale d'abord par son caractère conjoncturé* (1997, 5).

11 With this regard, as a Somali proverb asserts: '[We] live on meat and milk' (*Cad iyo caanaa lagu noolyahay*) (Ahmed 2018). Kusow explains that 'the most interesting aspect about the obscurity of the Somali name, though, is its different oral interpretations. In the north it is said to reflect *soo-maal*, which means "go milk", with an undertone of camel being the beast involved. In the south, particularly among Reewin clan families, it is said to reflect *sa-maal*, sa meaning "cow" and *maal* "milk", indicating cattle nomadism' (1995, 85).

12 The wealth of a shepherd, associated with power, was derived from the amount of hereditary possesses and the number of camels (Abokor 1987, 8).
13 Mohamed Diriye Abdullahi notes that the '*gabay* was mostly composed by men, while *buraanbur*, which is of a lighter measure, was mostly composed by women' (Abdullahi 2001, 75–7). It would have been interesting to know if, in the case *Il latte è buono* were told by Shakhlan herself, Garane would have used the term *buraanbur* to describe his novel.
14 'The victory of Ethiopia, aided by Russia and Cuba, coupled with his own arrogance of power, rapidly led Siad Barre back to the dependency upon the clan which he had claimed to repudiate when he came to power. In succession he turned on the Majerteen, the Isaaq, the Ogaadeen and the Hawiye, using other clan militias, in particular those of his own Marehan clan. Before he finally fled Mogadishu in January 1991, all the main clans had created their own militias as well as political organisations' (Gilkes 2002, 93).
15 Along the same axis, Derek Wright has already questioned the connection between supposed good traditional values and orality (1991).

5

Resistance and *impegno*

Postcolonial Somali Novels in Italian and *Letteratura della Resistenza*

Introduction

As we leave behind the history of the Ajuran, pre-colonial Somalia and Dante's role in shaping Gashan's identity, we turn to another aspect related to language and nationhood as to show, once again, how texts, authors and contexts of the diaspora are mutually intertwined. This chapter explores the Italian shores by looking specifically at two well-established authors of Somali descent, Igiaba Scego and Ubax Cristina Ali Farah, to analyse the relationship between their novels and the Italian canon, beyond the already discussed role of Dante. In particular, this chapter will explore correspondences between Scego and Ali Farah's novels and the *Letteratura della Resistenza* (Resistance Literature or Literature of the Resistance), an umbrella term which includes those texts flourished after – and from – the experiences of resistance against Fascism after the Second World War.[1] I propose reading Italian postcolonial literature and Resistance Literature comparatively to show the network of formal and thematic features that links them, using as a starting point the funding principles of the *Letteratura della Resistenza* as outlined by Italo Calvino in the Preface to *The Path of the Spiders' Nests* (1947), published in 1964.[2]

These two literary productions have never been examined together so, hopefully, the following inquiry will be a first attempt towards recognizing the postcolonial production in Italian as part of the national literary tradition and not as 'unrelated' to it. As underlined in Simone Brioni's *The Somali Within*, Somali Italian authors have been located between trans-cultural and transnational influences (with Anglophone, Francophone and Latin American literatures), but not in relation to their 'Italian' and 'Somali' sides (2015, 141–2). The question thus emerges of how to position Scego and Ali Farah in the Italian literary tradition and, moreover, why this 'Italian side' has been neglected so far. These questions surrounding the positioning of Somali Italian authors have broader implications for contemporary debates relating to the relationship between language and national identity in the Italian literary – but also sociopolitical – context. This chapter, accordingly, suggests that postcolonial Somali novels in Italian can *also* be analysed according to the influences coming from Italian literature. The following analysis, aims to critically engage with the Italian literary canon arguing that Somali Italian authors, on the one hand, position themselves in relation to multiple affiliations and, on the other, they challenge, dramatize and problematize the concepts of *identità italiana* (Italian identity) by showing connections with canonical authors of Italian literature. As they investigate the meaning of Somaliness from a diasporic standpoint, they also interrogate Italianness, claiming their presence in Italy as citizens and, in the Italian literary scenario, as professional authors.

This approach does not wish to underplay the transnational and multilingual framework of the texts or to anchor them to a singular and well-defined national or domestic belonging. As we have seen in the previous chapters, diasporic texts and authors show multiple connections and shared sensibilities, being produced in a context that, by definition, 'places the discourse of "home" and "dispersion" in creative tension, *inscribing a homing desire while simultaneously critiquing discourses of fixed origins*' (Brah 1996, 192–3). Paraphrasing Salman Rushdie's words used to illustrate the case of Indian authors writing in English, Somali Italian writers 'have access to a second tradition', which is made up of displacement, cross-cultural networks and multilingualism. At the same time, they are related to the history, the culture and the society of the 'host' country (1991, 124). This 'second tradition' allows us to consider them not just as 'Somali' or 'Italian' but both, at the same time, as 'they position their narratives interstitially, […] strategically claiming multiple affiliations' (Gerrard 2016, 156). In other words, postcolonial Somali novels in Italian take in global aspects of the diaspora and incorporate, thematically and aesthetically, local features related to the contexts in which they are produced and read. Both characters and authors show how they move in fluid space entailing 'roots and routes' and a shifting set of relations between languages, cultures and literary references (Clifford 1994, 308).

Evidently, the argument made here does not imply a teleological or linear development from *Letteratura della Resistenza* to Somali novels in Italian. Instead, it proposes a rhizomatic relation between these two branches of the Italian literary tradition, highlighting a shared ethical commitment and aesthetic practices. Therefore, this analysis wishes to reveal how several formal strategies used by Scego and Ali Farah – usually looked at in relation to the Anglophone postcolonial production in terms of appropriating and abrogating the former colonial language – show similarities with those strategies theorized by Italo Calvino in the Preface of his pivotal novel, *The Path of the Spiders' Nests*. The latter authoritative starting point is crucial to clarify the multiple literary paths taken during the complex period of the *Resistenza*, made up of countless novels, poems, short stories and memoirs. It is worth mentioning here that the analysis of the texts belonging to the *Letteratura della Resistenza* will be focused on the novel form and that the primary interest will not be the examination of the ideological perspectives of every single author of the *Resistenza*, but the ethical and aesthetic scope of their novels.[3] In doing so, *impegno* is a useful concept to show the relationship and continuity between the two literary productions. As Jennifer Burns has suggested, *impegno* ('commitment' or 'engagement') implies and requires a responsibility from the writer to the society, as writing should be considered an 'activity which has an ethical dimension' (2001, 5). In her excursus from the 1960s to the 2000s, Burns has noticed how the term has changed over time, shifting from being the commitment to a political agenda –much present in the post-war period – to a fragmented engagement with specific issues. Interestingly, Burns studied the works of African immigrant authors writing in Italian and how they show a 'manifest and urgent sociopolitical referent – a literature which hopes to bring about change' (2001, 159). The following analysis draws upon this idea and expands it to include Somali Italian authors, who seem to recuperate this ethical commitment 'to convey their impressions of the shared socio-political panorama as seen through their own lens' (Burns 2001, 184).

In doing so, authors like Beppe Fenoglio, Italo Calvino and Luigi Meneghello may find common ground in how they employed forms of commitments and how they translated them into formal aspects such as, for example, the liberating and subversive use of the English language. 'orality' and dialects against the protectionist rules of Fascism and the literary norms of the written languages.

This comparative approach aims to show the fluidity of texts and paradigms to expand the concepts of both 'postcolonial literature' and *Letteratura della Resistenza* beyond their traditional area of influence. This approach highlights that both post-war and postcolonial authors were 'committed to producing literature that was engaged with the society in and about and for which it was written' (Burns 2000, 992). Also, Somali Italian and *Resistenza* novels share a comparable feature in the way they both deal with civil war contexts. This aspect has been critically neglected, but it emerges as a strong tie between Italy and Somalia as both nations underwent dictatorship (Benito Mussolini and Siyaad Barre) and civil war. Despite the differences at the historical level, this study shows that, in fact, the two literary productions which followed these events share similar aesthetic and thematic features.

Postcolonial Authors: A Conundrum in Italian Literature?

Whereas postcolonial novels have been studied concerning their transnational influence with non-Western or non-European writings, little work has been done about the references between postcolonial Somali novels in Italian and their position within the Italian literary tradition. This aspect needs to be critically addressed, especially from *Italianistica*, which is still reluctant to include postcolonial writings in Italian as part of the Italian tradition (Comberiati and Mengozzi 2022, 11). For example, within the influential work *Scrittori e massa* (Writers and the Masses, 2015), authored by the distinguished literary critic Alberto Asor Rosa, there is a cautious effort to place postcolonial writers within the realm of Italian literature. He admits that the postcolonial production:

> [...] escapes, and continues to escape, despite its growing importance, any attempt to positioning it, both for the multiple knowledge it entails (there are now two, three, four stories and contemporary cultures at play), both for the difficulty of

connecting these attempts, of different origins, to the «national» framework that, according to tradition, we still strive to build.

(Asor Rosa 2015, 406)

Even though Asor Rosa points out the theoretical effort in linking postcolonial production to the 'national framework', due to the 'multiple knowledge' it involves (being cross-cultural and multilingual), in the end he renounces such an effort, thus leaving these connections unexplored. It is worth noting, though, that Asor Rosa's engagement with the postcolonial paradigm seems problematic, if not suspicious. He suggests that one of the effects of postcolonial writings may be that it 'strengthens the loss of those links with the Italian literary tradition so deeply connected [...] with what we cannot otherwise call nothing else but «Italian identity»' (Asor Rosa 2015, 407). With this assumption, Asor Rosa hints at the well-established idea that national literature is the product of a national identity or of a somehow recognizable national character that postcolonial production seems to threaten.

This chapter, instead, shows how 'those links with the Italian literary tradition' are far from lost or in danger: quite the reverse, they are reinforced by Somali postcolonial authors, as they participate in (or commit to) the making of new self- and national identities by retrieving links and strategies of *impegno* that belong to the Italian literary tradition. This starting point offers a new perspective on the *Letteratura della Resistenza* itself: by comparing it with postcolonial Somali novels in Italian, we can read the former as having something akin to anti-colonial and postcolonial aesthetics. In other words: not only do Italian postcolonial writings need to be acknowledged as part of the Italian literary tradition, but we also need to re-examine the latter by tracing analogies and resonances with the Italian postcolonial production.

It is important to emphasize that the marginalization of postcolonial writings from the literary tradition has been triggered, also, by modes of selection, validation and endorsement deeply rooted in factors of assessment based on aesthetic principles. In this regard, Graziella Parati notices that:

Traditional Italianists would downgrade the texts written by migrants to being non-literary expressions [...] that have no place in a canonical classification of the narratives that define Italian literature. This protectionist approach to literary studies has a place in very normative approaches to aesthetics and runs the risk of limiting the role of literature in interpreting the culture in which it interacts.

(2005, 175)

Owing to these 'normative approaches', *Italianistica* has dismissed postcolonial authors from its agenda, thus retrieving the ostracism toward 'marginal' and 'minor' voices according to the same principles at work during the Risorgimento. Daniele Comberiati and Chiara Mengozzi have pointed out that this attitude has remained unchanged in the *Italianistica*, still reluctant to consider this *corpus* as part of the national literature (2022, 11–12).

This chapter, as said, aims to consider postcolonial literature in Italian not as marginal, exceptional or subaltern but in dialogue with and as part of the national canon, 'located in the heart of the reflections about Italian identity, thus forcing Italian scholars to a revision of the canon' (Cometa 2010, 97). Accordingly, I aim to show how Somali novels in Italian employ aesthetic strategies and ethical concerns developed by authors and texts that much contributed to the making of the 'Italian identity', namely those included in the so-called *Letteratura della Resistenza*.

These normative approaches promoted an excessively generalized idea of postcolonialism and neglected the complexity of cultural, historical or geographical influences and overlooked the relationship between authors. Scholars Cristina Lombardi-Diop and Caterina Romeo have observed that Italian postcolonial studies have engaged with several perspectives, such as gender and cultural studies, but struggled to conceive a coherent and specific theoretical system (2014, 16–17, 54). Also, according to Fabrizio De Donno and Neelam Srivastava, Italian postcolonial studies have relied on concepts and theories shaped in the Anglophone academia; they have noticed that 'postcolonialism as a scholarly field [...] needs to extend its scope of enquiry beyond the Anglo-French models of the colonial (and postcolonial) relationship, which to some extent determine the theoretical directions taken by critics' (2006, 372). In this regard, two telling examples may be presented to point out the limitations of applying this logic to the Italian context: first, in the Italian literary tradition, the novel did not play the same role performed in the English literary tradition of 'cultural artefact of bourgeois society' imbued by imperialism (Said 1993, 88). Second, Italian postcolonial authors (from Somalia, Ethiopia, Libya or Eritrea) have rarely – if ever – published from the colonies or the metropole during colonialism, as happened, for example, in the Francophone and Anglophone contexts. In the period of the Italian Empire (1936–41), no voices emerged from the African territories so influential to make an intervention in the metropole, as in the cases of, for example, Chinua Achebe, Aimé Césaire or Frantz Fanon.[4]

These examples show that the development of Italian postcolonial literature has followed a different route from the Anglophone one. Whereas the latter stemmed from the subversion of colonial discourse – buttressed, ratified and validated by canonical novels from Defoe to Conrad – in the Italian case, postcolonial texts emerged without authoritative and canonized novel production that had endorsed Italy's imperial ambitions over time (Tomasello 2004; Venturini 2010).[5] Besides, postcolonial authors could not rely on archival documentation until recently, so the only memories or reports of the colonial past were the personal accounts of the witnesses. The absence of an official historiography about the events occurred overseas, neither documented nor openly available and taught at any education level, prevented the construction of a stable postcolonial social consciousness (De Donno and Srivastava 2006, 371–9).

The so-called 'Italian colonial literature', appropriately written for consumption or for propaganda to build and support the imperial project, never achieved the status of 'canonical' literature. In the Italian novels, Somalia, Libya, Eritrea and Ethiopia did not reach the literary prominence of, to say, India or South Africa in the English fiction. Even though Italian authors developed and sustained exotic and orientalist images of Africa, the latter has been consistently represented as part of the colonial discourse mostly during Fascism. Even then, the colonies surfaced in fiction as ahistorical, undefined and mythical places. When Massimo Bontempelli (1878–1960), an Italian intellectual who wrote on the Fascist magazine *L'Azione coloniale*, was asked to define whether Italy possessed a colonial literature, he tellingly pointed out that to have one, 'it is hardly enough to simply centre a plot in Tripoli that might have happened in Perugia' (Finaldi 2009, 142).

This suggests that, until at least the Fascist period, Italian authors were unfamiliar with the geographical vastness and the topographical, historical and political understanding that underpinned English fiction and reverberated in the novels by Kipling, Conrad or Forster. Moreover, the novel In Italy did not play a role as predominant as in the English literary landscape. During the early colonial period up to the full expansion of the Empire, poems, articles, diaries or memoirs, chronicles and travel books contributed significantly to supporting colonial discourse and orientalist representations of colonized subjects, especially after the Italian defeat at the hands of Ethiopian forces at Adwa in 1896. The literary production of the late nineteenth century, related to the so-called African argument and remarkably successful during that time, was then made up of reportage, private accounts and travelogues of non-professional writers, missionaries and explorers, and a few fictional works. Again, it should be noted that, at this stage, the novel represents a latent form in the production of knowledge about Africa, because several popular novels appeared only later, during the 1930s and 1940s and under the direction of Fascist literary policies (Venturini 2010, 7–8). As a result, the novels that explicitly endorsed colonialism have been eventually forgotten or disappeared from both the literary and the publishing scene, mostly because of their mediocre quality and the regrettable ideological stances they imply. The whole production of the Fascist period, which includes by-then-famous authors such as Mario Appelius, Vittorio Tedesco Zammarano, Mitrano Sani and Orio Vergani, has never been reprinted in post-war Italy after the downfall of the regime.

In this sense, the Anglophone corpus of novels fashioned during the prolonged period of colonialism and imperialism can hardly be compared, in terms of legacy and artistic outcomes, to the Italian one. Accordingly, scholar Giuseppe Finaldi underlines that, in the late nineteenth century, 'Italy's most prominent contemporary writers [...] did not write 'colonial' novels [...] but many lesser-known authors did turn to the African wars or at least to colonial-style events to create the backdrops for their novels and to turn Africa into an Italian literary scenario' (2009, 137).

This lack of fictional production by renowned – or canonical – authors made it impossible, for Italian postcolonial writers, to rewrite 'great colonial masterpieces, which not only misinterpreted [colonised subjects] but assumed they were unable to read and respond directly to what had been written about them' (Said 1993, 35). The absence of canonical novels that, implicitly or explicitly, have represented or sustained colonialism by embodying its practices and visions, delayed the development of Italian postcolonial literature and influenced how postcolonial authors have looked at literature, colonialism and its legacy.

In this scenario, Italian postcolonial authors did not look at Italian colonial novels or historiography as their primary sources for reappropriating and rewriting them but drew upon artistic practices and literary influences coming from the Anglophone world. In the case of Scego and Ali Farah, underlined in the previous chapters, among these influences is Nuruddin Farah. Nevertheless, within this Anglophone and Francophone network, it is possible to retrieve some yet uncovered connections with the Italian phenomenon of the *Letteratura della Resistenza*. Although this literary movement is unrelated to the representation of the colonial endeavours overseas, it serves as a significant framework for interpreting postcolonial authors through an Italian (literary) perspective; such an approach could also underscore the specificity of the Italian context, its genesis and development, different from the postcolonial production in Anglophone world.

Letteratura della Resistenza: A Historical and Literary Overview

As we have seen, the events occurred amid and after colonialism, along with the processes of decolonization, have found little space in the Italian literary production, thus receiving limited representation through the novel form. Colonialism, as a literary subject, pales in comparison to the Italian resistance movement, an extensively fictionalized period in the post-war Italian scene and the object of political, historical, cultural and literary inquiry. Significantly, these two events, namely the discussion about the *Resistenza* and the AFIS trusteeship in Somalia (1950–60), are concomitant. At the time of the publication of Calvino's *The Path to the Spiders' Nest* in 1947, Italy was engaged in negotiations concerning the political future of Somalia, hoping to receive a much-desired administration of the former colony leading up to its independence (Morone 2011). During the 1950s, when the Italian literary scene saw the publication of the vast experiences of the *Resistenza*, Somalia was recognized as a UN trust territory under the Italian government, starting a complex and contradictory administration marked by a paradoxical 'democratic colonialism' (Del Boca 1984; Morone 2011). However, while the anti-colonial debate appeared rarely in Italian fiction and in the public scene, the partisan fight emerged as one of the most prolific literary subjects. The *lotta partigiana* (partisan fight) gave rise to a whole new literary movement, which eventually came to be known as *Letteratura della Resistenza*. In post-war Italy, the literary construction of the *Resistenza* and the debate around the country's trajectory after Fascism during the post-war period eclipsed the Italian colonial experience, and indeed disavowed the emancipation movements of the former colonies.[6] Even today, the *Resistenza* remains a contentious and disputable period in Italian history, provoking debate at both historical and political levels, still more discussed than colonialism, despite the long wave of postcolonial production spanning over thirty years.

The post-war period has been considered a pivotal moment of political and economic renovation, but also of cultural reconstruction after the Fascist era.[7] In the late 1940s, 'literary and testimonial texts around the Resistance came to define an idea, a lived experience and a narrative of Italy's ruinous civil war' (Srivastava 2018, 211). On retelling the events that occurred during the partisan struggle, the novel form played a significant role in representing and understanding the Resistenza, anticipating ideas that historians would acknowledge and discuss only later. Moreover, the post-war period engendered a generation of skilled and prolific writers who have since become integral figures in Italian literature, including notable names such as Italo Calvino, Cesare Pavese, Pier Paolo Pasolini, Beppe Fenoglio, Luigi Meneghello, Renata Viganò, Carlo Cassola and Ignazio Silone, to name a few.

Whereas the Resistance emerged as the epic and founding moment for the new post-1945 national identity, thus holding 'pride of place in public ceremonial, political debate and to a point also in historical writing in Italy', colonialism and anti-colonial movements did not achieve the same prominence concerning their very role in the making of national identity (Pezzino 2005, 396–7). The two historical moments have been polarized over time in antithetical extremes: on the one hand, the Resistance has been publicly promoted as 'the popular and national struggle [...] of an entire population to liberate the country from the German invader and its few Fascist allies', thus embracing its constructive features and all-inclusive scope (*ibid.*). On the other, colonialism has been related to a fleeting period, dismissed as Fascist rather than Italian and overlooked for decades by official historiography. As scholar Paolo Pezzino maintains, 'The Resistance [...] represented a classic example of the "public use of history", in which a historiographical discourse is construed to further the purposes of other orders of discourse (institutional, ideological, or party political)' (2005, 397). In the case of the *Resistenza* and the anti-fascist struggle, literature fostered discussions and re-interpretations among historians, politicians and intellectuals, but also generated interest in segments of the general public and scholars of Italian studies over time. Still, the debate on the Resistance continues to be controversial, mainly because of its inmost relation with the assessment of the Fascist period and the building of an 'official' memory of the Italian Republic (Pezzino 2005; Mammone 2006; Pavone 2006; Peli 2006). In the case of colonialism, as shown, the debate about its 'indelible wounds and mental disorders', to use Frantz Fanon's words, has been nullified for decades (2001, 181). In fact, the ruinous experience of colonialism has been cleverly pulled by politicians and institutions towards a recognized self-absolution (Del Boca 1984, 17). After the war, Italy emerged as unambiguously anti-fascist (as stated in the Constitution of the Italian Republic, 1948) but not as much explicitly anti-colonial.[8]

Before showing how the literary production about the *Resistenza* can be compared to postcolonial Somali novels in Italian, I will chart the major features of the so-called *Letteratura della Resistenza*, starting from well-renowned and canonical authors who represented the *lotta partigiana*, namely Italo Calvino, Elio Vittorini, Beppe Fenoglio and Luigi Meneghello. Their novels, despite differences in terms of content and style, all have a strong autobiographical matrix (Calvino 2013a; Re 2017). This determination to reconstruct facts through individual and collective memories, though depersonalized via fictional protagonists, led these authors to elect the novel as their privileged form of representation, a form that would not bind them to the precise re-enactment of historical events or the factual recollections of their personal experience. During the war, short stories and poems allowed *partigiani*, most of them inexpert or non-professional writers, to fulfil the need to testify an experience instantly understood as fundamental for the civil and political reconstruction of Italy after two decades of Fascism.[9] After the war, some intellectuals and professional writers embarked on a more complex and literary endeavour, looking back at the years of *lotta partigiana* not to note and report its main events but to delve into its ambiguities and complexities. The urge for testimony and documentation, which pushed witnesses and partisans to write down facts as personally experienced, was left behind in favour of a more fictionalized and detached representation of *Resistenza*. The autobiographical component was then concealed in the novel and disjointed in different characters; nevertheless, the writer's involvement in the partisan struggle remained unambiguous and emerged as the main subject of their narratives.

It is indeed in the novel that the Resistance found its uppermost literary representation. Elio Vittorini initiated this fruitful literary movement with *Uomini e no* (1945), a prose work made of numerous short chapters spaced out by the personal reflections of the author, in which he engages in a discussion with the protagonist, a partisan who fought in Milan in 1944. Italo Calvino, too, initially wrote autobiographical accounts between 1945 and 1949, published later in the short story collection titled *Ultimo viene il corvo* (The Crow Comes Last, 1949). He soon realized that the short story hindered the evolution from autobiographical testimony to fiction, so he developed the idea of the novel *The Path to the Spiders' Nests* while working on his short stories about the *Resistenza*, as he states in the Preface of the 1964 edition (Calvino 2013a, 9–29). After the first commemorative literary debuts, the Resistance began losing the celebratory tones and the rhetoric of the early stages, aiming for a more nuanced dramatization, as shown in the semi-autobiographical novel *La casa in collina* (The House on the Hill, 1948) by Cesare Pavese, *L'Agnese va a morire* (And Agnes Chose to Die, 1949) by Renata Viganò, *Fausto e Anna* (1952) by Carlo Cassola and *Una questione privata* (1963) and *Il partigiano Johnny* (1968) by Beppe Fenoglio. The latter has been considered as the author who penned the most prominent and authentic pages about the *Resistenza*; when Fenoglio's *Una questione privata* was published posthumously, one year before the Preface to *Il sentiero dei nidi di ragno*, Calvino descibed it as 'the novel that we had all dreamed of' (2013a, 27).

In these novels, the partisan struggle is de-mythicized, allowing the writers to fictionalize the difficulties of a movement whose complexity could not be acknowledged without further elaborations. According to David Ward, Fenoglio allowed for a more personal investigation of *Resistenza*, beyond the ideological underpinning of the struggle and more focused on the individual 'aspirations and desires' who led authors – and Italian people more generally – to join the resistance (1996, 123). In this regard, author Luigi Meneghello waited twenty years before drafting *The Outlaws*, published in 1964, the same year of Calvino's Preface. The novel tells the story of a small group of students from Vicenza, led by a young anti-fascist professor, who 1943 went into hiding on the Asiago plateau (in the Veneto region of Northeastern Italy) to try to organize the Resistance with the partisans. The autobiographical narrative voice unravels a long thread of ambushes, roundups, killings and escapes in which the characters become protagonists and victims. As Meneghello himself stated, he sought to represent the Resistance in an anti-rhetorical and anti-heroic tone, against the commemorative attitudes of the initial stages and the nostalgic tendencies of later representations (Meneghello 1998, 238).[10] A few lines at the very beginning of the novel, during a dialogue between the narrator and his lover Simonetta, markedly admit the author's aim:

> 'You know, fragments from one's past don't really add up to anything. What has been has been. A vague sensation remains, such as I am feeling now.'
> 'What sort of sensations?' she asked.
> 'I feel as I do when I'm at home,' I said. 'But more excited.'
> 'That's because you've been brave here,' said Simonetta.
> 'Brave?' I said. 'We run away.'
> 'I bet you were brave.'
> 'What are you talking about? Don't you see how I even abandoned the sten?'
> 'That's true,' she said. 'Why did you leave it here?'
> 'How should I know?' I said. 'We left stens all over the place.'
> 'Why?' asked Simonetta.
> 'To be perfectly honest,' I said, 'we weren't very good at war.'
>
> (Meneghello 1967, 12)

By investigating the multifaceted feature of the *lotta partigiana*, the abovementioned authors underscored a complex scenario that reveals the contrasts, ambiguities and personal aspirations in a civil war context. This aspect will be analysed in relation to postcolonial Somali literature in Italian, which portrays the inner conflict among Somali people before and during the civil war, even though without focusing on the armed military intervention. Both works of literature share the features of relying on divergent, personal memories, opposing to a coherent grand narrative in which to ground their novels. Despite the time gap from the loss of the colonies (1945 or, in the case of Somalia, 1969) and the first considerable postcolonial productions (the late-1990s), authors like Scego and Ali Farah have tried to investigate, demystify and rewrite the complexity of that period against the hegemonic narrative summarized with the self-absolving expression *Italiani brava gente*. Therefore, the following section aims to explain how these two literary outcomes (*Letteratura della Resistenza* and postcolonial literature) can be compared in the way they challenge the representation of the past through shared aesthetic forms and the use of the novel as their primary genre for retrieving the colonial period and the lack of public awareness about its crimes, effects and legacy.

In the preface of *The Path of the Spiders' Nests*, Calvino becomes both author and critic, discussing the genesis of his novel retrospectively. As Jennifer Burns has noticed, the Preface is a 'long *captatio benevolentiae* […] to inculcate the reader's sympathy' and shows his changed attitude towards literature and literary theory (2000, 1002). In the 1960s, the author-critic self-consciously looks back at his first novel in the attempt to revisit his early work in the new literary scenario. By nostalgically describing the context in which, as a partisan in his mid-twenties, he developed the idea of writing it, Calvino argues that 'life in the Resistance and its immediate aftermath was a narrative experience' (Burns 2000, 1003). There emerges an urgency to narrate the events that occurred during the occupation, the collapse of Mussolini's regime and the dramatic experiences of the partisans who fought against German Nazis and Italian Fascists during the brutal conflict known as the Italian Liberation War (1943–5).[11] Calvino emphasizes that the crucial necessity towards his and future generations – towards society, we could say – was not to inform, or provide documentary evidence or detailed facts in historical terms about the *Resistenza*. Instead, he highlights the urge to *esprimere* (to express) 'ourselves, life's rough taste which we had just experienced, the many things we thought we knew or were, and perhaps really did know and really were at that time' (Calvino 2013a, 10).

In doing so, Calvino addressed two concerns, one related to *impegno* and the other to poetics. Almost trying to detach himself from his first novel, he explains that:

> Nowadays when one talks about 'committed literature' one generally has a mistaken notion of the term, as though it were a kind of writing that is simply an illustration of a thesis already defined a priori, completely independently of any poetic qualities. Instead, what used to be called in French *engagement*, commitment, can come out at all sorts of different levels: here it is intended to emerge through the book's imagery and lexis, narrative drive, tone, style, nonchalance, challenge.
> (Calvino 2013a, 15)

Here Calvino seems to critically reassess a definition of *impegno* to include his *Il sentiero* as an example of committed literature, written with the aim to challenge the detractors of Resistance and the 'high-priests of a hagiographic Resistance that was all sweetness and light' (Calvino 2013a, 15). These objectives, analysed in the Preface in retrospection, are related to the question of poetics, namely the trouble to narrate something as new and recent as the *Resistenza* without complying the rhetoric of the 'positive hero' to fulfil a celebratory and didactic function (*ibid.*, 17). In his own words, he faced the unprecedented task 'to transform that world which for us was *the* world into a work of literature' (*ibid.*, 11). Essentially, Calvino points out the necessity to develop innovative literary practices that could ultimately lead towards a thematic and linguistic renewal of literature. Intending to achieve a new realism in which language, content and style were imperatively tied together, Calvino placed people's stories, dialects and landscapes as the three tenets of the new narrative. These ideas resulted in the theorization of the so-called Neorealism, a literary movement that Calvino defines, in the Preface, as 'many voices combined, mostly voices from the provinces, a many-sided revelation of the different Italys that existed, a revelation also –and in particular– of the Italys that had been least explored by literature' (11).

Calvino's self-reflections on his first novel, even though more similar to a critical reassessment of *Il sentiero dei nidi di ragno* aimed to justify its flaws, nonetheless present useful theoretical suggestions of poetics, which may be considered as the starting point to draw a parallel with the Somali Italian production; accordingly, the following comparative analysis will show how some stylistic and thematic features of Somali novels in Italian, usually associated with the influence of foreign authors, are in fact characteristics that appeared, for the first time in the Italian literary tradition, in the novels about the Resistance. After the experience of colonialism and, above all, the extended phase of reticence in debating and analysing it, Italian postcolonial authors faced the same problem of poetics that challenged the writers of *Letteratura della Resistenza*. In other words, they dealt with the representation of a relatively unexplored subject (being colonialism one of the 'least explored [topics] by [Italian] literature') and the necessity to find a suitable form to fictionalize, narrate and dramatize it.[12] As Calvino suggests in the preface, writers needed people's stories, a new language and landscapes to fulfil the aim of representing *la Resistenza*. Since these main aspects also show correspondences to a postcolonial poetics, which operates at both the formal and thematic level, they could be read comparatively.

As mentioned, due to the relatively little fictionalized topic of colonialism in the Italian novelistic tradition (and the total lack of postcolonial novels in Italian before the 1990s), Somali Italian authors inevitability looked at the vast corpus of postcolonial authors writing from around the world. However, some of them, such as Igiaba Scego, grew up in Italy or, like Ubax Cristina Ali Farah, studied in Italian schools and attended prominent universities, respectively Ca' Foscari (Venice), La Sapienza and Roma Tre (Rome). Their cultural background is *also* Italian due to their education and biographical reasons, so it may be fair to assume that their literary influences may also be found within the corpus of the Italian literary canon.[13] In this regard, Igiaba Scego herself places Italo Calvino among her models and, furthermore, Luigi Meneghello's short story *Il dispatrio* (1993) has been suggested as the antecedent for her *Dismatria* (2005), a made-up word that implies a possible relationship between the two, emphasizing the shared condition of people who have been displaced from their motherland (Brioni 2015, 33; Lori 2022, 121). Moreover, Cristina Ali Farah's novel *Il comandante del fiume* (The River Master, 2014) has been studied according to the fairy-tale texture of its prose, influenced by Italo Calvino and Cesare Pavese (Clemente 2015).

Since Ali Farah and Scego are authors and intellectuals who creatively engage with language and make interventions concerning sociopolitical and historical topics within and from the Italian context, they could be read multi-directionally, focusing on both their transnational influences (as the previous chapters have shown) and their locally bounded commitment. Their Italian side, indeed, emerges as a fruitful, yet slightly neglected source of reflection.[14] The following analysis, therefore, instead of looking at the Italian postcolonial production as the embodiment, in Asor Rosa's terms, of the 'loss of those links with the Italian literary tradition', might be considered as an attempt to reestablish and reinvigorate 'those links' instead of cutting them off (Asor Rosa 2015, 407).

For example, the insertion of foreign words in the Italian framework of the plot, as well as the references to Somali, American or Brazilian culture and literature, has been looked at as markers of their non-relatedness to the Italian literary tradition. However, if this stylistic feature can be understood as a sign of the transnational and cross-cultural feature of both texts and authors, it should be read as anything but exogenous or new in Italian literature. Calvino himself affirms that one of the new characteristics of post-war Italian literature is indeed its transnational trait. By including American writers such as Ernest Hemingway (1899–1961), and Soviet authors like Isaac Babel (1894–1940) and Alexander Fadeyev (1901–56) as main models, the new-born narrative endorsed foreign terms and references as a distinctive feature. Language was meant to be a wide-ranging medium in which dialects, everyday expressions and literary lexes were to be included to achieve a higher degree of verisimilitude and reproduce the spontaneity and directness of the spoken word, thus marking a departure from Fascist linguistic policies. Furthermore, the narrative techniques derived from American literature and cinema of the 1920s and 1930s, such as the use of concise and blunt dialogues to resemble ordinary speech, are key features in the novels by Calvino, Vittorini and Pavese (Casadei and Santagata 2007).

For instance, in Beppe Fenoglio's *Il partigiano Johnny* (1968), the juxtaposition of Italian and English through unglossed and not italicized words is a frequent practice, as the following explicative passages show:

> So mornings were diseased and nightmared. Il paesaggio ora lo nauseava, scontato il gusto del ritrovamento della terra natale e vitale. La letteratura lo nauseava. Come da quel surfeit di cibo e di sonno gli si cancellò tutto dalla vita militare, in capo ad una settimana non sapeva più da che parte si cominciasse a smontare un mitragliatore, ciò che una settimana prima sapeva fare a occhi bendati. Ed era male; qualcosa, dentro pungente e icefying, l'avvertiva che era male.
>
> [...]
>
> Prese a smaniare per sentire la voce di Candidus, gluttoning on his own accent. Quasi ogni giorno saliva suo padre, for several requests-annotations e riferirgli le notizie locali e nazionali.
>
> (2003, 8–9)

> So mornings were diseased and nightmared. The landscape now nauseated him, expected the pleasure of rediscovering his native and vital land. Literature sickened him. As thought from that surfeit of food and sleep, everything from his military life was erased; after a week he no longer knew which way to start dismantling a machine gun, what he had been able to do blindfolded a week earlier. And it was bad; something inside, stinging and icefying, warned him that it was bad.
>
> [...]
>
> He began to long to hear Candidus's voice, gluttoning on his own accent. Almost every day his father visited him for several requests-annotations and report local and national news to him.

English literature and language do not play a fundamental role in the prose of Beppe Fenoglio alone, but they are also relevant in Luigi Meneghello's writing; English actively contributed to shaping their unique style (Brian 2011, 149). About this relationship, Meneghello himself stated that:

È stato in Inghilterra, e attraverso la pratica dell'inglese, che ho imparato alcune cose essenziali intorno alla prosa. In primo luogo che lo scopo della prosa non è principalmente l'ornamento, ma è quello di comunicare dei significati. Questa per me era una novità. Faceva a pugni con l'intera temperie dell'educazione retorica a cui ero stato esposto.

(Meneghello 2006, 1307)

In was England, through the practice of the English language, that I learned some essential things about prose. First, the main purpose of prose is not to be an ornament, but to communicate meanings. This was a novelty for me. It clashed with the whole period of rhetorical education I have been exposed to.

And so, *Letteratura della Resistenza* brought about two innovative and quite radical additions to Italian literature: the open acknowledgement of Anglophone, French and Soviet influences as literary references and linguistic creativeness that promoted the inclusion of foreign terms in the Italian syntax and forms of bricolage and juxtaposition. This transnational pull represented a way to position Italian literature globally and shatter the fascist linguistic protectionism and cultural segregation. If we understand Fascism as a form of internal colonialism in terms of language, *Resistenza* literature's formal aspects, such as juxtaposition, relexification and cushioning, operate as both poetic principles and political stances as they do in postcolonial authors. In the light of post-war Italy, 'this movement of going-between languages and cultures against the norm of the official language carries imaginative as well as an ethical force: going between worlds; going between a writer in one context and a reader in another' (Boehmer 2018, 53).

The concept of 'ethical force' might be suitable to draw a comparison between postcolonial and *Resistenza*/anti-fascist writings: in Fenoglio's *Il partigiano Johnny*, the Italian language embodies the fascist tool of formal education, political propaganda, a language stuck in rhetoric and isolationism that works as a colonial, normative language for control and power. A foreign language such as English, as much as dialect, emerges as both an ethical and aesthetic tool to obstruct the linguistic policies of the regime and oppose censorship (Isella 1992; Montermini 2007). The use of multilingualism, then, upsets the power of the 'official' language; the contamination of the Italian prose with foreign terms, sentences and syntax resembles a process that can be broadly conceived as a postcolonial act of literary abrogation.

Anti-fascist intellectuals and writers like Fenoglio, Meneghello, but also Pavese and Calvino, after being silenced and marginalized during Fascism, developed new literary strategies to dismantle the regime's conceptual paradigms and challenge linguistic hegemony, thus aiming for transformation and liberation. Italian authors during dictatorship underwent what can be called 'exile of the mind'. As Meenakshi Mukherjee explains, the latter is experienced by those who 'without being physically away from home remain outsiders in their own country due to certain circumstances in their history, language or education' (1988, 8).

In both *Letteratura della Resistenza* and postcolonial Somali novels in Italian, authors 'abrogate any centralizing notion of the "correct", or standard, way of doing things and re-define the practice in a different setting' (Ashcroft, Griffiths and Tiffin 2000, 4). Italian (a language both fascist and colonial) is reinvented and enriched through unglossed foreign words (in English and French) and dialect against any normative standard. As noticed by Marisa Escolar, 'In the context of civil war, the Italian language becomes a site of contention', whereas foreign languages such as German (spoken in some regions of the North of Italy) and 'dialect – rejected by the Fascist regime's *Riforma Gentile* as an impediment to national unity – becomes an invaluable tool in establishing new boundaries' (2018, 73). As Fenoglio aims to resist the regime's linguistic policies and explore new linguistic possibilities for the novel and for the narrative of the Resistance, postcolonial authors attempt to abrogate and appropriate Italian as well, arguing for the parity and irreducibility of Somali towards the former colonial language.

These linguistic tools (explored in the novel *Little Mother* by Ubax Cristina Ali Farah in Chapter 1) can be read here along with the theorization of the 'real', as imagined by Calvino. He suggests that the so-called 'real' should be achieved through the renewal and rediscovery of dialect, with a strenuous opposition to the Fascist rhetoric, and the restoration of orality (Calvino 2013a, 8). In this sense, the spoken word is understood as the collection of the stories and the direct memories of the events that occurred during *Resistenza*. To represent the everyday experience, literary language should comprise oral features such as tales, common sayings and songs in a kind of *repertorio documentaristico* (documentary archive) (*ibid.*, 14).

The latter approach emerged as a prominent literary practice and expanded beyond language; oral tales and personal memories were in opposition to any detailed or precise investigation provided by historical or archival documentation. The biographical matrix plays a fundamental part in the process of writing the past, as in postcolonial authors, since they have no direct knowledge of the events (as the partisan writers do); the significance of personal memories, therefore, holds considerable value, serving as a bridge between the present and the past. This connection is established using flashbacks, juxtaposed with the narrator's present-time setting. The lack of a first-hand experience of colonialism is effectively counterbalanced by the biographical element within the novels, as their literary works resonate across generations by incorporating the recollections of their relatives. This deliberate choice aims to underscore the enduring impact of colonialism on contemporary society, thus shedding light on this historical overlooked period. In other words, despite Scego and Ali Farah lacking direct experience to colonialism, they manage to retrieve it through the account of their families and the fictionalization of the present struggles against the prevailing racist and colonial ideologies in contemporary Italy. Notably, this is evident in Scego's *Adua* and Ali Farah's 'A Dhow Crosses the Sea' (2017).

In *Letteratura della Resistenza*, memory, orality and language, as understood in Calvino's terms, are combined with the intent of ethical and civil testimony, and with *impegno* (engagement or commitment). After the Second World War, the demand for a concrete commitment to Italy's political and social reality was a key subject for writers, directors and intellectuals. The latter, after their involvement in anti-fascist movements or their enrolment in *lotta partigiana*, started to consider literature as a form of *impegno*. As previously shown and analysed by Jennifer Burns (2001, 5–6), in Calvino's theorization, the *engagement* should not be tethered to a political stance, because this approach might eventually risk turning literature into propaganda; similarly, such *impegno* should not be perceived as a predetermined construct dictating and driving the author's poetics. Instead, writers should use literature to engage with the ethical dimension of writing and address contemporary topics, more than allowing literature to be driven by their political engagement.[15] In opposition to idealized and didactic perspectives, Calvino suggests a novel form unbound from programmatic ideologies, in which narrative motifs are provided from 'what [the writer] had seen and experienced' (2013a, 19).

If we consider postcolonial Somali novels in Italian, the recovery of *impegno* and the recuperation of ethics through the dramatization of everyday experiences connected to racism, migrations and citizenship arises as one of the foremost literary features of their novels. In doing so, their attention focuses on the oral *repertoire* of stories and recollections of migration, displacement and resettlement, thus echoing the concept of *repertorio documentaristico* Calvino theorized. Polyphony, understood as both the multiplicity of points of view and multilingualism, which combines different languages but also dialects, is employed by Scego and Ali Farah through unglossed words, loan words and a multi-narrator structure. Whereas these features find models in Anglophone postcolonial literature, they also may be traced back to the literary practices developed in the *Letteratura della Resistenza*, thus showing how that these aesthetic features and ethical practices are inherent to the Italian literary tradition and can be looked at as forms of resistance and *impegno*, in both anti-fascist and postcolonial terms. The core idea of 'resistance' should then be regarded as necessary in the poetics of Italian postcolonial writers and post-war novels. Whereas Calvino, Fenoglio and Meneghello looked at the Resistance from an anti-fascist standpoint, Somali writers resemantize the term *Resistenza* from a postcolonial perspective. The commitment they carried on, then, deals with the persistent challenge of the dominant discourse about colonial history and the supposed homogeneity of the Italian society.[16]

Nevertheless, it is worth noting that, apart from the revival of *impegno* and the recontextualization of the concept of resistance, the two literatures could also be linked through an additional, often-overlooked trait aspect, namely their representation of civil war and dictatorship contexts. Even though grounded in diverse historical and political settings, Somali novels in Italian and *Resistenza* texts deal with the armed conflict between peoples of the same nation. Scego's *Adua* and, above all, Ali Farah's *Little Mother* dramatizes the fragmentation of Somali people after colonialism and the long-lasting period of conflicts in the 1990s, where different clans fought for the control of power after the fall of Siyaad Barre's dictatorship. Similarly, *Letteratura della Resistenza* portrays the struggle between *partigiani* and *repubblichini* after the fall of Benito Mussolini's regime.[17] In doing so, the novels reconsider and problematize the concepts of nationhood and belonging, thus making the 'concept of identity [as] always plural, and in process' (Brah 1996, 193). On the one hand, Somali novels in Italian fictionalize the challenging idea of belonging in the war-torn scenario of infightings and sectarianism; on the other hand, they also claim their Italian identity and their relation to the Italian culture. In other words, they dramatize their struggle to identify themselves with the fluid concepts of Somaliness and Italianness. The following sections will further delineate the representation and fictionalization of this process in Scego and Ali Farah's novels, paying specific emphasis on the elements of resistance and *impegno* discussed beforehand.

Resistance and *impegno* in Igiaba Scego's *Adua*

Igiaba Scego's novel *Adua* (2019) may be read in light of the aforementioned comparative and cross-historical approach to highlight the novel's connection with some aspects that shaped Italian post-war literature. *Adua* re-counts the colonial past in juxtaposition to the narration of the present. At the basis of the novels, there are two storylines set during fascist colonialism in Somalia and Mussolini's dictatorship in Rome in the 1930s (the father's plot), and in present times (the daughter's plot). Along these main temporal axes, the plot often digresses so that the reader is led to other time settings through flashbacks told by Adua, such as the 1970s in Italy and the 1960s in Magalo, a town in Somalia. At the structural level, the two main temporal levels coexist and are not displayed diachronically: events do not follow a chronological order but are dispersed according to the characters' recollections. Time, then, is continuously stretched and tightened. The three sections in which the novel is organized also represent different time settings, connected one to the other by the presence of Mohamed Ali Zoppe and his daughter Adua, portrayed at different ages. The plot continually goes back and forth in time so that the events narrated in the section 'Zoppe' are resumed after the segment with Adua's perspective. The former dramatizes the events in Zoppe's life while he worked as a translator in Rome in the 1930s; the latter narrates the story of his daughter, who escaped from Somalia and moved to Italy in the 1970s at the age of seventeen, chasing the promise of a career in cinema. It also tells the story of Adua's involvement with a refugee arrived in Lampedusa, whose real name is Ahmed but is ironically nicknamed Titanic, thus shedding light on the so-called European migrant crisis. In Adua's story, the civil war that shattered Somalia seems over, and her best friend Lul has returned to Mogadishu, making Adua feel torn between the responsibilities of her life in Italy and the possibility to return to her homeland.

A short section, entitled 'Paternale' ('Talking-To'), interposes 'Zoppe' and 'Adua' and shows Adua's father in the act of lecturing and scolding her. Scego, in the afterword to the book, acknowledges the biographical sources of her work and admits a certain degree of embellishment and fictionalization. Most importantly, Scego states that she developed the two plots by gleaning material from family memories and her direct involvement with refugees (Scego 2019). Using first-hand experiences should not be intended merely as a personal or artistic choice but should be read in relation to the cultural context and, I argue, with that recuperation of *impegno* previously discussed.

Adua indeed shows a 'manifest and urgent socio-political referent', engaging directly with the present and taking part in a literary production 'which hopes to bring about change' (Burns 2001, 159). Scego's commitment to discuss relevant issues such as relocation procedures and unwelcoming policies towards migrants aims to signal and explore the legacy of colonial practices in contemporary Italian – and European – politics. Far from being a concluded period confined in archival documents and historical records, colonialism is still present in both explicit and edulcorated forms, such as the derogatory and simplistic language of the media, citizenship laws, restrictive migration policies and xenophobic slogans of right-wing politicians who capitalize on public anxiety and fear of a possible invasion. The primary goal of both the narrative fragmentation and the juxtaposition of separate times and geographies, therefore, is to highlight correlations between different periods. As Gabriele Lazzari has observed, involuntarily retrieving Primo Levi's *zona grigia*, Scego:

> […] explores the historical causes and personal repercussions of racial and gender oppression, the gray area of collusion with its perpetrators, and the pervasiveness of power asymmetries among and within social collectives, often occurring despite a shared cultural background.
>
> (2017)

In *Adua*, more than factual descriptions of historical events conveyed through the detached standpoint of an omniscient narrator as in a historical novel, the focus on two perspectives and the shifting in time and space mirrors the unsolved question of colonialism and the enduring effect of colonial discourse. The protagonists' subjectivity is, indeed, influenced and traumatically shaped by the colonial encounter and its present vestiges.

Little Mother by Cristina Ali Farah is another example of the fragmented and polyphonic structure of Somali postcolonial narratives. In Ali Farah's novel, the three main characters, Domenica, Barni and Taageere, narrate in first person the experience of the civil war and the resettlement in Italy and the United States. Like Scego's *Adua*, *Little Mother* illustrates the involvement of the author's relatives in colonial history by mixing testimony, biography and fiction (Brioni 2015, 141). In their novels as well, the present-day racism of Italian society and politics is explicitly connected to the Fascist colonial period, and this link is suggested by the personal account of the protagonists, who endured the discursive and physical violence of contemporary Italian society, functioning in the forms of objectification, sexualization, racism, violence and, at the political level, in restrictive policies concerning citizenship and asylum.

As for the writers of the *Resistenza*, the individual experiences of the author-narrator enable the process of reworking historical events and disrupt the dominant discourse. In the case of *Adua*, the dominant discourse that the novel aims to debunk is the myths of *Italiani brava gente* and of Europe as a welcoming place. Postcolonial literature and *Letteratura della Resistenza* converge here in their attempt to deflate and downplay the self-image of Italians as good people, which constructed modern Italian identity. These novels are, therefore, making a political move and elaborating on the meaning and the making of Italianness from anti-colonial and anti-fascist positions. To point out how this process of demystification operates, I suggest starting with the analysis of the structure of *Adua*.

As shown, the novel is made up of multiple points of view, and, at the formal-stylistic level, displays the provisional perspective of each narrative with three different narrative voices, accordingly. The sections entitled 'Adua' are written using the first-person narrator, while those entitled 'Zoppe' are in the third person and, lastly, the 'Talking to' sections are in the second-person narrator since the father – who is speaking to Adua without receiving any answers – addresses his daughter directly with 'You'. While individual recollections and memories unfurl in the foreground, historical events loom offstage. Both Adua and Zoppe seem to be drawn into these events rather than actively engaging with them, giving the impression that their personal stories – as partisan Johnny's 'aspirations and desires' – are interrupted by the unfolding course of history (Ward 1996, 123).

In the Preface of *The Path of the Spiders' Nests*, Calvino seems to hint at the same idea when he indicates that the *Resistenza* (both historical and literal) was made by the participants' first-hand experiences and, often, their inability to grasp the gravity and the importance of that moment. In the literary practice, rather than representing grand events, Calvino underlines the importance of individual points of view to shape a common history, stating that:

> Those who began writing in that period found themselves dealing with the same subject matter as these anonymous storytellers: not only did we have the adventures that each one of us had endured personally or witnessed, but there were also tales which came to us already formed as narratives, with a voice, a cadence.
>
> (2013a, 10)

Calvino's words, which consider orality as the collection of different voices and the role of the writer as the gatherer of these stories –including his own– resemble those by Ali Farah regarding her novel and her role as a writer. She explains that diasporic people as scattered pearls that were once part of the same necklace and that

> My book *Little Mother* takes inspiration from the oral stories that have been told in my family for years or that I have heard on the telephone, as well as from a series of testimonies that I have collected through interviews. […] With my novel and my writing, I narrate the story of these pearls, like the tiles of a mosaic: my attempt is to ensure that the pearls return to being part of the same necklace.
>
> (2007)

The necessity to collect stories, amalgamating individual experiences with second-hand testimonies to represent a historical moment, emerges as a shared approach of both post-war and postcolonial authors. Similarly, in Meneghello's *The Outlaws*, the events that occurred during the partisan fight between 1943 and 1945 are narrated in the first person, letting the reader reckon a certain degree of proximity between the author and the narrator. In doing so, rather than fictionalizing grand historical episodes, Meneghello reuses his own experience to distil the plot's main events. Both Scego and Ali Farah opt to tell the history of colonialism and civil war via the stories of relatives, parents, friends and witnesses who personally went through these events. In Calvino's words, they collect the many voices of 'the same subject matter' and try to give them a form of unity and consistency, in other words, a narrative (2013a, 10).

In *Adua*, the structure of the novel reflects this focus on multiple individual stories weaved together against the backdrop of major historical events, which allows recurrent themes, such as violence and racism, to connect different periods. When we first meet Zoppe, he is a Somali young man who works as an interpreter for the Fascist administration in Rome.[18] Scego introduces him while three soldiers are punitively beating him because of his skin colour. According to the collective knowledge of that time, which eventually resulted in the supposed scientific studies about race condensed in the *Manifesto della razza* (*Manifesto of Race*, 1938), Black skin connoted inferiority, primitiveness and bestiality. Scego describes Zoppe's harsh life as a Black man in Rome during Fascism, a city increasingly hateful towards colonized subjects and Jews. In this regard, Scego's often-brutal and body-related vocabulary employed to describe Zoppe's condition is intertwined with dream-like and surreal passages, in which the author suggests the forthcoming antisemitic persecution but also the ferocity of the colonial subjugation and the outbreak of Second World War (Scego 2019, 19–32; 57–9; 143–7; 161–72).

Zoppe, who is a translator but also possesses the clairvoyant power of foreseeing the future, repeatedly finds refuge in visions and hallucinations, which hallucinations which further remark the fluidity of time. This oneiric element, most importantly, reflects the defence mechanisms against the trauma induced by colonial invasion. Interestingly, in Calvino's *Il sentiero*, the 'spiders' nests' represent the protagonist's 'secret place of retreat into a natural setting far from the pressure and turmoil of social existence' (Re 1990, 263). Pin and Zoppe share the same attempt to retreat away from society as a reaction to overwhelming events that they struggle to process. Their efforts to escape and avoid the painful present, however, remain unfulfilled. In the case of Pin, he ultimately recognizes, drawing a zoomorphic parallel, an eerie similarity between men and spiders, between their cruelty and intelligence, thus nullifying the safety of his secret place. Zoppe's hallucinations, too, often lead him to witness the future war in Somalia and the illegal chemical weapons used by Italian soldiers against his people. Through Zoppe's subconscious, Scego shows the violence of colonization and displays insights into the effects of such violence on both national and individual identity.

As in the case of Pin, Zoppe's prophecies and nightmares are denoted by bestiality, a feature that stands out as the main feature of his visions. Described with attention to corporeal details and the cumulative use of adjectives pertaining to the semantic field of death, these visions give sense to the ferocity of the invasion, standing in stark contrast to the narrative of civilization constructed by the Italians. Scego's consistent use of graphic and harsh imagery, facilitated through an expressionistic linguistic style, can be interpreted as her attempt to underscore the enduring impacts of both war and colonization. Nevertheless, I argue that it may be considered as both a rhetorical and political practice to counterbalance the too often minimized and underrated – if not entirely overlooked – representation of Italian colonialism at both the mediatic and sociopolitical levels. As noted, for decades, Italian public policy has omitted the role played by the Italians in the Eastern-African territories, thus fuelling a state-driven forgetfulness and a collective self-absolution. The expressionist style thus confronts any attempts to lessen the violence of colonialism and its traumatic effect but also addresses the reader, challenges their perspectives and exposes any edulcorated visions of Italians as *brava gente*. This strategy might be connected to the notion of *impegno* which, according to Jennifer Burns:

> dictates that the writer has some responsibility for the response she produces in the reader, and that this respondent treats responsibility the commitment thus made by the writer.
>
> (2001, 5)

In other words, Scego's novel exemplifies the author's conscientious commitment to the society in which she lives. *Adua*'s objective extends beyond mere representation, seeking instead to re-evaluate societal perceptions regarding colonialism and still-present self-absolving ideas related to Italianness.

In Calvino's *The Path*, similes and expressions related to bestiality are often employed in dialogues and descriptions. He himself, in a later interview published in the 'Notes to the 1998 Translation', affirmed to 'have written things that seemed too brutal or exaggerated' (Calvino 2013a, 2). Accordingly, the following passage from the Preface highlights this shared linguistic feature with Scego:

> There was the manner of depicting characters: they all had exaggerated, grotesque features, twisted grimaces, dark, deep-rooted phycological scars. If Italian literature and art had missed out on expressionism after the First World War, it made up for it at the end of the Second. Perhaps the correct label for that artistic epoch in Italy ought to be 'Neo-expressionism' rather than Neo-realism.
>
> (Calvino 2013a, 13)

As scholar Caterina Mongiat Farina suggests, this (neo) expressionism aims to point out both the cruelty and violence of the partisans' life and humanize them (2014, 421). The same symbolic and analogic function of language can be retrieved in *Adua* since Scego employs a remarkable variety of references to the animal world to describe colonial violence. In this regard, the physical component of Scego's style, made up of numerous references to corporeality, prevails over a nuanced emotional depth. The syntax of colloquial Italian allows us to draw a parallel with the 'Neo-expressionist' style theorized by Calvino, made up of short sentences, limited spatial descriptions and inflated psychological traits. In this economy of language, metaphors and similes then acquire particular significance. They provide the novel, characterized by a material and bare prose, with a symbolical weight.

For example, when Zoppe is in Regina Coeli – a prison in Rome – after being beaten and insulted ('darkie bastard', 'dumb n****r', 'maggot'), one of the Fascists 'touched him like a mother her young' (in Italian, Scego uses more specifically the word *cucciolo*, meaning 'cub' or 'puppy') (Scego 2019, 39–41). In the cell, the calm is 'rat-scented', and 'worms dropped from his mouth whole' (41–44). In other cases, animals are employed to point out the shared nature between men and beasts with a negative zoomorphic connotation: official count Anselmi's hands are compared to 'the 'paws of a warthog which is in heat'; he moves 'like a hyena that has spotted his prey' (183, 185). The elder Ethiopians' leader has fingers 'like the claws of a bird of prey' (185); Somali people are described as 'naked and thrashing around like snakes' (in Italian, *bisce*: 'grass snakes') (97). The French hotel owner in Addis Ababa has arms as long as the tentacles of the octopuses that Zoppe used to find on the seashore in Magalo (105). The inhabitants of Mogadishu are compared to African wild dogs that wail, waiting for their death (167). In some passages of the novel, nature itself is the harbinger of war and death: cedar fruits, thrown by Zoppe's friend Dagmawi for fun, become grenades in the thoughts of the two friends, who imagine themselves fighting the Italians soon. The presence of death during the meeting between Zoppe and Dagmawi is further suggested by the looming presence of marabou storks, birds of bad omen (125–127).

Animals, too, draw attention to the violence of colonialism by emphasizing the Italians' disregard towards both land and people. In the first meeting between Zoppe and Count Anselmi, in the latter's eighteenth-century house in Tivoli, horns of rhinos and a buffalo's head hang on the wall as emblems of colonial exploitation (Scego 2019, 97–7). However, violence is not confined solely to the context of the Fascist period but instead serves as a thread to connect the past to contemporary Italy. The recollections of Adua after she arrived in Italy in 1976 echo the violence of the colonizers, especially towards Black women and parallel, too, the violence perpetrated on Zoppe's body at the beginning of the novel (Volpato 2009). While Adua grew up after Somalia's independence, she has direct experience of the neocolonial ties with Italy; when an Italian film crew arrives in Magalo, seeking Somali actresses, she joins them, prompting her aspirations of pursuing an acting career. Once in Rome, she discovers a less promising, harsh reality. She recalls being sexually abused and exploited with the promise of playing a part in *Femina somala*, an erotic film that perpetuates stereotypes of Black/African women.[19]

Adua, therefore, as the recurrent violence on the two protagonists' Black bodies suggests, exposes patterns of discrimination that connect Adua's present 'to the brutal reality in which her father found himself enmeshed decades before' (Burdett 2022, 14). The fascist idea of Black people as non-human, and the making of the colonized subject as inferior, results in a continuation of colonial discourse, exemplified by the sexual objectification and exploitation of Black women in the 1970s. Scego's example of transgenerational violence surfaces when she presents Adua's role in the male-centred film industry, stigmatized and limited to roles in which she is always subjugated by her male counterpart or required to pose, undressed, without speaking.

The attention to the two characters' Black bodies and their brutalization can be read as a metaphor for the whole of Somalia. In particular, Scego refers to one of the most brutal moments of the colonial period, which explicitly emphasizes the damages of the Italian invasion: the so-called Walwal incident in the Ogaadeen region, a border zone between Italian Somaliland and the Empire of Ethiopia. The events dramatized in the section 'Zoppe' occur during this period, and Scego acknowledges this historical setting only in the afterword (2019, 200–3). However, the protagonist does not witness these events, so they linger in the background and surface only due to occasional references.

The structure of the novel, then, with temporal and geographic shifts, implies that retrieving Italian colonial history may occur only in a deferred way. The historical events are never addressed directly, but always told from a delayed perspective and brought to life by individual recollections. The main historical events remain circumstantial, while the single stories of the characters, rather than their involvement in the greater scene, emerge as key narrative subjects. In this case, a passage from Calvino's *The Path of Spiders' Nests* suggests another parallel with *Adua*: both novels share the same approach towards history, understood as a collection of single experiences intermingle into one universal grand event. For Calvino, the latter is the *Resistenza*, for Scego, colonialism:

> I, on the other hand, am walking through a larch wood, and every step I take is history. I think 'I love you, Adriana' and that is history, will have great consequences. I'll behave tomorrow in battle like a man who has thought tonight, 'I love you, Adriana.' Perhaps I may not accomplish great deeds, but history is made up of little anonymous gestures; I may die tomorrow even before that German, but everything I do before dying and my death too will be little parts of history, and all the thoughts I'm having now will influence my history tomorrow, tomorrow's history of the human race.
>
> (Calvino 2013a, 139)

In the passage, love and history, personal and collective, are intermingled. Kim, the young psychiatrist who joined the Resistance and the 'I' voiced above, identifies his wish to fight with a vague desire for social redemption, thus showing how aspirations and desires are mixed – if not subordinated to – with political reasons. In his reflection, historical reasons take turns with private reasons.

This focus on the individual experiences of the characters, as the starting point to arrange the plot and represent history, should be considered a distinctive element of postcolonial Italian literature, as the colonial experiences they fictionalize survived for a long time in the single stories of the witnesses or individual memories (Andall and Duncan 2005, 15). Scholar Karen De Léon-Jones notices that, in *The Path of the Spiders' Nests*, 'transmission is oral, written language nearly absent, and this causes political discourse to distort in the telling, as the language of ideology is not accessible to the uninitiated in party politics and reduces itself to slogans and easily repeated catch phrases' (1997, 365). The oral narrative is then a central means (and somehow necessary, given the public amnesia about colonialism) to tell and re-tell the past, preferred to the documented, archival and 'objective' reconstruction of historical novels (Calvino 2013a, 23). This emphasis on orality and recollections approximates Calvino's 'urge to *express*' he describes in the Preface.

In the case of *Adua*, Zoppe's act of translation during a meeting between the Ethiopian elders and Italian officials marks the betrayal of Ethiopians, who vow to support Italian soldiers and to assassinate the Ethiopian emperor Hailé Selassié. The language of the official documents is accessible to Zoppe but not completely intelligible: he perceives the threat hidden in the Italian words, but he can only obey and accomplish his role of a translator (Scego 2019, 25–7). However, Scego challenges this submissive position of the translator by affirming, on the one hand, the impossibility for colonized subjects to fight back against colonial discourse and, on the other hand, Zoppe's ambition and self-fulfilment, which he places before his country. Zoppe himself describes his aspirations and desire and being 'the envy of everyone', so that people will kneel at his feet, in contrast to his father's will (*ibid.*, 53). His fascination for Rome (the same as Adua, years later) is associated with the alluring power of the metropole and the misplaced possibility of achieving power by working for the colonizers. This ambition could be read as an example of mimicry, or the adoption of the colonizer's cultural habits, values and beliefs (Bhabha 2004, 131). However, Scego does not draw much attention to Zoppe's interest in the language, clothes or cultural attitude of the colonizer to the detriment of his own. He loves Dante, but the Italian language is listed among others (Arabic, Somali, Kiswahili, Amharic, Tigrinya and several dialects of the Horn of Africa) without accentuating its ascendancy on Zoppe or its higher hierarchical status. While displaying evident pride in his khaki suit and lauding his role as a translator serving the ruling authorities, his fundamental objective in imitating the colonizer is centred on financial gain: 'All he wanted from the Italians was the money to buy a big house […] for his Asha. Everything else was of no consequence to him' (Scego, 24; 93). Zoppe's opportunistic behaviour prevails over the suppression of his Somali belonging to emulate a supposed (and inaccessible) Italianness; his main goal is to achieve wealth through the colonizers and, ultimately, wed Asha.

Zoppe's unscrupulousness may be associated, as well, with the conduct of several Italians who were ambivalent towards Fascism, non-ideologically aligned to the regime but not explicitly against it. According to historian Paul Corner,

> between 1943 and 1945, the great majority of Italians had not participated in the Resistance and, more significantly, had 'remained at the window', in what was, in effect, a great display of civil cowardice and amoral familism, in the sense of opportunistically waiting to see how things turned out before deciding to support one side or the other.
>
> (2012, 210)

The attitude of 'opportunistically waiting' cuts across the demarcation between colonizers and colonized, shedding light on the integral complexities and ambiguities of contexts marked by war or colonialism, which mix up power dynamics and produce a *zona grigia* (a gray area). In Primo Levi's term, in this gray area the line between victims and perpetrators becomes blurred (Levi 2017, 31). In a passage of *Adua*, Scego describes this ambivalence through the character of Idris Shangani, whose lure towards power leads him to switch allegiances during the Italian invasion. After the war, he takes over a cinema built by the Fascists, repurposing it for personal financial gain:

> Idris Shangani was one of those Somalis who had made money during colonialism by sending bodies to the front during Italy's war against Ethiopia. Then after the end of World War II, when the United Nations decreed that Italy and the newly formed Trust Territory of Somaliland would ferry us to independence, Mr Shangani got even richer.
>
> And you would always find people like Idris Shangani who would happily tell you how life wasn't so bad under the Italians.
>
> (Scego 2019, 80, 83)

Scego explicitly addresses the concept of 'collaborationism', which can be read along with mimicry in the fact that both attitudes reassess established hierarchies and expose the inconsistency of power dynamics. For example, Zoppe's work as a translator for the Italians is seen as a form of betrayal and as a way to achieve personal success; however, while admitting being a traitor and acknowledging his treachery by drawing a parallel to the biblical figure of Judas, 'who sold [himself] for a pile of money', Zoppe maintains a contemptuous view of Idris Shangani, considering him as a collaborator (*ibid.*, 171). In the case of Zoppe and Idris Shangani, their personal ambitions prevail over ideological motivations, leveraging the political situation to place themselves in proximity to power. Only towards the end of the novel Zoppe feels ashamed for his betrayal, struggling to come to terms with his conscience (Rand 2020; Burdett 2022).

In Calvino's novel, partisans too are liable for collaborationism due to personal motives. Pin's sister, for example, faces accusations of being sympathetic to the Nazi and is eventually side-lined from the group; however, it is Pelle – one of the youngest partisans of the group – who ultimately betrays his fellow partisans after arguing with one of them, named *il Dritto* (lit. 'the sly one'). The following section will further analyse this aspect, comparing Ali Farah's *Little Mother* and Meneghello's *Piccoli maestri*, both underpinned by questions that address the thin line that separates 'right' and 'wrong' choices and personal and national belongings considering catastrophic events such as the civil war.

The idea of collaborationism then addresses the fact that national identity was built upon the unified effort to fight dictatorship in the name of clear, undisputed values. In this sense, the reassessment of national identity represents a shared theme both in postcolonial Somali novels in Italian and *Resistenza* novels. The former claim both a reworking of Somalis' responsibilities during colonialism and dictatorship and, at the same time, a re-examination of Somaliness and Italianness in a transcultural and transnational context. This latter aspect brings back the question of national identity at the centre of Italian literature, considered 'missing' by Asor Rosa as rarely addressed again in novels after the post-war period. While intellectuals and writers considered rethinking the notion of Italianness as a primary necessity in their writings after Fascism, in the 1990s, postcolonial writers challenged the same notion dramatizing their experience of being both Somali and Italian. This issue about identity operates on multiple fronts and allows a further comparative reading between the fictionalized representation of Somali and Italian people, as they both experienced dictatorship and civil war, events in which nationhood becomes compromised and undergoes a severe review. In both the Italian and the Somali cases, citizens of the same nation fought against themselves after the fall of a totalitarian regime.

While comparing these historical events, the analysis has shown how postcolonial and post-war writers employ analogous aesthetic features and ethical standpoints to represent characters who become embroiled in the complex skein of history that, at times, eludes their complete comprehension but nonetheless requires them to act and take sides. The novels of Calvino and Scego show the ambivalence of the main characters, split between personal choices and historical events, thus making their texts a place of tension between several positions which do not necessarily succeed one upon the other. At the same time, they engage with readers, making them part of the realities of complex historical events, questioning any narrative that simplifies the *Resistenza* as an event solely orchestrated by heroic partisans, unaffected by doubts or personal aspirations, and colonialism as a civilizing mission where Italians exclusively play the part of *brava gente*. This tension is also underscored in Ubax Cristina Ali Farah's *Little Mother*, which elaborates on the civil war and the consequences of colonialism. The following analysis points out aspects of *impegno* and nationhood with the support of another novel about the Resistance: Meneghello's *The Outlaws*.

Ali Farah's *Little Mother* through the Lenses of Language and Autobiographical Testimony

In *Little Mother*, Cristina Ali Farah focuses on language and its power in shaping identities that experienced traumatic events. Language acts as a prolific tool to both retrieve the former Italian colonial presence in Somalia, through the characters' memories, and explore the impact of the civil war upon individual and national identity formations. This section extends the previous analysis concerning the aesthetic similarities and ethical concerns between *Resistenza* and Somali novels in Italian, but it also reconnects with the analysis of Roma Termini and linguistic appropriation made in the first chapter regarding *Little Mother*. Whereas Scego's novel foregrounds the responsibilities of the Somali people in endorsing colonialism and investigates the gray area where the roles of master and servant become blurred, Ali Farah problematizes the idea of belonging during the period of the civil war, an event fuelled by sectarianism and Siyaad Barre's ambiguous policies towards clannism. The parallel with *Letteratura della Resistenza* is conveyed by the need to represent an historical event, traumatic and harrowing, with both individual and collective perspectives after a period of reflections. The act of writing is then seen as an ongoing but necessary process to merge subjective experiences into the grand narrative of the making of national identities in Somalia and Italy. Both *Little Mother* and *The Outlaws* reflect this tension, aesthetically achieved through a specific use of language, a non-sequential plot structure and a metanarrative reflection on the act of writing as a way of making sense of traumatic events.

The three narrating characters of the novel, Barni, Domenica and Taageere, grapple with the psychological impact of their traumatic displacement and losses resulting from the civil war and the subsequent forced resettlement; Ali Farah reproduces their struggle by using different linguistic registers to elaborate on the disruptive consequences of the war at the emotional level. Barni's erudite vocabulary emphasizes her attempt to show her proficiency and fluency in Italian, as well as to claim approval in an unwelcoming society that marginalizes her. Barni's cousin, Domenica Axad, mixes Somali with Italian in a continual flow between the two idioms. This variation expands the linguistic range of the novel, showcasing her movements around the diaspora's multiple centres, where Barni wanders to reunite her family scattered after the war. Barni also moves between different times, retrieving the past relations between Italy and Somalia as her story is told *in absentia* to an interlocutor who is never mentioned and never speaks. She admits having a 'selective memory' while telling them her 'own version of what happened' in Mogadishu during the war (Ali Farah, 14). Lastly, Taageere's informal and paroxysmal language reveals the challenges in navigating a meaningful role within the diaspora, in precarious new settings. After the breakdown of Somali societal structures, Taageere struggles to keep alive the cultural values shaped in a nation that eventually collapsed, a nation in which his role as a man, husband and father was comprehensible.[20] Taageere's sentiments, in remembering his life back in Somalia during phone calls from the United States, blur the line between distrust and patriotism, as he shows a sense of disillusionment towards a country that cannot give him a future (Tembo 2017, 66).

At the structural level, each chapter tells the story of the three protagonists in first-person as monologues, but on two occasions, Barni's account becomes a one-sided dialogue infused with several questions and reflections about the colonial past. Assuming that the wholly silent addressee is, in fact, the reader, allows us to think about the novel as a way to retrieve a form of *impegno* that aims to undermine the power relations between colonizers and colonized.[21]

This strategy is further emphasized when Barni ironically asks:

You're impressed by my Italian? I've spoken this language since I was a child. I started studying it in primary school, together with my cousin Axad. But you probably already know that we Somalis can almost always speak Italian. At least my aunts and uncles did, people of that generation.

(Ali Farah, 13)

Similarly, the linguistic fluency and competence of Barni, who claims her Italian belonging having managed to build herself a house and earned a living in Rome as an obstetrician, deflate the supposed sameness and purity of Italian culture and language.[22] As we have seen in *Adua*, this attention to language involves both narrators and readers, the latter being part of the creative process; while in *Adua* expressionist language attempts to counteract the belittlement of the colonial experience present in the media and political rhetoric, in *Little Mother*, the destabilization of a supposed familiarity with the Italian language is played out with the insertion of Somali words that appropriate Italian common nouns.

In the case of *Little Mother*, language also arises as a fundamental tool to inventing the self, which is indeed at the centre of the novel. Ali Farah, in particular, describes Domenica's struggle with belonging. In Italy, due to her mixed background, half Italian and half Somali, she is 'welcomed with lively curiosity' by her classmates but soon ends up being 'relegated to the anonymous group of "all the other children"' (Ali Farah, 209). In Somalia, instead, Domenica is 'excluded from those activities that would have made her belong' (Tembo, 72).

But the idea of belonging is further problematized beyond skin colour or birth, as it is contingent, too, on clan affiliations. Through Barni's story, the novel explicitly shows the tendency among Somali refugees to categorize each other as either friends or foes based on clan belongings, as Nuruddin Farah highlights in *Links*.[23] Barni married a young man hailing from a faction involved in the violence of 1991, disregarding the objections of her family who viewed her husband as a member of an opposing clan. However, after several years of marriage, when Barni and her husband separated, his reason to make sense of their divorce echoed the previous detractors of their union. In his accusation directed at Barni, he now claims that the fault lies in her belonging to the wrong clan. She tells him they can no longer share a bed, because of 'all the murders we – my genealogy – had committed' (Ali Farah 2011, 144). It takes time for Barni to reject the simplistic dichotomies that underpin such collective blaming: 'us and you, murderers and victims, victims and murderers, who is who, if all you have to do is switch perspectives' (144). Once again, these words suggest a rejection of any Manichean divisions between good and evil and echo Levi's idea of:

> una zona grigia dai contorni mal definiti, che insieme separa e congiunge i due campi dei padroni e dei servi. Possiede una struttura interna incredibilmente complicata, e alberga in sé quanto basta per confondere il nostro potere di giudicare.
>
> (Levi 2017, 31)

> a gray area, poorly defined, where the two camps of masters and servants both diverge and converge. This gray area possesses an incredibly complicated internal structure and contains within itself enough to confuse our need to judge.

The historical (and fictionalized) context of large-scale violence that raises the ambiguity between victims and perpetrators fosters a theoretical approach based on the concept of a 'civil war literature', which sheds light on shared poetics between Somali novels and *Resistenza* literature, despite different historical contexts.[24] Somali Italian writers, accordingly, 'show that the positions of perpetrator and victim have never been static and are occupied by different individuals and groups at different times' (Kapteijns 2013, 239).

A parallel can then be drawn between the ambiguity expressed in *Little Mother* and a specific passage from Luigi Meneghello's *The Outlaws*, published in 1964 (and translated in 1967), the same year of Calvino's Preface to *The Path to the Spiders' Nests*. The novel tells the story of a group of young students taking part in the Resistance during the last stretches of the Second World War. It is interesting to notice that, in Italian, the novel is entitled *Piccoli maestri*, little teachers, suggesting an evocative parallel with Ali Farah's title, *Little Mother*. Meneghello's protagonists have formed their own partisan band, and their story, told by one of them with a dry irony and colloquial style to deflate the celebrative tone of the partisan fight, describes the anti-heroic, and often contradictory realities of the Resistance (Donazzan 2022, 70).

In one episode, Meneghello's take against the 'official' rhetoric of the Resistenza is epitomized in the description of a character called *il Vaca*, a dialect term that, when used with the female article, literally means 'cow'.

> Vaca was clever [...] and some time afterwards [...] he had decided to resolve once and for all the problem of how not to be captured by the partisans, simply going and joining them [...] When I was told this, I was scandalised. I felt cheated, because I had made a personal enemy of this Vaca; but when I thought it over, it seemed that our position was not so different to his after all. We too had been Fascists, and afterwards we became partisans; and it had been precisely the same with him.
>
> (1967, 93)

This passage shows how one's ideological standpoint becomes ambivalent and ambiguous in the context of the civil war, endorsing Calvino's aim to write against 'a hagiographic Resistance that was all sweetness and light' (2013a, 15). *Il Vaca*, for example, far from being an upright model of consistency, decides to join partisans and support their anti-fascist fight to avoid being caught in a round-up. The narrator's initial reaction of astonishment is then quietened down by the thought that Vaca was in the same position as other partisans, who might have been Fascists in the first place. This act of overstepping the feeling of resentment and betrayal occurred to Barni, too, after the same process of recognizing the self in the other. In *Little Mother*, this is described when Barni moves beyond clan-related resentment in her relationship with Ardo, a Somali girl she meets while travelling on the Roma-Giardinetti railway. Initially, Barni distrusts Ardo, who appears to be wearing the golden earrings that a young gunman had forcefully taken from Barni just before she fled Mogadishu. Hence, Barni connects Ardo with the clan responsible for her relatives' expulsion and death. Only later in the novel, when Barni is called upon to deliver Ardo's baby, she can finally release her resentment and look past clan ideology. Accordingly, she writes: 'We had settled our debt with the *nabsi*' (nemesis) (Ali Farah, 58). In the context of civil war, *Madre piccola* and *Piccoli maestri* point out how the concepts of 'Nemico' (capital letter in Meneghello, meaning 'enemy') and *nabsi* (in Ali Farah) denote many-sided and fluid positions, which may eventually turn into their opposite, such as comrade or associate, when the circumstances change.[25]

This process of understanding the other's position and suspending judgment requires a slow and often painful reassessment of one's self. *Little Mother* represents this process by disrupting the linearity of the plot and subverting any idea of time-based consistency, thereby mirroring the fragmentation of the characters' subjectivity after traumatic events and their need to reposition themselves under new circumstances. Even though the story develops along a chronological axis, the sections of both Barni and Domenica rely on several ellipses and flashbacks, which follow their memories and their attempt to place the pieces of their past together. In that sense, Meneghello's and Ali Farah's novels show how writing is an active act, as mentioned by the British Pakistani author Hanif Kureishi: 'The only way I could make sense of my confused world was to write' (qtd. in Kabir 2010, 145). In *The Outlaws*, memories do not surface in the novel because they are repressed, but are re-lived and re-experienced to reorder past events (Peters 2012, 59–60).

Little Mother's plot, roughly set in the 2000s, is continuously dragged back to the 1990s when the civil war erupted and forced the two protagonists to leave Mogadishu. The novel's structure, which is split into nine parts, stresses this temporal (and spatial) fluidity. Like in Scego's *Adua*, each chapter is titled with the name of the character who tells the story using a first-person narrator (Domenica, Barni and Taageere). These sections are spaced out by a 'Prelude', an 'Interlude' and an 'Epilogue', told by Domenica, Taageere and Barni, respectively. The 'Interlude' is entirely committed to representing Mogadishu during the 1990s, at the beginning of the civil war. As we have analysed in Chapter 2, the city, called by the original name of Xamar, is portrayed by Taageere according to his traumatic memories and addressed as a character itself, quoting the song 'Mogadishu, You Have Been Violated' (*Xamar waa lagu xumeeyeyeey*), written and performed by Somali songwriter Axmed Naaji Sacad (Ali Farah 2011, 127).

As well, memories are used as a supportive device by Domenica Axad to retrieve the past and tell her story from childhood, to give sense to her life and her ceaseless wandering around Europe in the attempt to reunite her family. In this regard, two relevant aspects should be noted: first, in retrieving the past, Domenica relies on the script to narrate her story of displacement, in opposition to the oral form preferred by Barni. The act of writing, for Domenica, is understood as a means to facilitate her emotional healing. This practice of self-discovery through writing echoes the words of Meneghello when, in the afterword of *I piccoli maestri*, he states that '*scrivere è una funzione del capire*' ('writing is functional to understand') (1998, 230). As Laura Peters underlines in *The Outlaws*, 'the desire to process one's life experiences by transforming them into a literary text is therefore driven by a cognitive ambition and the desire to delve into one's life story to better *understand*' (2012, 57). However, whereas Domenica decides to write a letter to retrace her challenging existential route and to give linearity to her story, Barni instead chooses the improvisation and the spontaneity of the oral form to recover her past and to describe the condition of Somali expatriates in Rome. Telling and re-telling the trauma of civil war and resettlement in a free-associative manner that resembles a confession is Barni's attempt to survive and surmount the trauma.

Second, there is another challenge to the linearity of the plot in terms of structure. The beginning of Domenica's story, which starts with the words: 'According to my birth certificate, I am Domenica Taariikh, born in Mogadishu in 1970', is placed at the end of the novel, before the epilogue (Ali Farah 2011, 294). It results that the conventional incipit can only be deferred, at that moment when Domenica is finally able to clear her mind. In this regard, Calvino's words suitably describe these circumstances:

> Ogni volta l'inizio è quel momento di distacco dalla molteplicità dei possibili: per il narratore è l'allontanare da sé la molteplicità delle storie possibili, in modo da isolare e rendere raccontabile la singola storia che ha deciso di raccontare.
> (2002, 138)

Every time the beginning is that moment of detachment from the multiplicity of the possible: for the narrator, it is to remove from the self the multiplicity of the possible stories, to close off and make the single story that he has decided to tell worth telling.

Only after reworking and remembering, Domenica is finally detached enough to make sense of her life through the writing process and a chronological structure. In *The Outlaws*, Meneghello tries, as well, to balance the multiplicity (the stories of the partisan fight) with the single story (his personal, double account of the *Resistenza*, told from the perspective of the self when he experienced it and his later recollection). Domenica's words in the closing chapter of *Little Mother* reverberate those written by Meneghello in the afterword to the Italian edition of *I piccoli maestri* (in italics in the original):

> *Mi accorsi che finalmente ci vedevo abbastanza chiaro, era nato il distacco, l'intera faccenda di quei nostri dolori di gioventù si schiariva, potevo scriverla.*
> (1998, 231)

I realized that finally, I could see clearly, the detachment occurred; the whole matter of our juvenile sorrows lightened, I could write it.

After a visit to the same place where in 1944 he participated in a round-up, Meneghello started to write *The Outlaws*, a novel about a historical event that occurred twenty years earlier – the direct first-hand experience of the partisan fight – but it is fictionalized and explained through the filter of memory. Meneghello re-elaborates the resistance movement after years by employing a detached perspective in which the narrator partially conceals the author. To paraphrase a famous line by Meneghello's beloved poet William Wordsworth, *The Outlaws* 'take[s] its origin from emotion recollected in tranquillity' (2003, 21). Only decades after the partisan fight, the author-narrator remembers his youth as a *partigiano*, thus undertaking a process of reworking past events through writing. By narrativizing his experience, he tries to exorcise the 'moral shock – so many years ago –of coming to understand what Fascism was and after one had been brought up as a Fascist' (Meneghello 1967, 5).

Accordingly, Meneghello began writing *The Outlaws* when he 'eventually felt that [he] had pardoned himself and his friends, in January 1963' (*ibid.*, 5). The novel, as the Author's note in the Italian edition states, has '*un esplicito proposito civile e culturale*' ('an explicit purpose, civic and cultural'), as Meneghello wanted to write about the Resistance with an anti-heroic and anti-rhetoric approach, in different way than the one 'popularized' ('*divulgato*'), (Meneghello 1998, 228). Making immediately clear the commitment of the novel, Meneghello retrieves and fosters that 'ethic dimension of writing' discussed thus far, namely the close relationship between literature and *impegno* that believes that the author should engage with society and 'aims in some way to represent it' (Burns 2001, 5).

The Outlaws begins with an analepsis (the narrator in 1964 remembers his experience in 1943) and then continues with the account of prior events structured across eleven chapters, made up of sections split by ellipses and unbalanced in terms of length and content. Language represents a flexible device to portray the narrator's direct experience and aims to demystify the rhetoric, conventionality and pretentiousness of the official culture (Meneghello 1967, 5; Donazzan 2022, 70).[26] As Maria Corti explained, the orality of the group, made up of recollected memories and events, becomes a script (1987). The polyphony of *The Outlaws*, which mirrors the disorder and richness of the partisan fight and represents the variety of social, linguistic and cultural backgrounds of *partigiani*, does not come from different narrators, but originates from the combination of dialect expressions, literary quotations, poems, songs and bureaucratic terms related to the semantic military field.

The following short quotation provides an example of the variety of linguistic registers in the novel; it also shows how the experience of the *Resistenza*, made by people belonging to different classes, education and cultural backdrop, is encompassed in the polyphony of the novel:

'E chi sareste voi altri?' disse l'ufficiale a un certo punto. Io risposi senza pensare: 'Fucking bandits', ma subito mi venne in mente che c'era un risvolto irriguardoso nei confronti della Simonetta, e arrossî nel buio. L'ufficiale gridò: 'I beg your pardon?' e io gridai: 'Ho detto che siamo i Volontari della Libertà'.

'Libertà?' gridò l'ufficiale, e io glielo confermai, e poi aggiunsi: 'E adesso canto una canzone che vi riguarda, se non le dispiace'

'Sing away' disse lui, e io attaccai:

Sono passati gli anni
Sono passati i mesi
Sono passai i giorni
E ze rivà i inglesi.

(Meneghello 1998, 226)

'And who are you?' said the officer after a bit.

'Fucking bandits,' I replied without thinking: But suddenly I realized I shouldn't say such things in front of Simonetta, and I blushed; however, it was dark, and no one noticed. The officer shouted: '*I beg your pardon?*' and I shouted back: 'I said we are Freedom Volunteers.'

'Freedom?' shouted back the officer, and I confirmed this.

Then I added: 'Now I'll sign a song. About you. Do you mind?'

'Sing away,' he said, so I started:

> *Years have passed*
> *Months have passed*
> *The English are here*
> *At last, at last.*

(Meneghello 1967, 236–7)

This particular use of the Italian language (and Venetian dialect: '*I ze rivà i inglesi*') does not aim merely to represent the composite linguistic and social background of the partisans; indeed, through irony, derived here from the juxtaposition of styles and forms (free indirect speech and, as the passage shows, songs), Meneghello rewrites the story of the *Resistenza* in the key to anti-heroism and anti-rhetoric.

It is important to note another stylistic parallel between Somali novels in Italian and Resistance novels. In the former case, the Italian language is the colonial language while the latter, the Fascist one, is abrogated in both cases by inserting unglossed words or variations that challenge the normative standard. The tools to achieve this process of appropriation and abrogation are dialect (the Venetian one, in the case of Meneghello) and Somali (for Somali Italian authors).

In Meneghello, then, the aim to debunk the dominant narrative of heroism and self-celebration, built around the partisan fight, goes along with the attempt to recollect, in the form of the novel, the complexities and contradictions of the post-war phase in Italian history. The means to achieve this twofold aim are a disruptive and inventive use of language and the employment of individual memories that merge into the grand narrative of the *lotta partigiana*. As I have shown, these key features resemble the poetics that Italo Calvino outlines regarding Resistance literature: personal memories, orality, stylistic polyphony and the active presence of autobiographical material, all combined in the novel form, arise as discursive devices to elaborate on traumatic events and reassess previous configuration of the self.

In this regard, the analysis of the similarities between Meneghello's and Ali Farah's novels allows us to read them as two texts that explore the issue of collective and personal identity in two post-totalitarian nations, which have dealt with a period of civil war. In *The Outlaws*, Meneghello represents a period of collapse, both from the institutional and societal perspective, in which the idea of national identity should be re-founded with a new system of values that risk reproducing certain rhetoric of heroism and self-celebration. Instead of turning this pivotal moment into a triumphant event, the narrator senses its complexities and incommensurability and uses the act of writing to reflect on individual and national responsibilities. The fall of Mussolini's regime appears to the narrator so distant as to be unbelievable, but the harsh reality of its occurrence, nevertheless, is soon described as the loss of a centre and disorientation, which follows a crisis in terms of personal identity (Meneghello 1967, 19–21). After the *Ventennio* (the two decades of Fascism) and the totalitarian control towards culture and society, the idea of Italy as a nation was shaped according to Fascist principles, which have made Italy a place of censorship, racism, concentration camps and political purges. Fascist policies shaped a specific idea of *Italianità*, according to which the concept of race was grounded in spiritual and cultural foundations; Italians, according to Mussolini's assumptions, had achieved racial unity and full political consciousness through the Fascist ideology.

This approach fostered the idea of the homogeneity of Italian society, attaching the concept of nation to Fascism. After the regime's collapse, this equivalence unwinds, as well as the idea of being *italiano*, an Italian, split between being a Fascist, once, and a *partigiano* (at least for some), later. Meneghello addresses this lack of unity in terms of identity by showing that a coherent ideological or political view did not bind the partisans. Some of them fought for opportunist reasons, such as in the case of *il Vaca* who, nonetheless, embodies the same uncertainty as the other partisans.

This intellectual, political, social and emotional ambiguity, stemming from the nation's collapse and its related complex body of principles, rules and customs, can be retrieved in the *Little Mother* as well, and in the dissolution of Somalia as a unitary sovereign state. Somalis of the diaspora, who arrived in Italy as regular migrants or asylum seekers, look back at Somalia's collapse through their recollections. However, they do not share the idea of Somalia being shaped by clan ideology, which thrived on filling the political vacuum after the fall of Siyaad Barre. As in the case of Italy, Mussolini and Barre 'arrogated the imagined national space for themselves by inscribing their personal stories in the narrative of the nation in the guise of collective history' (Yewah 2001, 47). Somali authors, as described here, challenge this national construction based on clan ideology and totalitarianism, attempting, from the diaspora, to reshape the concept of the nation along alternative trajectories, in which traumatic personal events are collected and gathered in a sort of communal narrative of the civil war, dominated by the constant shift between victims and perpetrators. The question that spreads throughout *Little Mother* concerns the meaning of being both Somali and Italian and how nationhood could be understood after the upsurge of clan ideology. In this regard, *Little Mother* begins with a telling, almost self-describing sentence, written in Somali: '*Soomaali baan ahai*' (I am Somali) (Ali Farah 2011, 1).

Conclusion

This chapter has explored possible links between texts written in two different literary and historical periods to show how postcolonial authors and texts, far from being incompatible with Italian national literature, aesthetically and ethically engage with issues related to nationhood, Italianness and the representation of complex and multi-sided historical periods, dictatorship and civil war. Somali novels in Italian have been compared and related to the literature of *Resistenza* in terms of formal features (non-linearity of the plot, multiple registers, orality, fragmentation of points of view, first-person narrator, reappropriation of language and memory as a structural principle). The use of language to disrupt the normative standard of the Italian and challenge main narratives (*Resistenza* as a homogeneous movement and *Italiani brava gente*) has been analysed as a shared feature of both post-war and postcolonial novels. In doing so, the unrelatedness of postcolonial texts to the Italian tradition has been questioned. Postcolonial texts, in fact, show the possibility of reinterpreting them as part of and in conversation with canonical authors who shaped Italian literature in the post-war period.

The theorization of the new modes of expression during post-war fiction, as suggested by Calvino in the Preface of *Il sentiero dei nidi di ragno*, has been the starting point to relate postcolonial and post-war texts which, nonetheless, show remarkable similarities when looked through the lenses of *impegno*. The latter has been understood as a commitment to make, through literature, an intervention at the sociopolitical level with a direct engagement with readers. Scego's and Ali Farah's resemantization of the idea of *Resistenza* has been read according to Calvino's suggestion that 'the real Resistance is not only a struggle against a foreign invader: it has to be a battle for a profound renewal within the society of one's own country' (2013b, 258–9).

Specifically, the chapter has examined how the anti-fascist trajectory traced by Calvino, and followed by other Resistance authors, has significantly contributed to the elaboration of aesthetic paradigms and the idea of *impegno* in Scego's *Adua* and Ali Farah's *Little Mother*. As Jennifer Burns has stated, 'it is reasonable to say that after the 1950s, *impegno* went "underground", but it is still there, diffused under the surface' (2001, 183). Indeed, rather than leaving commitment underwater, postcolonial authors have actively recovered it and skilfully demonstrated its relevance in addressing contemporary issues and complex historical periods. As shown, these aesthetic modes and ethical commitment should be understood as tools to re-tell history and problematize concepts of nationhood, belonging and identity, emphasizing the close relationship between literature and society.

As a result, this analysis has retrieved a neglected line between the anti-fascism of *Letteratura della Resistenza* and postcolonial Somali novels in Italian, thus showing that the criteria according to which the postcolonial production has been excluded from the categories of 'national' and 'canonical' are the same that can, instead, inform their inclusion. As the analysis has shown, postcolonial Somali novels in Italian are related to the 'national' literary-historical development as they recover an idea of commitment stemmed from the anti-fascist ideals of the writers of the *Resistenza*.

Notes

1   The *Resistenza italiana* or *la Resistenza* (Italian resistance movement) is an all-encompassing term for Italian resistance groups during the Second World War. It opposed both the Nazi forces and the local regime, the Italian Social Republic, especially after the German military occupation of Italy between 1943 and 1945. The movement arose among Italians of various social classes, and it is also known as the

Italian *lotta partigiana* (partisan fight). The modern Italian Republic was declared to be founded on the struggle of the Resistance.

2   Calvino's first novel is a coming-of-age story set against the backdrop of the Second World War. The protagonist Pin, an orphaned cobbler's apprentice, lives alone with his sister, who is known as the town's prostitute. While his sister sleeps with a German sailor, Pin dares to steal his gun, hiding it among the spiders' nests in an act of rebellion that entangles him in the adults' *lotta partigiana*. The novel develops the story of Pin joining a partisan group to fight against the Nazis and to endear himself to the grown-ups of his town in Liguria.

3   I have considered here the novels emerging from the Resistance movement as a collective *corpus* due to their unifying factor of being texts written by prominent Italian canonical figures who notably shaped the post-war literary scenario and were actively involved in the *Resistenza*, understood as both a historic-political event and a literary subject. While each text possesses distinct characteristics, my analysis aligns with the chapter's objective, which centres on exploring ethical and aesthetic correlations between post-war and postcolonial novels to show how the latter are deeply connected with the Italian literary tradition. Therefore, my attention is directed towards novels that most closely exemplify the principles of the 'literary' *Resistenza* elaborated by Calvino in the Preface of *Il sentiero dei nidi di ragno*.

4   This does not mean that there were no forms or resistance during colonialism or no Somali voices against Italian rule. For example, as E. R. Turton explained, armed resistance of Somali pastoralists to colonial rule was already active in 1893 and, in different forms and aims, could be traced back until the 1960s, a period characterized by the emergence of mass nationalism and Somali irridentism (1972, 120).

5   In arguing this point, I would not suggest that the Italian literary tradition lacked canonical authors who wrote about colonialism and its civilizing mission or dramatized nationalistic issues and described Africa from an exoticizing perspective. The main point here is that renowned authors who dealt with the vast topic of colonialism have fictionalized the latter's vision, policies and attitude unsystematically in their literary production. Furthermore, this production embraced Africa more like an idea than a real place. It should be noted here that Giovanni Pascoli (1855–1912) wrote one of the most famous endorsements of colonial enterprise in Libya. However, his *La grande proletaria si è mossa* is not a fictional work, but a public oration that Pascoli published in 1911. Pascoli's rhetoric, like that of Gabriele D'Annunzio, aims to foster feelings of fraternal pride, patriotism and imperialism. It was extraordinarily successful at that time because it promoted unity and a shared destiny for all Italians towards modernization in a still culturally divided nation. Giosuè Carducci (1835–1907), too, regarded as the Poet Laureate of modern Italy and Nobel Prize in 1906, showed equivocal opinions about colonialism: if in 1887 he condemned the colonial ambitions of Prime Minister Agostino Depretis, in 1890 he supported the government of Francesco Crispi and his aggressive policy to make Italy a colonial power (Baranello 2011).

6   In this regard, we should mention the few novels published after the War about colonialism. Mario Tobino's *Il deserto della Libia* (The Libyan Desert, 1952), a semi-autobiographical novel about the war in Libya between 1939 and 1941; the war-diary of Giuseppe Berto entitled *Guerra in camicia nera* (A Blackshirt's War, 1955) and Enrico Emanuelli's *Settimana nera* (1961, translated in English as *Black Dove*, 1964),

which is a story of an erotic obsession set in Mogadishu during the years of the Italian trusteeship. The most important, Ennio Flaiano's *Tempo di uccidere* (*A Time to Kill*, 1947) is set in Ethiopia during the Italian invasion (1935–6) and tells the story of an Italian officer who accidentally kills an Ethiopian woman and is ravaged by the memory of his act. A movie adaptation with the same title was released in 1989, directed by Giuliano Montaldo and starring Nicolas Cage and Giancarlo Giannini.

7   '*Resistenza* was later recast as a war of liberation against fascism, and the post-war period saw an attempt to reconstruct an idea of the nation that distanced itself from its fascist past' (Srivastava 2018, 3).

8   The left-wing and anti-fascist political party PCI (Italian Communist Party), on the one hand, encouraged the anti-colonial struggle for the Algerian independence against the French, but on the other hand it supported the trusteeship plan in Somalia by reclaiming the good work done in the colony by the Italians (Tripodi 1999, 49–50).

9   Except for a few texts such as *Per i martiri di piazzale Loreto* (1944) by Alfonso Gatto, *Alle fronde dei salici* (1945) by the forthcoming Nobel Prize winner Salvatore Quasimodo, the collections *Fisarmonica Rossa* (1945) by Franco Matacotta and *Galli notturni* (1952) by Elena Bono and the collected poems *Ad ora incerta* (1984) by Primo Levi (Casadei and Santagata 2007, 247–8).

10 One of the most famous examples of the representation of *Resistenza* comes from Roberto Rossellini's film *Roma, città aperta* (*Rome, Open City*, 1945). While the film brings up the collective memory of that period, it also portrays the post-war phase as a heroic war of national liberation, characterized by social homogeneity. The absence of class conflict and internal divisions implies that Italian society was uniformly anti-Nazi. Inasmuch as German soldiers embody the only antagonists, the movie dismisses the Italian's role in supporting Nazism, who eventually turned out to be victims rather than collaborators. In sharp contrast with Rossellini's representation, Meneghello raises the issue of the Italians' support to Nazis and Fascists against the prevailing propaganda according to which Italians were *brava gente*, while the antagonists were merely Germans.

11 This period, also called the Italian Civil War (*Guerra civile italiana*), saw the opposition between, on one front, the Italian Co-Belligerent Army (*Esercito Cobelligerante Italiano*) and the Italian Resistance (with the Allies) and, on the other, the Italian Fascist Social Republic (and the Axis powers) from 9 September 1943 to 25 April or 2 May 1945, the official date of the surrender of German forces.

12 In the previous section, it has been shown how colonialism, in comparison to the Anglophone narrative production, was rarely addressed and not included in the literary canon after the failure of the 'colonial novel' project.

13 As underlined in Chapter 3, Garane, who spent his youth in Mogadishu and studied in Italy only later, can be compared, accordingly, with the African writers of the post-independence period, with whom he shares similar discursive practices.

14 In a recent article, Laura Lori investigates the idea of *matria* in contemporary writers of postcolonial Somali literature in Italian, showing how the term has been previously used in the Italian literary production by authors such as Andrea Zanzotto and Mario Rigoni Stern (Lori 2022).

15 As in the case of Vasco Pratolini's novel entitled *Metello* (1955). In this example, the novel can be read according to the requirement of Socialist Realism, such as the representation of a positive hero and the victorious proletariat's struggle

16 In this sense, *Regina di fiori e di perle* by Italo-Ethiopian author Gabriella Ghermandi openly endorsed the affiliation between anti-colonialism and Resistance, supporting the double meaning of the latter term. She commits several episodes of the plot to narrate the role played by Kebedech Seyoum (1910–76), a fighter of the Ethiopian liberation front, against the fascist *talian soldati* [Italian soldiers] during the 1930s (Ghermandi 2015). Accordingly, Ghermandi's portrayal of the women who organized the anti-colonial resistance and fought against the Italian colonizers has been analysed comparatively with the representation made in *La battaglia di Algeri* (1966) by the Italian anti-colonial director Gillo Pontecorvo (De Vivo 2013).

17 The term *repubblichini* means those fascists who supported the Republic of Salò, a pro-German puppet state led by Benito Mussolini and lasted from September 1943 to May 1945, which exercised sovereignty in Northern and Central Italy.

18 A little emphasis should be placed here on the effects of traumatic experiences, which implicitly surfaces in the brief description of the characters. Zoppe is introduced as a twenty-year-old man who is already old. Also Pin, the protagonist of Calvino's novel, seems to inhabit different stages of his life at the same time, since he has 'the hoarse voice of a much older boy' (Calvino 2013a, 31).

19 *Femina somala* is a colonial novel written by Gino Mitrano Sani and published in 1933. The plot is centred on the relationship between an Italian officer and a Somali woman, a so-called *madama*. Sani's descriptions of her are drawn upon racist connotations, firmly entrenched in prevailing stereotypes about Black African women, encompassing notions of intellectual incapacity, animalistic attributes, and a proneness to fulfil the sexual desires of white men. A more detailed analysis of the representations of Black women in Sani's colonial fiction can be found in Bonavita (1999, 491–5).

20 'It's so difficult for our men to invent a role for themselves. To redefine themselves. To adapt. To accept themselves. To humiliate themselves. Because you see, for us women, in the end, those fixed points, our home, our daily life, motherhood, the intimacy of our relationships, they are like little signposts that save us from getting lost' (Ali Farah 2011, 29–30).

21 This strategy resambles the case of Mohsin Hamid's *The Reluctant Fundamentalist* (2007), a novel that stages a similar technique by making the protagonist, Changez, 'converse' with a silent American addressee. *Little Mother*, similarly, silences the former colonizer to give voice to the colonized (Hartnell 2010, 336; Koppisch 2018, 12). This process is also ignited by the creative appropriation of the Italian language and the insertion of Italian terms re-written according to Somali pronunciation, as shown in Chapter 1. The uncanny presence of Somali words in a colloquial Italian context locates the strangeness in the ordinary and fills the usual gap between what is self and what is Other. In the story told by Barni to the interviewer, *ciabatte* (slippers) is phonetically transformed into *jabaati*; the noun *peperoni* (peppers) becomes *barbaroni*, *tè freddo* (cold tea) turns into *deffredi* and *fazzoletti* into *fasoleeti* (tissue), while *trattoria* is *draddorio* and *kabushiini* is *cappuccino*.

22 'Me? I've lived in Rome for years now. I like it. My home is here, my friends, my profession. There is little left of my past' (Ali Farah 2011, 16).

23 Chapter 2 of this book and Nuruddin Farah's *Links* (36).
24 Also, it should be noted a significant difference in terms of media representation between the two civil wars, a difference that the novels (and this analysis) aim to rectify: while the Italian partisan fight emerges as the liberation struggle against the regime, endorsing ideas of freedom and anti-fascism, Somali civil war has been looked at as tribal infights fuelled by clan-ideology, and rarely as a reaction to the regime becoming increasingly totalitarian.
25 As I have shown in the case of Scego, who represents the ambiguity of her character's behaviours during civil war, also Nuruddin Farah's *Links* points out the ambivalence and the radical transformation of people who undergo periods of conflicts: '[…] all of us who've lived in this civil war have become someone another than ourselves for brief periods of time, in which we've entertained moments of doubt, or dropped into a deep well of despair. Have you too become someone other, in spite of yourself?' (*Links*, 247).
26 'Around the Resistenza there has arisen a rhetorical tradition that requires, and supplies, images of conventional heroes. This I find offensive. I was there, and there were no conventional heroes' (Meneghello 1967, 5).

Conclusion: Re-inventing *Somalias*

The future political landscape of Somalia remains uncertain, while the events of the past await thorough examination and reflection. The present five Federal Member States (Puntland State, Southwest State, Jubbaland State, Galmudug State and Hirshabele State) struggle to find a solution that could guarantee Somali people a political structure able to provide them with a long-lasting system that negotiates opposing tendencies: a unified and centralized state vs. clan-states' push for independence. To date, the difficulties for a public acknowledgement about what happened during the civil war further complicate the prospective political development. Likewise, the lack of forms of restorative justice for the crimes committed during the clan cleansing of post-regime initial stages does not help clarify the recent warlike events. The same silence embroils the war crimes and gross human rights violations that occurred during Siyaad Barre's dictatorship, which still weighs heavily in the present. Addressing these issues is undoubtedly a complicated long-term endeavour. It would mean, for Somali people, to find a way of 'unifying a divided historical memory, to provide healing and reconciliation between perpetrators, passive bystanders, and victims, or, more modestly, to help people coexist in peace' (Kapteijns 2013, 234).

A first, tentative attempt to find ways of coexistence and modes of narrating the civil war, thus fostering a dialogue between divided collective memories, has been undertaken by Somali diasporic authors, who elected Somalia and its recent past as the main symbolical and thematic horizon of their novels. Somali authors inhabiting the 'diaspora space' fictionalize the struggle to negotiate multiple belongings and identities, and conflicting tendencies about the potential sociopolitical structure of Somalia. Nuruddin Farah, the most eminent figure of Somali diasporic literature, expresses this aim in an interview, echoing Ali Farah's purpose to gather, through her novels, the stories of Somali people together:

> HG: So, in a sense, your current project is Somalia in the present – after Siad Barre? Put differently, your project on the diaspora is really about the need to construct a new community.
> NF: Yes, an alternative to the chaos.
>
> (Garuba 2017a, 3)

This book has drawn upon this 'project on the diaspora' and tried to explore how Somali authors have taken on the need to construct a new community by fostering a dialogue across languages and borders. As shown, Somali authors have not restored sectarian clan narratives, but attempted to speak and write as *Somalis*, avoiding any authoritative position and imposition of a single truth. In doing so, they have broadened and complicated the notion of Somaliness, but without trying to define it unequivocally; rather, they have unfurled alternative ideas of nationhood that include the voices from the diaspora and the ones of those who stayed put, imagining different modes of belonging and more inclusive articulations of social relations. What emerged from this multilingual dialogue within the diaspora is a literature that, despite the adoption of 'foreign languages' (nonetheless familiar to Somali authors due to education, colonial legacy and their multilingual locale), placed an overriding investigation of Somalia's past and present at its centre. Somali authors, whether writing in Italian or English from different places and backgrounds, have thus produced a transnational and multilingual corpus of texts characterized by a close connection to Somalia, which remains their unceasing source of inspiration.

Even though writing in multiple languages, across different countries and, in some cases, without having direct experience of migration, Somali writers have artistically responded to the large-scale violence of the civil war and the displacement that followed by representing, on the one hand, the difficulties of resettlement and, on the other, the complexities of a country that has not yet come to terms with its past and is still negatively depicted as a 'failed state'. Their task of fictionalizing the events after the national political crisis emerges as an endeavour, since there is no agreement on a consistent civil war narrative, neither at the political nor at the social level, but several memories. The title of Farah's last trilogy, 'Past Imperfect', emblematically conveys this idea of uncertainty and faultiness in Somalia's past, which arises as a still-unclear period intermingled with multiple legacies, from pre-colonial society formations to colonialism and dictatorship.

By placing at the core of the analysis the intertwined levels of intertextuality, transnationality and multi-localism of contemporary Somali literature, instead of focusing on single authors (Nuruddin Farah, for example) or single-language approaches (English or Italian novels), the comparative method employed in *Literature of the Somali Diaspora*, neither definitional nor exhaustive, has hopefully opened up a series of avenues for further research about contemporary Somali literature, postcolonial theory and Italian studies. Above all, by considering non-English literary material by diasporic authors sharing similar cultural and linguistic backgrounds, this theoretical approach has tried to expand the boundaries of postcolonial and Italian studies. Indeed, one of the ideas underpinning *Literature of the Somali Diaspora* was to expand what we mean by Somali literature and Italian literature. My starting point was to consider these two terms, Somali and Italian, more flexibly than how they are usually understood when they refer to terms such as literature or literary tradition. Given the sociopolitical status of Somalia, a country still struggling with stability after experiencing decades of emigration and a civil war, and its literature, produced also outside Somalia and in multiple languages, any understanding of Somali literature as made up of writers born in Somalia or texts written in Somali would have been reductive. As this book tried to show, Somalia has become a powerful signifier in the diaspora, a subject to be fictionalized and scrutinized from abroad, both from those who had direct experience with it and those who experienced it through the words, images and recollections of parents and relatives.

In the case of the Italian literature, I tried to show how a specific subject – Italian colonialism – has been addressed (also) by authors who do not write in Italian, such as Nuruddin Farah, Afdhere Jama and Fadumo Korn. The comparative approach has allowed us to overcome the idea of 'national' literature and to work on multilingual and transnational lines that advocate for a new line of inquiry that has been recently outlined by Italian scholars (Comberiati and Luffin 2018; Burdett, Havely and Polezzi 2020; Burns and Duncan 2020; Burdett 2022; Comberiati and Mengozzi 2022).

The book's approach aimed, therefore, to consider a variety of texts and authors, dissimilar and heterogeneous but, nevertheless, grounded in the idea – or project – of narrating Somalia. *Literature of the Somali Diaspora*, then, has investigated how this project of writing about Somalia, or rewriting Somalia, is achieved from the diaspora. The book has called attention to the points of contact between authors and texts, specific nodes that I identified as fruitful for a conversation surrounding nationhood. Having in mind that Somalia is a composite, problematic terms that should be understood in the plural form, the comparative approach I have used hopefully has shed light on the many *Somalias* represented in fiction. Drawing upon and rephrasing Emma Bond's critical approach of 'looking sideways to a place from elsewhere', I have suggested to look at how:

> the idea of [Somalia] has travelled worldwide to become a mobile cultural symbol, [that] shows how [Somalia], as a signifier, has become effectively detached from its original national parameters of territory.
>
> (2022, 97)

Of course, English and Italian novels do not represent a comprehensive picture of Somali diaspora, but they might be the starting point for a more holistic understanding of the Somali diasporic literary production, so far examined through nation-bound and language-related approaches. While I have considered a specific literary form (novel), and a specific time-period (novels published post-civil war) mainly in two languages, embracing other forms and languages might offer the possibility of looking at other convergences and differences on the idea of nationhood. As said, my analysis drew and focused on novels written in Italian and English, but other sources could also be considered. Consequently, some authors and texts have been excluded, such as those writing in Somali (both inside and outside the nation), in Arabic and in other European languages. These omissions, I think, are part of the nature of approaching a corpus of texts patently alive and still growing, which have been only recently addressed and examined comparatively. In my case, since the particular focus on the analysis relied on connections between texts, authors and contexts, I privileged those texts and writers which circulate globally, due also – but not exclusively – to translations and established publishing companies, and thus represent fruitfully examples to investigate literary connections within the diaspora.

This multilingual and comparative approach, far from being exhaustive and normative, will hopefully represent an initial step to include other voices and texts in the conversation about Somalia occurring across languages and geographies. For instance, the increasing significance of Nadifa Mohamed's literary works presents intriguing avenues for exploration, particularly regarding Italian colonialism and the notion of national identity stemming from northern Somalia. Mohamed's English-language novels offer potential insights that could further problematize the concept of Mogadishu as the nation's centre, given that in her fiction – especially *The Orchard of Lost Souls* (2013) – she primarily focuses on Hargeisa, which could be considered, the literary equivalent of Mogadishu for Farah and the authors considered here. Hargeisa is now the capital of a new, self-declared nation called Republic of Somaliland that, even though still considered internationally to be part of Somalia, shows nonetheless a distinct desire to disassociate itself from the southern region and the former capital city, Mogadishu. What is the relationship between the two cities? Do they function as antagonists and rivals in the making of the nation?

Given the recurrent presence of Mogadishu in the diasporic fiction and its historical relevance over time, both globally and locally, this book prioritized the capital city because of its significance in the memories, personal and second-hand experiences of Somali authors. It sought to examine how the capital city has emerged as a symbolic representation of the bygone cosmopolitanism of the 1960s and 1970s, but also as the epicentre of the civil war that eventually led to the collapse of the nation. In other words, the capital city of Somalia has become the epitome of both Somali modernity and unity, and the culprit of the current reality of political and social fragmentation. Somali authors, I argued in Chapters 1 and 2, saw the city as a petri dish for exploring the tensions of the past to outline – and understand – the evolution of Somali society until the ruinous civil war. At the same time, against Western narratives that condemned Mogadishu as a wasteland beyond saving, these authors used fiction to envision potential methods for reconstructing both the nation and the city, subtly suggesting alternative modes, distinct from clannism, to regenerate a collective sense of the nation.

Another aspect that might be investigated in relation to the work presented here is the role of ethnic minorities, often excluded from the national project and clan narratives. Somali author Mahmood Gaildon, for example, published the novel *The Yibir of Las Burgabo* (2005), a story about Amina and Ali, two children of a Yibir family set in the imaginary town of Burgabo. Yibirs are the most ostracized and despised group in Somalia and the novel narrativizes the conflict between Ali's search for a comfortable social position and the society determined to keep him out. How can this diasporic text, written in English, join the conversation about individual and collective identity against the backdrop of nationhood?

Another example aimed at expanding the scope of analysis within a comparative framework across diverse languages would involve scrutinizing Somali-language novels concerning the civil war or the post-war era, such as Ibraahin Yuusuf Axmed 'Hawd''s *Aanadii Negeeye* (2013), in which the every-day life of a Somali man is set against the backdrop of the post-independence Somali Republic, until the collapse of the state. Beyond English and Italian, the study of Somali literature produced in German, Dutch or Arabic would further contribute to considering the literary outcomes by Somali authors as part of the same diasporic community and foster the conversation between texts and contexts.[1] This book tried to achieve this objective in part by including a German-written text and poems in Somali thanks to their availability in English and, most importantly, their evident intertextual relevance with the primary texts examined here, chiefly focused on urban environments in the aftermath of the civil war. Above all, Chapter 4 critically engaged, if not directly with Somali texts, with a crucial aspect of Somali literary tradition, namely orature, revealing the relationship between oral and written expressions in the Somali context. The analysis, centred on Garane's novella because, I argue, stands as a *unicum* in the literary Italian tradition, being written outside Italy (and outside Somalia) but in Italian and about a former colony. The documentary *La quarta via* (2012) by Kaha Mohamed Aden, an Italian writer of Somali origin, could be a possible text to be analysed comparatively as it shows how Somali authors have revisited orature via different media. The documentary, directed by Simone Brioni, Graziano Chiscuzzu and Ermanno Guida, recounts Kaha Mohamed Aden's memories of Mogadishu, her hometown, from Italy, where she currently lives. In her recollections, the city is divided into five main streets, symbolizing different historical periods (the 'fourth road' of the title corresponds the period of the civil war), thus bringing to the fore the history of Mogadishu and questions on belonging and nationhood (Brioni 2013).

Along with films, a considerable number of online publications (of poems, short stories and performed songs through audio devices) are playing a significant role in connecting different experiences within the diaspora by scrutinizing and disseminating them in the public sphere. The languages and forms studied here represent a fraction of the many streams within the diaspora that could be investigated, but they are nonetheless useful to emphasize the importance to look at literary diasporas comparatively and multilingually, so to outline the multiple routes that the concept diaspora encompasses. Novels, especially, seem to serve as an effective form to dramatize the several voices that made up the fluid diasporic space and play an important part in sharing ideas across languages and geographies, but also to directly engage with ethical issues concerning nationhood and Somaliness, as Chapter 5 has shown.

Moreover, an additional line of investigation for the Italian studies, aligning with the concept of literature as a transnational and multilingual entity, might involve examining the connection between Nuruddin Farah, primarily an English-writing author, and the Italian literary tradition. This association is underpinned by the thematic interweaving in several of his novels, which delve into the historical context of Italian colonialism. These works portray the intricate cultural, political and economic connections between Italy and Somalia, exploring the nuanced dynamics between colonizers and colonized. This book has started scratching the surface of the possible influences between Farah's vast production and Italy, showing his reworking of Dante's *The Divine Comedy* but also the several ways, both aesthetic and thematic, in which he addressed the legacy of the Italian colonial past in Somalia.[2] However, it also shows the possibility of looking at Italian literature transnationally, as recently proposed by scholars such as Charles Burdett (2022) and Emma Bond (2022).

Furthermore, regarding the Italian language, Chapter 5 has pointed out how Somali postcolonial production in Italian could actively contribute to shaping Italianness. By comparing *Letteratura della Resistenza* and Somali novels in Italian, this book retrieved overlooked common aspects between these literary productions, thus proposing an entirely new reading of the Italian literary tradition. Through an examination of shared formal elements and the idea of *impegno*, as appeared in Calvino's Preface to *The Path of the Spiders' Nests*, my aim was to challenge the notion that postcolonial novels are unrelated to the Italian literary tradition. Additionally, I sought to establish a critical framework that integrates Somali authors, more specifically Igiaba Scego and Cristina Ali Farah, within the realm of *Italianistica* and in relation to the Italian literary canon.

Most importantly, this book has tried to reveal and investigate how diverse diasporic fictions, with variable emphases, present analogous formal strategies and points of contact, but also multiple local influences, which are not necessarily regulated by dualistic dynamics, such as centre/periphery or home/host country. The idea underpinning the analysis is that diasporic literary production should be read with a multi-angular perspective that considers the network of relations between texts, authors and contexts – the local and global realities they simultaneously occupy. Accordingly, the first two chapters have delineated the process through which global sites of consumption and transport could acquire locally shaped characteristics and be deeply constitutive of the time-setting in which they exist. Also, the chapters show how the Italian toponymy shaped the protagonists' idea of belonging and underscore the uneasy necessity of confronting the past to comprehend the current situation. Rome, at the same time, from being the former capital of the Italian Empire, emerged in the late 1980s and early 1990s as one of the hubs of the Somali diaspora, a familiar site within a hostile country, Italy, which did not show particular interest in welcoming Somali refugees during dictatorship and civil war. Mogadishu's and Rome's spatialities have been read through key spaces, against exclusive and clan-based formations, and against the dominant Western-centred narrative.

The fictionalization of space has then been connected to language through the idea of novels as *architexts* and palimpsest. Italian toponymy played a key role in Somalis' identity as much as the Italian language, which represents another fundamental point of contact within the diaspora. Space and language are linked also through the strong symbolical references to Dante's *The Divine Comedy*, as it provides an important intertextual source to fictionalize the civil war. Mogadishu has been represented (and examined) through Dante's journey in Hell; the overall state of confusion and bewilderment expressed by the pilgrim has been used by Somali authors to describe the sense of loss after the traumatic event of the civil war.

As shown, the use of the Italian language is not limited to the intertextual references to Dante's poem but is constitutive of the cultural horizon of those Somalis who lived soon after the end of Italian rule and during the AFIS, when Somalia transitioned from being a colony to an independent country. The third chapter, accordingly, has shown that the use of multilingualism may suggest a new line of enquiry, as it has investigated how Farah employs the colonial languages (Italian and English) with a nuanced approach, since the protagonist's adoption of the latter is not forced upon him because of colonial education. Rather than emphasizing the protagonist's struggle in positioning himself between the former colonial culture and native background, Farah brought to the fore his problematic American belonging and, as well, his 'unhomeliness' towards Somalia in the civil war context (Bhabha 2004, 9). Multilingualism also plays a key role in describing Somalia's pre-colonial history, as in the case of Garane's novella, *Il latte è buono*. Once again, with an approach based on multilocal aspects and multilingual features, Chapter 4 has explored how Somali and Italian work together at the formal level to retrieve the political role of orature. The latter, as shown, underwent an overall simplification when related to its intertextual relationship with the script, becoming an emblematic marker of Africanness. Taking a different approach, the chapter has analyzed the oral traits that are *specifically* Somali to show how they are reproduced and recontextualized in Italian in the novella.

As a final remark, it is as important to note, once again, that this book can only partly contribute to the analysis of the ever-expanding corpus of texts produced by Somali diasporic authors. Many works have been published recently, either within the conventional frames of nationwide publishing companies or through independent publishing or online media, so this book has skimmed the surface of the material available. Still, I hope to have provided a helpful picture to further investigate how literary diasporas work across geographies and languages, thus pointing towards a feasible way of approaching texts, authors and contexts.

One last note: as researcher with a white Western background, I would like to acknowledge the potential limitations in understanding experiences coming from different contexts. As a result, there might be blind spots in my analysis and theorization. I recognize that my perspective may not always be complete and that I cannot claim to speak for the views of racialized communities. My primary goal, as a scholar of postcolonial and comparative studies, is to contribute to the critical dialogue about diasporic writing and shed light on the complexities of such literary production which, among other things, has the merit of providing a valuable vantage point on Italian colonialism, a too-often neglected and misrepresented historical period.

Notes

1 For the production in Dutch, see the recent essay 'The Transnational Writers of the Somali Diaspora in the Netherlands' (Luijnenburg 2018).
2 Christopher Fotheringham moves in this direction, as he shows how Farah, 'despite his choice to write in English, is one of the most important contributors to the tradition of postcolonial Italian literature. I understand this to be not a national literature that is necessarily written in Italian, as has traditionally been the case, but rather as literature that contributes towards, to use Ato Quayson's terms, postcolonializing the Italian cultural sphere' (2018, 2).

Appendix

List of Italian words and references in Farah's *Links*. Page numbers and translations are provided in parentheses.

Group 1: single words/phrases

Spaghetti all'amatriciana (44, 138); *momenti della verità* (moments of truth) (169); *liceo classico* (high school) (202); '*Che maledizione!*' (What bad luck!) (210); *carbonara* (330) and *arrivederci* (goodbye) (334).

Group 2: proper names

Mogadiscio (with the Italian spelling in all Farah's novels); Inferno (23, 57, 193); Fiat Cinquecento (64, 150), Pisa (71); 'Parmesan cheese' (116, 330); Villaggio Arabo (133); Fellini's *8½* (316) and Geronimo Verroneo (318).

Group 3: sentences and general references

'A large sign, handwritten in [...] Italian' (37); 'the words for fate and place of birth, sex [...] were written in Italian, and spelled incorrectly' (40); 'For some years they had lived together in an apartment in Padua, in Italy' (56); 'I remember Seamus and the three of us in Italy' (86); 'Was it because Bile had quietly spun Jeebleh's Italian nostalgia back to Mogadiscio?' (86); 'in a vulgar Italian gesture of a fig' (88); 'school text in Italian' (116); 'An attached note advised him, in Italian, of the numbers' (125); 'receiving awards from an Italian monsignor' (155); 'the opportunity to go to Italy on scholarship' (170); 'an Italian-made affair' (179); 'It reminded him of their days in Padua' (181); 'in the apartment in Padua' (183); 'Mira's father [...] was a diplomat based in Rome' (183); 'When they met last, in Padua, they used Italian' (185); 'In Padua, Seamus used to describe himself as "a colonial"! [...] he was at a loss to find an equivalent word in Italian' (189); 'Jeebleh would have to run a fever of nerves before reintroducing the see-sawing games of their younger days in Italy' (191), 'I recited a verse from Dante's "Inferno"' (193); 'He [...] saw a slim book in Italian written by Shirin Ramzanali Fazel' (226); 'A wine of bottle of excellent Italian vintage, bought in Rome' (258); 'Jeebleh remembered Italian youths making on their motorcycles through the streets of Padua' (294); 'We communicate only in pidgin Italian, which he could barely use to order a meal at an eatery in Turin' (318).

Bibliography

Abdi, Ali A. 1998. 'Education in Somalia: History, Destruction, and Calls for Reconstruction'. *Comparative Education* 34 (3): 327–40.

Abdulaziz, Mohamed H. 2003. 'The History of Language Policy in Africa with Reference to Language Choice in Education'. In *Towards a Multilingual Culture of Education*, by Adama Ouane, ed., 181–200. Hamburg: UNESCO Institute of Education.

Abdullahi, Mohamed Diriye. 2001. *Culture and Customs in Somalia*. Westport: Greenwood Press.

Abokor, Axmed Cali. 1987. *The Camel in the Somali Oral Traditions*. Uppsala: Somali Academy of Sciences and Arts.

Achebe, Chinua. 1975. *Morning Yet on Creation Day*. London: Heinemann.

Adan, Amina H. 1981. 'Women and World'. *Ufahamu: A Journal of African Studies* 10 (3): 115–42.

Aden Mohamed, Kaha. 2010. *Fra-intendimenti*. Roma: Nottetempo.

Afrax, Maxamed Dahir. 2009. 'The "Abwaan" as a Beacon: The Centrality of the Message in Somali Literature with Special Reference to the Play *Shabeelnaagoog*'. *Horn of Africa* 22: 1–63. yumpu.com /en/document/read/16505530/ the-abwaan-as-guidance-provider-wardheernews.

Ahad, Ali Mumin. 2004. 'Italian Culture Influences in Somali. A Reciprocity?'. In *Quaderni del '900. La letteratura postcolonial italiana. Dalla letteratura dell'immaginazione all'incontro con l'altro*, by Tiziana Morosetti, ed., 13–24. Pisa: Istituti Editoriali e Poligrafici Internazionali.

Ahad, Ali Mumin. 2007. 'Could Poetry Define Nationhood? The Case of Somali Oral Poetry and the Nation'. *Journal of Historical and European Studies* 1: 51–8.

Ahad, Ali Mumin. 2008. 'Il dualismo Sab/Somali e la definizione della identità nazionale somala'. *Africa* LXIII (1): 429–68.

Ahad, Ali Mumin. 2012. 'Da un emisfero all'altro'. *Kuma & Transculturazione*. March. Accessed 30 October 2023. https://www.academia.edu/15099269/DA_UN_EMISFERO_ALLALTRO._PERSONAL_RECOLLECTIONS.

Ahad, Ali Mumin. 2017. 'Towards a Critical Introduction to an Italian Postcolonial Literature: A Somali Perspective'. *Journal of Somali Studies* 4: 135–59.

Ahad, Ali Mumin. 2019. 'The Historic Sins of Colonialism in Somalia'. *Journal of Somali Studies* 6 (1): 9–40.

Ahad, Ali Mumin. 2020. 'The Marathoner Not Yet at the Finish Line: Nuruddin Farah in Rome'. *Tydskrif vir Letterkunde* 57 (1): 30–6.

Ahmed, Ali Jimale. 1996a. *Daybreak Is Near ... Literature, Clans and the Nation-state in Somalia*. Trenton, NJ: The Red Sea Press.

Ahmed, Ali Jimale. 1996b. 'Daybreak Is Near, Won't You Become Sour?'. *Ufahamu: A Journal of African Studies* 22 (1–2): 11–24.

Ahmed, Ali Jimale. 2018. 'The Somali Oral Tradition and the Role of Storytelling in Somalia'. *Literature Culture Studies*. 30 October. Accessed 30 October 2023. https://momentliteratureandculture.wordpress.com/2018/10/30/158/.

Ahmed, Mohamed A. 2012. 'Cultural Heritage at Risk. Challenges and Opportunities'. *Momentinhistory.wordpress*. 5 December. Accessed 30 October 2023. https://momenthistory.wordpress.com/2012/12/05/the-past-for-the-future-the-protection-and-conservation-of-somalia-historical-coastal-towns-the-case-of-mogadishu/.

Ahmed, Osman Hassan. 1993. *Morire a Mogadiscio*. Roma: Edizioni Lavoro.

Aidid, Safia. 2011. '*Haweenku Wa Garab* (Women Are a Force): Women and the Somali Nationalist Movement, 1943–1960.' *Bildhaan* 10: 103–24.

Aidid, Safia. 2015. 'The New Somali Studies'. *The New Inquiry*. 14 April. Accessed 3 October 2023. https://thenewinquiry.com/essays/the-new-somali-studies.

Alden, Patricia, and Louis Tremaine. 1999. *World Authors Series: Nuruddin Farah*. Woodbridge, CT: Twayne Publishers.

Alden, Patricia, and Louis Tremaine. 2002. 'How Can We Talk of Democracy. An Interview with Nuruddin Farah'. In *Emerging Perspectives on Nuruddin Farah*, by Derek Wright, ed., 22–45. Asmara: Africa World Press.

Ali, Ayaan Hirsi. 2010. *Infidel: My Life*. London: Simon & Schuster.

Ali Farah, Cristina Ubax. 2007a. 'WikiAfrica intervista Cristina Ali Farah'. *WikiAfrica*. 19 September. Accessed 30 October 2023. https://it.wikinews.org/wiki/WikiAfrica_intervista_Cristina_Ali_Farah.

Ali Farah, Cristina Ubax. 2007b. *Madre piccola*. Roma: Frassinelli.

Ali Farah, Cristina Ubax. 2011. *Little Mother*. Bloomington: Indiana University Press.

Ali Farah, Cristina Ubax. 2014. *Il comandante del fiume*. Roma: 66thand2nd.

Ali Farah, Cristina Ubax. 2015. 'An Interview with Cristina (Ubax) Ali Farah'. *WardheerNews*. Edited by Abdelkarim Hassan. 7 August. Accessed 30 October 2023. https://wardheernews.com/wp-content/uploads/2015/08/WDN-Interview-with-Cristina-Ali-Farah.

Ali Farah, Cristina Ubax. 2017a. 'A Dhow Crosses the Sea'. *Asymptote*. Accessed 3 October 2023. https://www.asymptotejournal.com/special-feature/ubah-cristina-ali-farah-a-dhow-crosses-the-sea/.

Ali Farah, Cristina Ubax. 2017b. 'Between Two Worlds: An Exclusive Interview with Ubah Cristina Ali Farah'. *Asymptote*. 15 March. Accessed 30 October 2023. https://asymptotejournal.com/blog/2017/05/15/between-two-worlds-an-interview-with-ubah-cristina-ali-farah/.

Ali Farah, Cristina Ubax. 2018a. 'To Leave in the Afternoon Inheriting the Language of a Civil War?'. In *Scritture postcoloniali: Nuovi immaginari letterari*, by Francesca Tomassini and Monica Venturini, eds, 197–209. Rome: Ensemble.

Ali Farah, Cristina Ubax. 2018b. *Il teatro popolare somalo. 1940–1990*. Rome: Roma TrE-Press.

Ali Farah, Cristina Ubax. 2021. *Le stazioni della luna*. Rome: 66thand2nd.

Ali, Rashid, and Andrew Cross. 2016. *Mogadishu Lost Moderns*. London: Mosaic Rooms.

Alighieri, Dante. 1991. *La Divina Commedia*, by Anna Maria Chiavacci Leonardi, ed. Milano: Mondadori.

Alpers, Edward A. 1995. 'On Critiques of the Invention of Somalia'. In *The Invention of Somalia*, by Ali Jimale Ahmed, ed., 223–32. Trenton, Asmara: The Red Sea Press.

Andall, Jacqueline, and Derek Duncan, ed. 2005. *Memories and Legacies of Italian Colonialism*. Bern: Peter Lang.

Andindilile, Michael. 2014. 'English, Cosmopolitanism and the Myth of National Linguistic Homogeneity in Nuruddin Farah's Fiction'. *Forum for Modern Language Studies* 50 (3): 256-74.
Andrzejewski, Bogumił Witalis. 2011a. 'The Rise of Written Somali Literature'. *Journal of African Cultural Studies* 23 (1): 73-80.
Andrzejewski, Bogumił Witalis. 2011b. 'Modern and Traditional Aspects of Somali Drama'. *Journal of African Cultural Studies* 23 (1): 85-95.
Andrzejewski, Bogumił Witalis., Stanisław Piłaszewicz and Witold Tyloch, eds. 1985. *Literatures in African Languages. Theoretical Issues & Sample Surveys*. Warszawa: Cambridge University Press.
Antle, Martine, Roger Celestin and Eliane DalMolin. 2015. 'J. M. G. Le Clézio or the Challenges of the Intercultural'. *Contemporary French and Francophone Studies* 19 (2): 123-7.
Appiah, Kwame Anthony. 1997. 'Cosmopolitan Patriots'. *Critical Inquiry* 23 (3): 617-39.
Appiah, Kwame Anthony. 2004. 'Interview with Nuruddin Farah'. *Bomb* 84: 54-9.
Appiah, Kwame Anthony. 2006. *Cosmopolitanism: Ethics in a World of Strangers*. London, New York: W. W. Norton & Company.
Armitage, David. 2017. *Civil Wars: A History in Ideas*. New York: Alfred Knopf.
Ashcroft, Bill. 2008. *Caliban's Voice. The Transformation of English in Post-Colonial Literature*. London, New York: Routledge.
Ashcroft, Bill. 2014. 'Bridging the Silence: Inner Translation and the Metonymic Gap'. In *Language and Translation in Postcolonial Literature*, by Simona Bertacco, ed., 17-31. London, New York: Routledge.
Ashcroft, Bill, Gareth Griffith and Helen Tiffin. 1995. *The Postcolonial Studies Reader*. London: Routledge.
Ashcroft, Bill, Gareth Griffiths and Helen Tiffin. 2000. *Post-colonial Studies. The Key Concepts*. New York: Routledge.
Ashcroft, Bill, Gareth Griffith and Helen Tiffin. 2002. *The Empire Writes Back*. London, New York: Routledge.
Asor Rosa, Alberto. 2015. *Scrittori e popolo*. Turin: Einaudi.
Augé, Marc. 1995. *Non-Places. Introduction to an Anthropology of Supermodernity* [*Non-lieux. Introduction à une anthropologie de la surmodernité*]. Translated from the French by John Howe. London: Verso.
Augé, Marc. 1996. 'Paris and the Ethnography of the Contemporary World'. In *Parisian Fields*, by Michael Sheringham, ed., 175-81. London: Reaktion.
Augé, Marc. 2000. 'Airports, Roundabouts, Yellow Lines'. In *City A-Z*, by Steve Pile and Nigel Thrift, eds, 8-9, 206-7, 297-8. London: Routledge.
Bakhtin, Mikhail. 1981. *The Dialogic Imagination: Four Essays* [*Voprosy literatury i estetiki*]. Translated from the Russian by Caryl Emerson and Michael Holquist. Austin: University of Texas Press.
Ball, John C. 2004. *Imagining London: Postcolonial Fiction and the Transnational Metropolis*. Toronto: University of Toronto Press.
Bammer, Angelika, ed. 1994. *Displacements: Cultural Identities in Question*. Bloomington, IN: Indiana University Press.
Baranello, Adriana. 2011. 'Giovanni Pascoli's 'La grande proletaria si è mossa': A Translation and Critical Introduction'. *California Italian Studies* 2 (1). Accessed 30 October 2023. https://escholarship.org/uc/item/6jh07474.

Barnes, Cedric. 2007. 'The Somali Youth League, Ethiopian Somalis and the Greater Somalia Idea, *c*.1946–48'. *Journal of Eastern African Studies* 1 (2): 277–91.
Barolini, Teodolinda. 2018a. '*Inferno* 6. The City and Its Citizens'. *Commento Baroliniano*, Digital Dante. New York: Columbia University Libraries. Accessed 30 October 2023. https://digitaldante.columbia.edu/dante/divine-comedy/inferno/inferno-6/.
Barolini, Teodolinda. 2018b. '*Inferno* 10: Love in Hell'. *Commento Baroliniano*, Digital Dante. New York: Columbia University Libraries. Accessed 30 October 2023. https://digitaldante.columbia.edu/dante/divine-comedy/inferno/inferno-10/.
Barolini, Teodolinda. 2018c. '*Inferno* 24: *Metamorphosis* (Ovid)'. *Commento Baroliniano*, Digital Dante. New York: Columbia University Libraries. Accessed 30 October 2023. https://digitaldante.columbia.edu/dante/divine-comedy/inferno/inferno-24/.
Barolini, Teodolinda. 2018d. '*Inferno* 34: Satanic Physics and the Point of Transition'. *Commento Baroliniano*, Digital Dante. New York: Columbia University Libraries. Accessed 30 October 2023. https://digitaldante.columbia.edu/dante/divine-comedy/inferno/inferno-34/.
Bauböck, Rainer, and Thomas Faist, eds. 2010. *Diaspora and Transnationalism: Concepts, Theories and Methods*. Amsterdam: Amsterdam University Press.
Baumann, Martin. 2010. 'Exile'. In *Diasporas. Concepts, Intersections, Identities*, by Kim Knott and Seán McLoughlin, eds, 19–24. London, New York: Zed Books.
Benvenuti, Giuliana. 2011. 'Letteratura della migrazione, letteratura postcoloniale, letteratura italiana. Problemi di definizione'. In *Leggere il testo attraverso il mondo. Vent'anni di scritture della migrazione*, by Fulvio Pezzarossa and Ilaria Rossini, eds, 247–60. Bologna: CLUEB.
Benvenuti, Giuliana. 2012. 'L'italianità nel tempo della letteratura della migrazione'. *Moderna* 14 (1): 207–18.
Besteman, Catherine. 1999. *Unraveling Somalia: Race, Violence, and the Legacy of Slavery*. Philadelphia: University of Pennsylvania Press.
Beswick, Jaine. 2010. 'Diasporas and Language'. In *Diasporas. Concepts, Intersections, Identities*, by Kim Knott and Seán McLoughlin, eds, 134–8. London, New York: Zed Books.
Bhabha, Homi. 1984. 'Of Mimicry and Man: The Ambivalence of Colonial Discourse'. *October* 28 *(Discipleship: A Special Issue on Psychoanalysis)*: 125–33.
Bhabha, Homi. 2004 [1994]. *The Location of Culture*. London: Routledge.
Biles, Peter. 1992. 'Anarchy Rules'. *Africa Report* 37 (4): 30–3.
Blaagaard, Bolette B., Sabrina Marchetti, Sandra Ponzanesi and Shaul Bassi, eds. 2023. *Postcolonial Publics: Art and Citizen Media in Europe*. Venezia: Edizioni Ca' Foscari.
Blum, Alan. 2003. *Imaginative Structure of the City*. Montreal & Kingston: McGill-Queen's University Press.
Boehmer, Elleke. 2018. *Postcolonial Poetics. 21st-Century Critical Readings*. Basingstoke: Palgrave Macmillan.
Bonavita, Riccardo. 1999. 'L'amore ai tempi del razzismo. Discriminazioni di razza e di genere nella narrativa fascista'. In *Nel nome della razza. Il razzismo nella storia d'Italia 1870–1945*, by Alberto Burgio, ed., 491–5. Bologna: Il Mulino.
Bond, Emma. 2014. 'Towards a Trans-national Turn in Italian Studies?'. *Italian Studies* 69 (3): 415–24.
Bond, Emma. 2016. '"Let Me Go Back and Recreate What I Don't Know": Locating Trans-National Memory Work in Contemporary Narrative'. *Modern Languages Open*: 1–21.

Bond, Emma. 2022. 'Looking Sideways to Italy in Contemporary World Literature'. *Italian Culture* 40 (2): 95–111.
Bowden, Mark. 1999. *Black Hawk Down*. New York: Atlantic Monthly Press.
Bradatan, Cristina, Adrian Popan, and Rachel Melton. 2010. 'Transnationality as a Fluid Social Identity'. *Social Identities* 16 (2): 168–78.
Brah, Avtar. 1996. *Cartographies of Diaspora*. London: Routledge.
Brian, Giulia. 2011. 'Nel «brolo» di Luigi Meneghello, là dove fioriscono le parole'. *Studi Novecenteschi* 38 (81): 149–69.
Brioni, Simone. 2013. 'Migrant Stories and Italian Colonialism: A Report on Two Documentaries'. *The Italianist* 33 (2): 321–4.
Brioni, Simone. 2015. *The Somali Within. Language, Race and Belonging in 'Minor' Italian Literature*. Cambridge: Legenda.
Brioni, Simone. 2017. 'A Station in Motion: Termini as Heterotopia'. *Italian Studies* 72 (4): 443–54.
Brioni, Simone, and Lorenzo Mari. 2019. 'Postcolonial Dante. Reading the *Commedia* in Mogadishu'. In *Dante Worlds Echoes, Places, Questions*, by Peter Carravetta, ed., 113–29. Rome: L'Erma di Bretschneider.
Brioni, Simone, Graziano Chiscuzzu and Ermanno Guida. 2012. *La quarta via*. 5e6 film and REDigital. 37m. https://openddb.it/film/la-quarta-via/
Brown, Matthew. 2008. '*Knots* by Nuruddin Farah'. *Harvard Review* 33: 203–5.
Bryan, George, and Wolfgang Mieder. 1997. *The Proverbial Charles Dickens*. New York: Peter Lang.
Burdett, Charles. 2022. 'The Transnational Study of Italian Culture and the Ghosts of Empire'. *Journal of the British Academy* 10: 1–19.
Burdett, Charles, Nick Havely and Loredana Polezzi. 2020. 'The Transnational/Translational in Italian Studies'. *Italian Studies* 75 (2): 223–36.
Burns, Jennifer. 2000. 'Telling Tales about "Impegno": Commitment and Hindsight in Vittorini and Calvino'. *The Modern Language Review* 95 (4): 992–1006.
Burns, Jennifer. 2001. *Fragments of* impegno. *Interpretations of Commitment in Contemporary Italian Narrative 1980–2000*. Leeds: Northern University Press.
Burns, Jennifer. 2013. *Migrant Imaginaries. Figures in Italian Migration Literature*. Bern: Peter Lang.
Burns, Jennifer, and Derek Duncan. 2020. *Transnational Modern Languages: A Handbook*. Liverpool: Liverpool University Press.
Bwesigye, Brian. 2013. 'Is Afropolitanism Africa's New Single Story?'. *Aster(ix) Journal*. 22 November. Accessed 30 October 2023. https://asterixjournal.com/afropolitanism-africas-new-single-story-reading-helon-habilas-review-need-new-names-brian-bwesigye/.
Bystrom, Kerry. 2014. 'Humanitarianism, Responsibility, Links, Knots'. *Interventions* 16 (3): 405–23.
Calchi Novati, Gian Paolo. 1999. 'L'Italia e il Corno d'Africa. L'insostenibile leggerezza di un colonialismo debole'. In *Africa Italia. Due continenti si avvicinano*, by Stefano Bellucci and Sante Matteo, eds, 100–16. Santarcangelo di Romagna: Fara.
Calchi Novati, Gian Paolo. 2005. 'National Identities as a By-Product of Italian Colonialism'. In *Italian Colonialism: Legacy and Memory*, by Jacqueline Andall and Derek Duncan, eds, 47–74. Bern: Peter Lang.
Calchi Novati, Gian Paolo. 2011. *L'Africa d'Italia. Una storia coloniale e postcoloniale*. Rome: Carocci.

Calvino, Italo. 1999 [1947]. *Il sentiero dei nidi di ragno*. Milan: Mondadori.
Calvino, Italo. 2002. *Lezioni americane*. Milan: Mondadori.
Calvino, Italo. 2004. *Hermit in Paris: Autobiographical Writings*. Translated from the Italian by Jonathan Cape. New York: Vintage.
Calvino, Italo. 2013a. *The Path to the Spiders' Nests*. London: Penguin.
Calvino, Italo. 2013b. *Letters, 1941–1985*. Translated from the Italian by Martin McLaughlin. Princeton, NJ: Princeton University Press.
Cantone, Helena. 2016. 'Italy-Africa: A Contradictory Inventory of Modernity'. *Critical Interventions* 10 (1): 5–27.
Cappelli, Antonio. 2011. *Somalia. Il sangue e l'incenso*. Rome: Gangemi Editore.
Caprotti, Federico. 2011a. 'Visuality, Hybridity, and Colonialism: Imagining Ethiopia through Colonial Aviation 1935–1940'. *Annals of the Association of American Geographers* 101 (2): 380–403.
Caprotti, Federico. 2011b. 'Profitability, Practicality and Ideology: Fascist Civil Aviation and the Short Life of Ala Littoria 1934–1943'. *The Journal of Transport History* 32 (1): 17–38.
Carazzolo, Barbara. 2002. *Ilaria Alpi: un omicidio al crocevia dei traffici*. Milan: Baldini&Castoldi.
Carbonieri, Divanize. 2014. '"Please Don't Judge Us Too Harshly!" The Exile's Return to Contemporary Somalia in *Links* by Nuruddin Farah'. *Acta Scientiarium* 36 (1): 83–91.
Casadei, Alberto, and Marco Santagata. 2007. *Manuale di Letteratura Italiana Contemporanea*. Bari: Laterza.
Cassanelli, Lee. 2009. 'The Partition of Knowledge in Somali Studies: Reflections on Somalia's Fragmented Intellectual Heritage'. *Bildhaan: An International Journal of Somali Studies* 9: 4–17.
Cassanelli, Lee, and Farah Sheikh Abdikadir. 2008. 'Somalia: Education in Transition'. *Bildhaan: An International Journal of Somali Studies* 7 (1): 91–125.
Casti Moreschi, Emanuela. 1998. 'L'altrove negato nella cartografia coloniale italiana: il caso Somalia'. In *Culture dell'alterità. Il territorio africano e le sue rappresentazioni*, by Emanuela Casti Moreschi and Angelo Turco, eds, 269–304. Milan: Edizioni Unicopli.
Cawl, Faarax M. J. 2012 [1974]. *Ignorance Is the Enemy of Love [Aqoondarro waa u nacab jacayl]*. Translated from the Somali by Bogumił Witalis Andrzejewski. Madar Books.
Chakrabarty, Dipesh. 2000. *Provincializing Europe: Postcolonial Thought and Historical Difference*. Princeton: Princeton University Press.
Chiapparoni, Alfredo. 2009. *Quanti denti ha il pescecane*. Milano: Mursia.
Chiavacci Leonardi, Anna Maria, ed. 1991. *La Divina Commedia*. Milano: Mondadori.
Ciocca, Rossella, and Neelam Srivastava, eds. 2017. *Indian Literature and the World. Multilingualism, Translation, and the Public Sphere*. London: Palgrave.
Clemente, Annamaria. 2015. 'Ubah Cristina Ali Farah tra Calvino e Pavese'. *Dialoghi Mediterranei*. 13 May. Accessed 30 October 2023. www.istitutoeuroarabo.it/DM/ubah-cristina-ali-farah-tra-calvino-e-pavese/.
Clifford, James. 1994. 'Diasporas'. *Cultural Anthropology* 9 (3): 302–38.
Comberiati, Daniele. 2010. *Roma d'Abissinia. Cronache dai resti dell'Impero: Asmara, Mogadiscio, Addis Abeba*. Cuneo: Nerosubianco.
Comberiati, Daniele, and Chiara Mengozzi. 2022. *Storie condivise nell'Italia contemporanea*. Rome: Carocci.

Comberiati, Daniele, and Xavier Luffin. 2018. *Italy and the Literatures from the Horn of Africa. Ethiopia, Eritrea, Somalia, Djibouti. Beyond the Language and the Territory*. Canterano: Aracne editrice.
Cometa, Michele. 2010. *Studi culturali*. Napoli: Guida Editore.
Concilio, Carmen. 2016. 'Italy in Postcolonial Discourse. Jhumpa Lahiri, Michael Ondaatje, Nuruddin Farah'. *English Literature* 3: 113–25.
Coppola, Manuela. 2011. '"Rented Spaces": Italian Postcolonial Literature'. *Social Identities* 17 (1): 121–35.
Coquery-Vidrovitch, Catherine. 2005. 'Introduction'. In *African Urban Spaces in Historical Perspective*, by Steven J. Salm and Toyin Falola, eds, XV–XL. Woodbridge: Boydell & Brewer.
Corner, Paul. 2012. 'Luigi Meneghello and the Resistance: Motives and Memories'. *The Italianist* 32 (1): 209–15.
Corti, Maria. 1986. 'Sullo stile de *I piccoli maestri*'. In *Anti-Eroi. Prospettive e retrospettive sui I piccoli maestri di Luigi Meneghello*, by G. Vitali and G. O. Bravi, eds, 97–103. Bergamo: Lubrina.
Cousins, Helen, and Pauline Dodgson-Katiyo. 2016. *Diaspora & Returns in Fiction*. Woodbridge, UK; Rochester, US: James Currey.
Cresswell, Tim. 2015. *Place. An Introduction*. Oxford: Wiley & Son Ltd and Blackwell.
Crowley, Dustin. 2015. *Africa's Narrative Geographies. Charting the Intersection of Geocriticism and Postcolonial Studies*. New York: Palgrave Macmillan.
Curti, Lidia. 2007. 'Female Literature of Migration in Italy'. *Feminist Review* 87: 60–75.
Curti, Lidia. 2016. *La voce dell'altra*. Rome: Meltemi.
Dahinden, Janine. 2010. 'The Dynamics of Migrants' Transnational Formations: Between Mobility and Locality'. In *Diaspora and Transnationalism: Concepts, Theories and Methods*, by Rainer Bauböck and Thomas Faist, eds, 51–71. Amsterdam: Amsterdam University Press.
Dal Lago, Alessandro. 2004. *Non-persone. L'inclusione dei migranti in una società globale*. Milan: Feltrinelli.
Davies, Rick. 1987. *The Village, the Market and the Street: A Study of Disadvantaged Areas and Groups in Mogadishu, Somalia*. Municipality of Mogadishu UNICEF OXFAM CCFD-France, Mogadishu: British Organisation for Community Development.
Davis, Colin. 2018. 'Diasporic Subjectivities'. In *The Routledge Diaspora Studies Reader*, by Klaus Stierstorfer and Janet Wilson, eds, 119–25. London, New York: Routledge.
De Donno, Fabrizio, and Neelam Srivastava. 2006. 'Colonial and Postcolonial Italy'. *Interventions* 8 (3): 371–9.
De Léon-Jones, Karen. 1997. 'Language and Identity in Calvino's *Il sentiero dei nidi di ragno*'. *Forum for Modem Language Studies* 33 (4): 360–8.
De Luca, Mariagrazia. 2020. 'From Forced Readers to Freedom Writers: Responding to Dante in Postcolonial Somalia'. *Dante Studies* 138: 26–48.
De Napoli, Marco. 2018. 'La trasformazione italiana di Mogadiscio tra le guerre. Piani e progetti per una visione europea della capitale somala (1905–1941)'. In *La città altra*, by Francesca Capano, Maria Ines Pascariello and Massimo Visone, eds, 349–58. Napoli: Federico II University Press.
De Vecchi, Cesare Maria. 1935. *Orizzonti d'Impero: cinque anni in Somalia*. Milan: Mondadori.

De Vivo, Barbara. 2013. 'Alla ricerca della memoria perduta. Contro-memorie della colonizzazione in Etiopia nel romanzo *Regina di fiori e di perle* di Gabriella Ghermandi'. In *Postcoloniale Italiano. Tra letteratura e storia*, by Franca Sinopoli, ed., 120–46. Aprilia: Nova Logos.

Del Boca, Angelo. 1984. *Gli italiani in Africa Orientale. Nostalgia delle colonie*. Bari: Laterza.

Del Boca, Angelo. 1993. *Una sconfitta dell'intelligenza*. Rome: Laterza.

Deleuze, Gilles, and Félix Guattari. 2013 [1980]. *A Thousand Plateaus* [*Mille plateaux*]. Translated from the French by Brian Massumi. London: Bloomsbury.

Deplano, Valeria. 2014. 'L'impero colpisce ancora? Gli studenti somali nell'Italia degli anni Cinquanta'. In *Quel che resta dell'impero. La cultura coloniale degli Italiani*, by Valeria Deplano and Alessandro Pes, eds, 331–50. Milan: Mimesis.

Deplano, Valeria. 2017. *La madrepatria è una terra straniera. Libri, eritrei e somali nell'Italia del dopoguerra (1945–1969)*. Florence: Le Monnier.

Detmers, Ines, Birte Heidemann, and Cecile Sandten. 2011. 'Introduction: Tracing the Urban Imaginary in the Postcolonial Metropolis and the "New" Metropolis'. *Journal of Postcolonial Writing* 47 (5): 483–7.

Di Maio, Alessandra. 2011. 'Introduction: Pearls in Motion'. In *Little Mother*, by Cristina Ali Farah, ed., XV–XXV. Bloomington, IN: Indiana University Press.

Di Maio, Alessandra. 2017. 'Postcolonial Intersections: Transnational Women Voices from Minor Italy'. *InVerbis. Lingue, Letterature, Culture* 7 (1): 101–12.

Dirie, Waris. 1998. *Desert Flower*. London: Virago.

Dodgson-Katiyo, Pauline. 2016. 'The "Rubble" & the "Secret Sorrow": Returning to Somalia in Nuruddin Farah's *Links* and *Crossbones*'. In *Diaspora & Returns in Fiction*, by Ernest N. Emenyonu, ed., 77–81. Boydell and Brewer: Woodbridge.

Dodgson-Katiyo, Pauline. 2020. 'Anxiety and Influence in Nuruddin Farah and Younger Somali Writers'. *Tydskrif vir Letterkunde* 57 (1): 67–76.

Donazzan, Francesca. 2022. '"Non eravamo mica buoni, a fare la guerra". L'opposizione alla retorica del conflitto in Luigi Meneghello'. *Finzioni* 4 (2): 65–77.

Doyle, Mark and Binaifer Nowrojee. 1993. 'A Dangerous Place'. *Africa Report* 38 (6): 38v45.

Draper, Robert. 2009. 'Shattered Somalia: Can the World's Number One Failed State Reverse Its Course?'. *National Geographic* 216 (3): 70–99.

Duale, Ahmed Yusuf. 2004. 'Education in Somaliland'. In *War Destroys, Peace Nurtures. Somali Reconciliation and Development*, by Richard Ford, Hussein M. Adam and Edna Adan Ismail, eds, 281–3. Lawrenceville, NJ: Red Sea Press.

Ďurišin, Dionýz. 1984. *Theory of Literary Comparatistics*. Bratislava: Slovak Academy of Sciences.

Eade, John. 2010. 'Diasporas and Cities'. In *Diasporas. Concepts, Intersections, Identities*, by Kim Knott and Sean McLoughlin, eds, 107–11. London, New York: Zed Books.

Ega, Abdi Latif. 2012. *Guban*. New York: Panafriklitpress.

Einashe, Ismail. 2021. 'How Somali Women Are Breaking Tradition to Write Novels'. *BBC*. 9 October. Accessed 3 October 2023. www.bbc.co.uk/news/world-africa-58845340.

Eliot, T. S. 1923. 'Ulysses, Order, and Myth'. *The Dial* 75: 480–3.

Eno, Omar A. 2005. 'Somalia's City of the Jackals: Politics, Economy, and Society in Mogadishu 1991–2003'. In *African Urban Spaces in Historical Perspective*, by Steven J. Salm and Toyin Falola, eds, 365–80. Woodbridge: Boydell & Brewer.

Enwezor, Okwui. 2010. 'Modernity and Postcolonial Ambivalence'. *South Atlantic Quarterly* 109 (3): 595–620.
Escolar, Marisa. 2018. 'Beppe Fenoglio's *Partigiano* Archive: Translation, *Resistenza*, Testimony'. *Quaderni d'italianistica* 39 (2): 61–83.
Faist, Thomas. 2010. 'Diaspora and Transnationalism. What Kind of Dance Partners?'. In *Diaspora and Transnationalism: Concepts, Theories and Methods*, by Rainer Bauböck and Thomas Faist, eds, 9–34. Amsterdam: Amsterdam University Press.
Falola, Toyin, and Hetty ter Haar, eds. 2010. *Narrating War and Peace in Africa*. Woodbridge: Boydell & Brewer.
Fanon, Frantz. 2001[1961]. *The Wretched of the Earth* [*Les Damnés de la Terre*]. Translated from the French by Constance Farrington. London: Penguin.
Farah, Nuruddin. 1988. 'Why I Write'. *Third World Quarterly* 10 (4): 1591–9.
Farah, Nuruddin. 1989. 'A Combining of Gifts: An Interview'. *Third World Quarterly* 11 (3): 171–87.
Farah, Nuruddin. 1992a. *Sardines*. Saint Paul, MN: Graywolf Press.
Farah, Nuruddin. 1992b [1979]. *Sweet and Sour Milk*. Saint Paul, MN: Graywolf Press.
Farah, Nuruddin. 1992c [1983]. *Close Sesame*. Saint Paul, MN: Graywolf Press.
Farah, Nuruddin. 1993a. *Gifts*. London: Penguin.
Farah, Nuruddin. 1993b. 'Nuruddin Farah Interviewed by Armando Pajalich'. *Kunapipi* 15 (1): 61–71.
Farah, Nuruddin. 1998. 'A Country in Exile'. *World Literature Today* 72 (4): 713–15.
Farah, Nuruddin. 1999a [1998]. *Secrets*. London: Penguin.
Farah, Nuruddin. 1999b [1986]. *Maps*. London: Penguin.
Farah, Nuruddin. 2000a. *Yesterday, Tomorrow. Voices from the Somali Diaspora*. London, New York: Cassell.
Farah, Nuruddin. 2002. 'Citizens of Sorrow'. *Transition* 81–2: 10–20.
Farah, Nuruddin. 2003 [1970]. *From a Crooked Rib*. London: Penguin.
Farah, Nuruddin. 2005 [2003]. *Links*. London: Duckworth & Co.
Farah, Nuruddin. 2007. *Knots*. London, New York: Penguin.
Farah, Nuruddin. 2008. 'The Family House'. *Transition* 99: 6–16.
Farah, Nuruddin. 2010. 'Of Tamarind and Cosmopolitanism'. *African Cities Reader* 1: 9–12.
Farah, Nuruddin. 2012. *Crossbones*. London: Granta.
Farina Mongiat, Caterina. 2014. '«Mostruosi e incomprensibili come gli uomini». La Resistenza della persona in Calvino e Fenoglio'. *Italica* 91 (3): 419–36.
Fazel Ramzanali, Shirin. 2016. *Far from Mogadishu*. Self-published.
Fazel Ramzanali, Shirin. 2017a [1994]. *Lontano da Mogadiscio*. Self-published.
Fazel Ramzanali, Shirin. 2017b [2014]. *Nuvole sull'Equatore*. Self-published.
Fenoglio, Beppe. 2003. *Il partigiano Johnny*. Rome: La Biblioteca di LaRepubblica.
Ferguson, James, and Akhil Gupta. 1992. 'Beyond "Culture": Space, Identity, and the Politics of Difference'. *Cultural Anthropology* 7 (1): 6–23.
Finaldi, Giuseppe Maria. 2009. *Italian National Identity in the Scramble for Africa*. Bern: Peter Lang.
Finaldi, Giuseppe Maria. 2017. *A History of Italian Colonialism 1860–1907: Europe's Last Empire*. New York: Routledge.
Florio, Jason. 2012. 'Facing Mogadishu. Portraits of Life in the Capital of Violence'. *VQR* 8: 5–19.

Forbes, Dean. 2008. 'Metropolis and Megaurban Region in Pacific Asia'. *Tijdschrift voor Economische en Sociale Geograpfie* 88 (5): 457–68.
Fotheringham, Christopher. 2018. 'Publishing, Politics and Literary Prizes: Nuruddin Farah's Reception in Italy'. *African Studies* 77 (4): 568–83.
Fotheringham, Christopher. 2019a. 'History's Flagstones: Nuruddin Farah and Other Literary Responses to Italian Imperialism in East Africa'. *Interventions* 21 (1): 111–30.
Fotheringham, Christopher. 2019b. 'Tourism and Imperialism in Italian East Africa: The Discursive and Practical Functions of *The Guida dell'Africa Orientale* (1938) in Constructing a Colony'. *Italian Studies in Southern Africa* 32 (1): 51–82.
Fotheringham, Christopher. 2020. 'A Nation of Narratives: *Soomaalinimo* and the Somali Novel'. *Tydskrif vir Letterkunde* 57 (1): 56–66.
Frow, John. 1990. 'Intertextuality and Ontology'. In *Intertextuality. Theories and Practices*, by Michael Worton and Judith Still, eds, 46–55. Manchester: Manchester University Press.
Fuller, Mia. 1994–1995. 'Carlo Enrico Rava. The Radical First Formulations of Colonial Rationalism'. In *Environmental Design: Journal of the Islamic Environmental Design Research Centre* 1–2, by Attilo Petruccioli, ed., 150–9. Rome: Dell'oca Editore.
Fuller, Mia. 2007. *Moderns Abroad: Architecture, Cities and Italian Imperialism*. London, New York: Routledge.
Gadhweyne, Rashiid Sheekh Cabdillaahi, ed. 2009. *War and Peace: An Anthology of Somali Literature (Suugaanta Nabadda iyo Colaadda)*. London: Progressio.
Gagiano, Annie. 2006. 'Surveying the Contours of a Country in Exile: Nuruddin Farah's Somalia'. *African Identities* 4 (2): 251–68.
Gagiano, Annie. 2020. 'Male "Somaliness" in Diasporic Contexts: Somali Authors' Evaluative Evocations'. *Tydskrif vir Letterkunde* 57 (1): 77–87.
Galadeta, Giulia. 2006. 'Intervista a Garane Garane'. *El Ghibli* 3 (12). Accessed 30 October 2023. https://archivio.el-ghibli.org/index%3Fid=1&issue=03_12§ion=6&index_pos=2.html#top.
Garane, Garane. 2005. *Il latte è buono*. Isernia: Cosmo Iannone Editore.
Garuba, Harry. 2002. 'Mapping the Land/Body/Subject: Colonial and Postcolonial Geographies in African Narrative'. *Alternation* 9 (1): 87–116.
Garuba, Harry. 2008. 'No-Man's Land: Nuruddin Farah's *Links* and the Space of Postcolonial Alienation'. In *Literary Landscapes. From Modernism to Postcolonialism*, by Attie de Lange, Gail Finchman, Jeremy Lothe and Jacob Hawthorn, eds, 180–97. Basingstoke: Palgrave MacMillan.
Garuba, Harry. 2017a. 'Teacherly Texts: Imagining Futures in Nuruddin Farah's Past Imperfect Trilogy'. *Boundary* 2 44 (2): 15–30.
Garuba, Harry. 2017b. '"Dreaming on Behalf of the Community": A Conversation with Nuruddin Farah'. *Boundary* 2 4 (2): 1–14.
Gekas, Athanasios. 2009. 'Class and Cosmopolitanism: The Historiographical Fortunes of Merchants in Eastern Mediterranean Ports'. *Mediterranean Historical Review* 24 (2): 95–114.
Genette, Gérard. 1997a. *Palimpsests*. Lincoln: University of Nebraska Press.
Genette, Gérard. 1997b. *Paratexts*. Thresholds of Interpretation. Cambridge: Cambridge University Press.
Gerrard, Vivian. 2015. 'Mending Mogadishu'. *Arena Magazine* 139: 22–5.

Gerrard, Vivian. 2016. *Possible Spaces of Somali Belonging*. Victoria: Melbourne University Publishing.
Ghermandi, Gabriella. 2015. *Queen of Flowers and Pearls*. Bloomington: Indiana University Press.
Ghorashi, Halleh. 2003. *Ways to Survive. Battles to Win: Iranian Women Exiles in the Netherlands and United States*. New York: Nova Science Publishers.
Gikandi, Simon. 1998. 'Nuruddin Farah and Postcolonial Textuality'. *World Literature Today* 72 (4): 753–8.
Gilkes, Patrick. 2002. 'Wars in the Horn of Africa and the Dismantling of the Somali State'. *Cadernos de Estudos Africanos* 2: 89–102.
Gilroy, Paul, Lawrence Grossberg, and Angela McRobbie. 2000. *Without Guarantees: In Honour of Stuart Hall*. London: Verso.
Giuliani, Anna. 2007. 'Fiabe vere e città immaginarie: Universi fittizi nella saggistica di Italo Calvino e Salman Rushdie'. *Quaderni del 900* 8: 107–15.
Giulaini, Chiara. 2021. *Home, Memory and Belonging in Italian Postcolonial Literature*. Cham: Palgrave MacMillan.
Glissant, Édouard. 1999. *Caribbean Discourse*. Translated from the French by J. Michael Dash. Charlottesville: University of Virginia Press.
Gnisci, Armando. 1998. *La letteratura italiana della migrazione*. Montescaglioso: Lilith.
Gnisci, Armando, ed. 2006. *Nuovo Planetario Italiano: Geografia e Antologia della Letteratura della Migrazione in Italia e in Europa*. Troina: Città Aperta Edizioni.
Gordon, Alastair. 2008. *Naked Airport: A Cultural History of the World's Most Revolutionary Structure*. Chicago, London: Chicago University Press.
Gorlier, Claudio. 1998. 'Nuruddin Farah's Italian Domain'. *World Literature Today* 72 (4): 781–5.
Gregory, Derek. 1994. *Geographical Imaginations*. Cambridge: Blackwell.
Guglielmo, Matteo. 2013. *Il Corno d'Africa*. Bologna: Il Mulino.
Guida dell'Africa Orientale Italiana. 1938. Milano: Consociazione Turistica Italiana.
Gupta, Akhil, and James Ferguson. 1992. 'Beyond Culture: Space, Identity and the Politics of Difference'. *Cultural Anthropology* 7 (1): 6–23.
Hall, Stuart. 1994. 'Cultural Identity and Diaspora'. In *Colonial Discourse and Postcolonial Theory: A Reader*, by Patrick Williams and Laura Chrisman, eds, 392–403. New York: Columbia University Press.
Hamid, Mohsin. 2007. *The Reluctant Fundamentalist*. London: Penguin.
Hamid, Mohsin. 2014. *Discontent and Its Civilizations*. Dispatches from Lahore, New York and London. London: Penguin.
Harley, John Brian 1992. 'Deconstructing the Map'. In *Writing Worlds: Discourse, Text and Metaphor*, by Trevor J. Barnes and James S. Duncan, eds, 231–47. London, New York: Routledge.
Hartnell, Anna. 2010. 'Moving through America: Race, Place and Resistance in Mohsin Hamid's *The Reluctant Fundamentalist*'. *Journal of Postcolonial Writing* 46 (3–4): 336–48.
Hassan, Mohammed Sh. 1998. *Gurmad. Diiwaanka gabayada soomaaliyeed*. Järfälla: Scansom Publisher.
Hayes, Kevin. 1999. *Melville's Folk Roots*. Kent: Kent State University Press.
Hoben, Susan J. 1988. 'Language Issues and Education in Somalia'. In *Proceedings of the Third International Congress of Somali Studies*, by Annarita Puglielli, ed., 403–10. Rome: Il Pensiero Scientifico Editore.

Hodapp, James. 2020. *Afropolitan Literature as World Literature*. New York, London: Bloomsbury.
Huggan, Graham. 2008. *Interdisciplinary Measures: Literature and the Future of Postcolonial Studies*. Liverpool: Liverpool University Press.
Hussein, Shamis. 1988. 'The Transition of the Education in the Somali Democratic Republic in the Post-Colonial Years System'. In *Proceedings of the Third International Congress of Somali Studies*, by Annarita Puglielli, ed., 412–13. Rome: Il Pensiero Scientifico Editore.
Huyssen, Andreas 2003. *Present Pasts: Urban Palimpsests and the Politics of Memory*. Stanford, CA: Stanford University Press.
Ibitokun, Benedict M. 1991. 'The Dynamics of Spatiality in African Fiction.' *Modern Fiction Studies* 7 (3): 409–26.
Ilott, Sarah, Ana Cristina Mendes and Lucinda Newns, eds. 2018. *New Directions in Diaspora Studies. Cultural and Literary Approaches*. London, New York: Rowan & Littlefield.
Ingiriis, Mohamed Haji. 2016. 'Many Somalia(s), Multiple Memories: Remembrances as Present Politics, Past Politics as Remembrances in War-torn Somali Discourses'. *African Identities* 14 (4): 348–69.
Ingiriis, Mohamed Haji. 2018. 'From Pre-Colonial Past to the Post-Colonial Present: The Contemporary Clan-Based Configurations of Statebuilding in Somalia'. *African Studies Review* 61 (2): 55–77.
Isella, Dante. 1992. 'La lingua de *Il partigiano Johnny*'. In *Romanzi e racconti. Edizione completa*, by Beppe Fenoglio, ed., XIII–XLIV. Turin: Einaudi.
Ismail, Abdirashid A. 2010. *Somali State Failure: Players, Incentives and Institutions*. Helsinki: Hanken School of Economics.
Jaggi, Maya. 2012. 'Nuruddin Farah: A Life in Writing'. *The Guardian*. 21 September. Accessed 3 October 2023. www.theguardian.com/culture/2012/sep/21/nuruddin-salah-life-in-writing.
Jama, Afdhere. 2018. *Liido Beach*. Self-Published.
Jussawalla, Feroza, and Reed Way Dasenbrock. 1992. *Interviews with Writers of the Post-Colonial World*. Jackson: University Press of Mississippi.
Kabir, Ananya Jahanara. 2010. 'Diasporas, Literature and Literary Studies'. In *Diasporas. Concepts, Intersections, Identities*, by Kim Knott and Seán McLoughlin, eds, 145–50. London, New York: Zed Books.
Kachru, Braj. 1983. *The Indianization of English: The English Language in India*. New Delhi: Oxford University Press.
Kalliney, Peter J. 2008. 'East African Literature and the Politics of Global Reading'. *Research in African Literature* 39 (1): 1–23.
Kapteijns, Lidwien. 2013. *Clan Cleansing in Somalia. The Ruinous Legacy of 1991*. Philadelphia: University of Pennsylvania Press.
Kapteijns, Lidwien, and Annemiek Richters, eds. 2010. *Mediations of Violence in Africa: Fashioning New Futures from Contested Pasts*. Leiden: Brill.
Khan, Nyla Ali. 2005. *The Fiction of Nationality in an Era of Transnationalism*. New York: Routledge.
KiMani, Martin. 2011. 'Airport Theatre, African Villain'. In *African Cities Reader: Mobilities and Fixtures*, by Ntone Edjabe and Edgar Pieterse, eds, 24–9. Vlaeberg: Chimurenga and the African Centre for Cities.

King, Anthony. 2000. 'Postcolonialism, Representation and the City'. In *A Companion to the City*, by Sophie Watson and Gary Bridge, eds, 260–9. Oxford: Blackwell.

Kirk, Jens. 2015. 'Non-Place and Anthropological Place: Representing the M25 with Special Reference to Margaret Thatcher, Gimpo and Iain Sinclair'. In *Non-Place. Representing Placelessness*, by Mirjam Gebauer, Helle Thorsøe Nielsen, Jan T. Schlosser and Bent Sørensen, eds, 195–220. Aalborg: Aalborg University Press.

Koppisch, Michael S. 2018. 'Mohsin Hamid's *The Reluctant Fundamentalist*: Mimetic Desire in a Geopolitical Context'. *Contagion: Journal of Violence, Mimesis, and Culture* 25: 119–36.

Korn, Fadumo. 2005. *Born in the Big Rains [Geboren im Grossen Regen]*. Translated from the German by Tobe Levin. New York: The Feminist Press at the City University of New York.

Kusow, Abdi M. 1995. 'The Somali Origin: Myth or Reality'. In *The Invention of Somalia*, by Ali Jimale Ahmed, ed., 81–106. Trenton, Asmara: The Red Sea Press.

Kusow, Abdi M. 2004. 'Contested Narratives and the Crisis of the Nation-State in Somalia. A Prolegomenon'. In *Putting the Cart before the Horse. Contested Nationalism and the Crisis of the Nation-State in Somalia*, by Abdi M. Kusow, ed., 1–14. Trenton, Asmara: The Red Sea Press.

Laachir, Karima, Sara Marzagora and Francesca Orsini. 2018. 'Significant Geographies: In Lieu of World Literature'. *Journal of World Literature* 3 (3): 290–310.

Labanca, Nicola. 2005. 'History and Memory of Italian Colonialism Today'. In *Italian Colonialism: Legacy and Memory*, by Jacqueline Andall and Derek Duncan, eds, 29–46. Bern: Peter Lang.

Larcom, Shaun, Sarr, Mare and Tim Willems. 2018. 'Dictators Walking the Mogadishu Line: How Men Become Monsters and Monsters Become Men'. *The World Bank Economic Review* 32 (3): 1–33.

Lazzari, Gabriele. 2017. 'Somalia and Italy across a Century'. *Public Books*. 6 May. Accessed 30 October 2023. https://www.publicbooks.org/somalia-and-italy-across-a-century/.

Lazzari, Gabriele. 2021. 'Rethinking Diaspora through Borders: Contemporary Somali Literature in English and Italian'. *Comparative Literature* 73 (1): 61–83.

Lazzari, Gabriele. 2023. 'Methodologies of Blackness in Italy: Past, Present, and Futures'. In *Postcolonial Publics: Art and Citizen Media in Europe*, by Bolette B. Blaagaard, Sabrina Marchetti, Sandra Ponzanesi and Shaul Bassi, eds, 57–77. Venezia: Edizioni Ca' Foscari.

Lee, Yoon Sun. 2015. 'The Postcolonial Novel and Diaspora'. In *The Routledge Diaspora Studies Reader*, by Klaus Stierstorfer and Janet Wilson, eds, 196–200. New York: Routledge.

Leetsch, Jennifer. 2021. *Love and Space in Contemporary African Diasporic Women's Writing: Making Love, Making Worlds*. Cham: Palgrave Macmillan.

Lefebvre, Henri. 1991. *The Production of Space*. Oxford: Blackwell.

Levi, Primo. 2017 [1986]. *The Drowned and the Saved [I sommersi e i salvati]*. Translated from the Italian by Raymond Rosenthal. New York: Simon & Schuster.

Lewis, I. M. 1988. *A Modern History of Somalia: Nation and State in the Horn of Africa*. Boulder: Westview Press.

Liberatore, Giulia. 2017. *Somali, Muslim, British. Striving in Securitized Britain*. London, New York: Bloomsbury.

Lombardi-Diop, Cristina, and Caterina Romeo. 2014. 'The Italian Postcolonial: A Manifesto'. *Italian Studies* 69 (3): 425–33.

Longhi, Vittorio. 2023. 'The African Descendant, an "Invisible Man" to the Media'. In *Postcolonial Publics: Art and Citizen Media in Europe*, by Bolette B. Blaagaard, Sabrina Marchetti, Sandra Ponzanesi and Shaul Bassi, eds, 223–8. Venezia: Edizioni Ca' Foscari.

Lori, Laura. 2013. *Inchiostro d'Africa. La letteratura postcoloniale somala fra diaspora e identità*. Verona: Ombrecorte.

Lori, Laura. 2016. 'Rome: The Former Caput Mundi between Postcolonialism and Cosmopolitanism'. *New Scholar: An International Journal of the Humanities, Creative Arts And Social Sciences* 4 (1): 77–88.

Lori, Laura. 2022. '*Matria* in Contemporary Somali Literature in Italian: Mapping Articulations of Female Solidarity and Resistance'. *Nordic Journal of African Studies* 31 (2): 118–35.

Luijnenburg, Linde. 2018. 'The Transnational Writers of the Somali Diaspora in the Netherlands'. In *Italy and the Literatures from the Horn of Africa. Ethiopia, Eritrea, Somalia, Djibouti. Beyond the Language and the Territory*, by Daniele Comberiati and Xavier Luffini, eds, 139–60. Canterano: Aracne editrice.

Mahaddala, Hassan. 2004. 'Pithless Nationalism: The Somali Case'. In *Putting the Cart before the Horse: Contested Nationalism and the Crisis of the Nation-State in Somalia*, by Abdi M. Kusow, ed., 59–74. Trenton: Red Sea Press.

Mahoney, Desmond. 1990. *Trees of Somalia. A Field Guide for Development Workers*. Operational Report. Oxford: Oxfam.

Mammone, Andrea. 2006. 'A Daily Revision of the Past: Fascism, Anti-Fascism, and Memory in Contemporary Italy'. *Modern Italy* 11 (2): 211–26.

Mansur, Abdalla Omar. 1995. 'The Nature of the Somali Clan System'. In *The Invention of Somali*, by Ali Jimale Ahmed, ed., 117–34. Trenton, Asmara: Red Sea Press.

Marchal, Roland. 1993. 'Les "Mooryaan" de Mogadiscio: Formes de violence dans un espace urbain en guerre'. *Cahiers d'Études Africaines* 33 (130): 295–20

Marchetti, Marilia. 2015. 'J. M. G. Le Clézio: Une Littérature de l'Exil et de l'Errance'. *Contemporary French and Francophone Studies* 19 (2): 162–74.

Mari, Lorenzo. 2018. *Forme dell'interregno. Past Imperfect di Nuruddin Farah tra letteratura post-coloniale e World Literature*. Rome: Aracne.

Mari, Lorenzo, and Teresa Solis. 2017. 'Mighty Mouth, Minor Literature: Siad Barre's Dictatorship in Italian Postcolonial Literature'. In *Fictions of African Dictatorship*, by Charlotte Baker and Hannah Grayson, eds, 235–50. Lausanne: Peter Lang.

Markovitz, Irving L. 1995. 'Camels, Intellectuals, Origins, and Dance in the Invention of Somalia: A Commentary'. In *The Invention of Somalia*, by Ali Jimale Ahmed, ed., 63–70. Lawrenceville: Red Sea Press.

Marzagora, Sara. 2015. 'Re-writing History in the Literature of the Ethiopian Diaspora in Italy'. *African Identities* 13 (3): 211–25.

Massey, Doreen. 2005. *For Space*. London: SAGE.

Materson, John. 2013. *The Disorder of Things: A Foucauldian Approach to the Work of Nuruddin Farah*. Johannesburg: Wits University Press.

Maxamuud, Yasmeen. 2009. *Nomad Diaries*. Encinitas, CA: NomadHouse Publishing.

Mazrui, Ali A. 1993. *General History of Africa VIII*. Oxford: Heinemann Educational.

Mbembe, Achille. 2001. *On the Postcolony* [*Notes provisoires sur la postcolonie*]. Translated from the French by A. M. Berrett, Janet Roitman, Murray Last and Steven Rendall. Oakland, CA: University of California Press.

Mbembe, Achille, and Sarah Nuttall. 2004. 'Writing the World from an African Metropolis'. *Public Culture* 16 (3): 347–72.
McLaren, Brian. 2008. '*Casa mediterranea, casa araba* and Primitivism in the Writings of Carlo Enrico Rava'. *The Journal of Architecture* 13 (4): 453–67.
McLeod, John. 2018. 'Preface'. In *New Directions of Diaspora Studies*, by Sarah Ilott, Ana Cristina Mendes and Lucinda Newns, eds, XIII–XVII. London, New York: Rowman& Littlefield.
Mellino, Miguel. 2006. 'Italy and Postcolonial Studies'. *Interventions* 8 (3): 461–71.
Meneghello, Luigi. 1967. *The Outlaws*. Translated from the Italian by Raleigh Trevelyan. London: Michael Joseph.
Meneghello, Luigi. 1998 [1964]. *I piccoli maestri*. Milan: Rizzoli.
Meneghello, Luigi. 2006. *Opere scelte*. Milan: Mondadori.
Milton, John. 2007. *Paradise Lost*. Oxford: Blackwell.
Mohamed, Iman. 2023. 'Colonial Amnesia and the Material Remains of Italian Colonialism in Mogadishu'. *Interventions* 25: 1–23.
Mohamed, Nadifa. 2010. *Black Mamba Boy*. London: HarperCollins.
Mohamed, Nadifa. 2012. 'The Way to a New Somalia'. *The Guardian*. 4 March. Accessed 3 October 2023. https://www.theguardian.com/commentisfree/2012/mar/04/way-new-somalia-london-conference.
Mohamed, Nadifa. 2013. *The Orchard of Lost Souls*. London: Simon & Schuster.
Mohamed, Nadifa. 2022. *The Fortune Men*. London: Penguin.
Mohamed-Abdi, Mohamed. 2001. 'De Gaashaanqaad à Mooryaan: Quelle place pour les jeunes en Somalie?' *Autrepart* 18: 69–84.
Montermini, Fabio. 2007. 'La creatività lessicale nel Partigiano Johnny'. In *Les enjeux du plurilinguisme dans la littérature italienne*, by Cécile Berger, Antonella Capra and Jean Nimis, eds, 127–40. Toulouse: Universitaires du Mirail.
Moolla, Fiona F. 2012. 'When Orature Becomes Literature: Somali Oral Poetry and Folktales in Somali Novels'. *Comparative Literature Studies* 49 (3): 434–62.
Moolla, Fiona F. 2014. *Reading Nuruddin Farah. The Individual, the Novel, the Idea of Home*. Woodbridge: James Currey.
Moolla, Fiona F. 2020. 'Reflecting Back, Projecting Forward: A Conversation with Nuruddin Farah'. *Tydskrif vir Letterkunde* 57 (1): 23–9.
Moreira, Paul, director. 2010. *Toxic Somalia: l'autre piraterie*. ARTE and Premières Lignes. 52m. https://mubi.com/en/gb/films/toxic-somalia-lautre-piraterie
Morin, Didier. 1997. *Littérature et politique en Somalie*. Bordeaux: Centre d'Étude d'Afrique Noire.
Morone, Antonio. 2011. *L'ultima colonia. Come l'Italia è tornata in Africa. 1950–1960*. Bari: Laterza.
Mubarak, Jamil A. 1997. 'The "Hidden Hand" behind the Resilience of the Stateless Economy of Somalia'. *World Development* 25 (12): 2027–41.
Mukherjee, Meenakshi. 1988. 'The Exile of the Mind'. In *A Sense of Exile: Essays in the Literature of the Asia-Pacific Region*, by Bruce Bennett, ed., 7–14. Nedlands: Centre for Studies in Australian Literature.
Mukhtar, Mohamed Haji. 1995. 'Islam in Somali History: Facts and Fiction'. In *The Invention of Somalia*, by Ali Jimale Ahmed, ed., 1–28. Trenton: Red Sea Press.
Mukhtar, Mohamed Haji. 2003. *Historical Dictionary of Somalia*. Lanham, MD: Scarecrow Press.

Murray, Stephen O., and Will Roscoe. 1998. *Boy-Wives and Female Husband. Studies in African Homosexualities*. New York: Palgrave.

Musa, Mark. 1995. *Dante's Inferno*. The Indiana Critical Edition. Bloomington: Indiana University Press.

Musila, Grace. 2015. 'Part-Time Africans, Europolitans and "Africa lite"'. *Journal of African Cultural Studies* 28 (1): 109–13.

Muthuma, Gitau. 2007. 'Clans and Crisis in Somalia'. *The Guardian*. 6 May. Accessed 30 October 2023. http://www.theguardian.com/commentisfree/2007/may/06/clansandcrisisinsomalia.

Myers, Garth. 2011. *African Cities. Alternative Visions of Urban Theory and Practice*. London, New York: Palgrave MacMillan.

Mzali, Ines. 2010. 'Wars of Representation: Metonymy and Nuruddin Farah's *Links*'. *College Literature* 37 (3): 84–105.

Naletto, Andrea. 2011. *Italiani in Somalia. Storia di un colonialismo straccione*. Verona: Cierre Edizioni.

Negro, Maria Grazia. 2013. '"Un giorno sarai la nostra voce che racconta": la questione linguistica nella letteratura postcoloniale italiana'. In P*ostcoloniale italiano. Tra letteratura e storia*, by Franca Sinopoli, ed., 55–76. Anzio-Lavinio: NovaLogos.

Newcastle Centre for the Literary Arts (NCLA). 2015. 'Nuruddin Farah and Abdulrazak Gurnah'. *The NCLA Archive*. Accessed 3 October 2023. www.archive.nclacommunity.org/content/?p=1872.

Ngaboh-Smart, Francis. 2004. *Beyond Empire and Nation: Postnational Argument in the Fiction of Nuruddin Farah and B. Kojo Laing*. Amsterdam: Rodopi.

Niemi, Minna. 2012. 'Witnessing Contemporary Somalia from Abroad: An Interview with Nuruddin Farah'. *Callaloo* 35 (2): 330–40.

Niven, Alastair. 2016. 'An Overview of African Cities and Writing'. In *The Palgrave Handbook of Literature and the City*, by Jeremy Tambling, ed., 481–97. London, New York: Palgrave Macmillan.

Nora, Pierre. 1996. *Realms of Memory: The Construction of the French Past*. New York: Columbia University Press.

Norridge, Zoe. 2012. '*Crossbones*, by Nuruddin Farah'. *The Independent*. 6 July. Accessed 30 October 2023. www.independent.co.uk/arts-entertainment/books/reviews/crossbones-by-nuruddin-farah-7917720.html.

Nyabola, Nanjala. 2018. 'War and Literature in Mogadishu'. *Al Jazeera*. 19 August. Accessed 30 October 2023. www.aljazeera.com/indepth/opinion/war-literature-mogadishu-180819082812165.html.

Omar, Mohamed Osman. 1993. *The Road to Zero. Somalia's Self-destruction*. UK: Haan Publishing.

Orsini, Francesca. 2015. 'The Multilingual Local in World Literature'. *Comparative Literature* 67 (4): 345–74.

Orwin, Martin. 2007. 'Reflections of the Somali Situation in the Novel *Waddadii Walbahaarka* [The Road of Grief] by Xuseen Sheekh Biixi'. In *The Road Less Travelled: Reflections on the Literatures of the Horn of Africa*, by Ali Jimale Ahmed and Taddesse Adera, eds, 329–40. Trenton, Asmara: The Red Sea Press.

Osman, Abdirazak Y. 1996. *In the Name of Our Fathers*. London: Haan Publishing.

Osman, Idil. 2017. *Media, Diaspora and the Somali Conflict*. London: Palgrave Macmillan.

Pandolfo, Michele. 2013. 'La Somalia coloniale: una storia ai margini della memoria italiana'. *Diacronie* 2:14. Accessed 30 October 2023. https://doi.org/10.4000/diacronie.272.

Parati, Graziella. 2005. *Migration Italy: The Art of Talking Back in a Destination Culture*. Toronto: University of Toronto Press.
Parati, Graziella. 2010. 'Where Do Migrants Live? Amara Lakhous's "Scontro di civiltà per un ascensore a piazza Vittorio"'. *Annali d'Italianistica* 28: 431–46.
Parker, Adele and Stephenie Young, eds. 2013. *Transnationalism and Resistance: Experience and Experiment in Women's Writing*. Amsterdam, New York: Rodopi.
Pavone, Claudio. 2006. *Una guerra civile: saggio storico sulla moralità nella Resistenza*. Turin: Bollati Boringhieri.
Peli, Sandro. 2006. *Storia della Resistenza in Italia*. Milan: Einaudi.
Pericoli, Matteo. 2014. *Windows on the World*. New York: Penguin Press.
Peters, Laura. 2012. 'Narrazione e memoria ne *I piccoli maestri* di Luigi Meneghello'. *The Italianist* 32 (1): 56–73.
Petrucci, Pietro. 1993. *Mogadiscio*. Turin: Nuova Eri Edizioni RAI.
Pezzino, Paolo. 2005. 'The Italian Resistance between History and Memory'. *Journal of Modern Italian Studies* 10 (4): 396–412.
Polezzi, Loredana. 2006. 'Mixing Mother Tongues: Language, Narrative and the Spaces of Memory in Postcolonial Works by Italian Women Writers (Part 2)'. *Romance Studies* 24 (3): 215–25.
Ponzanesi, Sandra. 2005. 'Beyond the Black Venus: Colonial Sexual Politics and Contemporary Visual Practices'. In *Italian Colonialism. Legacy and Memory*, by Jacqueline Andall and Derek Duncan, eds, 165–90. Bern: Peter Lang.
Ponzanesi, Sandra. 2014. 'La "svolta" postcoloniale negli Studi italiani. Prospettive europee'. In *L'Italia postcoloniale*, by Cristina Lombardi-Diop and Caterina Romeo, eds, 47–60. Milan: Le Monnier.
Portelli, Alessandro. 1999. 'Mediterranean Passage: The Beginnings of an African Italian Literature and the African American Example'. In *Black Imagination and the Middle Passage*, by Maria Diedrich, Henry Louis Gates Jr. and Carl Pedersen, eds, 282–304. Oxford, New York: Oxford University Press.
Procter, James. 1998. 'Descending the Stairwell: Dwelling Places and Doorways in Early Post-War Black British Writing'. *Kunapipi* 20 (1): 21–31.
Proglio, Gabriele. 2011. *Memorie oltre confine. La letteratura postcoloniale italiana in prospettiva storica*. Verona: Ombre Corte.
Puglielli, Annarita, Francesco Agostini and Ciise Maxamed Siyaad, eds. 1985. *Dizionario somalo-italiano*. Rome: Gangemi Edtiore.
Quayson, Ato. 2013. 'Postcolonialism and the Diasporic Imaginary'. In *A Companion to Diaspora and Transnationalism*, by Ato Quayson and Girish Daswani, eds, 140–59. Oxford: Blackwell.
Rabasa, Jose. 1985. 'Allegories of the Atlas'. *Europe and Its Others: Proceedings of the Essex Conference on the Sociology of Literature*, July 1984. Colchester: University of Essex. 1–16.
Radcliffe, Sarah A. 1997. 'Different Heroes: Genealogies of Postcolonial Geographies'. *Environment and Planning: Society and Space* 29 (8): 1331–3.
Radical Books Collective. 2023. 'Writing Somalia: Nuruddin Farah'. *YouTube*. 30 October. Accessed 30 October 2023. https://www.youtube.com/watch?v=HJHEEWOeU3I.
Rand, Lucy. 2020. '*Transgenerational Shame in Postcolonial Italy: Igiaba Scego's Adua*'. *Journal of Postcolonial Writing* 56 (1): 4–17.
Re, Lucia. 1990. *Calvino and the Age of Neorealism: Fables of Estrangement*. Stanford: Stanford University Press.

Re, Lucia. 2017. 'Italy's First Postcolonial Novel and the End of (Neo)realism'. *The Italianist* 37 (3): 416–35.
Rift Valley Institute. 2013. 'Nuruddin Farah and Binyavanga Wainaina in Conversation'. *YouTube*. 15 May. Accessed 30 October 2023. https://www.youtube.com/watch?v=UbNk_uztZ8s.
Roble, Abdi. 2008. *The Somali Diaspora: A Journey Away*. Minneapolis: University of Minnesota Press.
Roy, Ananya. 2011. 'Postcolonial Urbanism: Speed, Hysteria and Mass Dreams'. In *Worlding Cities: Asian Experiments and the Art of Being Global*, by Ananya Roy and Aihwa Ong, eds., 307–35. Hoboken, NJ: Blackwell.
Rupiya, Martin R. 1997. 'The Bakara Market Arms Clearance Operation of 1993: The Zimbabwe National Army in Somalia'. *International Peacekeeping* 4 (1): 115–21.
Rushdie, Salman. 1991. *Imaginary Homelands: Essays and Criticism 1981–1991*. New York: Viking.
Said, Edward. 1993. *Culture and Imperialism*. London: Chatto & Windus.
Said, Edward. 2000. 'Invention, Memory, and Place'. *Critical Inquiry* 26 (2): 175–92.
Said, Edward. 2003 [1978]. *Orientalism*. London: Penguin.
Samatar, Abdi Ismail. 2016. *Africa's First Democrats: Somalia's Aden A. Osman and Abdirazak H. Hussen*, 39–85. Bloomington, IN: Indiana University Press.
Samatar, Ahmed I. 2001. 'Interview with Nuruddin Farah'. *Bildhaan* 1: 87–106.
Samatar, Said S. 1980. 'Gabay-Hayir: A Somali Mock-Heroic Song'. *Research in African Literatures* 11 (4): 449–78.
Samatar, Said S. 1993. 'Historical Setting: From Independence to Revolution'. In *Somalia: A Country Study*, by Helen Chapin Metz, ed., 26–36. Washington, DC: Library of Congress.
Sapegno, Natalino. 1981. *La Divina Commedia. Inferno*. Florence: La Nuova Italia.
Saro-Wiwa, Noo. 2012. *Looking for Transwonderland: Travels in Nigeria*. London: Granta.
Sauli, Luciano. 1954. 'Il nuovo stadio di Mogadiscio'. *Corriere della Somalia*, 14 October.
Scego, Igiaba. 2010. *La mia casa è dove sono*. Bologna: Loescher.
Scego, Igiaba. 2015. *Adua*. Florence: Giunti.
Scego, Igiaba. 2019. *Adua*. Translated from the Italian by Jamie Richards. London: Jacaranda Books.
Scego, Igiaba. 2023. *Cassandra a Mogadiscio*. Milano: Bompiani.
Schaberg, Christopher. 2012. *The Textual Life of Airports. Reading the Culture of Flights*. London: Continuum.
Scott, Ridley, director. 2001. *Black Hawk Down*. Columbia Pictures Corporation, Revolution Studios, Jerry Bruckheimer Films, Scott Free Productions, 2006. 2h 24m. DVD.
Sheikh Aden, Mohamed. 1994. *Arrivederci a Mogadiscio*. Roma: Edizioni Associate.
Singh, Amardeep. 2021. 'Diaspora'. *BioScope* 12 (1–2): 61–3.
Smith, Andrew. 2004. 'Migrancy, Hybridity, and Postcolonial Literary Studies'. In *The Cambridge Companion to Postcolonial Literary Studies*, by Neil Lazarus, ed., 241–61. Cambridge: Cambridge University Press.
Soyinka, Wole. 2012. *Of Africa*. New Haven, London: Yale University Press.
Spears, Ian. 2010. *Civil War in African States: The Search for Security*. Boulder: FirstForumPress.
Spina, Alessandro. 2015. *I confini dell'ombra*. Brescia: Morecelliana.
Spina, Alessandro. 2016. *The Confines of the Shadow*. Translated from the Italian by André Naffis-Sahely. London: Darf Publishers.

Spina, Alessandro. 2018. *Colonial Tales*. Translated from the Italian by André Naffis-Sahely. London: Darf Publishers.
Srivastava, Neelam. 2008. *Secularism in the Postcolonial Indian Novel*. New York: Routledge.
Srivastava, Neelam. 2018. *Italian Colonialism and Resistances to Empire, 1930-1970*. London: Palgrave Macmillan.
Stock, Femke. 2010. 'Home and Memory'. In *Diasporas. Concepts, Intersections, Identities*, by Kim Knott and Seán McLoughlin, eds, 24-8. London, New York: Zed Books.
Tally, Robert T. Jr. 2013. *Spatiality*. London, New York, Routledge.
Tembo, Nick Mdika. 2017. 'Reduced to Rubbish: Trauma and Migrant Identities in Cristina Ali Farah's *Little Mother*'. *Scrutiny2* 22 (2): 65-81.
Thieme, John. 2016. *Postcolonial Literary Geographies*. London: Palgrave Macmillan.
Tölölyan, Khachig. 1991. 'The Nation-State and Its Others: In Lieu of a Preface'. *Diaspora: A Journal of Transnational Studies* 1 (1): 3-7.
Tomasello, Giovanna. 2004. *L'Africa tra mito e realtà Storia della letteratura coloniale italiana*. Palermo: Sellerio.
Touval, Saadia. 1963. *Somali Nationalism: International Politics and Drive for Unity in the Horn of Africa*. Cambridge, MA: Harvard University Press.
Tripodi, Paolo. 1999. *The Colonial Legacy in Somalia: Rome and Mogadishu from Colonial Administration to Operation Restore Home*. London, New York: Palgrave Macmillan.
Triulzi, Alessandro. 1996. 'African Cities, Historical Memory and Street Buzz'. In *The Post-Colonial Question: Common Skies, Divided Horizons*, by Ian Chambers and Lidia Curti, eds, 78-91. London: Routledge.
Trokhimenko, Olga. 2003. '"If You Sit on the Doorstep Long Enough, You Will Think of Something": The Function of Proverbs in J. R. R. Tolkien's *The Hobbit*'. *Proverbium* 20: 367-78.
Trunji, Mohamed. 2015. *Somalia. The Untold History 1941-1969*. Leicester: Looh Press.
Tuan, Yi-Fu. 1977. *Space and Place*. Minneapolis: University of Minnesota Press.
Turton, E. R. 1972. 'Somali Resistance to Colonial Rule and the Development of Somali Political Activity in Kenya 1893-960'. *Journal of African history* 13 (1): 119-43.
Ubax, Ismaaciil C. 2017. *Gaax*. Leicester: Looh Press.
Urbano, Annalisa. 2016. '"That Is Why We Have Troubles": The Pro-Italia Movement's Challenge to Nationalism in British-Occupied Somalia (1946-9)'. *Journal of African History* 57 (3): 323-44.
Venturini, Monica. 2010. *Controcànone. Per una cartografia della scrittura coloniale e postcoloniale italiana*. Rome: Aracne.
Vimercati, Giovanni. 2018. 'Alessandro Spina's Anti-Colonial Hospitality, Then and Now'. *Los Angeles Review of Books*. 4 March. Accessed 30 October 2023. lareviewofbooks.org/article/alessandro-spinas-anti-colonial-hospitality-then-and-now/.
Vivan, Itala. 1998. 'Nuruddin Farah's Beautiful Mat and Its Italian Plot'. *World Literature Today* 72 (4): 786-90.
Volpato, Chiara. 2009. 'La violenza contro le donne nelle colonie italiane. Prospettive psicosociali di analisi'. *DEP. Deportate, Esuli, Profughe* 10: 110-31.
wa Thiong'o, Ngũgĩ. 1986. *Decolonising the Mind. The Politics of Language in African Literature*. London: James Curry.
Waberi, Abdourahman A. 1998. 'Organic Metaphor in Two Novels by Nuruddin Farah'. *World Literature Today* 72 (4): 775-80.

Warah, Rasna. 2012. 'A Dangerous Job. Interview to Maxamed Nuur'. *Cityscapes Magazine*. Accessed 30 October 2023. https://cityscapesmagazine.com/articles/the-most-dangerous-job-in-the-world.

Warah, Rasna, Mohamud Dirios and Ismail Osman. 2012. *Mogadishu Then and Now. A Pictorial Tribute to Africa's Most Wounded City*. Bloomington, IN: AuthorHouse.

Ward, David. 1996. *Antifascisms. Cultural Politics in Italy, 1943–46: Benedetto Croce and the Liberals, Carlo Levi and the 'Actionists'*. Cranbury, NJ and London: Associated University Press.

Weheliye, Alexander G. 2009. 'My Volk to Come: Peoplehood in Recent Diaspora Discourse and Afro-German Popular Music'. In *Black Europe and the African Diaspora*, by Darlene Clark Hine, Trica Danielle Keaton and Stephen Small, eds, 161–80. Champaign, IL: University of Illinois Press.

Weinberg, Grazia S. 2013. 'The Italian Legacy in Post-colonial Somali Writing: Nuruddin Farah's Sardines'. *Italian Studies in Southern Africa* 26 (1): 26–47.

Woods, Tim. 2011. 'Giving and Receiving: Nuruddin Farah's *Gift* or the Postcolonial Logic of the Third World Aid'. In *Literature and Globalization*, by Liam Connell and Nick Marsh, eds, 202–17. London: Routledge.

Wordsworth, William, and Samuel Taylor Coleridge. 2003. *Lyrical Ballads and Other Poems*. Ware: Wordsworth Editions.

Wright, Derek. 1990. 'Zero Zones: Nuruddin Farah's Fiction'. *Ariel* 21 (2): 21–42.

Wright, Derek. 1991. 'Oligarchy and Orature in the Novels of Nuruddin Farah'. *Studies in 20th Century Literature* 15 (1): 87–99.

Wright, Derek. 2002. *Emerging Perspectives on Nuruddin Farah*. Trenton, Asmara: Africa World Press.

Yeoh, Brenda S. A. 2001. 'Postcolonial Cities'. *Progress in Human Geography* 25 (3): 456–68.

Yewah, Emmanuel. 2001. 'The Nation as a Contested Construct'. *Research in African Literatures* 32 (3): 45–56.

Yusuf, Aweys Warsame. 2006. 'Somali Enterprises: Making Peace Their Business'. In *Local Business, Local Peace: The Peacebuilding Potential of the Domestic Private Sector*, by NGO International Alert, ed., 468–507. London: International Alert.

Zabus, Chantal. 2014. 'Writing with an Accent. From Early Decolonization to Contemporary Gender Issues on the African Novel in French, English, and Arabic'. In *Language and Translation in Postcolonial Literature*, by Simona Bertacco, ed., 32–47. London, New York: Routledge.

Index

AFIS 15, 17, 21, 41, 70, 77, 79, 129–31, 135, 141, 169
Africa Orientale Italiana (AOI) 55, 81
  in *Guida dell'Africa Orientale Italiana* 21, 75, 81–4
airport
  in Boosaaso 38–9
  in Fiumicino (Rome) 29, 40–1, 45–7
  in Mogadishu 32–8
  see also culture of flights
Ajuran (clan) 74, 144–6, 153–8
Al-Shabaab 2, 28, 38, 136
amnesia 41, 185
  see also colonial amnesia
architexture 14, 208
Azania 143–4, 148, 153, 158

Barre, Maxamed Siyaad 1–2, 16, 28, 47, 50, 53, 116, 120, 129, 203
  see also Scientific Socialism; dictatorship; censorship
Black 29, 43, 184
  Black Skin, White Masks 79
  Blackness 40–3, 46, 77, 182
  masculinity 156
  women 184

Calvino, Italo 12, 18, 20, 183
  Preface of *The Path of the Spiders' Nests* 163, 172–82
  The Path of the Spiders' Nests 182–7
camel
  in oral poems 94, 150–2
cartography 21, 83–4
  see also map and mapping
censorship 1, 39, 52, 107–8, 128, 176
  see also Barre, Maxamed Siyaad; dictatorship; censorship
chronotope 56, 63
clan, or clannism 20, 22, 29, 36–7, 49–50, 52–3, 73–4, 76, 90, 93, 98–9, 100, 118–19, 120, 125, 133, 150, 155, 188, 190–1
  see also qabyaalad; qabiil
collaborationism
  in *Adua* 187
  in *The Path of the Spiders' Nests* 187–8
colonial amnesia 40–1, 79
colonial discourse 13, 16, 21, 41, 46, 75, 81–2, 84, 90, 107, 156, 167–8, 180, 184, 186
cosmopolitanism 34, 42, 47–53, 70, 72, 78, 94–6, 206
culture of flights
  in Christopher Schaberg 46–7

Dante 17, 22, 52, 106, 111–2, 132, 159, 186
  Dante Alighieri Society 114, 128
  Dante's language 126
  The Divine Comedy 111–27
  De Monarchia 124
decolonization 14, 47, 59, 80, 74, 90, 94, 99, 142, 147
democratic colonialism 169
deterritorialization 17, 58–9, 106, 137, 159
  see also reterritorialization
dialect 119, 165, 175–6, 177
diaspora 5–6, 8, 10, 31, 63, 196
  diaspora space/place 4, 7, 31–3, 44, 110, 128
  diasporic community 55, 59
  diasporic identities 37, 39, 41, 44, 45–6, 47, 63, 132–3, 181
  diasporic imaginary 10–1, 13, 69, 203
dictatorship 1–2, 16, 23, 34, 118, 132, 165, 176, 178, 187
  see also Barre, Maxamed Siyaad; censorship
donkey 94, 150–2, 159

epigraph 111–24
  in Gérard Genette 115

Fascism 41, 75, 86, 129, 165, 169, 176, 182, 186
Fenoglio, Beppe 170–1
    Il partigiano Johnny 175–7

gabay 15, 148–9, 160
    see also orality
qabiil 75, 96
    see also clannism; *qabyaalad*
qabyaalad 20, 50
    see also clannism; *qabiil*
gray area (*zona grigia*) 180, 188
    in Primo Levi 36, 186, 190

hybridity 61, 128, 134

Imam 77–8, 144, 157
    see also Islam
impegno (commitment) 19, 164, 166, 173, 178, 183, 189, 197
indigenization 22, 111, 143, 145
intertextuality
    in *Links* 17, 111–14, 123, 137
    in *Il latte è buono* 151, 153, 159
Islam 124–5, 135, 158
    see also Imam
Islamic Courts Union 2, 29, 51, 70
Italian Empire (*Impero Italiano*) 13, 27, 75, 84, 167–8, 208
Italiani brava gente 40–1, 84, 127, 172, 180, 183, 197
Italianness 40, 43, 55, 89–91, 106, 127, 164, 181, 183, 186–7

landscape
    in Édouard Glissant 21, 70–1, 99
lotta partigiana 169–72, 178, 195
    see also *partigiano*

map and mapping 21, 70, 75, 80–1, 83–4, 86, 88, 100
market
    Bakhaaraha 20, 28, 30, 47–53
    Tamarind 47–52
Meneghello, Luigi 176
    The Outlaws 172–96
milk (*caano*) 150–1

multilingualism 15, 17, 22, 106–7, 141, 176, 178
    multilingual local 13
Muslim 125, 134
Mussolini, Benito 19, 55, 136, 178, 196
    Leggi Razziali (Racial Laws) 129
    Ventennio 196
    see also Fascism

nabsi (nemesis) 191
nationhood 3, 9, 12–13, 19–20, 74, 79, 93–4, 97, 100, 153, 188, 204
nomadic (life, culture) 41, 78, 99, 149–52, 155–7

orality 17, 148, 150–1, 153, 159, 160, 165, 177, 181, 194
    see also orature
orature 17, 22, 137–8, 141–59, 207, 209
    see also orality

partigiano 106, 178, 196
    see also *lotta partigiana*
pastoralist 53, 78, 149, 152

Resistenza 18–23, 163–5, 169–88
reterritorialization 4–25, 27–31, 53, 59–65, 106, 122
    see also deterritorialization

Scientific Socialism 72, 120
Somaliness 3, 7, 22, 28, 37, 60, 73, 90, 123, 129, 133, 152, 164, 187, 204
    see also *Soomaalinimo*
Soomaalinimo (Somaliness) 3
space/place
    anthropological place 30, 33
    lieu de mémoire 70
    luoghi di ritrovo 60
    luoghi prediletti 89, 94, 99
    metonymic spatiality 31, 46, 61
    non-lieu, or non-place 13, 20, 30–1, 46
    place(s) 30, 32, 39, 60, 63, 88–9, 94
    relational place 46
    spatiality 11–14, 20, 29, 33, 35–6, 41, 47, 53–4, 61–2, 64, 72–3, 75, 81, 86, 92, 110
    supermodern place 30–1

Termini (Train Station) 13, 53–64, 188
tol 96, 100
toponymy 64, 69, 71, 73–6, 79–80, 84, 86, 88, 99, 131, 208
transnational 3–4, 47, 58, 63, 110, 163–4, 174–6
  ghetto 13, 63
  identity 29, 39
  studies 5, 6–7, 19
  transnationalism 11

urban planning 48, 71, 75
urbane civility (*ilbaxnimo*) 49–50
urbanscape 7, 12–13, 21, 27, 53, 71, 73, 84, 88, 90, 96
  see also urban planning

warlord 28, 33, 39, 48, 92, 125

Xamar 76, 84, 92, 97, 105, 192
  Reer Xamar 99

www.ingramcontent.com/pod-product-compliance
Lightning Source LLC
Chambersburg PA
CBHW050327020526
44117CB00031B/1823